METAMORPHOSIS

Ernest G. Schachtel

META

MORPHOSIS

On the Development

of Affect, Perception,

Attention, and

Memory

Basic Books, Inc., Publishers, New York

© 1959 by Basic Books, Inc.

Library of Congress Catalog Card Number 59-12367
Printed in the United States of America

DESIGNED BY ALFRED MANSO

Foreword

THE PURPOSE OF THIS BOOK IS TO CONTRIBUTE SOME IDEAS TO A CEN-
tral problem of psychology: How does adult man become what he
is, how does his situation, how do his conflicts, his capacities and
their limitations become what they are. These are large questions,
and in the course of history, many and different answers have
been given to them. The contribution of psychology to these
questions is, relatively, quite recent, yet it already shows a similar
diversity of answers.

The human metamorphosis from birth to adulthood is much
greater than that of man's nearest relatives in the animal kingdom,
the higher mammals, and this is especially true of the developmental
changes during the first year of life. Whereas the higher mammals
(ungulata, whales, seals, apes, and monkeys) at birth look very
much like small replicas of the adult animal and behave and move
much as the adults do, man reaches this stage only at the end of
his first year of life.[1]

Yet, any attempt to understand man must take into account not
only the changes but also the continuities in his development, for
the later stages still show the traces of the earlier ones, and the
condition of the newborn shows the seeds of, the *Anlage* for, the
later developments. The studies presented in this volume examine
some crucial factors in the development of affect, perception, attention, and memory in an effort to throw some light, from these
vantage points, on the larger, more comprehensive question of
human development.

The developmental viewpoint is indispensable for an understanding of man. Psychoanalytic theory is outstanding among the psychological approaches to the knowledge of human nature in that
it accords to developmental factors the attention and the weight
which they deserve. But while the developmental constructs of

1] This difference and its far-reaching significance has been discussed in a most
illuminating way from the biological point of view by Adolf Portmann, *Biologische Fragmente zu einer Lehre vom Menschen* (Benno Schwabe & Co., Basel,
1951), pp. 26-81.

orthodox psychoanalytic theory and their modifications in ego-psychology have been fruitful in many respects, they do not suffice to account adequately for what we can actually observe in early development. This is especially true of the concepts of the pleasure and the reality principles and their relation to each other in the course of development.[2]

Careful observation and description of experiential data, for instance of emotional or perceptual experiences or of the quality of the data of memory, are as important for the understanding of man as is his developmental history. This approach has been emphasized lately by phenomenological and Daseins-analytic authors (such as Straus, v. Gebsattel, Binswanger, Merleau-Ponty, Bachelard, Buytendijk). However, it is in the nature of the phenomenological method that it does not and cannot raise the ontogenetic question of how certain modes of experiencing developed and became what they are. The understanding of adult man and his situation in the world requires both the careful, qualitative observation of his experiences and reactions and the genetic exploration of the ways in which he came to develop them in his interaction with the environment.

I want to thank several friends and colleagues who have helped me by their comments and criticisms and encouraged me by their interest in my ideas. I am especially grateful to Erich Fromm, from whom I have learned a great deal and whose friendly interest has contributed much to the development of my thinking. I want to thank Florine Katz, Lois and Gardner Murphy, and my wife for many suggestions and constructive criticisms in the revision of the manuscript.

I am indebted to the William Alanson White Psychiatric Foundation for permission to use in this book my articles, "On Memory and Childhood Amnesia" (February 1947) and "The Development of Focal Attention and the Emergence of Reality" (November 1954), both first published in the journal *Psychiatry*.

Part of the section "On Affect, Anxiety, and the Pleasure Principle," in a somewhat different form, was given as an address at the Freud Centenary Symposium at Brandeis University on December 15, 1956.   E. G. S.

2] The modifications of these concepts, required by the observable facts, will be discussed in detail. They demand, in turn, a revision of the concepts of ego and id and their relation to each other. This, however, goes beyond the scope of this book.

Contents

III On Attention and Memory

METAMORPHOSIS

Introduction

THE COMMON THEME OF THE FOLLOWING STUDIES CONCERNS THE great metamorphosis of man from embryonic life within the maternal womb to existence in the human and natural world. Only certain functions of the human mind are considered here: emotion, perception, focal attention, and memory; but the attempt is made to understand some aspects of their development in the light of the over-all significance of the change from foetal to adult state. The point of departure, in time, of these studies is that of the newborn infant, and while none of them pursues every step of childhood development, they all consider the implications of some of the major changes for the life of the adult.

Studies of this kind always raise two major questions: the question of *provenance,* of the links with the past, and that of the *direction* the development takes, including its implications for the future. Both questions have been considered within the ontogenetic framework, but in thinking about them one inevitably is struck by phylogenetic comparisons. They crop up everywhere, but their discussion has been limited to a few questions and remarks, partly because of the purpose of the studies, partly because of my lack of zoological knowledge.

Nobody can think about problems of development today without encountering the towering work of Darwin and Freud, which has influenced, directly or indirectly, most writers concerned with phylogenetic and ontogenetic evolution. Thus, the following studies all have been stimulated by Freud's work, and their origin lies in the attempt to think through some of his thoughts and their implications and to test them against others' and my own observations and experience.

Both Darwin and Freud stressed the ties with the past, both were mainly interested in origins, as even the title of Darwin's magnum opus says. In Freud, this interest led to the discovery of the child in man. Freud's contemporary, Nietzsche, once remarked that there is a child hidden in every man and that this child wants to play. But it was Freud who showed in rich and concrete detail the continuing link with infancy and childhood in man and demonstrated how every aspect of man's life is permeated and affected by them. While the full significance of the child's play for all later development escaped him, his discovery, nevertheless, enabled him to show the determining influence of the first years of life and furnished the clue to the interpretation of dreams. By deciphering the archaic, infantile modes of thinking and wishing, by discovering the "two principles of mental functioning," he unlocked the door not only to the world of dreams but also to many aspects of awake adult thought and affect and to the understanding of the neuroses and psychoses.

This discovery is all the more remarkable since it went counter to the spirit, the culture, and mores of the Victorian era. It has often been remarked that Freud's emphasis on the central role of sexuality was his great "offense" against Victorian morals. But this was not the only point where he clashed with the prevailing culture of his time, even though it aroused the loudest accusations. The Victorian burgher saw himself as a thoroughly rational, dignified adult, deliberate and sensible in action and enlightened in thought, miles removed from the joys and woes, the zest of discovery, the wonder, the magic hopes and the helpless anger and despairs of childhood. This was especially true of Victorian men who, by and large, would consider it beneath their dignity to be concerned with the world of children. This world was left entirely to women while the men had more "important" things to do.[1] A similar condescension is apparent in that period's attitude to the artist as crystallized in the concept of Bohème. The Bohemian world was viewed by the average burgher with a mixture of amused tolerance, sentimentality, contempt, and repressed envy, as was the world of childhood. Hence it was indeed an affront to this self-satisfied attitude when Freud asserted that grown-up men are driven by essentially the same forces as little children and that the same passions and affects govern the secret life that goes on under their dignified façade.

Freud's "offense" against the Victorian spirit consisted not only

1] Compare "On Memory and Childhood Amnesia," this volume, pp. 318-319.

in telling men about the infant and child in them, but also in attacking the sentimental myth of a false "innocence" of childhood. The child was not a little angel but a little animal to him, governed by many of the drives that society tabooed. But while, thus, he paved the way for a more natural and realistic view of child and man, and while he favored a more lenient attitude to the demands of sexuality, he shared his society's negative attitude to what he discovered in the child. He looked upon the infant as a "polymorph perverse" creature, helplessly governed by drives striving for discharge in passive satisfaction or in violent affect storms, a creature whose development depended entirely on the control, taming, or suppression of those drives and affects. What he did not see or did not emphasize in his rather negative view of childhood was that (1) the infant is not entirely helpless but shows from birth on steadily increasing capacities for active searching for satisfaction and for active discovery and exploration and that it enjoys these active capacities; and (2) that the child in many ways shows a promise which altogether too often is betrayed by adult man and his society and by the growing child itself when it yields to those forces and aspects of the culture, as transmitted by parents, teachers, and peers, which are crippling to its inherent potentialities. Perhaps Freud's primary interest in understanding pathology was partly responsible for this one-sided emphasis. But, probably, it is also related to the resigned and pessimistic tone pervading especially his later work which contrasts so curiously with the qualities of strength, courage, and confidence in the power of reason which also characterize his work and without which this work hardly could have been achieved.

The bitter and resigned pathos of the speculative essays of Freud's later years, however, is consistent with one of the early cornerstones of his scientific work, the doctrine of the pleasure principle which asserts that the fundamental movement of the living organism is toward an excitationless state of quiescence. This doctrine led him later to the hypothesis of the death instinct. In the abyss of these thoughts the question seems to hover why there is life rather than death, why movement, striving, creation, play rather than the lifeless calm of the cemetery and of inorganic nature. It is reminiscent of the question asked by modern philosophy why there is being rather than non-being.[2]

2] This question was first raised by Leibnitz, taken up again by Schelling, and in

Man lives throughout his life in a conflict which Freud at one time described as that between Eros, the principle of unification, and Thanatos, the death principle, and which I would describe as the conflict of emergence from embeddedness.[3] The movement of life, phylogenetically and ontogenetically, is toward increasingly greater mobility, relative separateness of the organisms from their immediate environment, and individuation. In man this means separation, first from the womb, then from maternal care, from life in the parental family, and progression to a position of relative independence. As the ties of embeddedness are weakened and dissolved, the person learns to relate to the environment in a new way, different from the way he related when he was nurtured and protected by and embedded in the womb and later in the immediate environment of the parental family. In this development the forces making for growth and maturation are more impressive, as a rule, during childhood than those conflicting with this movement. The latter arise from man's fear of emergence from embeddedness and of the new, as yet unknown way of life. The relative strength of, and the quality of the conflict between, the forces of growth and the anxiety of separation from embeddedness differ at different stages of development, in different individuals, and in conditions of mental health and sickness, but both forces are present in all men.

While the conflict of these opposing forces is most apparent in man, it is foreshadowed in the animal world. In an experiment, young starlings were fed regularly until the time when they usually start to search for their own food. Then one group was fed only once a day with a brush dipped in food, by means of which they had been fed since they were hatched, while another group, hatched at the same time, continued to be fed in this way once every one or two hours. The group fed only once a day stopped the gaping response and started to search and peck at their food many weeks before the others, who continued to gape.[4] Similarly, Konrad Lorenz reports that a brood of young birds which he raised and

---

our time revived by Heidegger. Compare Walter Kaufmann, *Existentialism from Dostoevsky to Sartre* (Meridian Books, New York, 1956), pp. 36, 220-221.

3] This concept is developed in the section on affect, this volume, pp. 19-77, especially 44-55 and 69-77.

4] Monika Holzapfel, "Analyse des Sperrens und Pickens in der Entwicklung des Stars," *Journal für Ornithologie*, 1939, 87:525-553.

on which he had imprinted himself as the parent started to peck and feed on grains when he had to leave on a trip for two days. When he returned and learned this, he stopped feeding them although in his presence they started to gape again. After a short time he noticed that they became weak and did not go after their food by pecking. His presence in the room had sufficed to let them "regress" to the childhood pattern of gaping. In order to prevent their death by starvation, he had to hand feed them again, and after doing this, to leave the room in which he and the birds usually stayed so that they would resume feeding themselves by pecking.[5]

Phylogenetically one might compare man's ontogenetic conflict in emerging from embeddedness with the clash between the conservative and the progressive forces in evolution, and think of the untold sacrifices of each step in evolution in which only those generations survived which, by virtue of favorable mutations, were better adapted to new conditions of life than those which remained tied to the old pattern. But while in phylogenesis the generations of animals doomed to extinction live without consciousness of the necessity to adapt to the changed conditions of the environment and of the fatal consequences of their individual lack of capacity for such adaptation, man in the course of his ontogenetic development can achieve some insight both into the steps necessary to make the transition from embeddedness to relative independence and into the crippling effects of the failure to do so. He can even take a conscious part not only in his own, individual development but, as Julian Huxley and others have pointed out, in the evolution of mankind.

Because in ontogenetic development the forces striving for a new, more mature and advanced way of life seem more conspicuous than those that cling to the past, it needed the penetrating mind of a Freud to perceive the surviving, infantile past in the grown-up, present adult. This made it possible for him not only to link the ontogenetic past with the life of mature man, but also to discover a unified principle connecting such seemingly diverse phenomena as the mental life of the insane with that of the neurotic, of the healthy, of primitive man, and with the dream. The sudden light that this unifying principle shed on many phenomena which

5] Konrad Lorenz, "Der Kumpan in der Umwelt des Vogels," *Journal für Ornithologie*, 1935, 83:137-213, 289-413.

hitherto had been considered quite unrelated still retains its power of illumination even if some of Freud's conclusions have later proved erroneous.

Freud's emphasis on the ontogenetic past was so strong that he tended to see in man nothing but the power of his past over his present life and that he often failed to see in the past the seeds and portents of the future. Similarly, in many books and papers on comparative and animal psychology, in spite of frequent protestations to the contrary, one gets the impression that the authors are interested only in that which man and animal have in common, but not in what differentiates them, as though man could be understood completely through the link with his phylogenetic relatives in the animal kingdom, however distant and obscure the common ancestry which establishes the relationship might be. These authors seem to tell the reader, implicitly, that man essentially is nothing but an animal.

Freud saw the ontogenetic beginnings of man as dominated completely by the pleasure principle, and his concept of this principle is such that it represents essentially a flight from or a fight against life and reality: it is the quest to return to a state without stimulation, excitation, tension, and striving. This principle, in spite of some later modifications and doubts, remained a crucial concept throughout Freud's thinking. Whether he conceived of it because he was impressed with the newborn's predominant wish to return to sleep and his at first predominantly negative reactions to the impinging stimuli of reality, or by the wish of so many mentally disturbed people to withdraw from life and reality, or whether his view of sexual activity as primarily a discharge of tension led him to his negative concept of pleasure as a ceasing or decrease of excitation, and whether all these views, in turn, resulted from some deep running source in his own life, we do not know. In any case, he assumed that only the necessity to come to terms with reality and the wish to retain or gain the love of the parents causes the infant, gradually and reluctantly, to relinquish or control the at first all-powerful striving for return to a tensionless state, perhaps for return to the womb. In order to bring about this compromise with reality the ego is formed, as a later offshoot of the id. By taking into account reality and by delaying fulfillment of the wish to return to the tensionless state of satiation, the ego attempts to secure later fulfillment by a detour via reality. Perception, attention, recall are among the ego's tools in this enterprise, while affect largely was seen by Freud as an expression and safety valve of the impatient and frustrated longings of the id under the sway of the pleasure principle, and only by being tamed and controlled could the affects help the ego in its policy of fulfillment by compromise and detours.

What Freud overlooked was that from birth on the infant and child also show an eagerness to turn toward an increasing variety of things in the environing reality and that the sensory contact with them is enjoyed rather than experienced as a disturbing excitation. While at first this is true of only relatively few, impinging stimuli, already in the first weeks the infant tries to seek them out or to recover them if they are lost. Most of these encounters are sought not in order to abolish the stimuli or the excitation caused by them, and increasingly not in order to still hunger or thirst or as a detour on the way to return to the comfort of sleep, but out of a growing urge to get in touch with and explore the world around the infant. This will be shown in detail in an analysis of the development of affect, perception, and focal attention, while the essay on memory and childhood amnesia deals mainly with the effect of the ontogenetic metamorphosis on memory and recall which, in turn, affects the development of perception and attention. Freud's negative pleasure concept blinded him to the significance of the phenomena, so striking in the growing infant and child, of the pleasure and fulfillment found in the encounter with an expanding reality and in the development, exercise, and realization of his growing capacities, skills, and powers.

Freud's pleasure principle is akin to Hull's drive reduction theory which has had a tremendous influence on learning theory. But there is a growing body of evidence that tension and drive reduction theories cannot explain adequately human and animal behavior and, especially, that they can account neither for man's nor for the animal's need to get in touch with, explore, and relate to the environment. This evidence comes from sources as divergent as neurological theory, biology, animal psychology, developmental and personality theory, and from psychologists as diverse in their orientation as G. Murphy, H. F. Harlow, D. O. Hebb, K. Goldstein, J. Piaget, and many others.[6]

6] Gardner Murphy, *Personality, A Biosocial Approach to Origins and Structure* (Harper & Brothers, New York, 1947); *Human Potentialities* (Basic Books, New

The concepts and language used by Freud to describe the great metamorphosis from life in the womb to life in the world abound with images of war, coercion, reluctant compromise, unwelcome necessity, imposed sacrifices, uneasy truce under pressure, enforced detours and roundabout ways to return to the original peaceful state of absence of consciousness and stimulation in foetal "sleep." Only under the pressure of need, such as hunger, or of the fear of loss of love and approval, is reality accepted reluctantly and only by a kind of superstructure (ego and superego) underneath which the unchanged, timeless forces of the id continue to demand the abolition of reality and its painful stimulation. While the somber, resigned, and tragic hues of the picture painted by Freud reflect important truths, they are one-sided, as many great discoveries are. Leaving aside the question of the personal causes of such a one-sided view, I believe that two main sources of it are discernible.

The first source lies in those objective aspects of modern society which make man's social reality crippling for his potentialities, destructive of his life, and oppressive.[7] These stifling and inhibiting social forces enter the child's life at first indirectly, through their effect on the mother's personality, later also through many other channels. However, the fact that many factors of social reality indirectly may have an inhibiting or outright destructive effect on the infant does not mean that all natural and social reality is at war with the child's potentialities and impulses and is accepted by him only as an unavoidable and necessary detour and nuisance which one has to put up with and cope with in order to get rid of it again.

The second source may have been an inadvertent confusion of phylogenetic, evolutionary hypotheses with ontogenetic, psychological motivations. It may well be that such capacities as active

York, 1958). H. F. Harlow, "Mice, Monkeys, Men and Motives," *Psychological Review*, 1953, 60:23-32. D. O. Hebb, *The Organization of Behavior* (Wiley, New York, 1949). K. Goldstein, *The Organism* (American Book Co., New York, 1939). J. Piaget, *The Origins of Intelligence in Children* (International Universities Press, New York, 1952). For an exhaustive survey of the literature on this question, see Robert W. White, "Motivation Reconsidered: The Concept of Competence," *Psychological Review*, 1959 (to be published).

7] From the vast literature of social criticism concerned with this problem I want to mention only two books which treat it in the context of psychoanalysis: Erich Fromm, *The Sane Society* (Rinehart & Co., New York, 1955), and Herbert Marcuse, *Eros and Civilization* (Beacon Press, Boston, 1955).

attention to and perception of reality developed phylogenetically to their high level in man because he needed them in order to survive. But Freud seems to assume that each infant learns to use his senses only under the coercion of the necessity to cope with reality and would prefer to shut out or abolish reality. Actually, however, it can be shown that at the present stage of phylogenetic development the child does not feel coerced to develop his senses but enjoys and exercises their growing capacity to perceive reality. And the same holds true of the development of all human capacities, as Goldstein has stressed in his concept of self-actualization.[8] The tragic and frustrating aspects of life and reality stem from the crippling and stymying of the development and realization of human potentialities rather than from the frustration of the striving to return to an excitationless state. Indeed, the wish to return to such a state, to remain in quasi-foetal embeddedness often becomes a powerful ally of the very forces in society which obstruct man's self-realization.

The recent development of orthodox psychoanalytic theory known as *ego psychology* has taken cognizance of the fact that the capacities ascribed by Freud to the ego are not merely a later offshoot of the id, developed under the impact of necessity. The proponents of ego psychology assume that the ego has greater autonomy than Freud thought and that it develops together with the id from a common, undifferentiated phase.[9] They also realized that the conflict between instinctual drives (i.e., drives to discharge tension) and reality is not the only source of the ego's development.[10]

However, they neither saw that in order to comprehend the nature of the capacities and forces which Freud had conceptualized as those of the ego, his concept of pleasure had to be revised, nor did they grasp the fundamental significance, for the development of these forces, of man's world-openness and of play in the realiza-

8] Goldstein, *The Organism*, pp. 197-207.

9] Heinz Hartmann, Ernst Kris, and Rudolph M. Loewenstein, "Comments on the Formation of Psychic Structure," *The Psychoanalytic Study of the Child*, 1946, 2:11-38. In one of his last papers Freud, too, had assumed that the ego and the id are originally one and that there are inherited, constitutional ego qualities. S. Freud, "Analysis Terminable and Interminable," *International Journal of Psychoanalysis*, 1938, 18:373-405, pp. 394-395.

10] Heinz Hartmann, "Ego Psychology and the Problem of Adaptation," in David Rapaport, *Organization and Pathology of Thought* (Columbia University Press, New York, 1951), p. 364, and Rapaport's comment in footnote 10.

tion of this world-openness. Thus they assumed (1) that the
energies at the disposal of the ego are basically sexual or aggressive
energies which have been neutralized, (2) that the pleasure experienced in the exercise of the ego's capacities consists, just as Freud
assumed with regard to libidinal pleasure, in discharge of tension
(i.e. return to a tensionless state or at least to decrease of tension),
and (3) that if the growth and development of the ego was not
due entirely to a conflict between instincts and reality, there must
be a conflict-free sphere of the ego.[11] For ego psychology the world
remains, as it was in Freud's thought, a need-object for man which
he uses merely for the discharge of tension in order to return,
directly or by a detour, to a tensionless state or to gain the pleasure
of a decrease of excitation. This goal is supposed to be common
to all organisms, and man differs from the animals, according to
this view, only because his adaptation in the pursuit of the common
goal proceeds by delays and detours which give rise to derivative
needs but do not change the ultimate goal.

But man's need to relate to the world leads to encounters which
are different from and go beyond those serving discharge of tension as described by Freud and by ego psychology. It leads to an
encounter with world and fellow men in which they are not
merely need-objects but in which they are experienced in their
own right and in which man, implicitly or explicitly, poses the
questions "Who are you?" "What is the world?" "Who am I?"
"What is and what ought to be my place in and my relation to
the world?" These questions arise because of man's openness toward
the world and toward himself, which distinguishes him from even
the highest mammals and the seeds of which are already visible
in his infancy and childhood, although they often wither away
during childhood and may be buried deeply and forgotten by the
adult.[12] Man's openness toward the world implies that the nature

---

11] *Ibid.*, pp. 364-366, 380-383, and p. 382, footnote 62.

12] Hartmann thinks of human adaptation as modeled after the way animals
"fit in" in their environment and of the conflict-free ego sphere as the human
equivalent of the animal's instinctive organization. Hartmann, "Ich-Psychologie
und Anpassungsproblem," *Imago*, 1939, 24:62-135. The relevant passages are
summarized briefly by David Rapaport, *Organization and Pathology of Thought*,
pp. 374-375, footnotes 37 and 39. While it is true that ego capacities in man to a
large extent take the place of the animal's instinctive organization and thus serve
adaptation to the environment, they go beyond the purpose of "fitting in" with
the environment. This is a decisive point in which man differs from the animal
because he is open toward the world. In wondering about his place in the world
he can never merely fit in, but always has to raise anew the question of his

of pleasure cannot be reduced to the decrease and abolishment of excitation, nor the strivings of man to sexual and destructive ones. He experiences the world not merely as a need-object, and his conflicts cannot be reduced to that between instinct and reality.

But this does not mean that he is ever free from conflict and that there is, as Hartmann and his followers assume, a *conflict-free sphere of the ego*. The presence of innate structures and dispositions characterizes all human energies and capacities, those conceptualized by Freud as functions of the ego as well as those which he ascribed to the id. But none of them can remain free of conflict. The fact that all people learn to use their senses, to speak, to walk, etc., and that most learn to do so in a way sufficiently effective for survival does not mean that the functioning of their perception, their gait, their speech will be free of conflict. Every human act bears the trace of the basic conflict of emergence from embeddedness even though neither the actor nor others who perceive the act may be aware of this. In motor behavior, kinesic analysis is potentially capable of revealing this;[13] in speech, it can be revealed by phonetic, kinesic, and linguistic analysis; in perception it is less readily available to observation. But if one includes in the study of perception not only what and how a person perceives but also what and how he fails to perceive, which from the perspective of the degree of self-realization is equally important, then the conflicts pervading the sensory sphere may become more accessible to thought, speculation, and observation. Perceptual attitudes, such as the autocentric and allocentric ones described in this volume[14] or the leveling and sharpening ones described by Klein,[15] are always the present result of a development fraught with conflicts and they are pervasive whether or not the person experiences conflict in the concrete, single act of perception.

---

relation to the world. His answers to this question, be they explicit or implicit, lead both to his tragic and destructive mistakes and to his greatest achievements.

13] This has been the basis of graphology even before kinesics became a special branch of behavioral science.

14] Pp. 79-248.

15] George S. Klein, "The Personal World through Perception," in Robert R. Blake and Glenn V. Ramsey, eds., *Perception: An Approach to Personality* (Ronald Press, New York, 1951), pp. 328-355. Klein found, for example, that those who show the "leveling" attitude prefer to ignore differences, retreat from reality, and tend to be passive. While this does not interfere with their practical capacity of recognition and perceptual orientation in their everyday world, i.e. with the major adaptative function of perception, it points to a conflict in the development of perception which pervades the present acts of perception.

The problem of human conflict cannot be understood merely from the smoothness or difficulty with which the person or a specific function fits into a particular situation, but only if the relation of actuality to potentiality is also taken into account. The openness of man toward the world means that he has potentially many ways in which to relate to and find his place in the world and that there is not just one but many kinds of personal worlds in which he can live depending on the direction he goes in and how far he goes in it. This means not only that he has the potentiality for adaptation to different cultures or ways of life, but that these potentialities are in everybody narrowed by the accidental fact that he is born and brought up in a particular culture and group. It also means that both circumstance and choice may enable him to look beyond the horizon of the culture and social group into which he has been born and thus relate both to aspects of the world transcending those defined by the environment of birth and to the "stranger"—the person who does not belong to the ingroup of family, home town, native country—thus experiencing the humanity of other men. But it means, above all, that within the world into which he is born he can remain tied to the past, to the ways of family, peer group, community, trying to fit in and thus to retain the security of embeddedness, or he can try to be born more fully, to emerge from such embeddedness and to become capable of interest in and love for the larger and richer world in which he lives, thus discovering its infinity and inexhaustible mystery. This discovery is possible only in the fully open encounter with the world when one does not cling to the protection of the familiar and the past. It does not necessarily depend on physical separation from one's home town or country. Neither the greater mobility of modern man nor the inventions of modern communication techniques have helped him to overcome his urge to seek protection in conformity with and dependence on the in-group. Only by emerging from such embeddedness and by becoming himself can man realize his potentiality, and this means, in Fromm's words, that "the whole life of the individual is nothing but the process of giving birth to himself."[16]

16] Fromm, *The Sane Society*, pp. 25-27. The same thought has been expressed in v. Gebsattel's analysis of the relation between human *time* and mental illnesses. He emphasizes that the basic neurosis (*Kernneurose*), psychogenic depression, obsessional neurosis, and some cases of schizophrenia involve a disturbance of *becoming* (*Werden*), of self-realization; he quotes Max Scheler's

The basic conflict of becoming, of emerging from embeddedness, of turning potentiality into actuality, of self-actualization (Goldstein) may or may not be obvious in the way in which a person fits in with a given, limited environment or situation. It may become apparent in a change of environment or situation, but it exerts its subtle influence on human behavior and experience in any situation. It is obvious that the environment, especially the most important factor in the earliest environment, the mother, plays a crucial role in the conflicts around the relation of the potentialities of the infant to the actualities he will realize.[17] But the significance of the environment's role in the developmental conflicts is not confined to the frustration of instinctive drives; it extends, more importantly, to its encouraging and discouraging influence on the development of the child's potentialities. Yet, even the most beneficial and encouraging environment cannot spare man the ever renewed birth pangs of emerging from embeddedness on the road to becoming what he could be.

Developmental studies attempting to trace the changes as well as the continuities and the effect of earlier on later forms of human life, and especially of human experience, encounter two major difficulties. One is that the earliest ontogenetic phase by its very

---

view according to which the human experience of time has its roots in the experience of the potency (*Können*) to change his state. V. E. von Gebsattel, "Störungen des Werdens und des Zeiterlebens im Rahmen psychiatrischer Erkrankungen," in *Prolegomena einer medizinischen Anthropologie* (Springer Verlag, Berlin, 1954), pp. 128-144, 138, 131. Fromm, too, believes that neuroses and many cases of psychoses are essentially a failure to be born fully and that the severity of the disturbance depends on the stage at which the development of the individual, i.e. the process of continuing birth, was arrested (personal communication from E. Fromm). The pain of this continuing birth is emphasized in Plutarch's saying that the child must die so that the youth may arise and the youth must die for the man to be born. This death is equivalent to the separation from embeddedness in a present form of life which ought to become past in order to yield to the actualization of the potentiality for a more mature form of existence; hence the anxiety often experienced about such dying. v. Gebsattel calls this the death immanent in life. See his "Aspekte des Todes," in *Prolegomena*, pp. 389-412.

To the whole problem of becoming, compare also May's introduction to *Existence, A New Dimension in Psychiatry and Psychology*, Rollo May, Ernest Angel, and Henry F. Ellenberger, eds. (Basic Books, New York, 1958), pp. 3-91. May discusses especially the important roles of Kierkegaard and Nietzsche in developing the concept of becoming. Compare also Gordon Allport, *Becoming, Basic Considerations for a Psychology of Personality* (Yale University Press, New Haven, 1955).

17] For a detailed criticism of Hartmann's theory of the conflict-free sphere of the ego, stressing particularly the mother's influence on the earliest developments of the ego functions, compare also Sylvia Brody, *Patterns of Mothering* (International Universities Press, New York, 1956), especially chapter 14.

nature can never be fully known to us and remains shrouded in mystery. Psychoanalysis has relied mainly on reconstruction based partly on memories, partly on speculative theory, in order to penetrate the earliest phase of development. This method will always be indispensable, but while it has led to important discoveries, it also has led to misinterpretations. Direct observation of infants, in which men like Preyer, Stern, and Piaget have done pioneering work, has only relatively recently joined forces with psychoanalytic theory (R. Spitz, S. Escalona, L. Murphy, Ch. Bühler, and others); this will give us a broader empirical basis and help to prevent speculation from going too far astray. But it will still not change the basic fact that the earliest experiences which are of great formative importance will remain hidden from us and an object of speculative inference.

The scope of experimental work, while far from exhausted, also has inherent limitations. These derive primarily from the fact that experiments in the area of sensory, intellectual, and emotional experience change the nature of the experience by the very method with which they study it. While the parallel phenomenon in physics is today recognized (Heisenberg's law of indeterminacy), in psychology, where this phenomenon is much more grossly palpable, its bearing on the science of man is still far from sufficiently appreciated. Many psychologists, of course, eliminate human experience as a possible object of study by asserting that only physiological or physical processes can be observed scientifically. But whether or not one accepts such a narrow definition of science, if one wants to understand man at all, his experience cannot be dismissed but is a matter of prime importance and concern. It is accessible to us only in introspection and through communication from others. Its careful description has been advanced much by the work of the phenomenologists, whose method, however, excludes the important and indispensable genetic viewpoint.

In presenting the following studies my main purpose is to raise some questions and to offer some hypotheses which may stimulate further thinking and research and thus contribute to the better understanding of that great miracle, the metamorphosis of man from embryo to adulthood, and to the appreciation of the direction of human development to which this metamorphosis points.

I

*ON AFFECT,
ANXIETY,
AND THE
PLEASURE
PRINCIPLE*

1

Freud's View of Affect

THERE IS A WIDESPREAD TENDENCY TO LOOK UPON THE UNIVERSAL human phenomenon of emotion as something negative, as a disturbance or a disorganizing influence on behavior. Often this view is propounded by contrasting affect with reason, emotional with reasonable behavior. The Enlightenment's apotheosis of reason and its belief that man himself could be understood as completely and mechanistically as a machine[1] did much to strengthen this view. Yet, Plato believed that no such inherent contrast exists between affect and reason and that there are reasonable and unreasonable emotions, true and false, beneficial and destructive feelings,[2] that philosophy itself is nourished by an emotion, the love for wisdom and truth.

The view of affect as a disturbance of behavior is prevalent also in the young science of psychology and has been questioned recently by Goldstein.[3] Freud, in whose work the theory of affect occupies a prominent place, shares the prevailing view of the disturbing nature of emotions. The present study proposes to re-examine Freud's theory of affect. When he turned his attention to

---

1] Compare J. La Mettrie, *L'Homme Machine*, 1750, and its modern descendant, cybernetics.

2] *Republic* 431, 485-486, 554, 571, 586-587; *Philebos* throughout.

3] Kurt Goldstein, "On Emotions: Considerations from an Organismic Point of View," *Journal of Psychology*, 1951, 31:37-49.

the problems of emotion, the psychology of his time was largely preoccupied with the perceptual and cognitive functions and with the rational, purposeful behavior of man. He did much to show the predominant position of drives and affects in human life. But at the same time he took a rather negative view of the affects.

The neglect of the integrative functions of affect and the emphasis on its disorganizing qualities are apparent in Freud's work in three major points.

First and foremost is Freud's view of affects as universal, congenital, hysterical attacks.[4] By this he means that all affects are reproductions of emotions originally generated by past traumatic experiences, vital to the organism, which possibly even antedate the individual existence of the person. These traumatic experiences are revived in situations similar to those in which they originally occurred.

The *second* point concerns Freud's tendency to view affect and action upon the outer world as radically different from each other, as if they were opposed to each other and mutually exclusive. This view, too, is shared by many other psychologists, especially those who subscribe to the conflict theory of affects. He writes: "Affectivity manifests itself essentially in motor [i.e. secretory and circulatory] discharge resulting in an [internal] alteration of the subject's own body without reference to the outer world; motility, in actions designed to effect changes in the outer world."[5] In contrast to this, I believe that there is no action without affect, to be sure not always an intense, dramatic affect as in an action of impulsive rage, but more usually a total, sometimes quite marked, sometimes very subtle and hardly noticeable mood, which nevertheless constitutes an essential background of every action.

Freud's view that affect results only in an alteration of the subject's own body without reference to the outer world probably

---

4] The idea that affects are similar to hysterical seizures was already voiced by Freud in 1917 in "Vorlesungen zur Einführung in die Psychoanalyse," *Gesammelte Werke* (Imago Publishing Co., London, 1940), Vol. XI, pp. 410-11. It recurs in 1926 in *Inhibitions, Symptoms, and Anxiety* (Hogarth Press, London, 1949), pp. 24 and 99. There Freud states that affects are precipitates "of primaeval traumatic experiences" and expresses again his opinion that all affects are innate hysterical attacks, but feels that this has been demonstrated only for anxiety, and that it would be desirable to prove it also for a number of other affects.

5] Sigmund Freud, "The Unconscious," *Collected Papers* (Basic Books, New York, 1959), Vol. IV, p. 111, footnote.

also accounts for the *third* point in which he neglected the positive function of affect, namely its tremendous role in communication and in effecting changes in the outer world by means of communication. Indeed, one might maintain that effecting changes in the outer world by means of communication is a primary function of affect, be it in the courtship, in the alarm or threat behavior of the higher animals, in the infant's crying which calls forth the mother's tender help, or in the constant, richly varied, affective communication by means of which we try to influence, and do influence, wittingly or unwittingly, the behavior of our fellow men. The function of affect can be fully grasped only if we do not confine our viewpoint to what goes on in the individual organism but take as the object of study the *life-scene* in which the affect arises and in which it affects not only the body of the isolated organism, but other organisms (animals, men) who perceive the expression of affect and react to it.

To study the communication function of affect would far exceed the scope of this presentation. Nor do I intend to present a comprehensive theory of affect. I shall confine myself to some thoughts and observations concerning the development of affect as an integrative and as a disintegrating force in human behavior and concerning the relation of affect to action.

2

Affect and Action

Embeddedness-affect and Activity-affect

MANY PSYCHOLOGISTS ASSUME THAT AFFECT AND ACTION ARE MU-
tually exclusive. According to this assumption, where there is
uninhibited action there is no affect and, conversely, affect arises
only where action is either inhibited, delayed, or not possible
for some other reason, e.g., conditions of reality. Among the
adherents of this view, which is consistent with a conflict theory
of emotions and which increasingly seems to dominate the field
of affect theory, are Bergson, John Dewey, Freud and many of
his followers, McCurdy, and, recently, Sartre and Nina Bull.[1]

1] Henri Bergson, "Essai sur les Données Immédiates de la Conscience," quoted
by Konrad Lorenz in Bertram Schaffner, ed., *Group Processes, Transactions of
the First Conference, 1954* (Josiah Macy, Jr. Foundation, New York, 1955),
p. 201. John Dewey, "The Theory of Emotion," *Psychological Review*, 1894,
1:553-569; 1895, 2:13-32; see especially 2, pp. 26 ff. J. T. McCurdy, *The Psychology of Emotion, Morbid and Normal* (Harcourt, New York, 1925), pp. 87-
88. Jean-Paul Sartre, *The Emotions: Outline of a Theory* (Philosophical Library,
New York, 1948). Nina Bull, *The Attitude Theory of Emotion*, Nervous and
Mental Disease Monographs, No. 81 (New York, 1951), p. 4. N. Bull (p. 87) also
quotes Coghill as making the assumption that where the automatic behavior of
the primitive organism was blocked the first awareness arose, in the form of
unpleasant emotion. G. E. Coghill, *Anatomy and the Problem of Behavior* (Cambridge University Press, Cambridge, 1929). Further references in David Rapaport,
Emotions and Memory (Williams and Wilkins, Baltimore, 1942), pp. 24-26.
    In contrast to these writers, two psychoanalytic authors, Jacobson and Rapa-
port, have pointed out recently that affects do accompany drive action. See
Edith Jacobson, "The Affects and Their Pleasure-Unpleasure Qualities, in Relation to the Psychic Discharge Processes," in Rudolph M. Loewenstein, ed., *Drives,
Affects, Behavior* (International Universities Press, New York, 1953), pp. 38-66;

Freud seems to hold this view both with regard to the drive action of the primary process and to deliberate, purposeful action intended to bring about changes in reality. He seems to assume that where the drive energy is used for action, no affect discharge occurs except the feeling of pleasure in relief of tension. For the drive action this is clearly implied in the psychoanalytic model of the primary psychic process. (See below pp. 23-24.) With regard to purposeful action he writes: "A new function was now [i.e. with the advent of the reality principle] entrusted to motor discharge, which under the supremacy of the pleasure principle had served to unburden the psychic apparatus of accretions of stimuli, and carried out this task by sending innervations into the interior of the body (mien, expressions of affect); it was now employed for the purposive alteration of reality. It was converted into *action*."[2]

At this point I want to examine the validity of this hypothesis only for the period of early infancy where, according to Freud's theory, the pleasure principle holds full sway and the primary process dominates the psychic life completely. What are the assumptions of his theory concerning affect and drive action for this stage and what can we actually observe in the behavior of the neonate and of early infancy?

The model of the primary psychic processes[3] consists of the following sequence: restlessness of the hungry infant—appearance of mother's breast and sucking action—subsiding of restlessness. This sequence is conceptualized as: mounting drive tension—appearance of and drive action on the drive object—gratification of drive. It is the restlessness in the absence of the drive object which, rightly, is considered as the expression of affect and it is assumed, I believe wrongly, that if the drive object were present and the drive action possible no affect would arise. As Rapaport

and David Rapaport, "On the Psychoanalytic Theory of Affects," in Robert P. Knight, ed., *Psychoanalytic Psychiatry and Psychology* (International Universities Press, New York, 1954), p. 287. Jacobson criticizes the view that affects are pathological phenomena arising from a damming up of psychic energy which cannot be discharged properly (p. 49).

2] S. Freud, "Formulations Regarding the Two Principles in Mental Functioning," *Collected Papers* (Basic Books, New York, 1959), Vol. IV, p. 16.

3] In the description of this model I follow Rapaport. Compare Rapaport, "On the Psychoanalytic Theory of Affects," in Knight, ed., *Psychoanalytic Psychiatry and Psychology*. See also Rapaport, *Organization and Pathology of Thought* (Columbia University Press, New York, 1951), pp. 689-91. Rapaport bases his description on Freud's remarks in "The Interpretation of Dreams." See *The Basic Writings of Sigmund Freud* (Random House, New York, 1938), pp. 508-509.

points out, this implies a conflict theory of affect. Indeed, he assumes that the "clash" between the drive tension and the reality absence of the drive object is the prototype of conflict.[4] Affect, at this stage, is considered entirely a discharge process which has the function of ridding the organism of excessive drive tension ("safety-valve" function of affect). While we have no direct way of knowing what goes on in the hungry infant, we will not go too far astray if we rely on our natural understanding of the expressive features of the infant's behavior and on our insight into phenomena analogous to the infant's crying and restlessness in adults. These two sources confirm the assumption of psychoanalytic theory that the affect we see in the restless infant is one of distress due to the rising need tension, and we also see that there is no apparent goal-directedness in the affective behavior but rather a general, non-directed motor activity, which may or may not be accompanied by crying. This corresponds very well to the concept of affect as a mere discharge of tension, without directedness. We are familiar, from our own experience and from observation of others, with similar, if milder phenomena in adults, e.g. the restlessness that overcomes us if we want or expect something and are prevented from goal-directed action. Then we may discharge some of the tension by restlessly walking back and forth, or by other nonpurposive motor activity. In pathological adult behavior the temper tantrum probably represents a fairly close analogy to extreme distress affect in an infant.

While the hungry infant's restlessness and crying is the most dramatic instance of its emotional[5] behavior, we can observe other instances which show a different kind of emotional behavior from the first or second day of the infant's life on. When we watch the sucking behavior of infants in nursing we can see in quite a few of them an attitude which shows all the signs of eager concentration. Here the picture is entirely different from the restless behavior. The torso and the limbs are held quite still and the whole energy is concentrated on the sucking activity. This activity itself is the eagerly pursued and gratifying goal of the infant.[6] The question

---

4] Rapaport, "On the Psychoanalytic Theory of Affects," *loc. cit.,* p. 285. About this assumption see below, pp. 31-32.

5] The words "affect" and "emotion" are used as synonyms in this presentation.

6] Piaget has given a detailed description of eager goal-directedness which he observed as early as the first and second day of life and which leads to an increasingly successful groping for the nipple in the following days. Jean Piaget,

arises why so many adherents of the conflict theory of emotions and some other students of affect, too, have failed to notice the affect which is so clearly apparent in this kind of action and which is present, if often less obviously and at times quite subtly only, in any other action. Perhaps it is because the affects arising from conflict, blocking, frustration are often more violent and dramatic (although by no means always) than those which I just described and which I propose to designate as *activity-affects*. Perhaps, also, the prejudice that affects are a more or less pathological, disturbing phenomenon has blinded some to those affects which appear in coordinated, goal-directed actions. Yet, each one of us is familiar from his own experience with the feeling of eagerness, zest, intentness that characterizes so many actions, be they actions to satisfy such a basic need as that for food when we are hungry, or be they any other kind of action in which we are strongly interested. I mean at this point not the relief from hunger, but the positive tension feeling of eagerness and the enjoyment in eating when hungry or drinking when thirsty. It is this affect which we encounter first in the eagerly nursing baby.

I want to draw attention especially to the fact that here we find in the very young infant an affect which does not impress as unruly, diffuse, violent, but as a kind of goal-directed, positive tension feeling, and this at a time when, according to classical psychoanalytic theory, no "taming," counter-cathecting, or controlling of drive or affect has yet taken place. Obviously, this neither implies nor suggests that in the total development of affect from infancy to adulthood counter-cathectic and other "taming" does not play a very important role. But it does point up the fact that we find, *before* these developments have started, right from the beginning of life, two types of affect, one of which impresses as the diffuse discharge of tension, familiar from Freud's theory, the other as a positive, directed tension phenomenon which seems similar to the activity-affects of later life, and is encountered first in connection with a basic, biological need. Probably, the development of affectivity proceeds both by counter-cathexis, repression, taming and by the growth, maturation, and spreading of an inborn capacity for striving (activity-affect). The activity-affects themselves undergo some change and development as they become

The Origins of Intelligence in Children (International Universities Press, New York, 1952), pp. 25-26. See also below, p. 72.

attached to an increasing number and variety of activities, interests, and acts of relating to others and to the world around us, and as the capacity for delay develops. But they are, right from the beginning of life, clearly different from the other type of affect, which Freud describes and which I shall designate as *embeddedness-affect*. This consists originally in diffuse discharge of tension, whereas the activity-affect can be described as a directed, sustained, and activity-sustaining tension.

While the eagerness of the nursing infant is the main example of activity-affect at this earliest stage of development, it is not the only one. Interested, attentive looking is another instance where the emotion is not a restless discharge phenomenon but again impresses as an eager directedness and is best described as an expression of interest. Some babies start to look at things in an interested, attentive way from the first or second week on, that is, even before their ability to focus their eyes on a particular object has matured. One observer has found that this looking takes place when the infant is neither hungry nor sleepy, and she describes it as involving "a comprehensive bodily effort; the whole body is still and the energy is concentrated in holding the head up for a moment or two and the baby keeps its gaze or stare steadily on an object, something bright generally, for some seconds."[7] Preyer as well as Piaget observed the baby's pleasure in soft light toward the end of the first week of life, and that he tries to prolong the sight of a luminous object and to recover it when it disappears from sight.[8] Here, the looking itself, i.e. the activity itself, seems to be the goal on which the baby concentrates eagerly.

This type of eager, zestful activity-affect is encountered with increasing frequency and in relation to an increasing variety of activities as the infant develops into a child. We can observe it as he learns to reach, to play with his fingers, to manipulate objects, to sit up, to crawl, and, in a particularly impressive way, when he learns to walk, toward the end of the first year. The child is indefatigable in his efforts to assume the upright posture and to walk. It is quite clear that in these efforts the goal is neither discharge of tension, the achievement of a tensionless state of satiation, or sleep,

7] Personal communication by Lois B. Murphy. Similar observations by F. Stirnimann, *Psychologie des neugeborenen Kindes* (Rascher Verlag, Zürich and Leipzig, 1940), p. 59. See also this volume, pp. 119-122.

8] Piaget, *The Origins of Intelligence in Children*, pp. 62-63.

nor a feeling of relaxed comfort, but the difficult activity itself of standing up and walking. The eagerness with which this goal is pursued, the concentration on the ever repeated efforts, the joy of the child when he succeeds are touching and impressive to watch.[9] I believe that these early instances in which the activity itself is the eagerly pursued goal of the infant are the prototypes of the adult's capacity to become interested in an activity for its own sake, without an ulterior motive such as money, prestige, etc.[10] Essentially, all such activities are new, expanding way of getting in touch with and relating to ever new aspects of the environment, of the world.

Before further considering the implications of our observations for the theory of affect, it will be useful to pay attention to their implication for our understanding of personality development. The psychoanalytic model of the primary psychic processes can be divided into two phases, which may be viewed separately. One phase consists of rising need tension ⟶ restlessness. The other of appearance of the breast to the hungry infant ⟶ sucking and swallowing action. The first phase leads to restlessness, i.e. diffuse affect discharge; the second leads to directed tension affect concomitant with drive action. The meaning of the first phase becomes more clearly apparent when we compare the infant's prenatal and postnatal situations. Before birth there was no, or relatively little, rising need tension and restlessness because all the needs of the foetus were continuously supplied by the mother's bloodstream. After birth, i.e. after the physical separation from the mother, the infant is severed from this continuous source of supply and is, at first, helpless to seek other sources. Compared to the intrauterine situation this is a radical change and one that constitutes an extremely stressful situation until the mother appears and feeds the infant.

The second phase, appearance of breast ⟶ sucking action, offers a very different picture. While the infant here, too, is no longer continuously fed through the placenta, it is not helpless and is able to get at a source of supply by means of its own activity

9] Compare the rich and thoughtful paper by E. Straus on the meaning of the upright posture. Erwin Straus, "Die aufrechte Haltung," *Monatsschrift für Psychiatrie und Neurologie*, 1949, 117:367-379.

10] I do not imply, of course, that parental gratification with the child's learning to walk is not a significant and important factor in the child's life and that it may even play a role as an added motivation. However, the child does not learn to walk to please his parents but mainly because he wants to stand up and walk.

once it has become aware of the presence of the breast. In other words, in the sucking action we find the first instance in the life of the neonate when, by his own active effort, in cooperation with the mother, he is able to satisfy his need. The activity in which the neonate has to engage in order to still his hunger is by no means simple. It involves a quite complex sensory and neuromuscular coordination which enables him to take hold of the nipple with his lips, to use lips and tongue in sucking, and to swallow. This active effort is characterized by the presence of the activity-affect described before.

I have emphasized the active quality of the sucking action because the classical concepts of the oral phase and the oral-receptive character have given rise to the erroneous idea that nursing amounts to being fed passively, to passive receiving, when actually it is the first instance of the infant's going actively after something for which, true enough, he needs also the cooperation of the mother.[11] Probably we have been inclined to overlook the active quality of the infant's nursing action because the adult thinks in terms of active search for satisfaction only when he overcomes obstacles or distance, either by moving from one place to another in search of an object or by reaching for it with his hands and arms. This requires the development of the sense of sight, in order to see the desired object, and the capacity to walk or to reach and grasp. In the sensory development of the neonate and very young infant, the sense of sight is not yet very important nor very developed. Tactile and olfactory cues play a predominant role. He becomes aware of the breast at first primarily through the senses of touch, smell, and taste. This does not alter the fact that even though the breast is "given" to him, i.e. brought into contact with his organs of touch, smell, and taste, he then still has to get the milk. For this, considerable motor activity of a directed and coordinated kind is required. If we think of an adult who, with a different sensory and motor organization, sees a tempting fruit in a tree and reaches for it, the difference does not lie so much in the active effort exerted as in the fact that in the infant the sensory cues release an instinctive

11] Compare Escalona's remark that feeding, breast-feeding more than bottle-feeding, is not merely a passive process but requires the active cooperation of the baby. Sibylle Escalona, "Emotional Development in the First Year of Life," in Milton J. E. Senn, ed., *Transactions of the Sixth Conference on Problems of Infancy and Childhood, 1952* (Josiah Macy, Jr., Foundation, New York, 1953), pp. 14-15.

activity while in the adult the activity is to a larger extent deliberate and purposive. Both adult and infant, however, have to overcome actively the gap between the hungry organism and the source of supply.

In nursing behavior, both the restless diffuse affect and the directed activity affect arise from drive tension. Only the hungry infant will get restless and only the hungry infant will be eager to suck.[12] Both types of affect are always present and observable, although their relative importance and strength varies considerably from one baby to another and from one occasion to another. When an infant is awakened from sleep in order to be fed, the diffuse discharge of drive tension in restlessness may not take place at all, but the baby to whom the mother gives the breast may start at once to suck eagerly. In "demand" feeding, on the other hand, the drive tension always leads to some restlessness, which serves as a signal to the mother to nurse the infant, at which point the action affect supplants the helpless, diffuse discharge of tension. I believe that we have in these two kinds of affect, which can be observed from the beginning of extrauterine life, the prototypes of two types of emotion which are destined to play a role throughout man's life. Their quality, relative strength, and relative frequency are important in the formation and functioning of the individual personality. The decisive difference between these two types of affect is that one is characterized by helpless distress (embeddedness-affect), the other by active coping with a drive tension or by active relating to the environment (activity-affect). They represent two different ways of dealing with the separation from the intrauterine situation of continuous supply and shelter. One implies basically the wish for the return to this stage or the frustration, anger, impatience that such a return is not possible; the other represents the adaptation to the new, separate form of existence. In reality, we find in every person a mixture of these two types of affect, although one of them may appear relatively pure on one occasion, the other on another.

In the neonate we can already observe quite marked differences both with regard to the congenital strength of these affect types in different individuals and with regard to their occurrence on different occasions. We are not concerned here with the very im-

---

12] I am not dealing here with the fact that sucking also comes to serve "pacifying" functions other than the stilling of hunger.

portant factor of the mother's attitude in nursing the baby.[13] For purposes of the present discussion we want to simplify matters by assuming that the mother is fully turned toward the infant in an attitude of tender care. Even then we can observe, and mothers who have nursed several children will tell us, that one infant nurses with great eagerness, energy, and concentration while another infant nurses only half-heartedly as it were, or haphazardly, or with many interruptions, restlessly, or is easily distracted.[14] These differences can be explained only if we assume congenital differences; they are not differences in physiological need for food. They are differences in the capacity actively to bridge the gap between the infant and the supply of milk in the mother's breast. I am inclined toward the hypothesis that these differences are related mainly to the channeling and quality of affect, and that in the eagerly nursing infant the activity-affect is congenitally stronger than in the haphazardly sucking one, in whom the transition from passive intrauterine receptivity to active going after the supply of milk has not taken place and the affect of helpless distress is more predominant. Obviously, this does not imply that subsequent learning from experience cannot change and even reverse the situation. If the active coping behavior is encouraged, the infant will learn to rely more on its own activity. Conversely, an overanxious, overprotective, or punitive mother may well prevent a congenitally active child from coping effectively with its environment. I am implying here that with the maturation of each faculty of the growing infant, such as grasping, focal regard and focal attention, reaching, upright posture and walking, we encounter the same difference of affect. One child will cry helplessly or lose interest when an object is taken from him or otherwise gets out of immediate reach; another child will reach for it or crawl or go after it with considerable determination, eagerness, and persistence. Similarly, Stirnimann reports characteristic differences in the reaction of the newborn to unpleasant stimuli, which closely resemble differences that we also find among adults: one baby will withdraw from the stimulus, another will cry restlessly, a third will actively try to do something against the cause of the unpleasant sensation.[15] The general course

13] For a discussion of this, see below pp. 50-51.
14] Compare also Piaget's observations of such congenital differences, in *The Origins of Intelligence in Children*, p. 25.
15] Stirnimann, *Psychologie des neugeborenen Kindes*, p. 98 and *passim*.

of development, especially during the first year or two of life, is one in which the infant acquires, partly by growth and maturation, partly by learning, a great many capacities, beyond the capacity to suck, which enable him to go actively after the satisfaction of his needs and to pursue his interests. Along with this development comes a shift in the relative frequency and intensity of embeddedness and activity-affect, respectively. This shift is dependent not only on the maturation of these capacities but also, throughout life, very much on the total psychic structure and the predominance in it either of the wish to continue the intrauterine existence or of the acceptance of separateness and the development of active ways of relating to and coping with the environment. We can assume that the relatively strong development of activity-affect (strong in relation to diffuse discharges of affect in restlessness) is one of the components which will lead to the development of ego-strength.

The recognition of the existence of and predisposition to activity-affects speaks against the validity of a pure conflict theory of emotions. The function of the activity-affects is to establish an effective emotional link between the separate organism and the environment, so that the organism will be able to engage in those activities which will satisfy his needs, develop his capacities, and further his life. In contrast, the main biological function of the embeddedness-affects is, originally, to arouse the attention and activate the care of the mothering one, that is, to induce the environment to do something about the organism's needs. This can be seen very clearly in the analysis of adult patients with strong embeddedness-affects, such as impatience, anger upon frustration, dependent demands. Their emotions usually still center around the child's cry for help or its restlessness and anger when meeting with obstacles or frustrations. The implication here is that the mere absence of the "drive-object," of the desired goal, constitutes the prototype of conflict only from the point of view of embeddedness. That is, only when the person's world is structured as an embeddedness world, a world which is experienced essentially as a uterus or a protective mother, does the affect arise out of a conflict, namely the conflict between the helpless "child" who wants something and the world conceived as a mother who withholds the satisfaction and help which she should give.[16] From

16] Of course, I do not imply by this that many of the frustrations in our civi-

the viewpoint of separate existence, however, the absence of the drive object or the distance of the sought-after goal does not constitute conflict, but mobilizes activity-affect and striving leading to the sustained efforts suitable to reach the goal in the environment.

The existence from birth on and throughout life of activity-affects also speaks against the theories that all emotions are reproductions of primeval traumatic experiences and that they are all basically a safety valve for the discharge of drive tension. Experientially the activity-affects—in contrast to the embeddedness-affects—have energetic, zestful, interested feeling tones and they are characterized by a positive tension feeling; they lend impetus to the ongoing activity and are felt to energize, activate, and sustain it, rather than to get rid of tension. If activity-affects, too, are the felt aspects of tension and discharge processes—which I consider quite likely—then these processes are comparable to the functioning of the steam engine or the internal combustion motor, i.e. to a continuous building up and discharge of energy by which the engine is driven. In other words, there are increasingly from birth on not only affects which are the representations in awareness, the felt aspects of discharge of drive tension for safety-valve functions, but also affects which are the felt aspects of the continuous building up *and* discharge of drive energy utilized for carrying out activities. Emotions have the function not only of letting off steam (embeddedness-affect) but also of creating an activity-sustaining mood (activity-affects).[17]

As the infant and child develop, the activity-affects take on

---

lization and our world are not based on actual conflict, e.g. the conflict between those wanting in the satisfaction of their legitimate needs and those who aim not at a just sharing of the available resources but at the maintenance of a position of power over others and of privilege for themselves. However, the mature person's reaction to this type of real situation is not the frustrated cry for a helping mother but the sustained effort to bring about changes which will remedy the situation.

17] Freud continued to consider affects as reproductions by the ego of traumatic experiences and inherited hysterical attacks, even at the last stage of his affect theory in which he emphasized their signal function. According to him, the signal consists in the tamed reproduction of a traumatic event, similar to a hysterical attack. Compare Freud, *Inhibitions, Symptoms and Anxiety*, pp. 24, 97, 99. Post-Freudian theory, too, sees the positive aspect of affects only in their signal function and assumes that this is the outcome of a taming, controlling, and restricting process imposed by the ego on the affects. It has overlooked the innate existence of the activity-affects and their increasing significance in adapting the organism to the extrauterine, higher form of existence. Compare Rapaport's synthesis, "On the Psychoanalytic Theory of Affects," in Knight, ed., *Psychoanalytic Psychiatry and Psychology*, especially pp. 305-306.

the increasingly important function of providing and sustaining the emotional link between the person and objects which do not impinge directly on his sense organs while at the same time they retain their original function of providing the emotional motivation to bridge the gap between the organism and the objects which do impinge on its sensorium. Piaget has shown that between the ages of nine and twelve months the infant first develops the idea that an object may continue to exist even if it cannot be seen, heard, or felt by him. Up to eight months the baby will try to grasp and manipulate an object which he sees but will not make any attempt to do so if, even before his eyes, one covers it with a cloth or places a screen between the baby and the object. But from eight months on he will seek the object under the cloth or behind the screen.[18] This observation implies not merely a purely intellectual development, namely the birth of the idea of object constancy, but primarily it signifies a very important expansion of activity-affect. The child remains *interested* in the object, even though he can't see it. Activity-affect from this stage on can be felt not only in relation to perceived objects but also in relation to ideas of objects and of activities, and it is this felt aspect of the drive or interest which links child and adult to the world.

18] Piaget, "Principal Factors Determining Intellectual Evolution from Childhood to Adult Life," in *Organization and Pathology of Thought*, pp. 163-164. A more detailed analysis in Piaget, *The Construction of Reality in the Child* (Basic Books, New York, 1954), pp. 3-96.

3

Analysis of
Specific Emotions:
Hope, Joy, Anxiety,
and Pleasure

SO FAR WE HAVE TRACED THE TWO TYPES OF AFFECT, EMBEDDEDNESS-affect and activity-affect, mainly in their early forms in the beginning of life, in the neonate and very young infant. We have to examine now what their roles are in later life, and whether and how they appear in the great variety of emotions in adult life.

Since it would require a whole book to analyze all the different emotions, we have to limit our discussion to a few examples. For these we shall choose some emotions which have found little or no treatment in the Freudian psychoanalytic literature, namely hope and joy, and two which are central to psychoanalytic thought, namely anxiety and pleasure.

Sartre's theory of emotions,[1] which is based exclusively on the observation of adult behavior, furnishes a good starting point for such an exploration. He asserts that emotion is the attempt to transform the world by magic when it becomes too difficult for us to cope with it in accordance with the deterministic pathways of reality.[2] It is true that we can often observe this magic

1] Jean-Paul Sartre, *The Emotions: Outline of a Theory* (Philosophical Library, New York, 1948).
2] *Ibid.,* pp. 58-91, especially pp. 58-59.

34

transformation of the world by emotion. In the ostrich policy of fear we like to blind ourselves against the difficulties, obstacles, and dangers of reality and to act as if they were nonexistent. In narcissistic feelings of omnipotence, in a similar way, we deny our own limitations and the difficulties to be overcome in reality and feel, magically, as *if* we had mastered all these difficulties. For example, people with psychogenic difficulties in working will sometimes have a feeling of power which at that moment makes them feel convinced that they can do the work they want to do without any effort, almost as if it had been accomplished already, although in reality they find it quite impossible to stay with their work for any length of time, often not even for ten or fifteen minutes. To some extent this feeling may reflect the awareness that they *can* do the work if it were not for their conflicts about it. But, primarily, this feeling of power is a quasi-hallucinatory fulfillment of the wish to return to infantile omnipotence, and is similar to Freud's description of the hallucinatory perception of food (or, as I would prefer to say, of the total satisfying feeling of being nursed) as resulting from the hungry infant's wish for food. In certain feelings of wishing and hoping we anticipate that reality and other people will conform to our fondest expectations, that fulfillment of our hopes will magically be granted by the world. All forms of wishful thinking contain this element of a reality transformed by the magic of emotion. Thus, undeniably, the magic function of emotion can be seen in many instances of adult behavior.

But when we analyze any of these instances more closely, then we see that this magic quite regularly consists of the (unconscious) phantasy of the return to a state similar to that of the foetus embedded in the uterus, i.e. to a state of being completely sheltered and of a continuous and constant satisfaction of all needs, without having to make any effort. This is as true of the denial of the dangers and difficulties of reality (or of the similar device of excessive sleeping in the face of a feared reality) as it is of the omnipotent feeling of being able to command fulfillment of every wish and ambition. In other words, Sartre's theory is not correct for all emotions but only for the embeddedness-emotions, that is, for all those which arise from the conflict of the person who persists in or reverts to the attitude that the fulfillment of his needs should be granted as it once was in intrauterine life and, to a lesser extent, after birth by a protective, nurturing mother.

It does not hold true, however, for the activity-emotions, which often accompany and sustain our active efforts in reality.[3] In them, too, we may anticipate satisfaction of a need, but this anticipation is consistent with reality and with a rational assessment of the effect of our activity on reality.

Obstacles and *frustrations* encountered in reality very often lead to a shift in attitude from active striving to embeddedness-affect. The readiness with which this shift occurs as compared with a realistic acceptance of and active fight against obstacles and frustrations is a good indicator of the relative strength of the tendency toward embeddedness-affect as compared with the relative strength of the striving attitude and the activity-affect. We can observe people who, in the face of very slight obstacles or frustrations, are ready to give up, feel unfairly treated, or adopt an attitude of reproachful injury or impatient anger. All these different affects have a common root in the underlying failure to develop beyond the stage of quasi-intrauterine embeddedness. Within the quasi-intrauterine world they make perfect sense: the foetus, by its biological structure, requires the relatively complete shelter and nurturing in the womb. In embeddedness-affect man reacts to *any disturbance* of this situation; he reacts as if the world were a womb for him. If the obstacles and frustrations are sufficiently great, most of us revert, to some extent, to this attitude, perhaps with the exception of those few who have traveled the difficult path to a profound and complete acceptance of man's situation in the world.

The person who resorts to magic feelings of omnipotence in the attempt to deny the difficulties of reality and to return, in phantasy, to the quasi-intrauterine phase where his wishes seemed magically to produce maternal care and fulfillment of the wish will be particularly vulnerable to the encounter of obstacles and frustrations, because they are in such glaring contrast to the narcissistic phantasy of omnipotence. Often, these people react with despair or hopelessness to realistic difficulties. I have the impression that their situation is comparable to that of certain drug addicts for whom the awakening from the euphoric stage induced by the drug is much harder to take than the confrontation of a difficult and painful reality was before they resorted to the escape from it by

3] By no means always. Active effort can be made with very ambivalent feelings, e.g. quite often with a feeling of coercion and resistance against coercion.

means of drugs. As long as it is undisturbed, the omnipotent phantasy is an escape from reality comparable to that in a drugged state, and therefore the encounter with the realistic difficulties of life often produces much stronger frustration affects (embeddedness-affects) in these people than in others.

Hope and Joy

The feeling of *hope* is of particular interest in the context of the difference between embeddedness- and activity-affect, because it can belong to both of them. Under the one word "hope" are concealed two profoundly different kinds of feeling, depending on whether we deal with hope as an embeddedness-affect or with hope as an activity-affect. Hope can be, and very often is, the mere wishful expectation and anticipation that somehow things will change for the better. Another person, God, fate, some event, such as marriage, the birth of a child, moving to another house or to another city, a trip, or—quite often—the mere flow of time, the beginning of a new year, the eternal tomorrow, will magically bring fulfillment without one's having anything to do about it.[4] Such hope may even be relegated to an imagined world after death. In all these instances hope is an embeddedness-affect, an expectation of and wish for magic change, to be brought about by some external agency or event, without one's own effort. It may range from an attitude of resigned and passive waiting, as described poignantly in Samuel Beckett's play *Waiting for Godot,* to a conscious or unconscious, insistent and often angry demand. Usually, such magic hope is also characterized by vagueness of the idea of what the change should be and what the realistic conditions for it are. To be happier, more satisfied, or some such general formula may be the hoped-for goal. This vagueness often is intrinsically related to the embeddedness state. The neonate and very young infant only feels general distress or discomfort without being able to locate the specific need or to think about the cause of the distress. His wish is for relief of distress, for comfort, which will be brought

4] This "tomorrow" of magic hope has been denounced eloquently by Camus. He sees in it man's worst enemy. Man longs for this tomorrow when everything in him ought to reject it. Albert Camus, *The Myth of Sisyphus* (Alfred A. Knopf, New York, 1955), pp. 13-14. Camus speaks of hope as such, but his penetrating remarks, it seems to me, apply only to magic hope. In this sense, he is right in pointing out that the absence of (magic) hope has nothing to do with despair. I would even say that, usually, where we find a strong element of magic hope we also find, upon closer analysis, a repressed despair.

about by the care of the mother. Similarly, the person who lives in a quasi-intrauterine world very often wishes for general relief to be brought about by somebody else or by some event. In the psychoanalytic situation this takes the form of the expectation that "psychoanalysis" or the analyst, without the active participation and effort of the analysand, will bring about the hoped-for happiness. The inability and the reluctance to make use of one's reason to find out more about the actual causes of the unhappiness and to invest active effort are part of the unconscious insistence on the continuation of quasi-intrauterine embeddedness.

Magic hope (which often goes together with magic superstitions the observation of which is expected to bring about change) forms a contrast to hope as an activity-affect. Here, no magic transformation of reality is expected, but the hope is based on the attempt to understand the concrete conditions of reality, to see one's own role in it realistically, and to engage in such efforts of thoughtful action as might be expected to bring about the hoped-for change. The affect of hope, in this case, has an activating effect. It helps in the mobilization of the energies needed for activity. By activity I mean not only motor activity but also the activity of thought or of relating to another person, e.g. in an attitude of loving concern. The person who feels hope, based on, to use Hegel's expression, *"real* possibility" (in contrast to merely phantasied, magic possibility) will usually act with more sustained energy than the person who acts without this affect. Of course, there exist all degrees of transition and mixture of magic and realistic hope, as is equally true of other embeddedness- and activity-affects. We have to picture these transitions on a continuum, on one end of which the quasi-intrauterine, embeddedness-affects would be located, on the other end the pure, realistic activity-affects. The affects which we find most frequently in reality usually are located somewhere between the two extremes of this continuum, with either the embeddedness or the activity quality prevailing.

Hope is closely related to *time.* In magic hope the time of the present is emptied and the emphasis shifts to the future. The present may be experienced as an unwelcome obstacle, as an empty span to be waited out, as time to be killed, time without meaning, fullness, weight. It may stretch endlessly in boredom, restlessness, or futility, or it may be felt as something to be kept free for the advent of the hoped-for future, but actually empty. In retrospect such empty time appears as shrunk, wasted, as though it had disappeared from one's life without leaving a trace. Pascal describes the emptiness of the time of the present in magic hope, as though it were man's universal experience of time: "Nous ne nous tenons jamais au temps présent. Nous anticipons l'avenir comme trop lent à venir, comme pour hâter son cours. . . . Le présent n'est jamais notre fin: le passé et le présent sont nos moyens; le seul avenir est notre fin. Ainsi nous ne vivons jamais, mais nous espérons de vivre; et, nous disposant toujours à être heureux, il est inévitable que nous ne le soyons jamais."[5] (We never take hold of the present. We anticipate the future as though it were too slow in coming and we wanted to hasten its arrival. . . . The present never is our goal: the past and the present are our means; only the future is our end. Thus, we never live, we only hope to live; and, in awaiting and preparing ourselves for happiness we inevitably never are happy.)

In the activity-affect of *realistic* hope, however, the present is not experienced as a desert through which one has to wander in order to arrive at the future. It receives its significance from the activities which make one's life meaningful and/or through which one tries to help bring about hoped-for change. While realistic hope, too, is directed towards the future it does not shift the emphasis from the present to anticipation of the future.[6]

The affect of *joy* is a stepchild of the conflict theories of emotion, including the classical psychoanalytic theory. It has found relatively little or no treatment by the proponents of these theories, probably because it does not seem to contain any elements of conflict and also because it is clearly different from the feeling of pleasure as conceived by Freud, who looks upon pleasure as being primarily relief from tension.[7] One finds the most contradictory statements about joy in the literature. Sartre emphasizes the element of *impatience* in joy and explains joy as the magical attempt to realize full possession of a desired object as an instantaneous totality.[8] N. Bull reports that in her attempts to induce different feelings

5] Pascal, "Pensées," *Oeuvres Complètes* (Bibliothèque de la Pléiade, Librairie Gallimard, Paris, 1954), pp. 1131-32, fragment 168.
6] See also below, pp. 73-74.
7] See below pp. 55-68 for a more detailed discussion of pleasure.
8] Sartre, *The Emotions*, pp. 68, 69. He distinguishes between "joy-feeling," a balanced, adapted state, and joy-emotion. At this point it becomes clear that only by explicitly denying to joy-feeling the character of emotion (p. 68), i.e. by arbi-

hypnotically she was least successful with joy, that it was very short-lived, often "forced," and often mixed with *triumph*. In fact, even in those subjects in which triumph and joy did not overlap, she feels that the difference between triumph and joy is largely a matter of orientation in time and space—"triumph carrying with it a sense of continuity while joy is only of the moment, without a future or a past" and thus more difficult for normal adults to achieve.[9] The joy that is linked to triumph or to good fortune is often regarded as *perilous* and extremely fragile.[10] Buytendijk distinguishes between a "leaping joy, a being animated when we shout, jubilate, dance" and a "silent, quiet joy, large, placid, voluminous, embracing as a climate." Of the former he says that it is allied to and impregnated with *impatience* and signifies the "reaching, longing for some value that is expected."[11] Goldstein emphasizes the "experience of infinite continuation" in joy, in contrast to those who stress its fleeting, momentary, precarious character, and considers it as a "productive disequilibrium leading to 'self-realization.' "[12] Obviously, the term "joy" as used by these different authors covers different phenomena, and we are as yet far from having a clear understanding of joy. All we can attempt here is to see whether the distinction between embeddedness- and activity-affects can shed some light on the complex problem of joy. From this viewpoint we can indeed discern two very different types of joy.

One type, magic joy, is based on the anticipation or the feeling of fulfillment of a drive, a wish. It is the joy of being about to get, or of having gotten something. During this state of joy, usu-

---

trarily limiting the sphere of emotion, can Sartre maintain his thesis that *all* emotions are magical behavior and arise out of conflict, out of defense against a peril.

9] Nina Bull, *The Attitude Theory of Emotion*, Nervous and Mental Disease Monographs, No. 81 (New York, 1951), pp. 71-76.

10] Compare Otto Friedrich Bollnow, *Das Wesen der Stimmungen* (Vittorio Clostermann, Frankfurt am Main, 1956), pp. 179-80. Bollnow attempts an analysis of the different feelings of happiness, and in contrast to Heidegger's exclusive stress on anxiety, emphasizes that their consideration is essential for a full grasp of the nature of man. His book contains many interesting quotations concerning the problem of joy and happiness.

11] F. J. J. Buytendijk, "The Phenomenological Approach to the Problem of Feelings and Emotions," in Martin L. Reymert, ed., *Feelings and Emotions* (McGraw-Hill Book Co., New York, 1950), pp. 127-141. His view of "leaping joy" coincides closely with Sartre's.

12] Kurt Goldstein, "On Emotions: Considerations from an Organismic Point of View," *Journal of Psychology*, 1951, 31:48-49.

ally short-lived, one feels as though the anticipated or present fulfillment has suddenly changed the whole character of life and of
the world. Everything seems or promises to be perfect—it is indeed
a magic transformation of the world. Obviously, in reality no single
event, whatever it may be, can change the character of life so
completely. What we see, then, in this kind of joy is the magic
overestimation of the joyful event that is anticipated or has taken
place. This joy sees in the present or in the immediate future the
fulfillment of what we described before as magic hope. Indeed, it
corresponds exactly to the kind of magic hope which expects from
a definite event a complete change in one's state of being, such as
a change from unhappiness and discontent to happiness and satisfaction. The only difference is that in magic hope the event hoped
for lies in the indefinite future, whereas in magic joy it either has
happened or is expected to happen in the immediate future. In
magic joy the impatiently anticipated fulfillment is expected to
come about not by the joyous person's activity, but to be given to
him by some outer event, be it the possession of the desired or
beloved woman, the passing of an examination, the acquisition of
a desired object, being of a certain age (like being grown-up or,
conversely, the wish to remain young), achieving success or fame,
etc. It may be objected that in some of these examples, especially
the last one, the achievement of some kind of success has not been
given to the person, but has come about by his own activity. This
is quite true, but the magic joy concerns not the achievement as
such nor the activity producing it, but the conscious or unconscious
expectations that are linked to the success. In these expectations
the future is magically changed, not by what one is going to do
in the future, not by our future behavior or way of life, but by
the event of success. It is as if fate were to give us a reward for past
labor in the form of success and this reward is to be a magic transformation of life.

Magic joy, thus, is essentially an expectation of future embeddedness, of a return to quasi-intrauterine existence: the joyful
event is expected to change the future in such a way that one will
be given all kinds of satisfaction. The relation of magic joy to
triumph lies in the feeling of being singled out, favored, and of
having achieved the hoped-for return to a state of being passively
rewarded, of having found, in some way, the good mother who
will take care of one so that he will be happier, more favored than

others. Hence the very frequent connection of magic joy and the *fear of envy*, or the feeling of the precariousness and perilousness of the state brought about by or expected from the joyful event. This fear of envy may be a fear that other people, or the gods,[13] or fate, will envy one, or the fear may have a more impersonal character, expressed in such superstitions as having to knock on wood lest the good fortune turn into something bad. In German a person favored by luck is called *Glückskind* (*child* of luck), which expresses the embeddedness quality of magic good fortune.

It is usually assumed that joy and the other happy emotions and moods bring people closer to each other, while anxiety, despair, sadness, and depression isolate them.[14] Actually, this is only partly true. Sadness, in contrast to depression, does not necessarily isolate, and joy, if it is magic joy with the component of feeling favored above others, does isolate. Even though on the surface the joyous person may want to announce his good fortune to everybody, this can be a quite egocentric activity without openness toward others, as we see it especially in hypomanic states. Where the element of triumph, of being singled out above others, becomes very pronounced, it may increase the fear of envy to such an extent that it tends to stifle or even prevent the feeling of magic joy.

However, the fear of envy and the feeling of triumph do not occur in connection with a different kind of joy, which is based, not on the expectation of return to quasi-uterine embeddedness, but in its highest form on the ongoing process of openness toward and affirmation of others and the world around one, on the activation of a feeling of being related to all things living. This joy lacks any feeling of impatience. It is the joy celebrated by Schiller in his *Ode to Joy*,[15] where he describes especially the connection between joy and the feeling of brotherliness. It is an activity-affect, in that it consists in continued acts of turning toward the world.

13] In Schiller's ballad, "The Ring of Polykrates," this connection between joy and fear of envy has found a classical description. Polykrates, the ruler of Samos, boasts about his happiness. One incident after another seems to prove the most incredible good fortune. But as these incidents pile up, his friend and guest, the king of Egypt, turns away from him with dread, convinced that such excess of good fortune can mean only one thing: the decision of the envious gods to destroy Polykrates, who is torn by fear in his "happiness."

14] This point is made especially by Bollnow, *Das Wesen der Stimmungen*, pp. 97-111.

15] Schiller's *Ode to Joy* furnished the text to the last movement of Beethoven's Ninth Symphony.

It is not linked to any expectation but is the felt experience of the ongoing acts of relatedness. This relatedness can take many other forms besides the one described so far, which constitutes joy in its profoundest, richest, and most embracing quality. It can be found in much more specialized, narrower forms of relatedness as the joy in any ongoing activity by which we get into contact, physically and/or mentally, with some aspect of the world around us, e.g. the child's joy in manipulating objects, the joy in walking through a woods on a fresh and clear morning, the joy in the exercise of any of our faculties. The essential characteristic which distinguishes this joy from magic joy is that it is not based on magic, passive expectation or anticipation, but on ongoing activity. It does not relate to the future, but is the result of the psychic activity of the moment. Like all activity-affects, it accompanies and sustains the ongoing activity. I propose to call it *real* (as contrasted with magic) *joy* because it is based not on a magic expectation but on the reality of the moment.[16]

So far we have dealt with affects which have received scant attention from classical psychoanalytic theory (hope and joy), possibly because they are not readily understandable on the basis of

---

16] The feeling of relatedness to the world in joy is also mentioned by Goldstein, when he says that in joy "we experience existence of ourself and the world" ("On Emotions," *loc. cit.*, p. 49). The concept of real joy as developed above is in essential agreement with Fromm's views on happiness and joy. Compare Erich Fromm, *Man For Himself* (Rinehart and Co., New York, 1947), pp. 186-191. Happiness and joy are closely related. Happiness refers to a basic mood (*Grundstimmung*) which pervades the person who, to use Fromm's term, excels in "the art of living," while joy refers to the activation or actualization of this basic feeling with regard to a temporally and quantitatively particular act or series of acts. In contrast to Fromm, who suggests (p. 187) using the term "joy" for the pleasure accompanying the satisfaction of appetite, I would speak in this instance of enjoyment. The distinction between enjoyment and joy is a fluid one and enjoyment can merge into joy. The enjoyment of the fine taste of food or wine is basically the receptive though attentive experience of how I am affected by the food on my tongue. This preponderantly receptive element has to do with the subject-centered quality of the sense of taste. The enjoyment of a work of art or a landscape is a much more active experience, due to the more active, object-centered quality of the fully developed human sense of sight. While in taste I enjoy the pleasant sensation on tongue and palate, in the full visual experience of the landscape, the work of art, etc., I am not merely affected by a pleasant sensation, but actively try to grasp the essence of the object seen. This kind of relation very often results in a genuine feeling of joy, with its heightened aliveness and relatedness to the object seen. Enjoyment sometimes can become a path to joy, and the joyous person is more capable of enjoyment than the joyless. But the gourmet, while enjoying fine food, very often does not know the experience of joy. The English word "enjoyment" stresses the kinship to joy. The German equivalent of "enjoyment," *Genuss*, emphasizes the difference from *Freude* (joy), and has more passive connotation than *Freude*. See also below, pp. 65-68.

Freud's concepts nor on the basis of any pure conflict theory of emotion. Let us turn now to those affects which are central to Freud's thought: anxiety and pleasure.

Anxiety

Anxiety was recognized by Freud, especially in his later years, as central for the theory of the neuroses. Its tremendous significance for the understanding of (normal) man had first been seen by Kierkegaard.[17] At about the same time that Freud published his book on anxiety (1926), Heidegger's *Sein und Zeit* (1927) tried to show that anxiety is the fundamental category of human existence.

From our viewpoint, anxiety is the embeddedness emotion par excellence. It arises with any separation from the state of embeddedness or with the threat of such a separation if the person is or feels helpless to cope with the situation of separation.

Such helplessness is experienced whenever in a particular "separation from embeddedness" situation the activity-affect aiming at the establishment of relatedness on the higher level of development (of greater differentiation and independence) is not sufficiently strong or persistent. The "trauma of birth" consists primarily in the difficulty of radical change and transition from one mode of life, the mode of embeddedness, to a different one. Hence, it recurs in changed forms and varying degrees, on a higher level of development at later points in life when there arises the necessity or desirability to emerge from a particular form or aspect of life in which one has become embedded and to make the transition to a new and different way of life, even in such relatively minor matters as changing a habit to which one has become accustomed, travel in foreign countries, etc. The danger of separation from embeddedness can arise from the outside, when some situation, event, or person poses a threat or challenge to this sheltered state, or it can arise because the individual himself tries to emerge from a state of embeddedness and feels entirely or partly helpless to do so.

In the latter case there is a conflict between the person's striving for growth and his clinging to embeddedness. The attempt to emerge from embeddedness sets off anxiety by which that side of the person which is afraid to leave the shelter of embeddedness warns him of the danger of helplessness in encountering the world.

17] See especially his book, *The Concept of Dread*, first published in 1844.

The areas in which the threat of separation is most readily experienced, the extent of these areas, and the kinds of events or situations which are most likely to constitute such a threat differ from one person to another, in accordance with their life histories and probably also with inborn predispositions toward anxiety[18] and toward activity-affect.[19] Although the areas in which and the means by which we try to maintain embeddedness differ individually, there exist such areas in all of us throughout life. Anxiety is ever present as a potentiality in all men. Indeed, the *potentiality* for anxiety is a much more powerful factor in the life of man than *acute* strong anxiety. The way in which man reacts to this potentiality—by anger, by trying to avoid anxiety at all cost, or by resolutely going into the activity and situation which might provoke the actualization of anxiety—is of crucial importance for his life. The threat of anxiety as a *potentiality* can be eliminated only by the *actual encounter* with the dreaded situation or activity, because until we actually meet the situation we do not know whether and how we will be able to live with it, master it, or perish in it, and thus we cannot transform the unknown and new into something knowable and known. Such encounter means leaving the embeddedness in the familiar and going forth to an unknown meeting with the world. The threat of *acute* anxiety can also be eliminated by *avoiding* the unknown situation, i.e. by restriction of the scope of life, by remaining in the embeddedness within the familiar and not venturing out. Obviously the threat of anxiety as a potentiality can never be eliminated totally since we cannot, and usually do not want to, encounter the infinite variety of situations possible for man. But the determination to go forward to such encounters keeps open the doors to an expanding life, while the seeking of protection in the embeddedness of the familiar makes for stagnation and constriction of life.

Anxiety appears in many gradations from a hardly perceptible twinge or a more or less constant mood of anxiousness of which the person often is not even conscious, to acute terror and panic. There is no clear demarcation line between anxiety and terror—they gradually merge into each other. The stronger the anxiety

18] Compare David Rapaport, "On the Psychoanalytic Theory of Affects," in Robert P. Knight, ed., *Psychoanalytic Psychiatry and Psychology* (International Universities Press, New York, 1954), p. 304.
19] See above, pp. 29-30.

and the closer it approaches terror, the less able will the person be to take anxiety upon himself in the attitude of resoluteness (Heidegger's *Entschlossenheit*). Hence the distinction between the signal function of anxiety[20] and the disruptive function of anxiety is a fluid one. One can think of increasingly strong anxiety as of increasingly loud signals which at a certain point of intensity stop being mere signals, i.e. signs upon whose perception man can still decide how he wants to react. At this point, which differs individually and with the situation, the signal function of anxiety changes into a disruptive, paralyzing function. Of course, man reacts to the signal function of anxiety, too, more often than not by disrupting the activity which might lead him to emerge from embeddedness and by scurrying back to the shelter of embeddedness (Sullivan's "security operations"). But this has still mainly the character of a flight activity, a more or less conscious or unnoticed giving up of something, turning away from something. At the point where anxiety becomes absolutely disruptive (paralyzing) there is no longer a possibility of choice. Thus, the signal function of anxiety is always an ambiguous one, signaling the danger of separation from embeddedness and, while tempting man to go back to embeddedness, still leaving open the possibility of the resolution to go forward and encounter the world. The disruptive, paralyzing function leaves no such choice; its function is to make man *avoid* the separation from embeddedness by paralyzing him and taking away from him the power of decision and action.[21]

20] This is the concept developed in Freud's later anxiety theory, *Inhibitions, Symptoms and Anxiety* (The Hogarth Press, London, 1949), p. 108 and *passim*, and foreshadowed by his view that the ego tames affects so that they reach only a minimal strength in which they serve as signals. "The Interpretation of Dreams," *Basic Writings* (Random House, New York, 1938), p. 536.

21] The disruptive function of anxiety relates anxiety to nausea, which also has the function of paralyzing all activity, but achieves it by different means, namely by an increasing loss of all interest and all emotional attachment with increasing degree of nausea until a state of complete indifference to the world is reached. This function of nausea has been shown in the significant work of Thure von Uexküll, "Untersuchungen über das Phänomen der 'Stimmung' mit einer Analyse der Nausea nach Apomorphingaben verschiedener Grösse," *Zeitschrift für klinische Medizin*, 1952, 149:132-210. He also shows that dizziness has the function of making activity impossible by taking away from us the *space* in which all our acts take place. Many people suffer from a more or less chronic slight anxiousness, often without being aware of the fact that they are feeling mild anxiety. This feeling often is hardly distinguishable from a slight feeling of nausea. Both lead to a withdrawal of interest in the world. This similarity of feeling and effect in nausea and anxiety points to their functional relatedness.

It has often been remarked that the difference between anxiety and fear is that while both are related to expectation, while both are about something, in anxiety the object of the expectation is unknown, while in fear it is known.[22] The unknown danger in anxiety is the new, unknown state of being when leaving a particular constellation of embeddedness. It tends to be the greater the more the child has been made to feel that life, the world, any new venture, any expanding beyond the already familiar are dangerous. Such a feeling can be aroused especially by the anxiety of parents who themselves are imbued with this feeling. In these cases the parents usually are not able to, and do not, specify the nature of the danger in any understandable, rational way, so that a vague distrust of the world and of life is engendered in the child. As a result, any concrete venture in which the child might engage is not only tied up with a concrete fear of its actual difficulty, or of a specific punishment, but also fraught with an unknown danger which adheres to the mere *beyond*, to the new state of being after leaving the familiar world in the daily routine of which both parents and child are embedded. It is this aspect which very often has the consequence that fear *opens into* anxiety.

I want to illustrate this openness of fear toward anxiety with a concrete example, familiar to many people. Suppose I have learned how to swim. Now I am learning how to jump into the water or how to dive. I have already jumped a few times so that I know that nothing will happen to me, that I can deal very well with the situation, that there is no danger. Yet, I hesitate before each new jump and I have to muster my courage to risk it. What is my "fear"? Is it not really anxiety? Supposedly what I am afraid of is the object "water," or that it will not carry me. But I know very well that it will. Am I not dealing, then, with anxiety, with the nameless threat of leaving the shelter of known safety and meeting the unknown? Leaving the firm, supporting earth and venturing into a different state of being, a state of being in which many of the trusted physical relationships with the environment will be radically changed? Probably many, perhaps most fears are in this peculiar way open toward the unknown, are not only fears of a concrete event but (in varying degrees according to the general anxiousness of the person and the degree to which different

22] See Freud, *Inhibitions, Symptoms and Anxiety*, p. 158.

situations mobilize it) at the same time anxieties about the *change in the state of being* which will be different from that before the event in a way which I cannot fully anticipate but which I will know only if and when I take the experience upon myself.[23] To this extent, they are anxieties connected with leaving a state of embeddedness and venturing into a new and always partly unknown kind of relatedness to the environment.

This *open-endedness of fear toward anxiety* can be observed in any number of situations where there is no question of such a drastic change of environment as in the example of jumping from land and air into water. For instance, the fear that in a fight I might get a bloody nose, or in a fall bruise my knee or break my leg, is not just the fear of these circumscribed events, but is open toward the anxiety of the unknown state of being into which I enter if any of these things should happen, augmented, of course, by the fact that we never know precisely in advance what will happen to us in living. E. Straus has described how in human walk, in contrast to the walk of the foor-footed animals, for one moment in each step the support of the ground is withdrawn from the body's center of gravity. The leg extended forward in walking prevents the threatening fall. He describes our walking as a movement "on credit": we do not wait until we have found a secure hold but trust, in swinging our body forward, that the next moment will bring the needed support to the stepping leg and to our body.[24] Walking requires faith in the future. I mention this example not only because it shows how so basic an activity as walking contains in it the fundamental human situation and its elements of risk, anxiety, and faith, but especially because of its developmental interest. Learning to walk entails the danger of falling. The child does not usually mind this danger. His eagerness (activity-affect) to master this new way of moving in and being in contact with the world is so strong that no amount of falling discourages it. But one can observe how parental anxiousness or parental faith in the child's capacity to master this new situation will make a great deal

23] Goldstein assumes that all fear is fear of the possible onset of anxiety, and that anxiety is the basic phenomenon from which fear derives. Kurt Goldstein, *The Organism* (American Book Company, New York, 1939), pp. 296-297.

24] Erwin Straus, "Die aufrechte Haltung," *Monatsschrift für Psychiatrie und Neurologie*, 1949, 117:371.

of difference in the way the child reacts to falling. This becomes even more marked when the child learns to walk downstairs, a situation where the moment of lack of support for the body's center of gravity is more marked. Indeed, if we could analyze fully the way in which people walk, on a level surface and especially downstairs, we would probably gain a great deal of information about the personality and its history with respect to the fundamental problems of anxiety, courage, confidence, and faith.

While anxiety is originally and often also later on connected with leaving embeddedness or the threat of separation from embeddedness,[25] embeddedness itself has *various stages* and a very great variety of forms according to the great variety of situations which men live in and encounter. The fundamental situation of embeddedness is the intrauterine situation (and in the animals which hatch from eggs it is the situation of the developing animal or its larva in the egg), where no separation from shelter and from the sources of energy supply (food, etc.) has taken place. Birth is the most radical of the many steps in life by which man leaves embeddedness and starts out in a more separate form of existence in which he has to adapt himself by means of a changed and changing system of relationships to his new situation. In birth he changes from a state in which he had no world, or in which he was sheltered within the world of the womb from any direct contact with the larger world, to a state where he is exposed to the world and where a great many physiological relationships suddenly have to be changed and adjusted to this new state of being. Because of the necessity of these adjustments the first two weeks after birth are, as Gesell puts it, "a critical period for all who survive the catastrophe of birth."[26] The difficulty and danger of this metamorpho-

---

25] Another cause of anxiety appears after infancy and early childhood. This is the anxiety about being strangled or suffocated in one's development by embeddedness. Its source is usually a mother who does not want her child to grow up into an independent person, separate from her, but who clings to the child for the satisfaction of her own embeddedness needs. This kind of mother-child relation usually results in a strengthening of the child's fear of separation from embeddedness, so that then the growing child's and eventually the adult's own neurotic needs to remain dependent gain a stranglehold on his healthy striving to emerge from embeddedness. Giving in to embeddedness anxiety, in these cases, causes a secondary feeling of helpless anxiety about one's wish and chances to grow and develop.

26] Arnold Gesell and Catherine G. Amatruda, *Developmental Diagnosis* (Paul B. Hoeber, New York, 1956), p. 217.

sis are shown by the rate of mortality, which is higher for the period of birth and the first two weeks of life than for any subsequent period until old age.

But while we do not know what the newborn experiences, it seems unlikely that he feels anxiety. Probably the distress resulting from separation from intrauterine embeddedness is at first felt as helpless global discomfort. As Freud has emphasized, there is, in spite of the "impressive caesura of birth," considerable continuity between intrauterine life and earliest infancy.[27] This continuity consists in the replacement of the womb by the mother's constant care. The mother now becomes the world of the infant by sheltering it from being too harshly exposed to the world and by supplying nourishment, although, as we have seen, there is the very important difference that the newborn baby now has to do something in order to get the nourishment (see pp. 27-28). At this stage, separation from the new form of embeddedness in the mother's care consists either in the inevitable interruption in the constancy of the care or in something going wrong with the care. The absence of the mother is at first experienced only in connection with rising need tension. The baby learns that its cry or restlessness usually has the power of making mother reappear to comfort it and to take care of its needs. But while the rising need tension (of hunger, etc.) or the exposure to a too direct impact of the environment (too low temperature, uncomfortable bedding, too bright light, too loud noise, etc.) is usually the cause of the infant's crying, we must beware of a too narrow conception of the mother's function in taking care of these needs. Freud thought that the danger which causes anxiety is merely one of non-gratification of a need, of growing need tension which causes a rise of stimulation (by the need) to an unpleasurable height, i.e. an economic disturbance in which the amount of stimulation cannot be disposed of by the helpless child.[28] We know, however, that if the mother appears upon the child's crying, but is angry, anxious, tense, or otherwise not capable of giving tender attention to the child and its needs, the crying may continue, feeding difficulties may set in, and even a not hungry child may not feel comforted when it is picked up by an anxious or tense mother. The reason for this, it seems to me, lies in the fact that the anxiety or tense-

27] Freud, *Inhibitions, Symptoms and Anxiety*, p. 109.
28] *Ibid.*, pp. 106-107.

ness of the mother causes a separation from embeddedness for the baby.

At this point of development, as we have seen, the embeddedness in the womb has been replaced by a much less complete and in very many respects different *embeddedness* in the *tender care* of the mother. Such tender care, e.g. in nursing, fuses into a global experience for the baby. While the infant is not, of course, able to distinguish between the elements of getting physical nourishment and the tender or not tender attitude of the mother, it is sensitive to the totality, the global character of the situation. We do not need to assume a special empathic transmission of anxiety or a transmission by contagion from the mother to the child.[29] It seems to me simpler and more likely if we assume that anxiety, tension, dislike on the part of the mother constitute a situation of *separation* between mother and child. True, the separation is not a physical but an emotional one. The mother can be *turned fully toward* the infant only if she has an attitude of tender care. Anxiety and tension disrupt such an attitude; dislike is the opposite of it. Hence, in anxiety and tension the mother no longer is fully there. This kind of "emotional absence" of a person is familiar to our adult experience, just as we can be aware of the suppressed hostility of another person. The infant probably experiences the global discomfort of separation from the mother and the resulting separation anxiety when one or the other of these emotions interferes with her full presence, i.e. with her being turned fully toward the child.[30]

To describe the various stages and forms of embeddedness in later life would be tantamount to writing a compendium of the various normal and neurotic security operations and forms of adjustment. In the present context, only the most sketchy and general statement is possible. Probably the most frequent *neurotic*

29] Empathic induction of anxiety in the child by the mother's anxiety is assumed by Sullivan. Harry Stack Sullivan, *The Interpersonal Theory of Psychiatry* (W. W. Norton & Co., New York, 1953), pp. 41-42. The same assumption is made by Escalona, who uses the term "contagion" for the "transmission" of anxiety from mother to child. Sibylle Escalona, "Emotional Development in the First Year of Life," in Milton J. E. Senn, ed., *Transactions of the Sixth Conference on Problems of Infancy and Childhood, 1952* (Josiah Macy, Jr., Foundation, New York, 1953), pp. 34-35.

30] One might speculate that feeding difficulties because of an anxious, tense, or otherwise averted mother are the prototype of separation anxiety that is disruptive of an activity-affect and of activity. Perhaps, in these cases, the trauma of loss of embeddedness paralyzes the nursling's capacity to strive for nourishment.

perpetuation of embeddedness consists of using other people as a kind of mother who will serve as a protective screen between the person and the world. But there are of course many other types of using, i.e. attempting to control other people so that they will serve as a protection against an immediate encounter with the world. The *normal* embeddedness in the sphere of interpersonal relations consists in relying on the relative stability of these relations, e.g. that the attitude of one's wife, husband, friends will not suddenly and unaccountably change. Man is also embedded normally in the countless patterns of routine, convention, more or less automatic behavior on his own part and on the part of others. He is embedded in his family, his home, his work, the circle of his friends, his town, his language, his culture, and his country. These publicly or privately "institutionalized" patterns, while created by man and changeable by him, in a way take the place of the instinctive behavior in which the animals are embedded. The embeddedness function of these patterns plays a large role, psychologically, in the conservative tendencies of man, in his fear of new individual as well as social ways of life.

Heidegger says that "anxiety is anxious about being-in-the-world."[31] If he means by this, as I believe he does, that being in the world, directly, without protection by some kind of embeddedness, is the "object" of anxiety, this would coincide with my conviction that anxiety is basically about separation from embeddedness, that is, in the adult person, about separation from the patterns of embeddedness just described, and/or from the perpetuated embeddedness of infancy and childhood.

But while man, as we know him, never emerges fully from embeddedness and always returns to some measure of embeddedness,[32] the possibility and actuality of acts of emerging and directly

31] Martin Heidegger, *Sein und Zeit* (Neomarius Verlag, Tuebingen, 1949), p. 187. My translation does not do full justice to the German text: "Wovor die Angst sich ängstet, ist das In-der-Welt-sein selbst."

32] In such figures as Christ and Buddha, mankind has crystallized the belief in the human potentiality for a full emergence from embeddedness. In saying that man as we know him never emerges fully from embeddedness I make a statement only about people of whom I have empirical knowledge, but do not want to say that full emergence is incompatible with human nature. From an evolutionary standpoint we can see that the higher up we move in the animal scale, the more we find an increase in active mobility and in independence from embeddedness in the most immediate and narrow environment. With the advent of the warm-blooded animals this independence is greatly increased. Also we find increasingly stronger and richer manifestations of an exploratory drive, i.e. of the first traces

encountering his fellow men and the world around him constitute an essential aspect of his humanity, an aspect which has been called aptly his *openness toward the world*,[33] in contrast to the closed world in which the animals live. This world-openness is most pronounced during infancy and childhood, when it leads to countless encounters with the world that increasingly opens beyond the quasi-uterine embeddedness during which mother constitutes the infant's world. These encounters are brought about by the exploratory drive and the very strong activity-affect, which is the felt aspect of this drive. They lead to an expansion of the child's world unparalleled in any later period of life.

Man's anxiety in leaving embeddedness is the one most powerful antagonist of his world-openness. It wants to confine him in the embeddedness of the familiar so that he will not experience the awe and wonder of the infinitely new and unknown.[34] And it

---

of world-openness, culminating in the primates. In man, independence from embeddedness and degree of world-openness are suddenly vastly increased over what we find in the primates. Owing to his gift of reflective consciousness, individual man has the possibility, within certain limits, to actively influence his own and others' development toward fuller emergence from embeddedness. Nobody can say how far mankind will be able to travel on this road.

33] This translates the word *Weltoffenheit*, which Adolf Portmann uses in his important and stimulating book, *Biologische Fragmente zu einer Lehre vom Menschen* (Benno Schwabe & Co., Basel, 1951); see especially pp. 59-64. The closed worlds of the animals have been described by J. von Uexküll's pioneering work in biology. He coined the term *Umwelten* for them. He extended this concept to man and described men as living in their individual *Umwelten* (as contrasted with the animals' *Umwelt*, which is more or less the same for the members of a species). Jakob von Uexküll, *Umwelt und Innenwelt der Tiere* (Berlin, 1921). Jakob von Uexküll und Georg Kriszat, *Streifzüge durch die Umwelten von Tieren und Menschen* (Berlin, 1934). While it can be fruitful metaphorically to speak of and describe the *Umwelten* in which the members of a particular civilization, or social class, or group, or, finally, individual people live, these *Umwelten* are essentially different from those of the animals. They are more or less identical with the various structures of embeddedness which men, culturally and individually, develop and they are different from the animals' *Umwelten* in that they are largely cultural and not instinct-bound. They do not, however, constitute all of man's world, because man can and does constantly transcend these *Umwelten* into the infiniteness of the world, thus encountering ever new aspects of world which then, in turn, may become assimilated and, as it were, petrified in becoming institutionalized parts of the culture. This process has its parallel in the individual person's emerging from embeddedness and encountering culture and world.

34] It is this awe of which Goethe has said, "Das Schaudern ist der Menschheit bestes Teil" (The feeling of awe is man's best part). *Faust II*, Act I, scene 5, "Finstere Galerie." Compare also Kierkegaard's words, "Anxiety is the dizziness of freedom." The word "familiar" expresses very well the significant connection between remaining embedded in the family and avoiding the encounter with the world. That which has to do with the family is the prototype of all that is "familiar," i.e. that requires no venturing into the openness of the world.

wants to confine him in the embeddedness of using other people for his needs, as he once was embedded in using his mother's care for his needs. His world remains open only to the extent to which time and again he can transcend such confinement in acts of object-centered interest and love, because only in such acts does he actually encounter the world and people around him, in their own right, without being blinded by the strength of his embeddedness needs.[35]

The emergence from embeddedness and the direct encounter with the world implies both being *open* to the impact of the world, and responding to this impact. Openness toward the world, while a primarily receptive attitude, is by no means identical with the passivity of embeddedness. Openness and responsiveness are the two aspects of encounter, of intercourse with the world. Embeddedness lets the person neither experience the world nor respond to this experience. In a particular act of encounter there may be more emphasis on the receptive openness or more on the response. In the former case we speak primarily of experiencing, in the latter of reacting. But every human encounter with the world pulsates or oscillates between these two aspects of receptiveness and response. In every act of experiencing there is also a more or less marked response, and in every activity, physical or mental, there is more or less receptiveness toward the environment with regard to which one acts. The threat of anxiety in separating from a state of embeddedness may be felt more with regard to the receptive or to the reactive pole of the encounter with the world, although usually it is felt to some extent with regard to both. The child, upon seeing a stranger, may hide behind its mother's skirt. Or one may hesitate to taste of a new, unfamiliar dish. In these cases the *exposure*, the opening oneself to the world, is in the foreground of the anxiety. Or anxiety may inhibit the response to an experience, may interfere even with being able to be actively attentive to one's own reactions to the impact of an experience. In this case the inhibition of responsiveness is the paramount effect of the anxiety. In the most frequent, culturally patterned form of embeddedness of our time, the embeddedness in automaton conform-

35] Since our topic here is anxiety as an embeddedness-affect, I must forego a more detailed analysis of the meaning of object-centered interest and love, which are closely related to each other. Compare Fromm's work on the meaning of love, *The Art of Loving* (Harper, New York, 1956), and the chapter in this volume on the development of focal attention, pp. 251-278.

ity, the crippling of the capacity for experience is at least as pronounced, if not more so, as the loss of spontaneous responsiveness. The anxiety which causes this phenomenon is the anxiety of loneliness, of being different from one's fellow men, without knowing how to overcome this loneliness in any way other than by conforming to the general cultural pattern.

Pleasure. Critique of the Pleasure Principle

The affect of *pleasure* was defined by Freud in a *negative* way: as the *relief* from excitation. Such excitation occurs either from the perceptive system in the perception of the environment, or from the interior of the organism, from its rising need tensions. Increasing stimulation is felt as unpleasure, decreasing stimulation as pleasure. The nervous system is conceived of as "an apparatus having the function of abolishing stimuli which reach it or of reducing excitation to the lowest possible level: an apparatus which would even, if this were feasible, maintain itself in an altogether unstimulated condition."[36] It is consistent with this negative definition, in which pleasure consists in the relief from or abolition of excitation, that originally Freud did not speak of the pleasure principle, but of the unpleasure principle.[37] The positive aspects of life—stimulation and activity—were seen as a disturbance, a nuisance as it were, which the organism tries to get rid of in order to return to a quiescent state which is felt as pleasure.

If we ask ourselves which phenomena this theoretical construct seems to fit, then we can think of several. It seems to fit the newborn infant and much in the infant's behavior during the first weeks of life, with the important exceptions described earlier (pp. 24-27). There we see that the greater part of the waking time is given to restlessness and unpleasure,[38] and that the blissful

36] Freud, "Instincts and Their Vicissitudes," *Collected Papers* (Basic Books, New York, 1959), Vol. IV, p. 63. It may be noted that the electroencephalographic study of the nervous system has not borne out this assumption on the physiological level. The delta waves show that in an unstimulated condition the nervous system itself produces a rhythmic alteration between charge and discharge of electric current.

37] Freud, "The Interpretation of Dreams," *Basic Writings*, p. 534. In this translation (by A. A. Brill) the German *Unlust* is rendered by "pain." The word "unpleasure," suggested by Strachey, is more accurate.

38] Stirnimann has observed that the proportion between pleasure and unpleasure feelings in the newborn is approximately 2:3. F. Stirnimann, *Psychologie des neugeborenen Kindes* (Rascher Verlag, Zürich and Leipzig, 1940), p. 69.

return to sleep looks like an expression of pleasure. It seems to fit some aspects of old age (although there we find considerable individual variation) where to rest undisturbed and peacefully again becomes a major goal; it seems to fit early stages of convalescence after severe illness when the organism is in a weakened condition; finally, we can observe it in all of us in our daily return to sleep when we are tired and when the stimuli reaching us from outside (noises, lights, etc.) are felt as a disturbance which we want to get rid of, just as we want to get rid of our own muscular or nervous tensions and to relax completely.

If we now ask ourselves which phenomena, at first glance, seem most inconsistent with Freud's construct, then we would think of the tremendous surplus energy which is so apparent, motorically and in every way, in the behavior of young children; we would also think of the great variety of ways in which youthful and adult zest for living, eagerness, interest, etc. characterize the awake grown person, whose major aim and condition for feeling well is the exercise of his capacities and energies in response to the environment, and who only at night, in preparing for sleep, wants to return to a quiescent state. Thus, a cursory survey of what strikes one phenomenologically reveals that there are certain states which seem to be governed, to a considerable extent, by Freud's concept of the pleasure principle, and others where the opposite seems to be the case, namely where we find a desire for, and enjoyment of, stimulation and activity rather than the wish to get rid of it. The former states—early infancy, old age, convalescence, sleep—are characterized by a weakened or immature state of the organism or by its need for rest; the latter—childhood, youth, maturity, awakeness—by heightened aliveness, intensity of interest, zest for living.

Thus, it becomes apparent that at different periods of life—or of a single day—there is a shift from the predominance of behavior that might well be governed by Freud's pleasure principle, where relief from stimulation is most sought after by the organism, to the predominance of behavior in which the opposite seems to be sought after, where the organism eagerly welcomes stimulation and enjoys the heightened tension of activity. We can observe this very clearly in man's behavior during the daily rhythmic cycle between day and night: At night, when one is tired, the noises and sights of the environment are felt as disturbing, and activity becomes an unwelcome effort and burden. In the morning, upon awakening, one enjoys the fresh and bright colors of the morning, the clear light of the day; and the healthy organism, refreshed and eager, seeks out tasks and situations which will offer an opportunity to exercise his capacities. Indeed, we would experience it as torture if we were condemned to do nothing all day long but rest, with all our appetites—sexual, for food, etc.—sated at the slightest desire, and with no physical or mental activity (i.e. heightened tension and stimulation) permitted. What is felt as pleasant by us at night, when we seek rest: the dimming and eventual disappearance of all outside stimuli, the relaxation of all heightened muscular or mental tonus, the abandoning of our upright posture, of our position of separateness vis-à-vis the world, and the return to the prone position which we occupied as infants before we had learned to sit up, to stand, and walk—entrusting ourselves again to the embeddedness of sleep—all this is not felt as pleasant when we awaken from sleep in the morning. Then the very things which were experienced as disturbing when we sought rest at night are eagerly welcomed and enjoyed by us: once again we *want* to look at the world of the day around us, we would hate to stay in a dark room, we enjoy the song of the birds, the voices of people (if not the honking of automobiles and the blare of the radio), we want to get up, to resume our upright posture, to walk, to think, to act. Pleasure, then, varies; it is not the same, does not always consist of the relief from excitation and tension; but at some times, under certain conditions, it does, and at other times the opposite holds true.

Freud emphasized only one side of the picture just sketched: the side that finds pleasure in relief from stimulation and tension, that is, the pleasures of rest and relaxation. It is a tribute to the consistency and depth of his thought that by this view he was driven to the inevitable conclusion that the pleasure principle, as conceived by him, is in the last analysis identical with the death instinct, the wish to return to a state of complete quiescence, to the state of inorganic matter.[39] In this view, life is seen as pain, disturbance, and want; death as relief from these; and the pleasure principle joins forces with the death instinct or becomes its main manifestation in seeking to abolish and to escape from the painful stimulation of life.

What Freud describes as pleasure actually is not based, in his

39] Kurt Goldstein also points this out in *The Organism,* pp. 332-333.

work, on an empirical analysis and study of the various pleasure-feelings nor on a study of the related feelings of joy and happiness.[40] Rather it is based (1) on a hypothetical reconstruction of what an organism accustomed to a state of complete embeddedness, like the intrauterine existence, might experience when forced to live in a state of greater separateness and independence, like that of the infant's extrauterine existence, and (2) possibly on his concept of sexual pleasure as consisting in the sudden discharge in orgasm of pent-up need tension.[41] Since the concept of pleasure is based pri-

40] The word *Glück* (happiness) appears very rarely in Freud's work. As far as I know he has defined it on one occasion only. There he says that it consists of the avoidance of pain and unpleasure (a striking recurrence of his negative definition for pleasure) and, in the narrower sense of the word, in the experience of strong feelings of pleasure, more strictly: in the sudden satisfaction of highly pent-up need tensions. Freud, "Civilization and Its Discontents," *Gesammelte Werke* (Imago Publishing Co., London, 1948), Vol. XIV, p. 434. Thus, he identifies happiness with pleasure as being the sudden decrease of the accumulated excitation of need tension.

41] In his later writings Freud began to question both the correctness of the observations that led to his original concept of pleasure and to the pleasure principle, and the basic concepts of his instinct theory. In 1924 he writes that pleasure and unpleasure *cannot* be related to the increase or decrease of stimulus-tension although "they clearly have a great deal to do with this factor." He believed at this point that they do not depend on this quantitative factor but on an *unknown* qualitative factor. ("The Economic Problem in Masochism," *Collected Papers*, Vol. II, pp. 255-268, 256.) In 1920 he developed the concepts of the life and death instincts, Eros and Thanatos. Eros as the principle of *unification* becomes the antagonist of the death instinct, which drives toward the return to the inorganic state of rest. Thereby Eros acquires a character entirely different from the original concept of libidinal pleasure, the aim of which was the return to an excitationless state. ("Beyond the Pleasure Principle," *Gesammelte Werke*, Vol. XIII, p. 66, footnote 1.) But although these developments pointed clearly to the necessity for a basic revision of the doctrine of the pleasure principle, neither Freud nor his followers took this step. Thus, in 1930, Freud again wrote that happiness and pleasure consist in the sudden decrease of accumulated excitation. ("Civilization and Its Discontents," *loc. cit.*, p. 434.)

Some of his followers have attempted to save the doctrine of the pleasure principle by divorcing it from the experiences and feelings of pleasure and unpleasure and to consider Freud's concepts of pleasure, pain, and wish as terms merely indicating energy distribution without correspondence to felt pain and pleasure. This is the position taken by David Rapaport (*Organization and Pathology of Thought* [Columbia University Press, New York, 1951], pp. 317-318, footnote 9), who quotes the following passage from Freud's "Interpretation of Dreams" (*Basic Writings*, p. 533) as expressing such a view: ". . . the accumulation of excitation is felt as pain, and sets the (psychic) apparatus in operation in order to bring about again a state of gratification, in which the diminution of excitation is perceived as pleasure. Such a current in the apparatus, issuing from pain and striving for pleasure, we call 'wish.'" However, this passage explicitly speaks of felt pain and perceived pleasure. But quite independently of the fact that in Freud's own thinking the pleasure principle was based on observations concerning experiential pleasure and unpleasure and conceived as a theory to explain the nature of pleasure and unpleasure, there does not seem much point in speaking

marily on the reconstruction of the primary-process phase of infantile existence, which in Freud's theory is completely dominated by the pleasure principle, it is necessary to examine the validity of basing the concept of pleasure on that hypothetical phase.

In speaking of the complete embeddedness of a living organism I mean a mode of existence in which the organism lives in a completely sheltering and nourishing environment from which it directly draws all its energy supply without having to go after it. In such a hypothetical organism-in-environment situation Freud's pleasure principle would apply. Since the organism's needs would be continuously supplied, there would be no need tensions. Since it would be completely sheltered, there would be no contact with an environment other than the beneficial sheltering and nourishing one. The organism would be at rest, without need tensions and without any cause for exploring or coming to grips with anything beyond the nourishing and sheltering immediate environment. If anything else intruded in this environment it would *disturb* the organism, i.e. stimuli from outside would be a disruption of shelteredness; the organism would want to avoid or abolish them. Interruption in the constant flow of nourishment would give rise to need tension and cause a disruption of energy supply; the organism would want to avoid this internal stimulation of need tensions. The only "pleasure" such an organism might experience would indeed be the negative pleasure described by Freud: the return after disturbance to the restful, tensionless, sheltered equilibrium of complete embeddedness. Every disruption of this state, whether it were by the intrusion of a larger environment on the shelter or the disruption of the automatic food supply, would be felt as pain, discomfort, disturbance. The encounter with the world as well as any need for goal-directed activity would be the main examples of such painful disruptions.

While probably no organism lives in such complete embeddedness, we have some knowledge of two conditions in which Freud's pleasure principle indeed seems to approximate what we can actually observe or assume with considerable probability. One is the

of a pleasure principle when it has nothing to do with the experience of pleasure. An understanding of the phenomena of pleasure which puzzled Freud in his later thinking cannot be gained, in my view, by discarding the connection between the pleasure principle and felt pleasure, but only by the insight into the development and change of the nature of pleasure and unpleasure in the course of phylogenetic and ontogenetic development.

condition of the foetus *in utero* (or, in animals hatching from eggs, of the foetus or larva in the egg); the other is the behavior of certain protozoa and, approximating it, the behavior of some other of the lowest animals. The foetus reacts with distress if prematurely taken from the sheltering womb or if too strongly stimulated in the womb. It dies if the premature birth takes place too early or if the conditions of the environment (incubator, etc.) are not sufficiently like the womb in their sheltering function. If the human embryo *in utero* is stimulated cutaneously it reacts with a movement which is probably a negative reaction of distress or avoidance. Among the protozoa the most frequent reaction is an avoidance or flight reaction. It has been said of them that their fundamental response to any stimulus is negative. Both in the embryo and in the protozoa who live in the nourishing water, the appearance of any stimulus means that something has *changed* in the hitherto sheltering and nourishing environment, that *embeddedness* has been *disturbed*. Hence, stimulation is indeed, as postulated by Freud, something that means discomfort, unpleasure, danger and that has to be avoided or abolished.

I believe that one can express these observations in a *law*, which would incorporate what is valid in Freud's law of the pleasure principle and would probably apply not only to man but to biology in general. While Freud assumed that the pleasure principle governs the psychic life of man at all stages of development, at first completely and directly, later less completely and indirectly, via the "detours" of the reality principle, the law of embeddedness does not state that increase of stimulation *always* is unpleasure, but that *the more nearly complete the state of embeddedness of the organism, the more strongly negative is the reaction of the organism to any change in the significant environment and the less does the organism want to stir from a state of quiescent equilibrium in relation to the environment.* The appearance of any new stimulus constitutes an unwelcome change in the environment. In other words, the pleasure principle does not hold true for all organisms nor for the human organism in all phases of its development, but it is inseparably linked to the prevalence of embeddedness. In the pleasure principle Freud has not defined pleasure as such, not all pleasure, but only pleasure from the viewpoint of the state of embeddedness. This pleasure is indeed a purely negative one: it is the elimination of any disturbance of embeddedness that has occurred. The undisturbed functioning of embeddedness is neither pleasurable nor unpleasurable. It resembles unnoticed comfort. The disturbance which consists in stimulation (that is, change from the state of smoothly functioning embeddedness) constitutes unpleasure; the return to embeddedness (that is, decrease, disappearance of stimulation) constitutes pleasure.[42] The keenest "pleasures" of this type in adult experience are the relief felt at the ceasing of physical pain which has lasted for some time, the relief from severe hunger and thirst, and falling asleep when exhausted. Freud has described, not positive pleasure, but relief from pain, from irritation (excitation) and tension.

In the ontogenesis of the metazoa and of man the phase of the most complete embeddedness is the phase of the foetus or larva in the egg or, in mammals, the intrauterine phase. With the act of birth (or of hatching) the physical separation from the most complete embeddedness is accomplished. Birth, thus, is physically the most impressive, relatively short act in the longer process of transition from complete embeddedness to relative separateness. It is a transition from living with biological equipment adapted to an environment of embeddedness to living with changing biological (including psychological) equipment—which was already developing *in utero*—in an environment of decreasing embeddedness and increasing separateness. That a transition of such magnitude can be accomplished at all is certainly one of the miracles of nature. It is not surprising that it is a difficult and complicated process. In the many physiological and psychological changes involved in this process we can also observe a shift in the valences of the environment for the organism, a shift of what constitutes a positive valence (pleasure, attraction) and what constitutes a negative valence. This shift is in all animals, and to a considerable extent also in man, a purely biological development, but in man it is also to a very large extent a cultural phenomenon.[43] It would contradict

42] Sullivan's concept of euphoria is, as far as I can see, identical with Freud's concept of pleasure. It, too, is not euphoria as such, but only euphoria from the viewpoint of embeddedness. Compare Harry Stack Sullivan, *The Interpersonal Theory of Psychiatry*, p. 34.

43] The distinction between biological and cultural factors in man constitutes a very difficult, perhaps unsolvable problem. The very fact that man has culture is part of his biological difference from the other mammals. For a biologist's viewpoint on this problem compare Portmann, *Biologische Fragmente zu einer Lehre vom Menschen*.

our entire biological observation if the nature of pleasure, as an important psychological phenomenon which mediates positive valences, did not develop and change together with all the other far-reaching developments and changes in the transition from complete embeddedness to relative separation.[44] Freud's position shows a profound disbelief in the phenomenon of change and development although, paradoxically, he is at the same time the man who in psychoanalytic therapy devised the most powerful tool for psychic development and change. His position is that pleasure remains throughout life what it was in the state of embeddedness and that development to maturity consists in the superimposition of a relatively thin layer governed by the reality principle which is an unwelcome and enforced detour to the same goal that governed the primary and basic phase, the phase of embeddedness dominated by the pleasure principle.

What can we actually observe when we study pleasure in the infant, the child, and the adult? In the first two weeks of life pleasure seems to be predominantly a matter of relief from disturbance and tension, as postulated by Freud. Probably this is related to the fact that in these two weeks a greater amount of physiological changes and adjustments to the new mode of existence in the new environment have to be made than at any other time in life.[45] But

44] The change of the nature of pleasure in ontogenetic development has an interesting parallel in phylogenesis. Because of their embeddedness, the lowest animals react almost exclusively in a negative way to external stimuli (see above, p. 60) and their memory (or learning) functions only in a negative capacity, as a warning agent. Thus, planaria can learn an avoidance reaction but not a positive reaction of going after something desirable. Only in the more highly developed annelides do we find the first instances of positive memory, of learning as a guide toward the encounter of a desirable stimulus. Werner Fischel, "Kleine Tierseelenkunde," *Sammlung Dalp* (Francke-Verlag, Bern, 1954), pp. 21-22. The reason for this seems clear: on the level of embeddedness the paramount biological need is for avoidance of disturbance and change in embeddedness. On the level of increasing separateness it becomes increasingly important that the organism be enabled to seek out and find that which is advantageous for its life.

45] Gesell and Amatruda give a catalogue of these fundamental physiological readjustments: "Pulmonary inflation, heightening of muscle tonus, sustained rhythmic breathing, elevation of blood pressure, reduction of heart rate, destruction of excess cells of plethoric blood; reorganization of cellular constituents of the blood; increase of systolic and diastolic blood pressure and reduction of heart rate, progressive reduction in the bleeding and coagulation time, the mobilization of antibodies in the blood plasma; a tenfold increase in gastric capacity in as many days; the establishment of gastric, biliary and intestinal secretions; massive bacterial invasion of the alimentary tract; sudden increase of demands on kidney excretion; equilibration of the fluid matrix of the body with respect to water and salt contents, blood sugar, proteins, fat and calcium; the regulation of body tem-

even in these first two weeks we can observe that infants are attracted to certain stimuli, in other words that they do not experience
all stimuli from the new environment as disturbance, hence feel
unpleasure, but that some have a positive valence for them. Thus,
Stirnimann, who has made a detailed and extensive study of the
reactions of newborn infants during the first two weeks of life
and especially during the first twenty-four hours, reports many
observations of the neonate's being attracted to certain stimuli
and apparently finding pleasure in them. This is most apparent in
those stimuli which are closely related to the infant's desire to
nurse, e.g. positive reactions when touched with a finger at the
lip, when stroked on the cheek, upon a warmth stimulus near the
cheek, upon tasting a solution of lactose. But it happens also with
quite a number of other stimuli, e.g. moderate warmth near the
sole of the foot, the smell of anise, a moderate light. Stirnimann
also observed that only in the prematurely born the so-called
grasping reflex when touched on finger or hand is a true reflex
and occurs regardless of whether the infant's hand is touched
with the human finger or with a small stick of 3 mm. diameter or
with a cylinder of the same size as the human finger. In contrast
to the prematurely born, half of the mature neonates discriminated
between stick, cylinder, and the human finger: they grasped and
held on to the finger, but either did not grasp, or soon let go of,
the stick or the cylinder. In other words: there was positive attraction to the stimulus of the human finger.[46]

In the following weeks and months the obviously pleasurable
encounters with reality and its many stimuli increase rapidly as
the infant's sensory and motor capacities develop and are exercised
in its exploratory *play*. I have described the significance of this
play for the infant's and child's growing relatedness to *reality*
elsewhere.[47] In the present context I want to emphasize especially
two aspects of it: (1) It is a *joyful* encounter with reality in which
the child enjoys both its own motor activity and the encounter
with the various "stimuli" of the environment which, in the course
of these repeated encounters, gradually become constituted as

perature and adequate oxygen supply; the acquisition of patterns and rhythms of
feeding, activity, and sleep. . . ." Gesell and Amatruda, *Developmental Diagnosis*,
p. 218.
46] Stirnimann, *Psychologie des neugeborenen Kindes*, pp. 23-27, 36-37, 43-46, 49,
58-60.
47] This volume, pp. 251-278.

objects; neither the tension in the activity nor the stimulation by the play-object are experienced as disturbances. (2) The activity does not lead to the satisfaction of a need (want) and therewith to the extinction of both the stimulus and the need tension, as is the case in eating when hungry. Instead, in the ever repeated approach of exploration, a *relationship* between the child and the object is formed, enriched, and deepened.[48] Not the reduction of a want tension nor the abolition of an intruding stimulus, but the maintenance of the relation to the object and the continuation of the ongoing activity itself with its fluctuating and enjoyable tensions are the goal of the playful activity. In other words, the nature of pleasure is changing: it is no longer restricted to the negative experience of relief from irritating disturbance of embeddedness, but now includes positive, joyful expansion of relatedness to the new and rapidly enlarging environment. The former kind of pleasure (relief) is an embeddedness-affect, the latter is an activity-affect; the former is a return to a stable state of rest, the latter the enjoyment of ongoing processes, of the process of relating to the world.

The increasing attraction by stimuli from the environment, the increasing positive pleasure in the play with them and in the playful exercise of the baby's growing energies and capacities go together with the growing *differentiation* between *sleep* and *wakefulness* and the increase of periods of wakefulness other than those brought about by the need tension of hunger or by other discomfort. In sleepiness and sleep the differentiation of the qualities of outside stimuli ceases or diminishes (even in adult life). The protective stimulus barrier of the organism becomes stronger, and those stimuli which penetrate it are experienced in an undifferentiated way as mere disturbance. In other words: the world of primary embeddedness in which Freud's pleasure principle governs once again prevails. In the first few weeks the baby not only sleeps practically all the time but also shows no clear differentiation between sleep and a drowsy kind of awakeness, except for the short periods during which it emerges from this state to nurse or for the kind of attentive looking described earlier. The growing differentiation between sleep and wakefulness means that the character of life

48] This point has been made by Bally. Gustav Bally, *Vom Ursprung und von den Grenzen der Freiheit. Eine Deutung des Spiels bei Tier und Mensch* (Benno Schwabe, Basel, 1945), p. 42.

is changing from a vegetating state of complete embeddedness to the rhythmic alternation between embeddedness (sleep) and periods of encounter with reality (wakefulness) which will characterize life from then on, with the exception of old age, which, in some people, shows a return to a less clear differentiation between sleep and wakefulness.[49] The periods of wakefulness are governed by psychological laws different from those of sleep, just as the state of separateness is governed by laws different from those of embeddedness. In the phenomenon of *pleasure* this difference consists in the fact that for the period of sleep (and sleepiness), pleasure is identical with Freud's concept of it, namely relief from disturbance (tension and outer stimuli), while for the period of wakefulness, pleasure has the *positive* character of enjoyment, joy, and happiness in encounter with the world and its stimuli, of relatedness to the world. In wakefulness the pleasure of relief plays a relatively minor role in the healthy person and comes to the foreground only in cases of deprivation (of food, sexual satisfaction, sleep).[50] This becomes even clearer if one analyzes the nature of pleasure connected with the satisfaction of the physiological needs (food, sex, rest, and comfort) where one might expect, as Freud postulates, that pleasure is relief from stimulation.

The positive pleasure in food is experienced in the *enjoyment* of the taste, tactile, and proprioceptive sensations in eating and drinking. This enjoyment, as distinguished from the relief from tension in stilling one's hunger, is characterized by *opening* oneself and being receptive to the specific quality of the stimulus encoun-

49] I must leave for another occasion the detailed analysis of the characteristic differences between adult people in the degree of differentiation between wakefulness and sleep. There are people who practically never seem to awaken fully but seem to live in a kind of permanent fogginess which does not permit any encounter with the world and in which, usually, the world is felt to be more or less of a disturbance. On the other extreme, there are people who during their waking hours show a degree of concentration, alertness, and sensitivity which is sharply differentiated from their periods of sleep and relaxation. The detailed analysis of the kinds of occasions on which one or the other state characteristically occurs in people is of considerable interest for the understanding of their personality structure. The lower animals, just like the embryo and neonate, do not show any differentiation between sleep and wakefulness. This differentiation is phylogenetically a relatively late phenomenon, encountered first in the vertebrates with their highly developed central nervous system.

50] This has been emphasized by Fromm, who distinguishes between *satisfaction* of psychological needs, which take place in the realm of *scarcity*, and pleasure and joy, which belong to the realm of *abundance*. Erich Fromm, *Man For Himself*, pp. 186-191.

tered, *staying* for a few moments in that encounter, and being *attentive* to what one feels. This is possible only when one is not in a state of deprivation, suffering from painful hunger or thirst. In extreme hunger or thirst the specific quality of the food does not matter, is hardly noticed; the hungry person eats so hastily[51] that he cannot stay with and notice, much less appreciate, any nuances of taste and he does not pay any attention to them, unless the taste is unpleasant or revolting. The goal of need satisfaction is so pressing and dominates the organism so completely that the urge to swallow does not permit the time nor the attention to taste fully. The discriminating enjoyment of food is the specifically human quality in eating and drinking, while man has in common with animals the negative pleasure of the relief from hunger.[52] The distinction between this enjoyment and need satisfaction is that the former is based on the *encounter* with the stimulus rather than on its abolishment. The gourmet wants to keep the mild tension of his appetite and to stay with the taste of the food, rather than to still the appetite as quickly as possible. The activity of eating becomes his goal rather than the state of satiation, the return to quiescence. But one does not need to be a gourmet to notice that in eating with good appetite it is the activity of eating itself rather than the subsequent ceasing of appetite which is enjoyable.

The developmental change in the nature of pleasure also becomes apparent if one analyzes the feelings of *restful undisturbedness, positive comfort*, and *well-being*. Just as the positive enjoyment of taste is based on the openness toward and the attentive staying with the stimulus of the food, beyond the mere attempt to still one's appetite, so positive enjoyment of *comfort* goes beyond the mere absence of excitation, beyond undisturbed embeddedness. It occurs when one is receptive toward and attentively staying with *particular* sensations of embeddedness, as in enjoying the softness and warmth of a balmy summer day, the pleasant feeling of the

---

51] This is also true of many people who eat to still a want of non-physiological origin. While they experience relief in eating or drinking, their capacity for the enjoyment of food is usually impaired. In drinking "hard liquor," in contrast to wine, the enjoyment of taste also often plays no role or a negligible role. In fact, recently one type of hard liquor was advertised as having absolutely no taste, which fact supposedly makes it superior to others.

52] In the higher animals one finds *preferences* for one kind of food over another. However, these numerically quite limited preferences compare in no way with the great variety of taste experiences appreciated by man.

warm water of a bath surrounding one's body, the cradling of the body in a comfortable chair, the pleasant passive tactile sensation of a fabric against the skin. Both in taste and positive comfort feelings the emphasis in the encounter is regularly not on the object encountered but on how it affects one; on how the *subject* is made to feel, not on what the *object* may be like. This is true of most experiences mediated through the so-called lower senses: thermal sense, taste, smell, passive sense of touch (as distinguished from active, exploratory sense of touch). They are *autocentric*, while the higher senses (sight, hearing, active sense of touch) are prevailingly *allocentric* (object-centered). But although the feeling of positive comfort and the enjoyment of taste or smell are autocentric and do not lead to a full encounter with the object, they do transcend the state of complete embeddedness. In them it is not that the relief from disturbance and return to quiescence constitutes pleasure (in Freud's sense), but rather that a *particular* stimulation is attended and enjoyed receptively.

The feelings of positive comfort are different from the feeling of *well-being*. Well-being is the feeling of energy potential, the feeling of heightened aliveness, of full awakeness and readiness to encounter the world with openness and alertness as well as with eagerness for activity, physical and mental. While the feeling of positive comfort has traces of activity-affect in that it requires a certain attentiveness and a temporary staying with the stimulus enjoyed, it comes to the fore in the context of man's natural daily swing toward embeddedness. It is most pronounced when one seeks rest and relaxation, goes to sleep at night, or in convalescence; it is an outgrowth of the normal embeddedness needs of man, consciously enjoyed. It can also become the object of irrational craving. In contrast to it, the feeling of well-being is an activity-affect which may be described as the feeling of readiness for the encounter with the world, both in receptive openness and in active response.

The analysis of *sexual pleasure* is particularly difficult because, in man, it is practically always inseparably tied up with other emotions such as love, power, return to childlike embeddedness, anger, search for approval or recognition, destructive-sadistic impulses, etc. These emotions play a large role in determining whether sexual pleasure has more the character of relief from tension (embeddedness-affect) or of the positive pleasure in the process of relatedness. In Freud's thought, sexual pleasure originally consisted entirely in the satisfaction due to the sudden decrease of tension. He explained the pleasurable character of sexual excitement, doubtless a state of increased tension, by minimizing it as mere forepleasure and contrasting it with the orgastic end pleasure, which he saw entirely as discharge gratification.[53] Later he began to doubt this position, but his doubt did not lead him to a reformulation of his theory of sexual pleasure.[54]

If discharge of tension were the only source of sexual pleasure it would neither be understandable why the sexual pleasure in intercourse is preferred by most people to the pleasure in masturbation, nor why individual variations of the sexual act are a source of pleasure. Furthermore, while it is true that forepleasure serves biologically as a step toward orgasm, just as the pleasure in the taste of food serves biologically as a step toward the satisfaction of the body's food needs, the significance of forepleasure is not exhausted with this explanation. Both the range in the subtle varieties of sexual behavior and the openness toward and temporary staying with the caresses and contacts preceding orgasm are the typically human elements which distinguish man's sexual pleasure from the sexual satisfaction of animals. Their significance parallels what has been said about the specifically human aspects of the positive enjoyment of food: In them not the mere discharge of tension, but the enjoyment of the ongoing process of encounter is the decisive factor.[55] In sexual pleasure this factor is heightened if there is genuine mutuality in which the giving of pleasure is enjoyed together with the receptivity toward pleasure.

53] Freud, "Three Contributions to the Theory of Sex," *Basic Writings*, pp. 605–607. Jacobson has pointed out, rightly, that the end pleasure of orgasm is not simply discharge of tension but oscillates in rhythmic waves of heightened excitement and relief. Edith Jacobson, "The Affects and Their Pleasure-Unpleasure Qualities, in Relation to the Psychic Discharge Processes," in Rudolph M. Loewenstein, ed., *Drives, Affects, Behavior* (International Universities Press, New York, 1953), p. 53.

54] See this volume, p. 58, footnote 41.

55] A similar view is expressed by Watts, who emphasizes that the fullest sexual enjoyment is in the total ongoing relatedness rather than in the relief from tension in orgastic discharge. Alan W. Watts, *Nature, Man and Woman* (Pantheon, New York, 1958), pp. 184–206.

4

Conclusion

DRIVES AND AFFECTS ARISE WITH THE SEPARATION FROM COMPLETE embeddedness, a state in which no separation exists between the organism and its sheltering and nourishing environment. Such embeddedness distinguishes plant from animal life; it also distinguishes the intraovine and intrauterine phases of animal and human life from the phase after leaving the sheltering egg or womb. The function of the drives and affects is to bring the organism, now separated from embedding shelter and energy supply, into contact with the sources of energy supply on its new level of existence and, within the larger environment, to maintain its contact with a favorable environment and avoid an unfavorable one.

The tremendous significance of this change becomes more apparent when one considers that space and time in their biological meaning (as contrasted with the abstract space and time measured by man) are born only with this separation from complete embeddedness.[1] Intrauterine life has no space, since the embryo is one with its mother and does not have to move in order to find nourishment or shelter. It has no time, since there is neither a rhythmic change between rising and falling need tension nor the tension between "now" in which the organism senses (sees, hears, feels) something and a future "then" in which it will incorporate it as food or use it in some other way. Only with the separation

---

1] The following remarks on space and time are based in part on Thure von Uexküll, "Der Mensch und die Natur," *Sammlung Dalp* (A. Francke Verlag, Bern, 1953), Vol. 13, pp. 206-218.

from intrauterine embeddedness does the spatial and temporal gap arise and develop between the human organism and the environmental aspects significant for its life. For instance, the nursing infant, when put to the breast, feels the tactile sensation of skin and nipple on his lips. But he is separated by a spatial and temporal gap from the satisfying flow of milk. This gap he has to overcome by the motor activity of sucking. The eagerness to suck (an activity-affect) arises because the infant must bridge this gap. All our affects arise from such spatial and/or temporal gaps which open between us and our aims in the world, after we have left the embeddedness of intrauterine life.[2]

In the animals, drives and affects remain to a very large extent tied to an inherited instinctive organization. The animal is embedded in this organization and in the closed world (J. v. Uexküll's *Merkwelt* and *Wirkwelt*) corresponding to this organization.[3] Man's relation to his world is an open one, governed only to a very small extent by instinctive organization and to the largest extent by man's learning and exploration, in which he establishes his complex, changing, and developing relations with his fellow men and with the natural and the cultural world around him. The newborn infant, compared with the newborns of the most

2] The development of life-space and life-time is a gradual one. They are the more varied and the more richly articulated, the higher the development of the organism. I believe that with every significant step in emergence from embeddedness throughout man's life the quality of his life-space and life-time undergoes a change. An analysis of these changes has yet to be made. Piaget's work contains many interesting findings on the development of space and time concepts in the child. However, his main interest is to pursue the gradual development of the concept of an abstract, uniform time and space, and he has not devoted any attention to the differences in psychological time and space due to the degree of embeddedness or autonomy rooted in personality differences. For pathological and normal conceptions of time and space and their changes due to the effect of moods and drugs, compare the work of L. Binswanger, E. Straus, E. Minkowski, G. Bachelard, K. Goldstein, and others.

3] I leave aside here the complex and very interesting phylogenetic development of learning by which the animal's world to some degree transcends embeddedness in a purely instinctive organization, the more so the higher the level of phylogenetic development. I also leave aside the equally complex and interesting phylogenetic development in which the more differentiated and highly developed the organism of the animal is, the richer and more differentiated his *Umwelt* becomes. This omission is justified because there is a much greater gap or jump in this respect from the most highly developed mammal (the primates) to man than there is within the phylogenetic development from any one animal to the next higher, however great the mysterious jumps in this development may be. Also, the consideration of animal embeddedness and its phylogenetic development would completely exceed the scope of this presentation.

highly developed mammals, has far fewer innate reaction patterns at his disposal. Hence the human infant is much more helpless than, e.g., the newborn monkey, kid, calf, or foal. But the other side of this infantile helplessness is man's freedom in the sense of an immensely greater variety of potentialities of development. As Portmann says, "The free play of the limbs which gives to the human nursling so much richer possibilities than the newborn monkey or ape have reminds us that our state at birth is not simply helpless but is characterized by a significant freedom."[4]

The practically infinite openness of man's world rests physiologically mainly on the jump in cerebralization from primate to man, and probably also on the jump in the ratio of the (large) association area to the sensory cortex of the human brain compared with this ratio in animals. The large association area makes for a less direct control of behavior by the immediate environmental stimulus of the moment.[5] Psychologically, this means that there is an infinity of aspects of the world potentially accessible and significant for man, and that there is an enormous number of ways in which he can get in touch with these aspects. One would get some idea of the unimaginable richness and depth of the world and its possible meanings for man if one knew all languages and cultures, not merely intellectually but with one's total personality. This would comprise the historically knowable world of man, but not the infinity of future possibilities. Obviously, this is not possible for any man. The imagination gets dizzy at such a prospect. Being born and growing up in a concrete society and culture drastically narrows the patterns of relatedness to the world offered to the growing child. On the other hand, it makes it possible for him not to get lost in the infinite possibilities of his world-openness, but to find, within the framework of his culture and tradition, his particular structure of relatedness to the world. The often observed originality of children is due to the fact that they are still more open to the many possibilities of relating to the world and are not yet so completely embedded in the ways of their culture and particular group as the average man.

4] Author's translation from Adolf Portmann, *Biologische Fragmente zu einer Lehre vom Menschen* (Benno Schwabe & Co., Basel, 1951), p. 30.
5] For the meaning of the sudden increase in cerebralization in man as compared with animals, see Portmann, *op. cit.* For the significance of the large association cortex of man, see D. O. Hebb, *The Organization of Behavior* (John Wiley & Sons, New York, 1949), pp. 124-126.

World-openness is the distinctly human characteristic of man's awake life. To some extent, it penetrates even his sleep in his dreams. But apart from his dreams, man returns in sleep to embeddedness. Thus, in the normal rhythm of day and night the growing child and adult man alternate between the *natural* embeddedness of sleep and the emergence from embeddedness into the open world of the day. In the natural embeddedness of sleep man returns to a state which closely parallels intrauterine embeddedness, where stimuli and tension are felt as disturbance, activity is suspended, and no encounter with the variety of differentiated stimuli takes place. This state is approached in tiredness and need for rest, before sleep sets in. The affects germane to the pre-sleep state may therefore be designated as natural embeddedness-affects. In the world of the day, however, man emerges from the natural embeddedness in sleep and relates to the world on the higher, more separate level of (extrauterine) existence in the world. In this situation two basic ways of reacting are open to him. He can establish, develop, and expand his relatedness to the world on the new level of a relatively independent and autonomous existence. The affects germane to such activity are the activity-affects. Or he can, consciously or unconsciously, refuse to accept his relatively separate existence and the challenge it offers to him, and instead feel frustrated and angry or long impatiently for some magic substitute for the lost paradise of the adualistic prenatal state. The affects germane to this reaction are the embeddedness-affects.

The biological prototypes of the activity-affects are those affects which accompany consummatory activity. They can be seen first in the newborn who nurses, provided that the nursing activity goes on successfully within an adequate relation of the nursling and the nursing mother. K. Lorenz has pointed out that in the realm of instinctive behavior in animals and men the motor behavior in consummatory activity is an end in itself, is performed for its own sake and accompanied by pleasure.[6]

6] Konrad Lorenz, "The Nature of Instinct," in Claire H. Schiller, ed., *Instinctive Behavior* (International Universities Press, New York, 1957), p. 144. I differ from Lorenz's viewpoint, however, in that I do not believe that any of man's activities are purely instinctive, not even consummatory behavior in sex and in eating. Very often disturbances of the capacity for full sexual enjoyment are due to the fact that the sexual relatedness is not an end in itself but that sexual activity is in the service of, for example, neurotic status or acceptance needs or of hostile or ambivalent impulses. Compare also this volume, pp. 211-212.

In their purest form, the activity-affects are connected with an activity performed for its own sake. They are found also in activities other than those consisting of the release of innate motor coordinations discussed by Lorenz. They are limited neither to innate reaction patterns nor to motor activities. They can accompany predominantly mental as well as predominantly motor behavior, e.g. the activity of ongoing relatedness between two people or the activity of contemplation. Thus, the attentive gazing of some newborns at mild light or at a luminous or pleasantly colored object has the same quality as their nursing activity in that it, too, is an end in itself, namely sensory relating to something in the environment, and it seems to be accompanied by a similar affect which may be described as zest, wholeheartedness, and satisfaction in engaging in the activity. In the sphere of the basic visceral needs (food, sex), the consummatory activity is usually accompanied, in addition, by the physical pleasure peculiar to the autocentric senses (commonly designated as the lower senses) involved.[7] Such pleasure occurs also in many other sensory activities.

In man the activity-affects are by no means limited to those consummatory activities which serve the satisfaction of hunger and sexual desire. Not only do we see that the newborn and the infant already engage in a rapidly increasing variety of sensory-motor activities in which the activity itself is the end, satisfying the need to relate to the environment. But in the growing child and in adult man almost any activity can assume consummatory character, that is to say become an end in itself. It is no accident that the language speaks of "consummate" skills. They are acquired most readily in those activities which man pursues for their own sake, so that consummation lies in engaging in the activity with wholehearted interest and without being distracted or pressed by ulterior purposes or needs. Similarly, the activities of relating to another person, or to nature in the contemplation of a tree or a landscape, are accompanied by pure activity-affect, i.e. by a feeling of wholeheartedness, when they are an end in themselves.

This may sound as though any purposive activity performed as a means to an end could not be accompanied by an activity-affect. But if a man wants to build a house it is quite possible for him to devote himself wholeheartedly to each activity which is neces-

7] For a discussion of the concept of autocentric senses and of the quality of the pleasure peculiar to them see this volume, pp. 89-95.

sary as a step toward the ultimate goal of the finished house, and yet not lose sight of that goal. Each activity may be fully and wholeheartedly engaged in while it lasts. In fact, the more one is capable of devoting oneself to each step as though it were an end in itself while one is engaged in it, the better will it serve the purpose of completing the house. Impatient longing for the final result, the finished house, will not permit the activities necessary to that end to be performed with the pure activity-affect of wholehearted devotion to them, and will quite likely lead to an impairment of the quality of the work and the house. The wish to be done with something so as to arrive at an ultimate goal does not allow the proper doing of it.

The person who is engaged with pure activity-affect in an activity which is a means toward an end does not experience, while thus engaged, the feeling that meanwhile he has to *delay* reaching the end for which he may wish. Paradoxically, where the capacity to delay reaching an ultimate goal or fulfilling a wish is fully matured, the experiential *feeling* of delaying that which one wants all but vanishes and the present has its own fulfillment. Where the feeling of delaying satisfaction of a need or wish remains vivid and is felt as an impatient waiting or longing, the emphasis of life shifts to the future, leaving the present empty, thus changing the structure of experiential time. Usually, this shift involves the embeddedness-affect of magic hope.[8] In these cases the specific conscious goal whose attainment has to be delayed (e.g. marriage, success in a love affair, reaching adulthood, traveling abroad, finishing some work, financial success) very often conceals the hope for the satisfaction of much more comprehensive, unconscious wishes. In contrast to this, the person capable of giving himself fully to what he is doing at the moment, even if it is a step to some future goal, does not have the feeling of delaying anything but lives at each moment with his full presence in the present.

While the activity-affects culminate in the feeling of relatedness (openness and responsiveness) in the ongoing processes of the person's encounter with the world and with his fellow men, the embeddedness-affects result from wishes and attempts to remain, at least partly, in a state of quasi-uterine embeddedness and

8] See above, pp. 37-39.

from rejecting and resenting the relatively separate existence in the postnatal state. One can distinguish two major forms or aspects which such fixation in embeddedness takes, and which usually are found together, one or the other prevailing. One form, which in its extremes is found in many neurotic and psychotic patients and in milder forms in many normal people, is the attempt to remain in or return to familial embeddedness, mainly embeddedness in the protection and parental love and care of a mothering person or of a mother or father substitute. The principal effect of this return to embeddedness is that the person does not become able to love and to encounter other people in their own right, but attempts to use them as providers of quasi-parental care and protection. Hence he sees others as potential aids or threats to his wish to remain in a state of childlike embeddedness. The other form, which might be called cultural embeddedness and which constitutes what Fromm has called a culturally patterned defect, is the abandoning of world-openness, usually sometime during childhood before adolescence, and the attempt to find the safety of embeddedness by completely accepting the closed pattern of relatedness to the world institutionalized in the particular culture or cultural subgroup into which the individual is born and in which he is living. The affects germane to these states of embeddedness, particularly striking in their neurotic and psychotic forms, may be designated as embeddedness-affects in the narrower sense of the word, i.e. not based on the natural swing to embeddedness with the need for rest, but on a failure to emerge from embeddedness in the awake part of life. These affects usually take the form of a passive longing (impatience, magic hope, dependent demands, etc.), of frustration, anger, disappointment, reproachfulness because of the non-fulfillment of such longing, and of excessive anxiety about emerging from embeddedness.

Most affects accompanying the activities of people who are not suffering from severe mental sickness usually are neither pure embeddedness- nor pure activity-affects but a mixture of both. Often only a detailed and careful analysis can show whether the activity or the embeddedness quality prevails in a specific emotional experience. For example, the intensity or eagerness with which one engages in some work activity may stem from the interest in doing the work for its own sake or from the impatient and/or anxious longing to reach some goal of security or status by means of the work, or it may be the result of a mixture of these two different affects.[9]

The concepts of embeddedness-affect and activity-affect are developmental concepts in two respects. First, in the development of the infant and child there always is a shift from massive predominance of embeddedness-affect to increasing significance of activity-affects. Second, if man continues to grow mentally, i.e. emotionally and intellectually, throughout his life, as some people do, then at each significant step of such development a similar shift will occur, while conversely, if he regresses, a shift from activity- to embeddedness-affect will take place. While the early shift from embeddedness- to activity-affect always occurs, although in individually widely varying degrees, the later shifts depend to some extent on man's own decisions within the margin of freedom which he has. To that extent the individual evolution from embeddedness to emergence and encounter with the world is not an automatic development but is dependent on the conscious effort of man, an effort which involves his total being.

The developmental nature of the concepts of embeddedness- and activity-affect implies that there are no absolute criteria for them, except in their extreme forms of massive embeddedness or else in the case of the sage or saint who has freed himself from embeddedness. But for the developing child and for man in his struggle to grow, the question of whether a particular affect has predominantly embeddedness or activity character depends on the analysis of the stage and direction of development which the person is in at the moment. To illustrate: The affect of directed anger is an activity-affect at the stage of development where it begins to supersede the diffuse, temper-tantrum-like discharge of anger. It signifies the growing capacity of the small child to assert his demands and to fight for them. At a somewhat later point of development the question whether directed anger against the mother is an activity- or embeddedness-affect depends on whether the anger is due to the mother's frustrating the growth toward independence of the child or to the frustration of a neurotic embeddedness need, e.g. the mother's refusal to be the servant of the child in an area where the child is quite capable of meeting his needs by his own activity. At a still later point, in young adulthood,

9] Compare also above, p. 38, regarding the mixture of magic and realistic hope.

the anger at a possessive parent who tries to interfere with the grown-up child's autonomy begins to acquire the quality of an embeddedness-affect, since at this point the anger is due to a feeling of helplessness in relation to the parental possessiveness, a helplessness which in turn is caused by excessive dependence on the parents, i.e. continuing embeddedness in parental protection and approval.[10]

Man is forever on the road between embeddedness and emergence from embeddedness. Where he is on this road at each moment of his life determines, and finds expression in, the kind of emotions which he experiences. Thus, the prevalence of activity- or of embeddedness-affect is both a result and an indication not only of the impact of a particular situation but also of how far man has gone in his development toward emergence from embeddedness and toward relatedness to the world open to him.

10] Even the stage of development cannot be determined according to a fixed schedule, but only on the basis of the total life situation of the person. Suppose the emotion of anger, due to severe parental taboos, had become repressed to the extent that the person had never been able to feel and express directed anger, but instead felt only a diffuse depression and reproachfulness. In the course of psycho-analytic treatment the patient for the first time feels strong anger against a parent or parent substitute. In this case, even though we deal with an adult, this anger would be an activity-affect signifying the developing capacity of the patient to fight people who thwart his growth. But this does not mean, of course, that to be able to be angry is an ultimate goal of life. On the contrary, the more autonomous a person is, i.e. the less embedded in need for parent-like approval and acceptance by others, the less is he likely to feel threatened and helpless and to become angry in response to these feelings.

II

ON THE TWO
BASIC PERCEPTUAL
MODES:
AUTOCENTRICITY
AND
ALLOCENTRICITY

5

The Two Basic Perceptual Modes

MAN'S NAIVE ASSUMPTION THAT WHAT HE PERCEIVES WITH HIS senses is reality, things as they really are, is so deeply rooted in his nature that almost three thousand years of epistemological doubt, since the teachings of the Indian Vedanta and the early Greek philosophers, have not changed the fact that each one of us believes his senses. What he perceives with them "makes sense" to him, and only in exceptional states of mind or by an effort of theoretical thought does he start to doubt them. The bulk of the vast psychological literature on the senses and on sensory perception shares, in different forms and ways, the tacit assumption of the basically cognitive nature of human perception. This is curious when one considers that, experientially, the senses differ markedly in what they convey to the perceiver. Whereas in sight the experience is usually one of "seeing the object as it really is," in taste and smell the recognition of an object plays a much lesser, often a quite negligible role, and the primary experience is one in which the specific quality of the taste or smell is linked with pleasure or displeasure. Yet, the words "pleasure" or "disgust" hardly appear even in the literature on smell and taste. The attention of most experimentalists who have worked in this field is directed, if not to the physiological functioning of these senses, to phenomena of threshold, discrimination, etc. Reading their accounts one would get no idea that one of the primary experiences connected with smell and taste is on the order of pleasure and displeasure.[1]

The cognitive bias of the literature on perception has its parallel in the dominating position of rationality in pre-Freudian psychology's image of man. In philosophy the Enlightenment's emphasis on the supremacy of reason in man had been questioned and attacked, first by the romantics, later by Schopenhauer, Nietzsche and the vitalists, and in our time by the existentialists. In psychology it was primarily Freud who, with his theories of the unconscious and of the two principles of mental functioning,[2] the pleasure and reality principles, effectively shook the fundaments of a too rationalistic concept of human nature.

The viewpoint from which sensory experience will be analyzed in this presentation is concerned not with differences between sense organs and their physiological functioning nor with the physical properties of the stimuli to which they react, but with modes of relatedness, mediated by the senses, between perceiver and the world around him and with the way in which the environment is given to the perceiver in these modes of relatedness. What E. Straus[3] has pointed out for the visual and auditory senses can be seen even more strikingly in the olfactory and gustatory as compared to the visual sense: They differ not only because they respond to different physical excitations, by means of differently functioning organs, and because they perceive different objects, but because of the *specific type of relatedness between subject and world* in each of these senses, because they are *different ways of communication* between subject and world.

Such an analysis of sensory experience reveals two basic modes of relatedness between perceiver and environment which are akin to, yet different from, Freud's two principles of mental functioning, the pleasure and the reality principle. A shift in the relative

1] Compare E. G. Boring's chapter on smell and taste in *Sensation and Perception in the History of Experimental Psychology* (D. Appleton-Century Co., New York, 1942). Freud's remark in 1905 that everything relating to the problem of pleasure and pain touches one of the weakest points of present-day psychology still holds true today, especially as regards the psychology of perception. "Three Contributions to the Theory of Sex," *Basic Writings* (Random House, New York, 1938), p. 605.

2] Freud, "Formulations Regarding the Two Principles in Mental Functioning," *Collected Papers*, Vol. IV (Basic Books, New York, 1959).

3] Erwin Straus, *Vom Sinn der Sinne*, 2nd ed. (Springer Verlag, Berlin, 1956), p. 210.

importance of these two perceptual modes characterizes the onto-genetic development of human perception, and the vicissitudes of their later transformation and development are closely linked with the psychic growth and maturation of man.

I shall designate these two basic modes of perceptual relatedness as the subject-centered, or *autocentric*, and the object-centered, or *allocentric*, mode of perception. The main differences between the autocentric and allocentric modes of perception are these: In the autocentric mode there is little or no objectification; the emphasis is on how and what the person feels; there is a close relation, amounting to a fusion, between sensory quality and pleasure or unpleasure feelings, and the perceiver reacts primarily to something impinging on him (although sometimes he may have brought about the impingement, for example by taking food into his mouth). In the allocentric mode there is objectification; the emphasis is on what the object[4] is like; there is either no relation or a less pronounced or less direct relation between perceived sensory qualities and pleasure-unpleasure feelings—that is, such feelings are usually absent or less pronounced or of a different quality; the perceiver usually approaches or turns to the object actively and in doing so either opens himself toward it receptively or, figuratively or literally, takes hold of it, tries to "grasp" it.

The distinction between these two basic perceptual modes both differentiates between and cuts across the different senses. It cuts across them in this way: developmentally the autocentric mode holds almost exclusive sway at the beginning of life in all the senses of the newborn, and later the allocentric (higher) senses

4] The word "object," for want of a better one, will be used to designate any thing, natural or man-made, and any plant, animal, or human being which can become the object of human perception, especially when it is perceived as having an existence of its own, independent of the perceiver and his needs. Its use does not imply that the perceptual relationship is characterized by the Cartesian subject-object dichotomy, nor does the term "objectification" correspond to Heidegger's concept of *Gegenständigkeit*, which, according to his more recent writings, increasingly pervades Western thought since its beginnings. In Heidegger's concept the objectification of everything means that man, for the sake of his own security, tries to secure his domination over everything that *is*, thus transforming everything into objects at his disposal or objects which he can be sure of and which he can account for by the laws of causality. Compare Martin Heidegger, "Nietzsches Wort 'Gott ist tot,'" in *Holzwege* (Vittorio Klostermann, Frankfurt a.M., 1950), pp. 193-247, 242-243; *Der Satz vom Grund* (Günther Noske, Pfullingen, 1957), 99-100, 115, 136-137. My use of the word "object" also differs from Freud's, for whom it means need-satisfying object, especially object of libido, i.e. other people in the role of need-objects. Where the word is used in a different way this will be indicated, as in "need-object" or "object-of-use."

can and do function also in the autocentric mode, while the autocentric (lower) senses are capable of a very limited degree of
allocentricity. Our distinction differentiates between the senses in
that the higher, or allocentric, senses usually function predominantly in the allocentric mode and are the only ones capable of
full-fledged allocentric functioning, while the lower, or autocentric, senses always function predominantly in the autocentric
mode and are not capable of real allocentric perception.

First, these differences between the two basic modes of perceptual relatedness will be shown in a discussion of objectification
and pleasure- or unpleasure-boundedness and their role in some
of the major senses in adult man. Second, the developmental shift
in infancy and childhood from predominance of autocentric to
increasing importance of allocentric perception and, third, the
development of a secondary autocentricity on the new, higher
level of objectification will be described. Fourth, the connection
between general attitude and perceptual mode will be discussed,
and examples of shift of perceptual mode in connection with
changes of general attitude will be given. The last chapter in this
section will discuss some implications of the two basic perceptual
modes and of their development for the difference between animal
and man and for the concepts of normalcy, regression, and creativity.

6

Objectification and Pleasure-Unpleasure-Boundedness in Different Sense Modalities

BY "OBJECTIFICATION" I DO NOT MEAN OBJECTIVITY, BUT THE PHE-
nomenon of man's encounter with more or less definite objects
as a certain type of relatedness emerges between him and his
environment. The degree of objectification is characterized by the
degree to which the object is perceived as existing independently
of the perceiver and the degree to which the richness of its qualities is perceived. Man takes it for granted that his environment is
structured into definite objects. This is what he experiences both
in his wakeful awareness and even in the hallucinatory world of
his dream life, although in the latter the objects become more
elusive and cannot be sought out and recaptured at will, as the
objects of reality can. Yet, objectification is a quite late phenomenon, genetically. It appears fully only in man, and in him it
develops only gradually in the course of infancy and childhood.
Neither man, ontogenetically, nor the living organism, phylogenetically, begins life with the objectifying type of related-

ness. The human embryo and the neonate do not distinguish between themselves and the outside world. In most of the protozoa, proper sense organs are as yet hardly to be found. If nevertheless they are sensitive to light, mechanical, chemical, and electrical stimulation, and to changes of temperature (although not all of them are sensitive to all of these stimuli), this seems to be due to an undifferentiated irritability of the whole protoplasma of the animal body. Ontogenetically and phylogenetically, when life begins it does not have an object world but proceeds only in degrees of well-being or ill-being, in degrees of nervous excitation, which, although often caused by agents of the environment, is not referred to the environment by the organism or probably does not even show, in the earliest stages, bodily localization. These excitations evoke reactive movements, but they do not lead to the perception of objects or even of an undifferentiated environment. The Swiss biologist Portmann has given a vivid account of the gradual emergence of an environment as we move up the evolutionary scale. He describes the world of the earthworm, in which there is only the change of light and dark, the experience of more or less hard obstructions (*Widerstand*), of humid and dry, of warm and cold, and of some scents. But no objects exist in this world and the worm never encounters the unending variety of plant and animal forms. In some, more highly organized worms of the ocean, in some snails, in many insects and crabs, the presence of simple eyes leads to the emergence of foreground and background, of distance, and of vaguely perceived shapes moving before this background.[1] With the increasingly higher development of the sense organs and increasing cerebralization, the distinctness and variety of sensory experience of the environment increase. The development of the so-called higher senses, sight and hearing, with the advent of a more highly developed eye and ear in the higher vertebrates (birds and mammals), constitutes an especially important step in evolution and brings about a considerable enrichment of the perceived environment. But even though man is surpassed by some animals in the acuity and range of some senses, only he has a full-fledged perception of objects as things and creatures existing independently of him and his needs.[2]

1] Adolf Portmann, *Grenzen des Lebens* (Verlag Friedrich Reinhardt, Basel, 1943), pp. 41-49; *Die Tiergestalt* (Verlag Friedrich Reinhardt, Basel, 1948), p. 247.
2] I have shown elsewhere why only man is able to encounter objects in the true

In the most primitive linkage between organism and environment, then, "perception" consists not of the perception of an environment but of changes in excitation. The neonate probably feels these mainly, but not entirely, as varying degrees of comfort and discomfort.[3] In contrast to this, adult man's perception shows the highest degree of objectification. In his perceptual experience he encounters a world of objects among which he moves and which he is able to perceive at any time during his waking hours, relatively independent of what momentary biological needs drive him and what temporary moods dominate him. Man's relation to the world is such that in his intersensory perception, the environment is given to him as a configuration of independently existing objects. But if we analyze his various sensory experiences more closely, we find that this is only true of perception with the totality of man's sensory equipment and of the more highly developed of his senses, especially sight. The experience of seeing is predominantly one of seeing independently existing objects, an environment structured into a variety of objects which are related to each other and to the perceiver. However, if we examine such senses as taste, smell, proprioception, or the thermal sense, then we discover that they are closer to the objectless primitive sensory organization which registers degrees and qualities of well-being or ill-being than to the objectifying organization of the more highly developed human senses.

What is the *taste* experience like, considered from the viewpoint of the relation between perceiver and environmental object? In order to answer that question, one has to isolate the pure taste experience from the natural unity of the sensory experience of tongue and palate in eating, and to disregard the tactile experience which, normally, is part of tasting food. Then it becomes apparent that in the experience of pure taste (sour, sweet, bitter, salty, etc., or any mixture of these qualities[4]) no object is perceived.

---

sense of the word. This volume, pp. 251-278. The above description of increasing objectification is in essential agreement with Révész's account of the development of spatial experience, which, according to him, coincides with objectification. G. Révész, *Die Formenwelt des Tastsinnes,* 2 vol. (Martinus Nijhoff, Haag, 1938), Vol. I, pp. 58-62.

3] For a more detailed analysis of the neonate's sensory experience see below, pp. 116-146.

4] These are the pure taste qualities which can be tasted without any help from the olfactory sense. The perception of most other tastes and flavors depends on the functioning of the natural unity of the olfactory and gustatory senses.

All I experience is that my tongue is made to feel these qualities, pleasantly or unpleasantly, by something that touches it. But what this something is, what kind of object, what structure it has, I have no way of learning from tasting it. No objectification takes place in the pure, isolated taste experience.

Even if we consider the natural unity of the experience of tasting foods or liquids, including the olfactory and tactile sensations, the degree of objectification, while somewhat higher than in pure taste, remains negligible, incomparably lower than in sight and considerably lower than in the experience of touch when the hand is engaged in active tactile exploration. The tongue and palate react only to liquid stimuli. Solid food has to be liquefied by chewing and by the action of the saliva before it can be tasted. In other words, the taste reaction does not even start before the object tasted, unless it was liquid to begin with, has lost its original structure. The tongue is exquisitely sensitive to the degree of viscosity of liquids and, according to Katz,[5] together with certain parts of the palate, is the only organ which has a specific experience of degrees of wetness and dryness. The tongue is also highly sensitive to texture. However, its capacities to taste and to explore the shapes of objects by its tactile nerves are mutually incompatible. When the tongue is tasting, the object, or part of it, is already liquefied. But even when, before tasting, one engages in tactile exploration of an object's shape and structure by moving it around in one's mouth, the range of such exploration is quite limited. It is possible only with small objects. But unless the object has a quite simple structure, like a sphere, a cube, a cylinder, etc., it is impossible to get a clear grasp of its structure. Furthermore, while engaged in oral tactile, structural exploration, one's attention fails to grasp more than a crude taste experience that may take place at the same time. And vice versa: as soon as one really tries to taste something, to be aware of the finer nuances of taste, the experience becomes one of how it *feels* on the tongue, and there is no objectification beyond the realization that *something*, of a certain texture and of greater or lesser viscosity and density, makes the tongue feel this way.

In *olfactory* perception the lack of objectification is equally evident. The experience of smelling is one which contains no

5] D. Katz, "Psychologische Untersuchungen an der Zunge," *Studien zur experimentellen Psychologie* (Benno Schwabe & Co., Basel, 1953).

clue at all about object structure. Only the directional element in smell, the fact that the sensation becomes stronger in the direction of the object from which it emanates, contains a clue that something impinges on the organism from outside. The fact that I can tell whether I smell an orange or tobacco is not due to a givenness (*Gegebenheit*) of these objects in the smell experience but because I *know* from former visual and tactile experience that the object which *looks* like an orange gives off a scent which, when I smell it again, reminds me of the object that I have seen and held in my hand. From the smell alone I cannot possibly tell whether it comes from an actual orange or from perfume distilled from orange peel in such a way as to smell exactly like an orange. Similar to pure taste, the experience of smell is one which feels more or less pleasant or unpleasant, a feeling that is inseparably linked with the specific quality of the fragrance. While I know (have learned) that smell emanates from an object, the object is not "given" in the olfactory experience. The linkage between perceiver and object is one in which the perceiver is affected by the object, experiences an excitation, pleasant or unpleasant, within his body, his nose, but in which he does not encounter an object.

A similar analysis of the *thermal sense* and of *pain* shows that there, too, the experience is one of the state of one's own body, pleasant or unpleasant, while the object causing the sensation is not "given" in the experience. Such an analysis requires the (artificial) separation of the thermal sensation from the tactile one. Both in thermal sensitivity and in pain caused by some object, the tactile sensation is of *something* impinging, without, however, any higher degree of objectification. The pain when I cut myself does not tell me anything about the structure of the object "knife" with which I have cut myself. It conveys, apart from the displeasure of pain, merely a localization of the pain.

The allocentric visual sense, as we have seen, shows a high degree of objectification while the autocentric senses (gustatory, olfactory, thermal, proprioceptive, pain) do not lead to objectification proper. Another group of differences between the autocentric and allocentric senses revolves around the more *physical quality* of autocentric as contrasted with the more *intellectual* and sometimes *spiritual quality* of allocentric perception. This contrast becomes apparent in the fact that the allocentric (or higher) senses have only a loose and often hardly noticeable connection with *feelings of sensory pleasure* and *unpleasure, comfort* and *discomfort*, while in the autocentric (or lower) senses this connection is intrinsically strong. It makes for a more *direct control of behavior* by sensory cues in the autocentric mode than in the allocentric one. Furthermore, perception by the autocentric senses is characterized by the localization of the sensory and pleasure-unpleasure sensations in or around the sense organ which mediates perception. Such *felt organ localization* is absent in the allocentric senses. Finally, the autocentric and allocentric senses differ in their relation to *memory, recall,* and *communication.*[6]

Language reflects the close linkage of the autocentric senses with subjective *feelings*. French has no separate word for the verb "to smell" but uses *sentir*, which otherwise mainly means "to feel" but can also be used for "taste." In English the word "to feel" can be used for tactile and thermal sensations as well as for emotions. The same holds true of the German *fühlen*.

Because of the feeling-boundedness, particularly the pleasure-unpleasure-boundedness of the autocentric senses, behavior responding to the perceptions received through these senses is often *more directly* and compellingly *controlled by the environment* than is the case for behavior responding to cues furnished by perception in the allocentric mode. This compellingness of the response is experienced subjectively as an almost irresistible attraction or repulsion which is not found in the allocentric senses, especially sight, to the same extent as it is in the autocentric senses of touch, proprioception, smell, taste, and pain. Examples of such repulsion are the reflex-like withdrawal from pain or the aversion that goes with the feeling of disgust fused with certain olfactory, tactile, or gustatory experiences much more strongly and frequently than with visual or auditory ones. Examples of the compelling force of positive, autocentric sensory cues are the sexual responses to tactile and proprioceptive cues, the chewing and swallowing response to gustatory, tactile, and proprioceptive cues, and the automatic distending of the nostrils and deeper breathing in response to a welcome scent or atmosphere. It is much easier, both in sexual and in eating behavior, to resist or turn away from an

---

6] This difference can be understood fully only in connection with the ontogenetic development of perception and will be discussed later on. See below pp. 158-165.

attractive visual cue than it is to do so once the tactile, proprioceptive, or gustatory sense modalities have taken over in the consummatory act or in behavior immediately preceding it. The sensual pleasure which characterizes, according to Lorenz, the consummation of probably all instinctive acts is in man pleasure of the autocentric senses. Its biological role is not only, as Lorenz has emphasized, to strengthen the motivation in the pursuit of these acts but also to ensure with compelling force their consummation.[7]

In both *taste* and *smell* each sensory experience has a more or less pleasant or unpleasant quality. This quality is not comparable to aesthetic enjoyment or rejection, but is immediately present and inseparably linked with the sensation. It distinguishes smell and taste from sight and hearing. Most visual perceptions have the neutral character of recognition, and similarly, in listening to speech, that is, in the most important use of the sense of hearing, the content of the speech, its meaning, may have a neutral, pleasant, or unpleasant effect on us, but the sensation of hearing itself is, as a rule, not accompanied by outspoken feelings of pleasure or displeasure. Of course there can be pleasure in seeing and hearing, too,[8] but by and large, a great deal of what we hear and see is characterized by the neutrality and "objectivity" of the sensory experience which, in these prevailing modes of hearing and seeing, serves mainly the function of recognition, that is, of orientation in reality. We want to understand the words spoken to us and their meaning, to recognize them. And, similarly, we recognize where we are, try to see whether we have taken the right way to the street toward which we are headed, or look for an object that we need until we see it. In all these instances, the sensations of hearing and seeing as such are indifferent, as far as their relation to pleasure and displeasure goes, quite in contrast to tasting and smelling, where the sensation itself is pleasant or unpleasant. A taste or smell is pleasant or unpleasant independent from one's ability to tell from it whether the object tasted is an orange or a peppercorn, whether the scent comes from a lilac bush or a skunk. Of course, anticipation and knowledge, or the lack of it, can have

7] Compare Konrad Lorenz, "The Nature of Instinct," and Konrad Lorenz and Nicholas Tinbergen, "Taxis and Instinct," in Claire H. Schiller, ed., *Instinctive Behavior* (International Universities Press, New York, 1957), pp. 153-154, 184.
8] See more about this below, pp. 110-111.

a suggestive influence on the pleasant or unpleasant character of what one tastes or smells. But this possibility does not alter the fact that the sensations themselves, whether or not linked with knowledgeable or other anticipation, have pleasant or unpleasant character.

In the *thermal* sense, too, the sensations of various degrees of warmth, heat, coolness, or cold have pleasant or unpleasant qualities. These become very marked and assume the quality of *pain* in the more extreme degrees of heat and coldness; in between these extremes they have the character of more or less pronounced *comfort* or *discomfort*. Little or no objectification takes place in perception by means of the thermal sense.

The sensations caused by the *pain* receptors also are characterized by lack of objectification, by displeasure, and by more or less distinct localization.

Proprioceptive (kinesthetic) perception of the muscles, tendons, and joints also functions largely in the autocentric mode. Their tension, relaxation, and position are registered automatically, most of the time unattended by central awareness, although of vital importance for the performance of any motor activity and the maintenance of any posture. But if they are consciously noticed, the sensation usually is slightly or distinctly pleasurable, comfortable or unpleasurable, uncomfortable; the motor or postural activity is felt as satisfying or as strained or cramped. The sensations range from hardly noticeable feelings of either well-being or strain in the activity or posture to outspoken pleasure or discomfort. They do not tell us anything about the shape, composition, and other qualities of the muscles, joints, and tendons whose messages they convey; nor do they reveal much about the objects encountered which give rise to them. They do not show the spatial arrangement nor the forms of the object world. All they tell us about the object concerns the effort required to handle it, the resistance it offers, the support it gives to the human body resting its weight on it. Thus, proprioception does not convey qualities of the object but states and changes of the body in contact with the object. Only if interest is focused on the object does proprioception indirectly permit, for instance, an estimate of the object's weight by the feeling of the effort required to lift it or to hold it in the outstretched hand.

In general, modern Western civilization has tended to atrophy the conscious awareness of the constant stream of pleasurable or unpleasurable sensations which the proprioceptive sense is built to arouse.[9] People often become aware of inappropriate motoric or postural activity only when chronic pain or discomfort arises from constant misuse of muscles and tendons, which they could have felt and corrected immediately if they had listened to the comfort as well as discomfort signals of the body in the way in which small children and, in some of the Eastern and in some more primitive civilizations, many adults do.[10] Nevertheless, the satisfaction that people experience in physical exercise is partly the pleasure intrinsic to the conscious proprioceptive experience of the appropriate use of one's body just as the discomfort of strained, cramped, or exaggerated activity is the conscious counterpart of inappropriate use. Of course, the pleasure in physical exercise usually is a much more complex phenomenon and sometimes proprioceptive pleasure may have no part at all in it. It may be based entirely or partly on the satisfaction of skillful and successful handling of an object, e.g. in bowling, archery, tennis, etc., on competitive success, on feelings of power or triumph, on the discharge of anger. Also, proprioceptive may combine with other sensory experience to create, for instance, what Novalis has called the *Wollust der Wasserberührung*,[11] where the proprioceptive pleasures of propelling oneself forward by using one's strength against the yielding resistance of the water, of resting the body's weight on the encompassing support of the water, goes together with the tactile and thermal pleasures of feeling the water gliding by and its refreshing coolness. One of the most obvious and unmixed examples of proprioceptive sensory pleasure is in stretching after awakening from sleep or after getting up from sitting for a long period of time in the same position. This stretch-

9] See below, pp. 208-210.

10] T. v. Uexküll makes a noteworthy comment on the similar phenomenon of unawareness and disregard of mood. He points out that mood disorders may consist in mood rigidity as well as in mood lability and that certain illnesses which are practically unknown in the great Eastern civilizations and among primitive people may occur so frequently in Western civilization because an attitude of purposeful performance which disregards and eventually excludes awareness of the person's changing moods is taken for granted. He calls them civilization-diseases (*Zivilisationskrankheiten*). Thure von Uexküll, "Das Problem der 'Befindensweisen' und seine Bedeutung für eine medizinische Phänomenologie," *Psyche*, 1951, 5:401-432, 415, 425.

11] The voluptuousness of contact with water. Novalis, *Schriften* (Eugen Diederichs, Jena, 1923), Vol. 3, p. 24.

ing is a muscular activity at which dogs, cats, and other animals seem to be much better than people. As a final example, in which, as in stretching, the biological importance of the reward inherent in sensory experience is very apparent, I want to mention chewing and swallowing, which, of course, usually combines with tactile and taste sensations to make eating pleasurable. The proprioceptive factor is distinct in the pleasure of the jaws' muscular activity or the tongue's pressure against the palate in overcoming various degrees and qualities of resistance offered by different kinds of food and also in the displeasure caused by the strain of coping with a very tough steak.[12]

In contrast to the kinesthetic sensations aroused by the proprioceptors, the sensations caused by the *visceroceptors* are much fewer. Most of the function of the visceroceptors never comes to awareness, as is true also of most of the work of the labyrinth and the semicircular canal receptors. But when the visceroceptors do cause sensations they are usually unpleasant, varying in degree from the slight discomfort after having eaten too much to acute pain; they do not lead to any objectification.

The pleasure and displeasure, comfort and discomfort or pain feelings linked with perception through the autocentric senses have a peculiarly *physical* quality, different for each sense. In most cases, this physical quality does *not* have the character of relief from tension. It also differs from other feelings such as pity, love, sadness, anger, and from the joy and fulfillment which may be experienced in the allocentric mode of perception in sight or hearing.[13]

Plato points to the pleasure linked with the sense of smell as an example of genuine pleasure and he opposes this to the experience of the mere ceasing of pain.[14] Freud, by attempting to explain all pleasure as a reduction or cessation of unpleasant tension (excitation), took a position diametrically opposed to Plato's view. But he did so at the price of omitting the analysis of many kinds of pleasure, among them especially the pleasures connected with some of the autocentric senses. These result not from a cessation

12] About the reward in proprioception compare Konrad Lorenz, "Behavior Patterns in Allied Species," in Bertram Schaffner, ed., *Group Processes, Transactions of the First Conference, 1954* (Josiah Macy, Jr., Foundation, New York, 1955), p. 188, and the whole discussion pp. 187-195.

13] See below, pp. 110-111.

14] Plato *Republic* 583B-584B. Similarly Aristotle *Ethics* 1173b.

of excitation but from the excitation itself, not from the abolishment of, but from the temporary staying with and the receptiveness toward the substance or the activity causing the pleasurable sensation.[15] Pleasure as well as displeasure in autocentric sensory experience arise from the excitation of the sense organ in contact with the environment. The experience of sensory pleasure can be fully realized only by the extension of the consciously attended contact over some period of time, while the experience of sensory displeasure usually leads quickly to the attempt to abolish the stimulus, to turn away from it, or in some other way to protect oneself against its impact.

Within a certain range, which differs in the different sense modalities and varies somewhat individually, the autocentric senses and also the autocentric functioning of the allocentric senses have the capacity for *adaptation* to any new stimulation. This means that the awareness of temperature, of tactile sensations caused by objects touching the skin, of the kinesthetic sensations of a certain posture, of smells, etc., recedes into the background and eventually ceases altogether, unless the stimulus is too strong. Concomitantly, the pleasure-displeasure and comfort-discomfort feelings also fade and finally disappear from awareness. The person now has become accustomed to or, as it were, embedded in the environment relevant to these senses and no longer notices it, until a change occurs or attention is redirected to the sensations for some other reason. Also, strong goal-directedness, with its focusing of energy and attention on the goal, has the effect of letting the autocentric sensations which are irrelevant to the goal recede and disappear. This is true even of not too severe pain. Both these phenomena, adaptation and goal-directedness, are not entirely naturally given, but are to a considerable extent historically, socially, and culturally determined and dependent on individual experience, personality structure, and constitutional factors. Different historical epochs, civilizations, social groups, and persons show considerable variation in the absolute and relative sensitivity to the various autocentric sensations. Obvious examples can be found in our own culture. Witness the American phobia of body odor, artificially and successfully nurtured by advertising campaigns. Another example is the adaptation of the greater part of

15] For a more detailed analysis of pleasure and critique of Freud's pleasure principle see this volume, pp. 55-68.

the urban population to industrial fumes and exhaust gases, of which many become aware only when they visit the country, and some not even then. On the other hand, many city dwellers are disgusted by the smell of a stable, a cowshed, a manure pile, which, objectively, are not harmful, as exhaust gases of automobiles are, and which the farm population either does not particularly notice or else likes. In many countries people live in the same room with cattle, chickens, a goat, without the feeling of objection or even revulsion that the odors and the tactile contact would arouse in the urban population of other countries. Different social classes also show differences in autocentric sensory reactions.[16]

The sociocultural history of the senses has yet to be written. The young Marx pointed to this task when he said that the formation of man's five senses is a work of the entire world history.[17]

The autocentric sensations, including their pleasure or displeasure qualities, are generally experienced not centrally[18] nor as a sensation pervading the entire person but as localized in, around, or near the particular sense organ through which the sensory perception takes place. This phenomenon I designate as *felt organ localization*.

We are wont to say, without giving it a second thought, that we see with our eyes, hear with our ears, touch with our hands or skin, smell with our nose, and taste with our tongue. While such a statement names the various sense organs from which the afferent nerves conduct the sensory excitations to the brain, it obscures a marked difference between the higher and lower senses with regard to the felt localization (or lack of it) of the sensory experience. It is a statement reflecting knowledge and learned rather than felt experience. I know that I see with my eyes because when I close them I cease to see or because I have learned about the way in which the retina, the lens, etc., function. And the same holds true for the other organs. But what is the felt experience in seeing, hearing, tasting, smelling, feeling warm or cold? The *olfactory* and *gustatory* excitations are actually *felt in* the nose and *on* the tongue and palate, respectively. *Tactile* sensa-

16] Compare this volume, p. 300.

17] Karl Marx, *Die Frühschriften*, ed. Siegfried Landshut (Alfred Kröner Verlag, Stuttgart, 1953), p. 242. Some significant historical and sociocultural factors in perception are discussed below, pp. 166-212.

18] This refers to the experiential quality of the sensation, not to the neurological fact that such experience is mediated by the central nervous system.

tions are felt to occur at a particular place on the skin. Sensations in the other autocentric senses are similarly localized. In *seeing* and *hearing*, however, the sensation is *not felt* to take place in or on the sense organs of eye or ear. Only indirectly, by closing my eye or blocking the entrance to the ear, do I *learn* that I see with my eye and hear with my ear. And only under unusual circumstances does the experience of seeing assume the character of a sensation *felt* to be localized in the eye, e.g. when the excitation becomes extreme so that it approaches the quality of pain, as in exposure to glaring light or in looking straight into the sun. But in the ordinary range of hearing and seeing, the experience does not involve localization of the sensation in eye or ear. The experience is not "my eye sees," but "*I* see," or the seeing "happens"; it is an ongoing process in a field which comprises both perceiver and percept, without any special, experiential reference to the perceiver's eyes.

The quality of a physical sensation which characterizes perception in the autocentric senses is accentuated in felt organ localization. The taste on the tongue, the pain on a bruised knee, the scent inhaled through the nose are actually felt as affecting me through these parts of my body. In these experiences I am made to feel something in these areas of my body. The word "sensation" expresses this quality better than does the word "perception," which describes more fittingly the allocentric experience of an I seeing an object.

Some autocentric sensations are more sharply localized than others. A pin-prick is felt in a quite definite area of the skin, but the shivering in cold temperature seems to pervade the whole body. The scent of a flower at which one sniffs, the irritation caused by the smell of ammonia are felt to be localized in the nasal passages, but the smell of freshly mowed grass on a meadow or of a fresh morning in the woods may be experienced as filling the whole chest because it becomes linked with the sensation of breathing deeply. Yet, whether distinctly or only vaguely localized, all these sensations have a physical quality and retain an experiential link with positive or negative bodily feeling which is absent in the typical experience of allocentric sight, for example of seeing a house or a person.

So far, the *difference* between *two groups of senses*, the autocentric and the allocentric, has been emphasized. This difference is not a matter of absolute alternatives, but rather of the relative predominance of objectification in the allocentric senses and of pleasure-boundedness and felt organ localization in the autocentric senses. Perception by means of the predominantly autocentric senses can and does at times shift back and forth between pure autocentricity and a somewhat more allocentric mode, although the limitations of the autocentric senses never permit a predominantly allocentric, objectifying mode of perception. Conversely, the predominantly allocentric senses can and do function also in the autocentric mode. In the autocentric senses, the shift to a measure of allocentricity usually occurs together with, and is caused by, a shift of attitude which is brought about by the *intention* of the perceiver. In gustatory experience, for instance, while the quality of the taste is characteristically fused with pleasure or displeasure, and what one eats tastes either good or bad, one can shift one's attitude to find out what ingredients may be contained in a dish or, as the professional wine or tea taster does, to compare critically different kinds of wine or tea. This causes the emphasis of the perceptual experiences to shift, as E. Straus has formulated it, from how something tastes *to me* to how *it* tastes.[19] Of course, the one-dimensional quality of taste never allows one to perceive many features of the object tasted, but the shift in attitude can loosen the usual pleasure-displeasure-boundedness of the sense of taste and focus the attention on the objective[20] taste qualities of the object. This loosening of the pleasure-displeasure tie finds its limits in the case of very unpleasant, revolting, or disgusting taste qualities, and in the same way there are probably few if any people who, even when their attention is focused on the ingredients of a dish or the distinctive quality of a wine, can avoid feeling pleasure if the dish is delicious or the wine superb. Similar objectifying tendencies in other autocentric senses can be observed when one tries, for example, to gauge the temperature of water or of the air or to find out in which of two containers the water is slightly warmer, or when, by holding two stones, one in each hand, one wants to find out which is heavier. In all these cases

19] Erwin Straus, *Vom Sinn der Sinne,* 2nd ed. (Springer Verlag, Berlin, 1956), p. 394.
20] "Objective" here means the experiential quality of "belonging to the object," not any objectivity which transcends human sensory experience. Thus "objective" here contrasts with the subjective feelings of delight, pleasure, or disgust.

there is an intention to find out something about the object and, while this is done by watching how the object affects one, the emphasis shifts from how I feel when the object impinges on me, to how "it" feels, namely the water, the air, the stone.

An example of an allocentric sense functioning in the auto-centric mode is furnished by the experience of looking at a glaring light; for instance, in looking into the bright sun the primary experience is one of an unpleasant, almost painful feeling which, in contrast to the usual experiences of seeing, is felt as localized in the eye and causes one to close the eye or turn away. A very loud or shrill noise close by has a similar effect on the otherwise predominantly allocentric sense of hearing.

In spite of the fact that the experiences mediated by the auto-centric senses vary between complete autocentricity and a some-what more objectifying attitude, and that the allocentric senses can also function in an autocentric mode, the basic differences between the autocentric and the allocentric senses remain. In the former, the autocentric mode of relatedness is the essential mode of sensory experience and the autocentric senses are incapable of true objectification, while in the latter the allocentric mode pre-dominates although the allocentric senses can and do also function in the autocentric mode.

The common, popular classification of the senses into the *higher* and the *lower* senses assumes new meaning and validity when viewed in the light of these distinctions of the predominant mode of relatedness in sensory experience. The so-called lower senses, taste and smell, are clearly autocentric, and so are the propriocep-tive, thermal and pain senses. The higher senses, especially sight, the highest, but also hearing, are predominantly allocentric. In order to be meaningful, the terms "low" and "high" have to be related to stages of development. Then it becomes clear that allocentricity, characterized by objectification and by a loose con-nection between perception and pleasure-unpleasure, comfort-dis-comfort, attraction-repulsion feelings, is a late development, phylogenetically and ontogenetically, and is to be found only in man, at the highest stage of evolution and after man has emerged from the infantile mode of relatedness. Autocentricity, with its lack of objectification and, in man and probably also in many animals, with its fusion with pleasure-unpleasure feelings, is the exclusive sensory mode of relatedness in earlier, lower stages of phylogenetic and ontogenetic development.[21]

Where the distinction between lower and higher senses has been used in psychology and physiology, the sense of *touch* has become an object of disagreement. Some definitely regard it as one of the higher senses,[22] while others classify it with the lower senses.[23] This puzzling contradiction is due to the unique position of the tactile sense from the viewpoint of the distinction between the allocentric and autocentric modes of perception. While in the other senses either the allocentric or the autocentric perceptual mode of functioning predominates in the waking life of adult man, this is not the case to the same extent in the sense of touch. Man encounters *objects* and learns something about their form, structure, and texture by means of the sense of touch. Developmentally, touch plays at first a more important role in the gradual emergence of the object world than sight does. Later, although we continue to explore objects also by tactile manipulation, sight becomes paramount and the degree of objectification mediated by the mature sense of sight is very much greater than that mediated by tactile exploration.[24] While, thus, there is definite objectification in tactile experience, touch is nevertheless closely tied up with pleasure and unpleasure, comfort and discomfort. The feeling of fabrics of cloth or of sheets or blankets touching the body and many other textural experiences usually are characterized by varying degrees of sometimes noticed, sometimes unnoticed comfort or discomfort. Tactile sensations in sexual contact contribute to the highest peak of pleasure in man's life. Pleasurable tactile experiences of the mouth in sucking play an important role in

21] See below, pp. 116-158. Compare also Boernstein, who bases the classification of the senses into higher and lower ones on their capacity to perceive strong or weak *Gestalten* and on neurological considerations. He, too, comes to the conclusion that the higher senses retain their low sensory function and thus can function both on a higher and lower level. Walter S. Boernstein, "Classification of the Human Senses," *Yale Journal of Biology and Medicine*, 1955-56, 28:208-215.

22] For instance Révész, *Die Formenwelt des Tastsinnes*, Vol. 1, p. 61; Boernstein, "Classification of the Human Senses."

23] F. Stirnimann, *Psychologie des neugeborenen Kindes* (Rascher-Verlag, Zürich and Leipzig, 1940), p. 50; W. Nagel, "Allgemeine Einleitung zur Physiologie der Sinne," in *Handbuch der Physiologie des Menschen*, Vol. III (F. Vieweg und Sohn, Braunschweig, 1904), quoted by Boernstein, *op. cit.*, p. 209; George Santayana, *The Sense of Beauty* (Random House, New York, 1955), pp. 68-69.

24] The most detailed analysis of this difference has been made by Révész, *op. cit.*

infancy and early childhood. Later, in the enjoyment of food, tactile experiences of texture and viscosity are almost as important as gustatory ones. Touch, furthermore, is characterized by felt organ localization; it is felt to take place in a definite area of the body.

Thus, the tactile sense would seem to defy classification under the concepts of autocentric and allocentric senses. However, if different tactile experiences and different stages in the development of the tactile sense are studied more closely, then it becomes apparent that *each single tactile experience* as a rule shows either a predominantly autocentric or a predominantly allocentric mode of relatedness and that experiences in which objectification, pleasure-boundedness, and felt organ localization are equally present are hardly to be found. Rather, we find that the neonate's tactile experiences and those of early infancy are in the autocentric mode, while in later stages of development some tactile experiences take place typically with a predominantly autocentric, others with a predominantly allocentric perceptual attitude.

Autocentric tactile experiences occur typically and regularly when any area of the skin is *being touched by something*. In such contact there is hardly any objectification if no other sense data, outside of tactile ones, come into play. One is aware only that *something* touches the body—aware of the object's thermal quality and its textural quality (smooth or scratchy, soft or hard, etc.), provided there is some movement, however slight.[25] In other words, there is a lack or a low degree of objectification just as in smell or taste. On the other hand, there is definite, felt organ localization: one feels which part of the skin is being touched. Also, in response to texture, there are usually feelings of more or less marked comfort or discomfort, pleasure or displeasure. In most people, these feelings probably are less marked than the pleasure-displeasure feelings in smell and taste. But in some people they are very pronounced. There are considerable individual differences with regard to the intensity of these feelings, the kinds of texture that are experienced as pleasant or as unpleasant, and the degree of fusion between touch and pleasure-displeasure, i.e. the degree to which this kind of tactile experience is tied to the

25] D. Katz, in *Der Aufbau der Tastwelt* (J. A. Barth, Leipzig, 1925), pp. 62-64, has shown that without movement it is not possible to feel the texture of objects.

comfort-discomfort and pleasure-displeasure experience. In some people this tie is, for some types of tactile experience, well-nigh unbreakable; for others it is fairly loose.

Allocentric tactile experience presupposes the possibility of objectification. A full-fledged perception of objects (rather than just the sense of something impinging) can be attained by means of the tactile sense only if some degree of structural exploration is possible. To carry out this exploration in its most primitive form, the various surfaces of an object, or a fairly large proportion of them, must be surrounded by some of the organism's tactile, sensitive surfaces so that something of the object's surface configuration can be felt simultaneously, or—for more elaborate exploration—they must be held and manipulated between at least two sensitive skin surfaces which are able to explore the various object surfaces successively by changing pressure of touch and by well-coordinated movements. These conditions are met minimally by the mouth cavity and the tongue and—in a much more elaborate and miraculously versatile way—by the human hand with its opposing thumb.

While oral tactile exploration plays a considerable role in infancy, its importance is soon superseded by manual exploration, and we must turn to the *hand* for the clearest examples of *allocentric* tactile experiences. When one manipulates and touches something in order to recognize what kind of object it is, while the eyes are closed or blindfolded, then the tactile experience is clearly an allocentric one. There is very definite objectification. The contact is not merely with a vague something that impinges, but with a definite object whose various surfaces the hands explore. The experience is a neutral one as far as the pleasure-unpleasure dimension is concerned. Organ localization is present, but recedes to the fringe of awareness. The experience is an active one, of touching and manipulating, rather than a reactive one, of being touched and reacting with an autocentric, tactile feeling. The example of blindfolded, manual object exploration was chosen only because it is best suited to bring the allocentric quality of this kind of tactile experience into sharp focus. Actually, any active manual object exploration has this allocentric character, provided that the intention of the perceiver is directed toward exploring the object and not toward how his hand feels in contact with the object. But since people who are not blind usually engage

in tactile object exploration concomitantly with visual exploration, the tactile experience tends to be overshadowed by the visual
one. Even in allocentric tactile exploration there remains a background sensation that it is *my* body, *my* hand which feels the
object. Thus, in contrast to allocentric vision, touch never is entirely without a trace of felt organ localization. While I touch I
am also being touched.

The twofold nature of tactile perception has been emphasized
also by Katz,[26] who speaks of its bipolar quality in which the
subjective sensation on the body surface seems inseparably combined with the perceived qualities of the object touched. He points
out that in the impressions received through the *moving* tactile
organ (the moving fingers), the object pole predominates; in those
received by the *static* organ, the subject pole predominates. It is
true that usually the moving, exploring fingers function in the
allocentric mode, the passively touched skin in the autocentric
mode, but this is due to the active, object-centered attitude in
manual exploration rather than to the mere fact of movement.
Although the shape and structure of an object cannot be fully
explored without movement of the hand, autocentric tactile perception can occur by means of the moving as well as the static
fingers and palm of the hand, as, for example, in the pleasant
sensation of stroking fur. There also can be a shift from autocentric to allocentric perception, and vice versa, in holding an
object in one's hand,[27] and an oscillation between the two perceptual modes. Thus, while tactile perception in most areas of the
skin takes place in the autocentric mode, in the hand, the most
important organ for tactile exploration, the perceptual mode can
be either allocentric or autocentric, depending on the intention and
attitude of the perceiver. These facts give to the sense of touch
the unique position which has led some to count it among the
higher, others among the lower senses.

Sight, man's highest and most developed sense, is clearly allocentric. People take it for granted that seeing means to see a
variety of distinct objects, and usually they do not experience
any particular pleasure or displeasure in seeing the ever-shifting
scene around them as they move about or glance from one object
to another. Thus, the predominant function of sight, the recogni-

26] Katz, *Der Aufbau der Tastwelt*, pp. 19, 124.
27] See below, p. 217.

tion of and orientation in the visible environment, shows eminently the quality of objectification and most of the time in most people also an absence of pleasure-displeasure-boundedness, a quality of "objectivity" in the sense of a neutrality of feeling.

The *objectification* in the sense of sight is apparent in a number of ways. Many more features of the object are grasped simultaneously, and by virtue of this, each object looked at is given to the perceiver more fully, in more dimensions than through any other sense. The autocentric senses have a one-dimensional character. Even touch, in its allocentric mode, lets the object appear only successively, as the exploring fingers move over its surfaces; the object does not show its color and shading, which, in sight, are grasped together with its shape and three-dimensional Gestalt. Many objects that can be seen are not accessible to touch, and many, even if they are accessible, do not reveal their structure and shape to manual exploration if they exceed a certain size. A tree, a house, a mountain, a landscape never would become a unified, clearly grasped Gestalt if man were limited to the sense of touch. Unless the two hands, in addition to exploring details, can move back and forth over the entire surface of the object in a relatively short time, the perception of the unity of the object touched is disrupted and its structure does not become clear. The congenitally blind are able to know about trees, houses, mountains, and landscapes only because their thinking is informed by a language and by concepts based on the total experience of man so largely dependent on vision, and by communication with others who tell them about the visual world.

Objectification in sight, furthermore, rests on a much more comprehensive and clearer perception of distance and spatial relations than touch can furnish, and especially on the possibility of seeing at one glance, or by a swift movement of the eyes, several different objects. Touch, a proximity sense, confines the perceiver to those objects which are within his reach, one at a time, while sight, a distance sense, not only reveals many features of each object but permits the glance to range over many objects in a very brief time and to perceive their spatial relations to each other and to the perceiver, and their movements in space, from the flight of a distant bird to the changing gestures and facial expressions of people close by.

The high degree of objectification in sight, however, does not mean that sight functions only in an allocentric way. Autocentric functioning of sight takes place in the newborn and predominates for a considerable period of time in infancy;[28] to a lesser degree it takes place in adult man both together and alternating with more allocentric functioning. If one compares the experiences of seeing form and structure with those of seeing light and color, it becomes apparent that the former tend to be more allocentric, while the latter have a comparatively more autocentric quality, as does also the experience of the total insistence (*Gesamteindringlichkeit*) of the visual field.

In sight the highest degree of objectification is found. Sight responds to a much greater wealth of sensory data than do the lower senses and thus makes accessible to the perceiver a greater variety and richness of object qualities, especially very highly differentiated spatial patterns. Thus, with the gradual development of the allocentric attitude, sight increasingly becomes the foremost medium for objectifying perception. It offers a wealth of identifiable, recognizable features characteristic of the object, particularly the object's form and Gestalt. In allocentric sight the perceiver is turned toward the object in an active and selective attitude. He *focuses* on a particular object within the totality of the impinging visual field, for however brief a moment, and follows, more or less attentively, its dominant lines, thus grasping its form and structure. The eye not only singles out a particular object among the multitude of objects in the visible environment, but furthermore, while looking at this object, selects and dwells on particular distinctive features of this object. The selective process, thus, not only lifts one object out of the total field but then abstracts from this object features which will make it possible to distinguish the object from others and, if these features have been grasped sufficiently, to identify, recognize, or recall it or similar objects in the future. In fact, the act of interested selective visual focusing is *constitutive* of the object: it makes what before was part of the total field into a distinct object for the perceiver, the object of active attention. In order to perceive clearly an object thus selected, the eye has to move, now following a line, now jumping from one point to another, wandering back and forth over the various features of the object so that its total configura-

28] See below, pp. 116-158.

tion and structure may be grasped. Perception of even such simple figures as a triangle, square, or circle tends to become amorphous if only one point is focused upon, e.g. one angle of the triangle. In order to see the figure distinctly, the eye has to follow its lines actively.[29] The active character of visual perception which leads to objectification lies in the motor activity of the eye as well as in the selective and active attention governing this activity. Attentive looking at something is a visual experience markedly different from gazing at the total impinging field. Klein found that the distinctness and definiteness with which the spatial object quality of size is perceived varies in different people; he distinguishes between a "sharpening" and a "leveling" perceptual attitude. People who have the sharpening attitude perceive differences in size (and presumably also other form differences) more distinctly and decisively and are generally more active and show what he calls "self-outwardness." Those who have the leveling attitude do not perceive the differences in size but act as if they "preferred to ignore, deny or suppress" them and show a pattern of "self-inwardness," a retreat from objects, and are generally more passive.[30] These findings confirm that sensory perception is partly determined by the mode of relatedness of the perceiver to the environment and that the degree of objectification depends on the allocentric attitude, particularly on the active and selective turning toward the object.

Aristotle accounts for the preferred position of sight among the senses of man by pointing to the fact that sight more than any other sense enables man to become aware of the *distinctions* between things,[31] in other words to select or abstract the distinguishing form of an object. Susanne K. Langer, on the basis of philosophical considerations, comes to conclusions regarding form perception similar to those of our experiential analysis. She writes: "A tendency to organize the sensory field into . . . patterns . . . , to perceive forms rather than a flux of light-impressions, seems

29] Compare the detailed discussion of this point by Hebb, who emphasizes particularly the genetic and learning aspects from the viewpoint of a neurological theory of perception. D. O. Hebb, *The Organization of Behavior* (John Wiley & Sons, New York, 1949), pp. 31-35, 80-106. For a discussion of the role of focal attention in the constitution of the object world, see this volume, pp. 251-278.

30] George S. Klein, "The Personal World through Perception," in Robert R. Blake and Glenn V. Ramsey, eds., *Perception: An Approach to Personality* (Ronald Press, New York, 1951), pp. 328-355, 336-339.

31] *Metaphysics* 980 a 26.

to be inherent in our receptor apparatus. . . . This unconscious appreciation of forms is the primitive root of all abstraction, which in turn is the keynote of rationality. . . . I believe our ingrained habit of . . . seeing *things* and not sense-data rests on the fact that we promptly and unconsciously abstract a form from each sensory experience, and use this form to *conceive* the experience as a whole, as a 'thing.' " And in another passage: "The power of . . . regarding everything about a sense-datum as irrelevant except a certain *form* that it embodies, is the most characteristic trait of mankind. It issues in an unconscious, spontaneous process of *abstraction* which goes on all the time in the human mind. . . . *Abstractive seeing is the foundation of our rationality.* . . ."[32]

Compared with the active and objectifying allocentric perception of form and structure, the perception of *color* and *light* does not require an active and selective attitude. They *impinge* upon the eye, which does not have to seek them out attentively but *reacts* to their impact. Goethe, whose descriptions of the experiential qualities of the different colors are outstanding, speaks of their sensual-moral effect and describes how one is, so to speak, "affected pathologically" by color and carried away by various feelings.[33] He does not mean pathological in the sense in which the word commonly is used today but refers to the pathic, passive, reactive quality of the color experience. Similarly, he speaks of the impact of light by comparing it to tremendous noise.[34]

Color and light affect the motionless eye as much as, if not more than, the eye in movement. The light of the day awakens one from sleep, penetrating even through the closed eyelids. The wide expanses of the green of the fields and woods, the blue of the sky and water fill the eye, and the vivid colors of flower beds or of the varicolored neon lights on the advertising signs in the night of the big cities strike, even assail it. Even a relatively small spot of a bright color on a neutral background "catches" the

32] S. K. Langer, *Philosophy in a New Key* (The New American Library of World Literature, New York, 1951), pp. 83-84, 70. Langer speaks generally of all sensory experiences. Actually, her conclusions apply only to the allocentric senses or the allocentric mode of perceiving, and it is no accident that the examples which she gives in her discussion are taken from the visual and the auditory senses, not from taste and smell.

33] J. W. von Goethe, "Zur Farbenlehre," *Sämtliche Werke* (J. G. Cotta, Tübingen, 1850/1), Vol. 28, §§ 758-920, 812.

34] *Faust II*, Act I, scene 1, A pleasant landscape: "A tremendous noise announces the approach of the sun."

eye. Goldstein has shown how the impact of color affects the entire organism and is especially marked in patients in whom the "objectifying" attitude is impaired.[35] The perception of color, by itself, does not permit objectification, while the perception of form does. Even when one is already familiar with a particular object, its color alone usually is insufficient to enable one to recognize it. To perceive an object with its distinguishing features for the first time as well as to recognize an already known object requires the perception of form. The basic perceptual experience of color changes its quality somewhat when colors are seen in connection with distinct object perception, especially in relatively small objects, for example when one focuses on a pencil lying on the desk and notices that its color is green; it also changes somewhat, in a different way, when one is attentive to subtle nuances of colors or to how different colors harmonize or contrast with each other, as for instance in a painting.[36]

The more allocentric quality of form perception and the more autocentric quality of color perception not only consists in the active and objectifying character of the former as contrasted with the lack of objectification and the impinging, passive character of the latter, but becomes apparent also if one analyzes the relation of form and color perception to feelings, especially the problem of *pleasure-displeasure* and *comfort-discomfort-boundedness* in *form* and *color* perception. The process of active, selective focusing on an object and of following its distinguishing features can be and usually is carried out in an emotionally neutral way. Such outstanding examples of form perception as recognition of the shapes of the different letters and numbers in reading or of the environmental objects on the street or in a room usually take place without pleasure or displeasure. Of course, the sight of something beautiful can lead to a feeling of profound enjoyment and appreciation. But this feeling has a different quality from that of the pleasure-displeasure feelings linked with autocentric perception.[37]

35] K. Goldstein and O. Rosenthal, "Zum Problem der Wirkung der Farben auf den Organismus," *Schweizer Archiv für Neurologie und Psychiatrie*, 1930, 26:3-26; K. Goldstein and W. Jablonski, "Ueber den Einfluss des Tonus auf Refraktion und Sehleistungen," *Graefe's Archiv für Ophthalmologie*, 1933, 130:395-410. K. Goldstein, *The Organism* (American Book Company, New York, 1939), pp. 263-265, 484.

36] See below, pp. 111-113.

37] See below, pp. 110-111.

In contrast to the emotionally detached or neutral quality of form perception and recognition, the impact of color is usually linked with definite, if often slight, feelings of pleasure or displeasure, comfort or discomfort. Colors are not only and usually not even primarily "recognized" but they are *felt* as exciting or soothing, dissonant or harmonious, clamorous or tranquil, vivid or calm, joyous or somber, warm or cool, disturbing and distracting or conducive to concentration and tranquillity. Every decorator knows how much the color of a room influences its "mood," that is to say how directly it affects the whole state of feeling of people in the room or, in Goethe's words, how it carries them away to various feelings.

The allocentric, objectifying character of form perception and the autocentric, feeling-bound character of color perception account for the symptomatic significance of so-called form and color responses which Rorschach derived from the results obtained from different types of mental patients and normal persons with his ink-blot test. He observed that responses based on the perception of the forms of his ink-blots and on their more or less accurate comparison with the form of remembered objects are essentially conscious achievements of intelligence, attention, and concentration, that they have to do with the *fonction du réel* (reality testing), and that a too high proportion of them indicates too much intellectual control. On the other hand, he found that responses based entirely or in part on the color of the ink blots represent emotionality and are indicators of the excitability of affect. These findings, although obtained by a quite different method, are consistent with, and understandable on the basis of, the experiential nature of form and color perception as shown by our phenomenological analysis.[38]

Phylogenetic and ontogenetic development, too, show that perception of color and of light and dark are already part of the more primitive, autocentric world of animals and the newborn infant and precede the perception of form, which, on a limited scale, is

38] Hermann Rorschach, *Psychodiagnostics. A Diagnostic Test Based on Perception* (Hans Huber, Berne, 1942). Compare also Ernest G. Schachtel, "The Dynamic Perception and the Symbolism of Form," *Psychiatry*, 1941, 4:79-96, and "On Color and Affect," *Psychiatry*, 1943, 6:393-409. In the latter article the relation between color and affect is explained in a somewhat different way from the one given here. The two explanations do not contradict but supplement each other. The article also gives a more detailed analysis of the emotional significance of different colors.

found only in the higher animals, and which achieves its dominant importance in the growing child and in man, where it makes possible the discovery of an infinitely varied and expandable world of objects.[39]

These remarks on the pleasure-displeasure-boundedness of color perception and the absence of this link in form perception may seem to imply that only color gives pleasure to sight while the world of form is always an abstract, neutral one, devoid of enjoyment. Although the pleasure and charm or the dissonance and gaudiness of color pervade everything man sees, obviously the sense of form, too, can be the source of delight; the grasp of form and structure gives a deep feeling of joyful satisfaction. This in spite of the fact that most of the time seeing has the neutral quality of everyday recognition and orientation and that many people after childhood completely lose their capacity for the enjoyment of seeing. But the immediate, reactive feelings of pleasure or displeasure linked with color perception are qualitatively different from the enjoyment in form perception. They resemble more the pleasure experienced in the predominantly autocentric senses. If they do not have the physical quality of the pleasures of taste and smell and of autocentric tactile experience they approximate this quality in their stimulating, exciting, or soothing and calming effect. The joy and the heightened sense of aliveness inherent in the grasp of *form and structure,* on the other hand, are akin to that in any activity by which man realizes and enhances his capacity to relate to the world around him. Santayana apparently had this difference in mind when he wrote that the beautiful effect of form "arises in the constructive imagination," but that prior to it is the "purely sensuous" effect of color which he calls "no better intrinsically than the effects of any other sense" (meaning the lower senses), and that "by a simplification of the organ of sense [the eye]" color may be perceived without form.[40]

To grasp and behold the forms and structure of a landscape, of the human body, or of an animal, a plant, a human face, or of a work of art, of architecture, or of craftsmanship, all this is on the visual level what understanding and penetration by thought are on the level of thinking. The pleasure and exhilaration experienced in all these activities are of the kind that Aristotle con-

39] For details of this development see below, pp. 144-145.
40] Santayana, *The Sense of Beauty,* pp. 76, 90.

sidered a sign of the true and perfect functioning of our powers.[41] To see in a fully allocentric way, that is, to see the essence of the object, is in the Aristotelian sense energeia and praxis. According to Aristotle, those actions which stop with the achievement of a goal are never an end in themselves but only a means to an end. They are not truly "praxis." Praxis is only that activity which is an end in itself. Hence, the contentment in such activity does not cease when a goal is reached, but the activity itself is the goal. The joy and fulfillment of seeing do not stop when one sees.[42]

In actual sight, perceptions of form, color, and light, of course, usually are not so neatly separated as they have been made to appear here in order to clarify some differences between them. Except for such activities as, for example, reading or looking at drawings, geometric figures, diagrams, or drafts, where form alone is perceived, the visible world appears to man as a world of light and dark and form and color. Man abstracts form from this unity. But in looking at his visible environment he may see it primarily as a world of color, as did the impressionists, who were "impressed" by color. But he may also see it primarily as a world of form, as Leonardo, Holbein, and Dürer did. The former view opens itself receptively to the play of light and color, the latter pursues and takes hold of form and structure yet sees the object also as colored. But color perception changes its quality when the perceiver's total attitude changes from full receptiveness towards light and color to active attention to definite objects. Then color assumes the character of surface color[43] and becomes the color of this particular object, subordinated to and confined within its Gestalt.[44]

41] Aristotle *Ethics* 1174 b-1175 a.

42] Aristotle *Metaphysics* 1048 b. Goldstein's concept of self-actualization is akin to Aristotle's. See also Erich Fromm, *Man for Himself* (Rinehart & Co., New York, 1947), pp. 172-197; Thure von Uexküll and Ernesto Grassi, *Wirklichkeit als Geheimnis und Auftrag* (Verlag A. Francke, Bern, 1945), pp. 112-13.

43] Katz's *Oberflächenfarben*, D. Katz, *The World of Colour* (Kegan Paul, Trench and Trubner, London, 1935).

44] This difference in attitude accounts also for the significant symptomatic difference which Rorschach found between the FC responses, on the one hand, in which form is the primary, color the secondary determinant and which represent adaptive emotional responsiveness, and the CF and C responses in which color is the main or predominating determinant and which point to egocentric and labile affectivity. In the typical FC response the Gestalt of the object is clearly seen and it also has the color which it has in reality. Rorschach, *Psychodiagnostics*, pp. 33-34.

The perception of color becomes atypical and objectified in artificial experimental situations in which the subject is asked to name or discriminate between various colors and color nuances shown to him. These conditions create an attitude of concentration in which the perceiver no longer is open to the experience of color but focuses his active attention on his knowledge of color designation or tries to discover barely perceptible differences. These attitudes usually effectively exclude the possibility of experiencing the natural impact of color.

The basic impact of color and light are changed in a different way by an attitude of conscious attention to the color values and to their aesthetic effect. This attitude results in a consciously heightened sensitivity to color in which the perceiver reflectively is attentive to how his sensibilities are affected by the combination and arrangement of various color values, as in painting or in choosing the colors for a room or for clothing. The achievement of a pleasing or effective color arrangement requires a careful, conscious "listening" to the impact the colors have on one. By such "listening," not only the color sense but also other autocentric senses, especially *taste*, can develop to a much higher degree of differentiation in adult man than they have, in spite of their predominant position, in infancy and early childhood. It is no coincidence that a person with a fine sensibility for arrangement of colors in a room is said to have *taste*, and that not only in English, but also in German (*Geschmack*) and in French (*goût*), the same word designates the gustatory sense, the capacity to make or appreciate pleasing visual arrangements, and, more broadly, a sensitivity with regard to what is fitting in general, the opposite of offensive, displeasing, or clumsy. Taste is the capacity to appreciate that which is fitting or pleasing, to discriminate between what goes well together and what goes ill. Perhaps the fact that both the French and the Chinese have an exquisite sense of color and light and dark in their painting, the most highly developed cuisine, and are masters of tact and politeness is no accident. All these capacities may have a common basis in a particularly differentiated taste, in a highly developed attitude of listening carefully and with discrimination to their reactions, be it in the sphere of the gustatory sense, of the sense of color, or the sense of social behavior. Of course, this does not imply that taste is the basis or the essence of art, but it can be a factor in art, and it plays a dominant role in interior decoration, a major purpose of which is to create a pleasant and harmonious atmosphere in terms of color and form, as well as in other ways. Taste is always concerned with making the physical and social environment agreeable and pleasing to people. This connection with pleasure makes for the subject-centered quality of taste and for its affinity to the autocentric component of sensory experience even on a highly conscious level.

The passive experience of something visually impinging, as contrasted with the active focal perception of an object, occurs not only in the perception of color and light but also in the *impingement of the total visual field* (Katz's *Gesamteindringlichkeit*). The total visual field impresses itself on the eye; it seems to come toward one and to lose the qualities of distance and spatial structure if one gazes at it without trying to see any particular object. At the same time, light and color and indistinct multitude become the outstanding qualities seen. The passive eye, especially on a bright day or even more on a day with the intense diffuse light from a slightly overcast sky or from a not too heavy fog, feels assailed as it were by this impinging field. But as soon as one focuses on an object, the rest of the visual field, which just before seemed to come towards the eye, now recedes into the background and periphery; the impinging field is changed into a structured one. This phenomenon, which can be produced by a shift of visual attitude, has been studied experimentally by Katz by means of glasses which prevent the perception of sharp contours or single surfaces and the effect of which cannot be overcome by accommodation of the eye's lens.[45] Something akin to the impingement of the total visual field may be an important part of the visual experience of earliest infancy. It can also occur as a dominant phenomenon in certain pathological conditions, such as in the case of Julie Weber,[46] a young girl of 24, with many phobic reactions, of which the most manifest was that she could not let her glance rest for more than the briefest moment on any single object without feeling overwhelmed by the masses of objects seen, which led to severe anxiety

45] Katz, *The World of Colour*, § 65, especially pp. 280-281.
46] The case of Julie Weber was first described by Hufeland in 1809 and is discussed in detail in a noteworthy article by V. E. von Gebsattel, "Zur Psychopathologie der Phobien (1935), *Prolegomena einer medizinischen Anthropologie* (Springer-Verlag, Berlin, 1954), pp. 47-74; see especially pp. 58-59. For the phenomenon of impingement of the total visual field, compare also Straus, *Vom Sinn der Sinne*, 2nd ed., pp. 216-221.

attacks. She avoided looking at anything, and if her glance accidentally rested for a moment, for example on a piece of fabric of a dress, she would see not only the dress but every single thread in the fabric; that is to say her vision lacked the capacity for active, selective structuring of the visual field. She therefore lived in a darkened room and often sat on the floor with her visual field further narrowed by a hat which she pressed deep down on her forehead so that its brim would cut down the visual horizon.

A full analysis of the allocentric and autocentric modes in the *auditory* sense would require as extended an exposition as for the sense of sight. Since the purpose of this presentation is the demonstration and analysis of the two basic perceptual modes rather than an analysis of all the different senses, a few remarks on the role of the two perceptual modes in hearing must suffice.

The *allocentric* mode of perception in hearing has its most important function in relation to the spoken word. In listening to *speech,* attention is usually focused on understanding the meaning of the communication and this requires the grasp of the words spoken. The words and sentences, that is, the structured units in a sequence of sounds, are the objects of active auditory grasp. Similarly, in listening to *music* the allocentric mode of perception functions mainly in relation to the structure of the music, its architecture, which reveals itself in time rather than in space. But the sounds of nature too can be heard in the allocentric mode.

Listening to speech in an attitude of wanting to understand what is being said and listening to music in an attitude of grasping its structure are comparable to the active, structuring, allocentric visual focusing on objects. Being affected by the timbre of the speaking voice or the sensuous quality of a singing voice, the sweetness of a melody, by the emotionally charged intonation of words spoken in anger or in tenderness, in command or in supplication, in hostility or friendship, is comparable to the more *autocentric* impact of the various colors. These emotionally expressive overtones are "understood" in a much more immediate way; their impact usually is linked with pleasure, displeasure, and other feelings, while the content of the words, as the sight of objects, may be grasped in an atmosphere of emotional neutrality. The infant responds to the friendly or angry, tender or hostile, tense or relaxed tone of the mother's voice with pleasure, anxiety, or discomfort long before he understands words. He is affected in an autocentric way by the tone of the voice, but cannot yet listen, in an allocentric way, to the content of speech. Similarly, a brain-injured adult patient reacted habitually more to the tone of the voice of a person speaking to him than to the content of the remarks made.[47]

Shrillness or dissonance or sudden very loud noises usually are heard in the autocentric mode, assailing the ear unpleasantly. *Noise,* especially the kind that consists of the combined sounds of a busy city street or a machine shop, impinges on the passive ear; but distinct, particular noises, once they have impinged, may then be listened to actively, in the allocentric mode. Steady noise produced by a single or by many different sources, if it is not too loud, leads to an adaptation of the ear. While it is still heard one becomes fully conscious of it only when it suddenly stops. The simultaneous noise from many sources resembles in the auditory sphere the impinging of the total visual field. As in vision, it recedes into the background as soon as the hearer focuses on a particular sound or series of sounds; for instance, when somebody speaks in noisy surroundings, the noise recedes when one listens to the speaker. Here, too, the active, selective auditory attention structures the total auditory field and changes it from something that impinges to a mere background for the spoken words attended to.

As in vision, so also in hearing, especially in hearing speech and music, the allocentric and autocentric modes of perception usually both function at the same time, although one or the other may predominate, according to the situation, the mood, and the personality of the perceiver.

47] Eugenia Hanfmann, Maria Rickers-Ovsiankina, and Kurt Goldstein, *Case Lanuti: Extreme Concretization of Behavior Due to Damage of the Brain Cortex.* Psychological Monographs, 1944, Vol. 57, No. 4, p. 11.

7

The Ontogenetic Development of the Two Basic Perceptual Modes

IN SURVEYING THE EXPERIENTIAL QUALITIES OF DIFFERENT SENSES in relation to the two basic perceptual modes in adult man, it has become apparent that the autocentric mode and the autocentric (lower) senses, because of their lack of objectification, tell the perceiver relatively little about reality and its spatial structure, but that they are closely linked to pleasure and displeasure feelings, many of which are physically localized on or in man's body. The allocentric (higher) senses, on the other hand, when functioning in the allocentric mode do not have this close link with pleasure and displeasure, but transmit to man all essential information about reality which he needs in order to orient himself in it. This comprises what man learns by *hearing* the words of others and *seeing* what they have written, including many things which he cannot grasp directly by looking at his environment and manipulating the objects in it. Even in the blind and deaf, as in the famous case of Helen Keller, only the high development of allocentric touch makes possible their sharing of the common world of man by enabling them to perceive the tactile communications of others.

The profound differences between, and peculiar qualities of, the two basic modes of perceptual experience suggest their relation to Freud's concepts of the pleasure and the reality principle. The autocentric mode, at first glance, seems to represent in the perceptual sphere a functioning of the senses more in accordance with the pleasure principle, while the allocentric mode seems to function more according to the reality principle. Freud assumes that in the earliest phase of development, the pleasure principle and its primary processes are the only kind of mental processes, and that at a later point the reality principle with its secondary processes is superimposed on the pleasure principle.[1]

Closer examination shows that Freud's concepts of the early development of sensory perception correspond only partially to the observable facts. They are correct in that full perception of reality is a relatively late achievement and that in the earliest developmental phase pleasure and unpleasure feelings are the most important if not the only phenomenon in the neonate's sensory contact with the world. They are wrong in that the early development does not proceed from the absence of sensory perception to its full development, but from the predominance of autocentric to that of allocentric sensory perception. This implies modification of Freud's view in four major points:

(1) While Freud thought that at first no sensory quality is perceived but that only pleasure or unpleasure are felt in the interior of the psychic apparatus, actually the exteroceptors function from the first day of life (and most of them already *in utero*) and convey sensory quality as well as give rise to comfort and discomfort feelings.

(2) From birth on the newborn does not wish merely to abolish external sensory stimuli, but also turns towards them and wants to prolong contact with them.

(3) Pleasure, even in the neonate, consists not only in the absence or decrease of excitation or in the return to an excitationless state, but also in sensory excitation itself.

(4) Hence pleasure and reality are not intrinsically or inevitably opposed to each other and the perception of reality does not serve merely as a necessary but unwelcome detour on the way to its abolishment in an excitationless state.

1] Freud, "Formulations Regarding the Two Principles of Mental Functioning," *Collected Papers* (Basic Books, New York, 1959), Vol. IV, pp. 13-21.

In Freud's view, perception is entirely linked up with the reality principle, which alone brings about the comprehension of "the qualities of sense," whereas in the earliest phase of development only pleasure and pain are felt consciously and, thus, are contrasted by Freud with sensory quality.[2] This implies that Freud, if he thought about it explicitly, must have assumed either that the exteroceptors in particular do not function at all in the earliest stage of infancy or else, more likely, that they do not transmit any quality of sense but arouse only pleasure or unpleasure.[3] Since pleasure, in Freud's view, arises from a discharge or decrease of excitation, and unpleasure from an increase of excitation, this would lead to the conclusion that in the earliest phase every excitation of the sensory apparatus from the external world, just as every increase in excitation from the interior of the organism by rising need tension, if consciously felt, would be felt as unpleasure. It would lead to the view that perception at first causes unpleasure and that the organism, under the pleasure principle, would try to avoid it. Pleasure, on the other hand, would be felt when excitation ended or decreased, when no stimulus excited the sensory apparatus. Several statements by Freud indicate that this indeed seems to have been his view. Thus, he writes that "the nervous system is an apparatus having the function of abolishing stimuli which reach it, or of reducing excitation to the lowest possible level: an apparatus which would even, if this were feasible, maintain itself in an altogether unstimulated condition," and that "external stimuli impose upon the organism the single task of withdrawing itself from their action."[4] The negative formulation of Freud's concept of pleasure as being relief from excitation or tension places the emphasis on the *avoidance* of the unpleasure of stimulation, excitation, or tension, and Freud originally did speak

2] *Ibid.*, p. 15.

3] The latter is also Rapaport's understanding of Freud's view. David Rapaport, *Organization and Pathology of Thought* (Columbia University Press, New York, 1951), p. 321, footnote 20.

4] Freud, "Instincts and their Vicissitudes," *Collected Papers*, Vol. IV, p. 63. In an earlier formulation of this thought he had written that at first the psychic "apparatus strove to keep itself as free from stimulation as possible, and therefore, in its early structure, adopted the arrangement of a reflex apparatus, which enabled it promptly to discharge by the motor paths any sensory excitation reaching it from without." Freud, "The Interpretation of Dreams," *Basic Writings* (Random House, New York, 1938), pp. 508-509.

of the pain (or unpleasure) principle rather than the pleasure principle.[5]

Both the concept of pleasure as relief from excitation and the tendency of the organism to avoid or withdraw from external and internal stimuli are consistent with, and seem to account for, very impressive phenomena in the behavior of the newborn infant during the first weeks of its life. These phenomena are (1) that the newborn spends the greatest part of his time in sleep; (2) that the brief periods of awakeness seem to be caused largely by the unpleasant sensation of hunger or some other discomfort; (3) that during the greater part of the brief periods of wakefulness, behavior and facial expression show restlessness and unpleasure; and (4) that the most blissful expression usually seems to appear when, after nursing, the infant returns to sleep again.

However, these observations do not tell the whole story. I believe that we have to assume that another tendency is already present from the first day of extrauterine life, that this tendency rapidly increases throughout the first years, and that eventually it is more important for the characteristically human qualities of man than Freud's pleasure principle is. This tendency can be seen in the fact that even in the earliest stage of development the infant does not only try to *avoid* stimulation, but also *seeks* it and *turns toward* it; that is, sensory excitation can be pleasurable as well as unpleasurable, and pleasure can consist in excitation itself as well as in the decrease of excitation.

This is apparent from the systematic observations which Stirnimann made with a group of fifty to one hundred newborn infants.[6] He found that besides the prevailing uncoordinated mass activity which involves the whole body of the infant, newborns show an impressive number of specific movements and that among these are both movements of *turning toward* an external sensory stimulus or trying to keep in contact with it, and movements of *turning away* from such a stimulus or attempts to get rid of it. These spe-

---

5] Freud, "The Interpretation of Dreams," *Basic Writings*, p. 534.
6] F. Stirnimann, *Psychologie des neugeborenen Kindes* (Rascher Verlag, Zürich and Leipzig, 1940). Compare also Karl C. Pratt, "The Neonate," in Leonard Carmichael, ed., *Manual of Child Psychology* (John Wiley & Sons, New York, 1949), pp. 190-254, especially pp. 203-226, with a survey of the literature on the neonate's sensory reactions. Pratt, too, points out that the neonate "responds to some sensory stimuli by movements which prolong stimulation, to others by withdrawal or rejection" (p. 241).

cific motor reactions to stimulation of the exteroceptors occur in the majority of the observed infants during the first ten or fourteen days and in quite a few *even on the first day* of extrauterine life. Among these reactions are:

(1) Reactions to *thermal* stimulations: Turning the head toward the side where a test tube filled with warm water (45° C.) was held near but not touching the cheek (39% of the infants); one infant lifted its hand and pressed the tube against its cheek; one infant, when the tube was held near its hand, grasped it and put it against its cheek; turning or moving the head away from a tube filled with moderately cold water (15-17° C.; 63% of the infants), pushing the tube away (16%); pressing the sole of the foot against the warm tube held near the foot (42%), grasping the tube with the toes (26%); withdrawing the foot from the tube with cold water (67%).

(2) Reactions to *tactile* stimulations: When touched with the finger on the lip or on the corner of the mouth, many infants respond on the first or second day with movements of the head or opening of the mouth so that the tip of the finger will glide into the opened mouth. This, of course, is the same specific motor reaction as to the nipple of the breast. When stroked with the finger on the cheek 32% of the newborns, *before* their first nursing experience on the first day, turned their heads toward the side from which they had been touched. When touched with the finger on the palm of the hand, 88% responded with the grasp reflex, grasping the finger, while a little wooden stick of 3 mm. diameter was grasped only by 18%, a cylinder of the same diameter as the finger only by 6%. About 50% of the infants flexed their fingers when touched with the little stick or the cylinder, but then let it go again, whereas they kept hold of the finger, thus showing a fine tactile discrimination, which was not present in 3 prematurely born infants. When touched on the sole of the foot most of the infants reacted by withdrawing the leg, some by pushing, that is by movements indicating the attempt to abolish the stimulus by withdrawal or by pushing it away. When a little stick of 3 mm. diameter and 3 cm. long was placed between the first and second toes, there was in most newborns at first a grasp reflex of the toes, but this was followed soon by attempts to get rid of the stick. On the first day of life 5 infants out of 50 succeeded in pushing it out with the other foot from between their toes on

both feet, 13 on one foot only, while toward the end of the neonate period 21 were able to push it out on both feet (on the 10th to 14th day). The movements made the impression of being goal-directed, in contrast to the flailing movements in mass activity. Stirnimann reports that distraction can interrupt them: 2 infants less than one day old looked at him for a while and resumed their leg movements only after he left their field of vision.

(3) Reactions to *gustatory* stimulation: Using distilled water in four solutions—one of 7% lactose, another of 0.5% citric acid, a third of 2% salt, and a fourth of 0.01% quinine sulfate—he found clear evidence of discrimination between sweet, sour, salty, and bitter, although to the adult tongue these solutions provide only weak, just barely perceptible sensations of the four basic taste qualities.[7] Again, he found both movements of attraction (sucking and swallowing) and of expelling, the latter being more frequent.

(4) *Auditory* reactions: On the first day quite a few infants turned their heads towards the source of a sound and opened their eyes. The sound of a bell had a calming effect on more than half of 50 crying infants, who stopped crying when they heard the sound.

(5). *Visual* reactions: One 16-hour-old newborn followed several people with his eyes; a 4-hour-old newborn gazed in the direction of several people, letting his eyes wander from one to another, but among them gazed for half a minute at a woman wearing a colored dress (all the other people were dressed in white). When they changed position, his eyes started to move until they came to rest again on the woman in the colored dress. The same observation was repeated with another newborn. Many newborns turn toward the direction of a mild source of light, such as the window on a clear day. But when the light becomes glaring they turn away. Stirnimann also found a tendency to differentiated reactions to different colors.

These observations show that in several of the exteroceptive senses, in some infants from the first day of life on and in an increasing number of newborns during the first two weeks of life, (1) certain sensory stimuli *attract* the infants and are experienced as pleasurable, while others *repel* them and are experienced

7] For a discussion of the literature, part of which assumes that there is no discrimination but only pleasure and unpleasure reactions to taste in the newborn, see Stirnimann, *Psychologie des neugeborenen Kindes.*

as unpleasurable; (2) *discrimination* occurs in relation to different *sensory qualities* (of taste, hearing, temperature, touch, sight), and the differentiated reactions are *coupled* with feelings of *pleasure* and *unpleasure;* (3) in some of the reactions, especially to touch, temperature, taste, sight, and sound, *directional* factors are involved which indicate that there is some experience of *whence* the stimulation comes, a localization, however vague, of something impinging which (4) in some instances evokes the first signs of a vague, directional *attention.*

Thus, in the brief periods of awakeness the newborn does not, it is true, initiate any sensory exploration. He reacts only to what sensory stimuli impinge on him. But once they impinge on him, he does not uniformly try to abolish them, as Freud assumed, but he selectively *turns toward* some of them while he turns away from others. This is the first, dim movement away from complete autocentricity, in which every stimulus is felt as an unpleasant disturbance of total embeddedness, in the direction of more allocentric sensory experience, in which the encounter with certain sensory stimuli is desired rather than avoided. This behavior is known to every mother, especially to a nursing mother. The movements toward gentle warmth, toward the finger stroking the cheek, toward the nipple or the tip of the finger touching the mouth, the taste of lactose solutions—all are reactions of vital importance which ensure successful nursing. Although Freud recognized the great importance of pleasure and unpleasure, which had been neglected by the psychology of his time, he did not pay attention to the concrete phenomena of sensory pleasure and unpleasure in the human senses. Probably his concept of pleasure prevented him from doing so, for this concept is inseparable from the observation of relief in discharge of drive tension. He at first construed sexual pleasure, to which he paid more attention than to any other, as being entirely relief from need tension, and only later modified this by recognizing that the increased tension preceding orgasm is also pleasurable.[8] But, just as he considered this as mere "forepleasure," so he may have felt that the taking of nourishment by adults and infants serves only the stilling of hunger, i.e. the relief from the tension of hunger. But in eating and drinking, it is not primarily the stilling of hunger which is pleas-

8] Compare the detailed discussion of pleasure and of Freud's concept of pleasure in "On Affect, Anxiety, and the Pleasure Principle," this volume, pp. 55-68.

urable, but eating itself, the taste, the chewing, salivating, and swallowing. While infants experience hunger as unpleasurable, they also experience the tactile, proprioceptive, thermal, taste, and, probably, olfactory sensations in nursing as pleasurable and not only the ceasing of hunger. The pleasure in these sensations, viewed teleologically, serves the purpose of assuring proper nourishment of the infant and proper functioning and learning of the complex pattern of motor activities necessary for successful nursing. But the biological goal is something very different from the subjective experience. What is most pleasurable and satisfying in taking food, both for the newborn infant and for adult man, are the sensations, gustatory, tactile, and proprioceptive, in sucking or eating and swallowing, and not the arrival and digestion of the food in the stomach, which is what stops the appetite and achieves the biological goal of taking nourishment. As Lorenz once put it succinctly: "My aim in having lunch is the pleasure I derive from eating and definitely not the biological consequence of my eating activity—which is only to make me still fatter."[9] In adults who do not starve or suffer from insufficient diets, the tension of appetite with its anticipation of a meal is actually often felt as pleasurable, just as is the meal itself. But the fact that in infants, in contrast to adults, the tension of appetite seems to be felt as unpleasure and causes restlessness and crying does not mean that in nursing or, later, in eating the infant experiences only the negative pleasure of relief from tension. The whole nursing behavior, when undisturbed, shows all the signs of eager attraction and pleasure in being held, turning toward the warmth of the mother's breast, touching and sucking and tasting and swallowing. The pleasure in the tactile and proprioceptive sensations of sucking also is apparent in the pleasure infants and children show in thumb-sucking. The fact that certain sensory stimuli are attractive and pleasurable for the newborn infant is the complement, in the perceptual sphere, to what I have called activity-affect in the emotional sphere.[10] The pleasurable sensory stimulus causes the infant to turn toward

9] Konrad Lorenz, "Behavior Patterns in Allied Species," in *Group Processes, Transactions of the First Conference, 1954* (Josiah Macy, Jr., Foundation, New York, 1955), pp. 188, 195. Compare also Lorenz, "The Nature of Instinct," in Claire H. Schiller, ed., *Instinctive Behavior* (International Universities Press, New York, 1957), pp. 129-175, 144.

10] "On Affect, Anxiety, and the Pleasure Principle," this volume, especially, pp. 22-33, 72-77.

it. It is not unlikely that, similarly, some of the repellent, unpleasant sensory stimuli also arouse an activity-affect, but in the direction of flight, turning away from, or trying to abolish the stimulus. Such directional turning away from a sensory stimulus is different and has to be distinguished from the mass activity of restlessness and crying which goes together with what I call embeddedness-affect[11] and is the phenomenon described by Freud in which unpleasant increase of excitation causes mere *discharge* of tension in uncoordinated motor activity and affect.

Observations of nursing infants as well as Stirnimann's observations show that infants react to sensory stimulation not only with feelings of pleasure or unpleasure, but that *specific sensory qualities are felt together with pleasure and unpleasure.* In this respect, their experience probably is similar to the adult's perceptual experience with the autocentric senses of taste, smell, thermal, proprioceptive, and passive tactile senses, which also show a combination of pleasure-unpleasure with sensory quality. It differs from the adult's experience in that it is more global; for instance, in the nursing situation there is not only a fusion of sensory quality from nipple, breast, and milk with pleasure (or unpleasure) feelings and proprioceptive sensations in the mouth, but also with the total postural and being-held experience. The newborn experiences not only the unpleasure of stimuli which change and disturb the quiescence of comfort (homeostasis) but also, and increasingly, specific pleasures and unpleasures caused by excitation of the autocentrically functioning senses (that is, in the earliest stage of development, of all senses) by welcome, attractive stimuli or by repellent stimuli. It is likely that in the growing infant and the young child such pleasurable as well as unpleasurable sensory stimulation is perceived more intensely and totally than in the adult. Thus, the exteroceptors as well as the interoceptors function from the moment of birth on, at least to some extent, as conveyors of sensory quality.

The fact that sensory quality is not perceived as being quality of an object does not imply that sensory quality is not felt at all. It is felt in different ways by the neonate and young infant and by the adult. But some of the adult's purely autocentric sensory experiences probably present a fairly good analogue to the object-

11] For the concepts of embeddedness and of embeddedness-affect see this volume, pp. 22-33, 72-77.

less combination of pleasure-unpleasure and sensory quality that the infant may feel, for instance the pleasure of sweet taste, of a warm bath, of mild light. If the adult does not make use of his capacity to distinguish between, for example, the pleasurable feeling of comfortable warmth or the savoring of a particular taste, and perceiving that this is the warmth of air or water and the taste of a fruit, but instead gives himself over to the pure sensation itself, then he experiences a fusion of pleasure and sensory quality which probably approximates the infantile experience, except for the conscious attention which the attitude of savoring implies. But this attitude, too, need not be a part of adult autocentric sensory experience. What these examples have in common is that the emphasis of the sensory experience is not on any object but entirely or almost entirely on feeling or sensation. This exclusive emphasis on the felt sensation of the organism precedes any subject-object and within-without differentiation. In it is rooted also the phenomenon of primitive synaesthesia in which sensory stimulation of one sense organ leads to sensations in more than one sense modality, so that a particular tone may be experienced not only as that tone but also as a particular color, temperature, etc.[12] It is likely that in the neonates, all of whose perceptions are in the autocentric mode, these sensations are more pervasive than in most adults, and it is possible that synaesthesia plays an even greater role in the newborn than it does in children, in whom it is generally more frequent than in adults. But even assuming the greater prevalence of synaesthesia in infancy, this does not imply that the newborn's sensory experiences consist of pleasure and unpleasure only and are altogether devoid of sensory quality. All of Werner's examples of synaesthetic perception are examples in which specific sensory quality is experienced in an intersensory mode and in most of which pleasure or unpleasure is not even mentioned. The common distinctions between warm and cool colors, high and low tones, etc. have their origin in intersensory perception (thermal and visual, spatial-visual-proprioceptive and auditory), but they convey definite sensory qualities. We have every reason to assume that from the beginning of extrauterine

12] Compare the detailed discussion of synaesthesia as an early mode of sensory experience pointing to the primitive unity of the senses in Heinz Werner, *Comparative Psychology of Mental Development* (Follett Publishing Co., Chicago, 1948), pp. 86-103.

life during awakeness sensory quality is experienced in combination with pleasure and unpleasure. If it is felt more pervasively, then this means, as Werner has pointed out, not that there is an absence of discrimination of sensory quality, but that different types of discrimination are involved at different levels of development, namely a sensory-motor-affective type on the earliest, more primitive level, and perceptual (or, as I would prefer to say, discrimination in the allocentric perceptual mode) and conceptual discrimination in later stages of development.[13]

Of great importance in this development is not only the distinct perception both of feelings and sensations *within* one and of qualities of the *external* environment, but also the capacity to differentiate clearly between these two. Freud has emphasized rightly that the distinction between within and without is acquired only gradually, and he assumes that the basis for this development lies in the fact that external perceptions can be made to disappear by motor activity while perceptions originating within one's body cannot.[14] According to him, during the earliest stage of development the infant experiences only sensations originating within its body, namely pleasure and pain, because in Freud's view these are at first the only ones attended by consciousness and they "emerge as the sole psychic qualities yielded by the transpositions of energy in the interior of the [psychic] apparatus."[15] This assumption is in line with his view that the qualities of sense mediated by the exteroceptors are perceived first at a later stage, at which the reality principle supervenes. But analysis of the sensory experience of the newborn and of early infancy makes it more probable that the development of the distinction between interior sensations or feelings and perception of external reality proceeds in a somewhat different way than Freud assumed. The newborn's perceptions probably are *fusions* of internal feelings (pleasure and unpleasure) and sensory aspects of the impinging external environment. This is also Werner's view, who, following Stern, describes the mental state of the newborn "as a mere state of feeling, a total sensation,

13] *Ibid.,* p. 101.
14] Freud, "Metapsychological Supplement to the Theory of Dreams," *Collected Papers,* Vol. IV, p. 148.
15] Freud, "Formulations Regarding the Two Principles in Mental Functioning," *Collected Papers,* Vol. IV, p. 15, and "The Interpretation of Dreams," *Basic Writings,* p. 515.

in which object and subject are merged.[16] Similarly, Piaget says that "at a certain level life organization and mental organization only constitute, in effect, one and the same thing."[17]

It would be just as wrong to describe the newborn's sensations as coming entirely from the interior of the body as it would be to say that external objects are perceived by the infant.[18] As the experiential and conceptual distinction between the internal and external gradually develops, the *fused perceptions* become increasingly differentiated into perceptions of feelings and states of being (comfort and discomfort, pleasure and unpleasure) and of something that comes from and exists without and that eventually is perceived as object, as part of the environment. Because the conceptual distinction between subject and object, internal and external, is so fundamental to adult thought, it usually permeates the entire consciousness of our perceptual experience. This is probably the reason why little attention has been paid to certain sensory experiences of adults in which perceptual fusion of the internal and external continues throughout life. I am referring not only to the already discussed fusion of pleasure-unpleasure feelings with sensory quality in the autocentric senses, but more specifically to sensory experiences in which the fusion between external world and state of one's own body are fused in one sensation and separated only by thought. This is particularly striking in the combination of tactile and proprioceptive qualities in perceptions of pressure and resistance, a phenomenon that is most distinct when, for example, the eyes are closed and the arm is pressed against the edge of a table or the arm rest of a chair. The contact of the buttocks with the chair on which one sits furnishes a similar

16] Werner, *Comparative Psychology of Mental Development*, p. 65.

17] Jean Piaget, *The Origins of Intelligence in Children* (International Universities Press, New York, 1952), p. 46.

18] Spitz, in an interesting paper, assumes that the inside of the mouth, which partakes of the perceptual qualities of the inside and the outside at the same time, fulfills the function of a bridge from internal to external perception. Because the mouth region is at birth the most highly developed sensory-motor region, the mouth plays a dominant role in the early development of perception. However, Spitz, like Freud, wrongly assumes that the newborn perceives only sensations originating *within* his body. But the distinction of within-without does not apply to the newborn, and Stirnimann's observations show that auditory, visual, tactile, thermal stimuli from the environment certainly affect the sensorium of the newborn. René A. Spitz, "The Primal Cavity," *The Psychoanalytic Study of the Child*, 1955, 10:215-240, 219-220.

example, especially if one does not touch at the same time the back of the chair or if one sits on a stool. Under these conditions it may happen that no object is perceived and the tactile and pressure sensations completely fuse with the sensation of the resisting "something" against which the arm presses or on which the weight of the body rests. When the pressure of the arm against the edge of the table is increased sufficiently, a slight feeling of pain fuses with these other sensations.

The sensory perceptions just described are in the autocentric mode: the proprioception of the muscular activity, the autocentric tactile and deep pressure sensations involved do not lead to any objectification unless one consciously starts to think about the object against which one presses. Without such thought the resisting environment (the edge of the table, the seat of the stool) and the pressing arm or buttocks are felt in a single percept in which there is a fusion of external and internal. If one compares this with the previously described observations by Stirnimann of the neonate's behavior in relation to the little stick placed between the first and second toes, it seems likely that there a similar perceptual fusion between interior and external may take place, since the directedness of the motor activity by which the infants try to get rid of the something pressing against their toes indicates that the tactile and pressure and discomfort sensations probably are fused with a feeling of something *impinging, resisting* the natural, free position of the toe. The same assumption seems justified for the many other tactile and pressure sensations in which the infant's body rests on something or his limbs press or are pressed against something. It is interesting that in the adult this fusion effect is not present as soon as, for example, one grasps the table top with the hand, placing the thumb on the underside and the other four fingers on the surface of the top of the table. This leads to allocentric perception in which the object grasped and the grasping hand, the resisting table and the fingers pressing against it, are clearly separated. Similarly, although not quite as fully and distinctly, if one sits on a chair and leans against the back of the chair, the contact with more than one area of the object by more than one surface of the skin leads in the adult to objectification of the chair because spatial structure is perceived. The limited contact of only part of the arm with part of the table edge or of only the buttocks with the seat of the chair does not permit the perception of spatial structure to the same extent.

The concept of *fused perception* (of within and without) is closely related to Werner's concept of *vital sensations* of which he says that they "are devoid of . . . objectivity . . . ; they are psychophysically undifferentiated and involve pervasive bodily reactions to stimuli."[19] The concept of fused perception emphasizes the fusion of within and without, and of pleasure-displeasure with sensory quality, while the concept of vital sensations emphasizes the synaesthetic phenomena and the motoric reactions as well.

Freud's sharp distinction, in time of development, quality of experience, and in function, between the pleasure and the reality principle, and the nature of his pleasure concept led him to a view in which pleasure and reality are seen too much as alternatives. The pleasure principle has as its goal undisturbed quiescence, culminating in death. According to the reality principle, reality is viewed as interfering with or delaying attainment of this goal and necessitating difficult detours on the road to it; the pleasure principle is seen as being concerned only with processes *within* the body, namely rising and falling tension, the reality principle foists upon this monadic existence the need to get in touch with the outer world. The former leads only to feelings of unpleasure with rising excitation and to motor-affective discharge and feelings of pleasure with falling excitation, the latter to perception of sensory qualities and to directed motor activity. Freud's concept of the infant as experiencing *only sensations within* himself is derived from the adult perspective which distinguishes within and without, from the Cartesian dichotomy of subject and object. There is no within, unless there is a without, too. Actually, the prevailing mode of experience of the neonate *precedes* this distinction and in it within and without, pleasure-unpleasure, and sensory quality are fused and only gradually become more differentiated. But there are already in this dim fusion the *Anlage* and the first traces of turning to the without and perceiving the sensory qualities emanating from it. Indeed, the pleasurable sensory qualities which lead the newborn to turn its head to the warm breast of the mother, to suck and swallow, function as guides directing the drive for nourishment to the source of satisfaction in the external world. Freud retains the veridical bias of the perceptual theory of his

19] Werner, *Comparative Psychology of Mental Development*, p. 96.

time and separates pleasure from perception of sensory quality. He overlooks the fact that the newborn's sensory organization is actually adapted to the great change from total embeddedness in the mother's womb to the state after birth in which the infant, now separated from the mother though still embedded in her care, from the first day of his life has to turn toward her. Such *turning toward* marks a decisive step both in phylogenetic and onto-genetic sensory-motor development. It becomes necessary because of the separation of the organism from the sources of his energy supply. It is scarcely found in those lowest forms of animal life which could be described as passive feeders. They either sift in their alimentary organs the environing water or soil or, if they are parasites, feed on the environing host. Thus they do not have to turn toward or seek their food; on the other hand, they perish when their immediate environment does not happen to be nutritious and otherwise favorable. But the infant, even though he is given the breast, also has to turn toward it when it is given, and thus starts what is at this stage the most vital part of his sensory-motor life with the directional groping and learning to find and keep hold of the nipple, to suck and swallow, all of which depends on the sensory cues furnished by thermal, tactile, proprioceptive, taste, olfactory, to some extent perhaps auditory and later increasingly also by visual receptors. They are the guides to the newborn's world, the world of the mother's care. But even at birth they already transcend that world and function in relation to aspects of the total immediate environment, for example when the infant turns toward light and sound, shows the first signs of attention, gets rid of disturbing contacts and pressures, as in removing a little stick from between his toes or in working his way out of confining mittens or blankets.[20]

While Freud felt that in the earliest stage of development the organism has only one task—to rid itself from any stimulation—others have acknowledged that there is not only stimulus avoidance but also "stimulus hunger." But Fenichel, who introduced this concept, nevertheless maintains that "the first acceptance of reality is only an intermediary step on the road to getting rid of it" and he believes that the phenomenon of longing for objects is a "complication" introduced by "the fact that external objects brought about the desired state of relaxed satisfaction"; hence

20] See Stirnimann, *Psychologie des neugeborenen Kindes*, pp. 30, 52, 60, 89, 103.

"they were sought only as instruments which made themselves disappear again. The longing for objects thus began as a detour on the way to the goal of being rid of objects (of stimuli)."[21] Two points are of interest in Fenichel's statement: (1) He speaks of longing only and not of perceiving and turning toward sensory stimuli that attract the infant. This is consistent with Freud's emphasis on the drive tension and the wish, as expressed in crying and helplessness, but the exclusive emphasis on the wish tension leads to the overlooking or neglect of concrete observations of the newborn's turning to attractive sensory stimuli. (2) He believes this longing for the "object" to be dependent on a preceding experience in which the object brought about a state of relaxed satisfaction. Actually, newborns often turn toward attractive stimuli even *before* their first nursing experience.[22] Thus we have to assume not only that the infant is born with the capacity to perceive a variety of sensory qualities, in the autocentric mode, to be sure, but also that some of these are felt as pleasurable and attractive before there has been any experience of satiation. It seems to me very questionable whether the fact that many of these innate perceptual capacities and motor patterns obviously, from a functional-teleological viewpoint, serve the newborn's capacity to nurse justifies the statement that the newborn who wants and enjoys their exercise really does so only in order to get rid of the stimulation leading to such exercise. The fact that the newborn sleeps most of the time cannot be used to explain his waking behavior as a desire to return to sleep. It is at least equally possible and, in view of the whole direction of the infant's development, I believe more justified to argue that in the waking behavior of the newborn we see at work an organization of strivings and capacities designed to play an increasingly important role in the infant's turning *toward* rather than *away* from the world, and that this organization exists together with the still predominating one of intrauterine life where every external stimulus was reacted to as a disturbance of complete embeddedness.[23] This is even more

21] Otto Fenichel, *The Psychoanalytic Theory of Neurosis* (Norton, New York, 1945), p. 35.

22] Stirnimann, *Psychologie des neugeborenen Kindes*, pp. 22, 25. He reports furthermore that *all* his observations regarding the skin-receptors, including the turning toward warmth, were made on the *first* day of life (p. 20).

23] Compare also "The Development of Focal Attention and the Emergence of Reality," this volume pp. 251-278.

likely because not all the stimuli which attract the newborn are related to nursing. Turning toward the sound of a toy bell on the first day of life, toward color four hours after birth, following moving people with the eye sixteen hours after birth, turning toward light—all this does not have any intrinsic connection with nursing.[24] In fact, all those pleasurable stimuli which transcend the maternal sphere and do not have a direct relation to nursing but are the precursors of autonomous interest in the environment have their greatest valence for the infant when he is *not* in a state of need tension.

The fused perceptions and vital sensations in which pleasure-unpleasure feelings are merged with sensory qualities of the external objects play an important role in the gradual emergence of the object world. A significant factor in this role is the pleasurable feeling aroused in the encounter with the objects of the environment which, together with the drive toward motor activity and the exploratory drive, attracts the infant and young child to ever repeated, increasing, and varied contacts with the environment. This can be observed at first particularly in the tactile, pressure, and proprioceptive senses and is a phenomenon very different from motor discharge in mass activity. As an impinging, passive experience it occurs first in the feeling of being comfortably supported, whether in the crib or, of greater significance for the development of the infant's relations to others, in being held. As an active experience it occurs first in the muscular activity of the mouth in taking hold of the nipple and sucking and in the grasp reflex of the hand which, from birth on, is not merely a reflex but is combined with sensory discrimination.[25] But while the hand of the newborn is already capable of the fused perception of sensory quality, pleasure, and unpleasure in contact with an object, and while tactile and proprioceptive sensations are combined in these experiences, developmentally the greater *emphasis* is on oral experience, which thus precedes manual contact in importance.

In the active contacts of mouth and hand with environmental

24] Stirnimann, *Psychologie des neugeborenen Kindes,* pp. 52, 59, 60. The positive reactions to sound were observed in the majority of the one-day olds. The directed gaze usually develops later. However, the fact that in some infants it occurs so early is significant because it shows that it is an innate Anlage which occasionally can mature even before the rise and fall of the need tensions of extrauterine life are incorporated in the newborn's experience.
25] See above p. 120.

objects which are not yet perceived as objects, the pleasurable tactile and proprioceptive sensations themselves are *rewarding* and thus lead the infant to repeat and vary them in relation to anything that is handy or "mouthy." These pleasurable rewards of activity itself infant and adult have in common with many of the higher animals.[26] But while in the animal the reward is tied to a fixed, instinctive motor pattern that never varies, the infant finds an ever increasing variety of movements which lead to, or consist of, such rewarding contacts with the environment. In the infant many different movements, many different kinds and degrees of pressure against and resistance by or yielding of environmental objects are experienced as rewarding, while others are felt as more or less unpleasant.

It would be quite misleading to characterize the nature of this sensory pleasure as libidinous in the sense of sexual libido, as sadistic, or as discharge of aggression. There is nothing sadistic in learning to bite by feeling pleasure in the muscular-tactile experience of chewing on something. There is nothing primarily sexual in the pleasure of the infant's grasping, with mouth or hands, of the mother's breast or in the pleasurable contacts with teddy bear, soft blanket, shaggy dog. There is nothing inherently aggressive in banging the rattle against a blanket or the side of a crib or the spoon against the table, or in tearing paper. All these and many other vital sensations or fused perceptions which occur in the course of motor activity leading to the infant's pleasurable contact with environmental objects are essential steps in the infant's self-actualization;[27] they furnish an important link in the infant's motivation for the continued exercise of its muscles and senses, its motor coordination, and its exploration of the environment as well as of its own body and physical capacities. The exercise of these increasingly varied activities, outside of the nursing situation, is the first step toward play, at first an objectless play; but out of this objectless play the object eventually emerges as that with which the infant and child play and which it explores in this play. All these varied, pleasurable activity contacts with environmental objects show that the pleasure principle is not always and not

26] Compare Lorenz's and others' discussion of the "tremble-shove" in the nest-building activity of many birds, in *Group Processes, Transactions of the First Conference, 1954*, pp. 185-198.

27] K. Goldstein, *The Organism* (American Book Co., New York, 1939), pp. 197-198.

necessarily the antagonist of the reality principle provided that one is not blind to the fact that there is pleasure other than that felt in relief from tension and excitation, that pleasure can and does arise from contact with reality, from sensory stimulation, and also that this pleasure is not merely a step towards getting rid of the pleasurably exciting stimulus but on the contrary can be and, in the course of a healthy development, increasingly is a step toward maintaining contact with it in play, in interest, and eventually in love. In contrast to Freud's relief-pleasure resulting from the attempt to get rid of the stimulus, the feeling of pleasure in sensory contact with environmental objects is in animal and man a tie to reality. It reinforces the eagerness to overcome the gap that—in contrast to the embeddedness of the plants—opens between the separate, mobile organisms and their sources of energy supply in the environment;[28] and it plays a stimulating role in the growing infant's and man's realization of his potentialities and in his total relatedness to the world.

The fact that the pleasurable vital sensations (fused perceptions) of the infant are not inherently libidinal (sexual) or aggressive does not mean, of course, that they do not at a later point in development enter into experiences of sexual pleasure, nor does it imply that the banging, biting, etc. of the infant cannot and does not at times also serve as a way of discharging anger and aggression. But the view of the activities of the infant and young child as intrinsically aggressive, sadistic, or destructive often is an adultomorph misinterpretation. Frequently, the adult's own aggressive-destructive tendencies lead him to feel that an activity which in him would have an angry or destructive motivation must have the same motivation in the child. Or the adult, often for good reasons, is concerned that the child may damage itself or may damage objects of value to the adult, or create a general mess or disorder. But while the child's activity may, from the adult's point of view, have destructive *effects*, this is not sufficient reason to assume that it arises from destructive *motivation* or from an aggressive drive.[29]

Another source of misunderstanding arises from a semantic con-

28] See this volume, pp. 69-70.

29] This, however, seems to have been Freud's assumption, who reduced all human energies to libidinal (Eros) and destructive (Thanatos, death-instinct) ones, the latter being discharged through the musculature. Freud, "Abriss der Psychoanalyse," *Gesammelte Werke* (Imago Publishing Co., London, 1941), Vol. XVII, pp. 71-72.

fusion which, probably, often is related to the points just discussed. The word "aggression" stems from the Latin *aggredi*, which originally meant "to go towards," "to approach." Even in present-day usage the word "aggressive" still has both connotations, the more prevalent one of hostile attack, but also that of an energetic approach. Similarly, one speaks of "attacking" a problem or a task. The described sensorimotor activities of the infant are approaches to, not attacks on, reality, the objects. This does not mean, of course, that they cannot also, at times, have hostile or angry implications. Only concrete observation and analysis can tell, in each case, whether the infant is engaged in pleasurable exploratory play or in discharge of anger.

The adultomorph misinterpretations of the infant's behavior and egocentrically affect-charged adult reactions to it can have a profound and sometimes all but irreversible effect on the infant's development. They can effectively stifle or inhibit the infant's exploratory drive and turn the pleasure in his expanding and varied contacts with reality into anxiety. They play an important, perhaps decisive role in the development of the feeling of disgust, and even more important, they reinforce and very much increase separation anxiety. The prohibitive gestures and behavior of the adult arouse the fear of loss of love and support in the infant if he follows his natural impulse of attraction to reality, his impulse for playful exploration. They also often change the lure of the pleasurable stimuli into the fear of a dangerous world, especially when the motivation of the parent is based on his or her own fear of the world or on egocentric worry about the infant rather than on encouraging love for the infant and its development.

The normal steps of the development from fused autocentric perceptions to play with a variety of objects can be described schematically. At first the autocentric sensations are caused only by stimuli which impinge on the infant, some of which are pleasurable while most are unpleasurable. But in some instances from the first day on, more often in the first two weeks, and with increasing variety the infant *turns* to some of the impinging stimuli. This leads later to a precursor or an early stage of play mainly characterized by the repetition of different kinds of vital sensations in the encounter with environmental objects, by gripping, banging, touching, pressing, mouthing, gazing, etc. These encounters are still objectless although they take place in contact with an object. They merely "feel nice." But gradually the infant starts to notice that there is *something* which resists, yields, is lost, reappears. This something is the first stage of what Werner has called a "thing-of-action."[30] At this point the thing-of-action is no more than the something in contact with which autocentric, pleasurable fused perception can arise, be repeated, or lost, depending on the availability of the object. It then becomes more definitely a thing-to-bite, or a thing-to-grip, or to bang, to squeeze, to stroke, or to throw. The growing attention of the infant soon discovers that all sorts of things happen to and with this something as he plays with it. He eventually realizes that his own activity not only produces the pleasurable sensations but is related to the things that happen to the object. The development goes from an almost complete state of embeddedness in which there is mostly a negative, unpleasurable vital sensation to impinging stimuli, to increasing pleasure in a largely autocentric vital sensation in contact with "something." These sensations are rewarding, and together with the pleasure in movement as such and the expanding exploratory curiosity, they motivate repetitions and variations of activity, thus bringing about diversified contacts with the object and revealing again and again a variety of its sensory aspects. Through this kind of play there eventually emerges an object existing for the child independently of his immediate contact with it. The infant and child now learn different ways of dealing with this object, thereby discovering and integrating new aspects of it. The various steps of this whole, complex development overlap, and only very gradually does the allocentric interest in and exploration of objects gain predominance over the autocentric pleasurable sensation of sensory contact with them. The latter, however, continues throughout life, mainly in the predominantly autocentric sense modalities.

Instances of pleasurable fused perceptions can be observed also as part of activities other than oral or manual contact in nursing and in the early stages of play. Toward the end of infancy, when the baby learns to walk, and continuing through the toddler stage of early childhood, the gait of the child has a thumping quality because of the difficulty of learning the right balance and motor coordination. But the joy of the child in his indefatigable efforts to walk and run is not only joy in the mastery of so difficult a task but often seems also to be the pleasure in the accentuated, firm

30] Werner, *Comparative Psychology of Mental Development*, pp. 59, 65-66.

contact of the foot with the ground, a pleasure in which tactile sensations in sole and toes combine with proprioceptive sensations of the leg and foot muscles and of pelvis and torso, and with pressure sensations from the force with which the contact with the ground is re-established with each step. Similarly, this kind of pleasure is often shown in the baby's firm sitting on the ground. It also plays a role in learning to speak. At the stage where the infant produces a great variety of sounds, not only does he delight in the fact that he can produce all these different sounds to hear, but also there is often a distinct pleasure in the proprioceptive and tactile sensations which their production causes in mouth, lips, tongue, and throat. This pleasure often continues in a less pronounced way throughout childhood.

The development from the predominance of the experience of impinging stimuli as disturbing the homeostatic state of comfortable embeddedness to the increasing importance of specific attractive and repellent stimuli in fused autocentric perception of specific sensory qualities, and eventually to the beginnings of the perception of objects and object qualities is of basic significance in the ontogenetic development of sensory perception and is closely linked with the development of attention. In the adult, too, attentive perception reveals object aspects qualitatively and quantitatively different from those yielded by inattentive, peripheral, and background perception. Thus, while the development of attention, especially focal attention, is very important in the great ontogenetic shift from completely autocentric to increasingly allocentric perception, there are other important factors of maturation and experience involved in this shift. In the course of infancy and early childhood there occurs a shift from the predominance of the autocentric senses (lower senses) to a predominance of the allocentric (higher) senses, and within the higher senses there occurs a shift from functioning on the autocentric level to increasing predominance of functioning on the allocentric level. Furthermore there occurs a development toward greater differentiation in some of the autocentric senses which, too, is linked to the growing capacity for attentive conscious experience.

At birth the lower, autocentric senses are more fully developed, and together with the tactile sense, they play a greater role in the newborn and in early infancy than do the gradually developing highest senses, sight and hearing. The tongue is the newborn's most highly developed sense organ, both with regard to taste and touch, and perhaps also proprioceptively.[31] Neurologically, the taste buds on the dorsal surface of the tongue, especially those sensitive to sweet taste (lactose!) are much more numerous in children than in adults.[32] Tactile sensations of the lips, too, are already highly developed at birth.[33] Autocentric tactile, thermal, pressure and proprioceptive sensations play a much greater role in early infancy than active manual exploration, which becomes possible only after palmar grasping has been supplanted in frequency by digital, finger-tip grasping in the thirty-second to fifty-second weeks.[34] Together with olfactory and, to a lesser extent, autocentric auditory sensations they are more important at first in the infant's "recognition" of the nursing situation and of the mothering one than are visual factors. Groddeck believed that the infant and young child "judge" people and objects by their smell even more than dogs do, and that, since the infant is often held on the lap and the young child, when standing, does not reach high, the smell of legs, lap, sexual, and excretory organs of the adult is particularly emphasized in these olfactory sensations.[35]

In the higher senses—touch, sight, and hearing—the gradual emergence and development of the allocentric mode of perception

31] David Katz, "Psychologische Untersuchungen an der Zunge," *Studien zur experimentellen Psychologie* (Benno Schwabe & Co., Basel, 1953); Stirnimann, *Psychologie des neugeborenen Kindes*, pp. 41-46.

32] Carl Pfaffmann, "Taste and Smell," in S. S. Stevens, ed., *Handbook of Experimental Psychology* (John Wiley & Sons, New York, 1951), pp. 1143-1171, 1145; Friedrich Brock, *Bau und Leistung unserer Sinnesorgane, I, Haut-, Tiefen und Labyrinthorgane, Dalp-Taschenbücher* (Francke Verlag, Bern, 1956), p. 36. Brock mentions a similar decline from 6000 tactile receptors on the tip of a finger in childhood to 1000 in later adulthood, p. 44.

33] According to Pratt, the cutaneous responses "constitute much of the neonate [sensory] repertoire" and tactile sensitivity is ontogenetically and phylogenetically the first to appear, arising prenatally first in the oral-nasal region. Pratt, "The Neonate," in Carmichael, ed., *Manual of Child Psychology*, pp. 220-221.

34] See H. M. Halverson, "The Development of Prehension in Infants," in Barker, Kounin, and Wright, eds., *Child Behavior and Development*, (McGraw-Hill, New York, 1943), pp. 49-66, 55.

35] Georg Groddeck, *The World of Man* (C. W. Daniel Co., London, 1934), p. 132. Compare also to the whole problem of the early sensory shift: "On Memory and Childhood Amnesia," this volume, pp. 298-301. The ontogenetic shift in perceptual organization was conceptualized there as a shift from the proximity to the distance senses. It is more correct to speak of a shift from the predominance of the autocentric senses and the autocentric mode to that of the allocentric mode and the allocentric senses. The sense of touch is a proximity sense, but its predominant mode of functioning after infancy and early childhood is allocentric, at least in the most important tactile organ, the hand.

from their early, completely autocentric functioning can be observed in a great many phenomena in infant and child behavior. Because the lower senses are not capable of allocentric, objectifying perception, their development after birth and early infancy compares in no way with the scope of the development of the allocentric (higher) senses, which assume ever increasing importance during early childhood.

The newborn's *tactile* sensations are entirely of the autocentric type. He experiences comfort or discomfort in being touched, in the way he is being held, swathed, in the contact with a smooth or a scratchy, a dry or a wet sheet or diaper. Also in the grasping reflex of the hand, which is fully developed at birth, the tactile experience is an autocentric one, not one of encountering and exploring an object, but of something that is good or not good to hold. The fine sensory discrimination of the newborn between the human finger and a rod of similar proportions, which leads to a firm grasping of the former and a quick letting go of the latter,[36] does not imply any awareness of two different objects, but two different vital sensations one of which feels good, the other not. Similarly, the fact that many newborns discriminate with their lips and tongue between the nipple, skin, an eiderdown quilt, or a human finger and accept some of these when sucking for the sake of sucking (skin, finger) while rejecting others (eiderdown quilt, coverlet), but accept only the nipple when in a state of hunger, means, in Piaget's words, the rediscovery of "a sensorimotor and particular postural complex" among several others "which constitute [the nursling's] universe and reveal a total lack of differentiation between subject and object."[37] At eight weeks the infant still grasps only objects that are put in his palm, that is to say he responds only to impinging tactile stimuli. Halverson found that of eight different objects (cube, rod, spoon, cup, bell, ball, pellet, string) only a rod and a ball were grasped in this way.[38] Perhaps this indicates that the rod, just as in Stirnimann's experiment, is

36] Stirnimann, *Psychologie des neugeborenen Kindes*, pp. 26-27.

37] Piaget, *The Origins of Intelligence in Children*, p. 37. Piaget observed this in his son Laurent when he was three days old. He assumes that this "elementary recognition consists . . . of assimilation of the whole of the data present in a definite organization which has already functioned and only gives rise to discrimination due to its past functioning." This does not seem to hold true for Stirnimann's experiment with finger and rod in the grasping reflex which he made on the first day of life; there discrimination took place without prior experience.

38] *Ibid.*, pp. 56, 62.

grasped because of its similarity to the human finger, while the ball may evoke a response because of some tactile similarity to the maternal breast. Only at sixteen weeks, when focal regard for not too small objects has developed, does the infant actively reach for and grasp objects within his reach. But since the grasp remains palmar until the thirty-second to thirty-sixth week, hence does not permit finer manipulation and exploration of the object, only autocentric tactile and proprioceptive sensations can occur at that period.[39] At about five months the infant carries everything he can grasp with his hand to his mouth for oral exploration. The palmar grasp, which by this time takes place with the thumb opposing (from the twenty-fourth to thirty-second week[40]), is similar to holding something in the mouth—the object is surrounded by sensitive skin but cannot be manipulated in a systematically explorative way. Actually, in the palm the object is held firmly in one position, while in the mouth, the tongue, lips, and jaws try more actively to get the feel of it. But neither palm nor mouth contact permits objectification in the sense of a perception of the structure of an independently existing object. At this stage, however, the mouth yields more richly varied sensitive discrimination of various things-to-be-mouthed and their particular, more or less pleasurable or unpleasurable feel. In this autocentric way the mouth is used by the baby to "recognize" various objects and, according to Stern and Piaget, even to compose his first notions of space ("buccal space").[41] The quality of such early autocentric recognition can be seen from the example of a six-month-old boy, quoted by Werner, who was given a round rattle instead of a square-edged one to which he was accustomed, and who tried in vain to find and bite the "corners" of the round rattle.[42] He did not perceive the roundness of one rattle and the angularity of the other. All he did was to experience that his accustomed rattle felt right when he put it in his mouth to bite, and that the round one did

39] Halverson, "The Development of Prehension in Infants," *loc. cit.*, p. 62, says that only in the course of the first year does the grasp change from a *holding* to a *feeling* grip. He equates feeling with digital exploration. Actually, however, the holding grip is also a "feeling" grip from the first day of life on. What changes is the quality of the feeling, namely from an autocentric vital sensation to more allocentric, objectifying, tactile exploration.

40] *Ibid.*, p. 55.

41] Piaget, *The Origins of Intelligence in Children*, p. 35. Compare also Spitz "The Primal Cavity," *loc. cit.*, pp. 215-240.

42] Werner, *Comparative Psychology of Mental Development*, p. 65.

not. A similar kind of autocentric perception continues, side by side with allocentric, in such adult experiences as that a certain fabric or an upholstered chair do not "feel right" when stroked with the palm of the hand or sat upon although in allocentric visual perception the adult was led to expect that they would.

Oral tactual exploration precedes manual because the muscular and nervous development of the oral zone (lips, tongue, palate, jaws) are much farther advanced at birth and during early infancy than that of the hand. Only gradually, after finger-tip grasping, holding, and manipulating have developed and, during the thirty-second to fifty-second week, have supplanted palmar grasping in frequency, does the mouth yield its predominant position in contact with objects to the hand. For quite a while to come the infant and young child supplement manual with oral exploration of objects. As the motor coordination of the fingers develops and permits manipulation and sensitive finger-tip contact with the object so that it can be shifted and varied at will, the child discovers that one can do and explore much more with hands and fingers than with the mouth. During the same time focal attention and visual perception develop, so that object-centered, allocentric perception becomes possible and plays an increasingly larger role after the first year. The tactile exploratory capacities of the mouth then become increasingly restricted to the enjoyment of food texture and eventually also to the sifting out of things that it is better not to swallow. But because of the autocentric character of taste and of most of the mouth's tactile sensations, even in the adult, pleasure and disgust reactions remain stronger in oral than in manual contact.

It is no coincidence that when Descartes wanted to prove that all the senses are deceptive, even the sense of touch, which he describes as usually considered the most reliable one, he resorted to an example of completely autocentric tactile experience. He refers to a child falling asleep and being tickled with a feather at the mouth and tries to prove his thesis by saying that the tickling sensation does not remind the child of anything that belongs to the feather.[43] But while he uses an inconclusive example to prove

43] Descartes, *Traité de la Lumière*, quoted by Erwin Straus, *Vom Sinn der Sinne*, 2nd ed. (Springer Verlag, Berlin, 1956), pp. 214-216. Descartes' example compounds several autocentric factors: (1) in falling asleep all perceptions revert to the autocentric mode, even in the adult (see below, pp. 214-216); (2) children's perceptions are more autocentric than adults'; (3) being touched, rather than touching actively and exploring by means of the tactile sense, is always predominantly autocentric.

the fallibility of tactile experiences, he touches on the distinguished position of the sense of touch as giving man a greater feeling of *certitude* than any other sense. By means of touch we are really and fully in con*tact* with an object. We refer to this sense, to being in *touch* with somebody or something, when we want to express a state of full and alive awareness, but also to indicate merely a continuing possibility of communication (hence "to get in touch"). Perhaps the fact that touch, phylogenetically and ontogenetically, is the foundation of all sensory experience and all the other extero-ceptive senses are but highly specialized variants of cutaneous sensitivity, gives to it a unique position. Kant described touch as the only sense of immediate outer perception, hence also the most important and the one that informs with the greatest certitude. For similar reasons Locke and Berkeley ranked touch higher than vision. D. Katz agrees with them because what is known through touch has most reliably the character of reality; for this reason he attributes to touch greater importance than to the other senses in the development of the "belief in reality."[44] It is the touchstone of reality. Doubting Thomas was convinced only by touching the wounds of Christ (John 20:25).

These considerations bear on the important problem of experiential as compared to objective reality and of the different degrees and qualities of experiential reality, which I shall call from here on "realness" in order to distinguish it from scientific and other more conceptual ideas of reality. Touch does, indeed, provide the most undeniable encounter with anything real. Children want to touch everything in order to get really acquainted with it, and when the adult does not feel quite sure whether his senses may not be playing a trick on him, he touches an object to make sure of its really being there. Many adults in encountering something new want to touch it; they feel, like most children do, that this will give them an undefined something which mere sight does not yield. Hence the printed admonitions in many museums and galleries not to touch the objects exhibited. The palpable physical impact of bumping into something or somebody leaves no doubt about the realness of the object with which one collides. This is the reason why many metaphorical expressions are taken from the tactile sphere to describe various qualities and degrees of experiential impact, as in being touched, impressed, shaken, moved,

44] D. Katz, *Der Aufbau der Tastwelt* (J. A. Barth, Leipzig, 1925), pp. 253-256.

struck, smitten, thrown. While all these refer to the psychic effect of something impinging, others refer to the realness mediated by active touch as in perceive, prehend, comprehend, grasp, manifest (that which is obvious to the hand).[45] Language seems to confirm that only that which has touched one or which one has touched can be fully experienced and clearly understood and assimilated. The feeling of realness ultimately derives from the autocentric phase of development in which only that is real which is in the immediate environment and of which the physical impact is felt on one's body.[46]

This first sphere of realness is later enlarged by the active mobility of the developing person who can bring his body into contact with the objects, can approach, touch, and grasp them. In a metaphorical sense, valid throughout life, only that becomes fully real to man to which he reaches out and to the impact of which he exposes himself. The degree of realness depends on the intensity, presence, and fullness with which he does so.

While touch, throughout life, remains the basic experiential test of realness, *sight* becomes increasingly more important than touch. As sight gradually develops into the most objectifying of all the senses, it assumes a dominant position because it tells man more than any other sense about reality, about the many objects in the midst of which he finds himself. The shift from the predominance of tactile and kinesthetic to visual factors continues for a long period and, as Werner has shown, can be observed in certain situations as late as at the eight-to-nine-year level.[47]

Sight, like hearing, develops more slowly and over a longer period of time than touch and the autocentric senses, and the use of sight in the service of the nursing situation occurs considerably later than the use of hearing. Autocentric recognition of the mother's voice in connection with the total, global experience of the nursing situation has been observed clearly in some infants by the second week,[48] while similar global recognition visually does not seem to occur before the third month. But Piaget reports in-

45] Compare also the German and French examples quoted by Katz, *Der Aufbau der Tastwelt*, p. 253.

46] Compare to this also Werner's characterization of the child's world as being "a world of nearness at hand." *Comparative Psychology of Mental Development*, p. 383.

47] *Ibid.*, p. 482, with further references.

48] Stirnimann, *Psychologie des neugeborenen Kindes*, pp. 54-55, 86.

stances, other than nursing, of pleasurable recognition of global situations involving a familiar face by the second half of the second month.[49]

Sight, the highest and most objectifying sense, the sense that contributes more than any other to a true picture of reality and of the objects in their spatial relations, thus seems to develop at first more independently from the basic nursing and comfort needs than any other sense. In its very beginnings the sense destined to be most important for perception's role in the grasp of reality seems to develop more autonomously, with less reference to any other vital need of the infant. Psychologically, the earliest development of sight is not enforced by supervening needs of reality adaptation but is advanced by the pleasure of encountering visual stimuli and by the wish to prolong such stimulation. The newborn and the young infant look for the sake of looking and for no other purpose. The newborn's gaze is attracted by soft light and by luminous objects. Piaget speaks of *light* being an aliment for visual activity and describes the newborn's tendency to preserve the perception of light and his groping to rediscover it when it vanishes.[50] He mentions Preyer's observations of the infant's expression of satisfaction at soft light during the first few days of life.

From Stirnimann's observations it seems likely that in addition to light, certain *colors* are attractive while others are repellent to the newborn, and that these sensorimotor-affective reactions to color become more pronounced in the second week. On the very first day of life, the newborn is more attracted by a visual field that is not uniformly colored than by a uniformly colored visual field. While the question of color sensitivity of the newborn and the infant has been controversial, autocentric discrimination of color occurs a considerable time before the child starts to perceive definite form and structure.[51] The infant is affected in a different way by different colors long before he recognizes different forms and, of course, long before the child *knows* the different colors.

49] Piaget, *The Origins of Intelligence in Children,* p. 60, 72.

50] *Ibid.,* pp. 62-63. Stirnimann, *op. cit.,* p. 60.

51] Compare Stirnimann, *op. cit.,* pp. 56-59; Peiper believed that even prematurely born infants are sensitive to color, A. Peiper, "Ueber die Helligkeits- und Farbempfindungen der Frühgeburten," *Archiv für Kinderheilkunde,* 1926, 80:1-20; Pratt, "The Neonate," in Carmichael, ed., *Manual of Child Psychology,* pp. 203-208, with further references to the literature. Werner, *Comparative Psychology of Mental Development,* pp. 97-100; Géza Révész, "Abstraktion und Wiedererkennung," *Zeitschrift für Psychologie,* 1925, 98:34.

As Werner puts it, "the early development of the color sense consists . . . of a gradually increasing domination of objective perceptual factors over a fused syncretic activity in which colors are experienced as responses of the body in its totality."[52]

Those functions of sight which are the more autocentric ones in the adult, the perception of light and color, are also the genetically earlier ones. This is also true of the development of vision in congenitally blind people who in adulthood have obtained sight through successful operations. Their vision has at first an amorphous, unified quality in which distinct forms are not recognized while color is. In these individuals, even conceptual recognition of color long precedes that of form. One such patient learned the color names and was able to identify the learned colors, but eleven months after the operation he still could not recognize the simplest forms.[53] Similarly, Meyer and Harlow have shown that colors offer more effective and more easily learned cues to monkeys than do forms, and Nissen and McCulloch report the same for chimpanzees.[54]

The first visual experiences of the neonate, thus, seem to be regulated by a pleasure principle which differs from Freud's in that excitation can be both pleasurable or unpleasurable. The neonate and infant respond to impinging visual stimuli by enjoying and seeking to prolong or recover the contact with some, while seeking to withdraw from or avoid others. Soft light, mildly luminous objects, some colors and, even more, color combinations are enjoyed; too much or too glaring light and some colors are rejected. All this takes place while the infant's gaze is still vague and not focused. In the first four weeks, especially around the end of the first month, the infant's vague gaze changes more and more to interested looking, and the capacity to follow the movement of an interesting sight with his glance develops increasingly. Moving objects excite the infant's interest. But these images have neither depth nor articulate form, and with the exception of the mothering

52] Werner, *op. cit.*, p. 100.
53] M. v. Senden, *Raum- und Gestaltauffassung bei operierten Blindgeborenen vor und nach der Operation* (J. A. Barth, Leipzig, 1932).
54] D. R. Meyer and H. F. Harlow, "The Development of Transfer of Responses to Patterning by Monkeys," *Journal of Comparative Physiological Psychology*, 1945, 42:454-462; H. W. Nissen and T. L. McCulloch, "Equated and Non-Equated Stimulus Situations in Discrimination Learning Chimpanzees III. Prepotency of Response to Oddity through Training," *Journal of Comparative Psychology*, 1937, 23:377-381.

one's face in nursing, at which the infant gazes steadily from the third or fourth week on, they do not belong to any significant, recurrent total situation in which they are combined with nursing, sucking, grasping, particular postures, or being held in a particular way. For this reason, as Piaget has pointed out, the interest which moving images so obviously hold for the infant can derive only from his *need* to look.[55] Moving, luminous units or spots are things-of-action in Werner's sense, namely things-to-look-at. They have as yet no distinct forms, but merely serve as objects for the enjoyable exercise of looking. Nor do they appear as yet in space, since the capacity for distance accommodation of the eye's lens has not yet developed.

If one speaks of sight and hearing as *distance* senses, as contrasted with the proximity senses of touch, taste, and smell, it is necessary to clarify the meaning of this term. It comprises two different meanings. One meaning of distance sense is that the sense organ can be stimulated by a source that is objectively distant from it. According to this meaning, which refers to concepts taken from physics and physiology, there are distance senses from birth on and, similarly, phylogentically from almost the lowest point of the evolutionary scale. In man these senses are as follows, in a descending order according to the length of the distances between the source of the stimulus and the sense organ: sight, hearing, smell. The other meaning of distance sense is an experiential one, that is, the sense conveys an experience, a perception of distance. This is an essential characteristic of the sense of sight, much less essential of hearing, and still less of smell.[56]

The perception of distance and of spatial structure and the perception of distinct objects are interdependent. They are a prerequisite for allocentric perception in which definite objects are seen in their spatial relation to each other and to the perceiver. Even in the adult, perception of distance becomes dim or disappears entirely in the autocentric mode, for instance when gazing without focus at the total impinging visual field. It is much less pronounced

55] Piaget, *The Origins of Intelligence in Children*, pp. 63-66. Piaget reports the first recognition of people at one month fifteen days, when his son recognized his nurse when she was wagging her head and singing, p. 72.

56] Since smell depends on gaseous (or, for some animals, liquid) diffusion of the smelling substance it cannot be called strictly a distance sense in terms of physics. But experientially, higher animals and men in following a scent to its source have some experience of distance connected with the olfactory sense.

in impressionistic painting with its emphasis on light and color than it is, for instance, in some Renaissance paintings with their emphasis on the main objects in the foreground and a distant landscape in the background, or in certain seventeenth-century Dutch landscapes, where distance and expanse seem to become the very themes of the artist.

From interested looking at the changing images which appear and disappear in the infant's visual field it is still a long way of many months to the perception of objects with distinct forms and detailed articulation of structure. This requires considerably greater activity of the eye and the mind than does the earlier perception of objects as mere global units set off against a background and separated from other such units. The eye now has to follow the distinguishing shape and the details of the object's structure.[57] This change is part of a total perceptual development which gradually leads to the discovery of independently existing objects and to their allocentric perception. Some of the major steps on the way are the perception of distance; the development of digital grasp with its possibility of manual, tactile exploration; the development of sustained focal attention which permits exploration of very small objects as well as detailed articulation of larger objects; the coordination of the different sense modalities so that the infant can discover that the object which he sees is the same as that which he can reach and grasp, put in his mouth and taste and smell, and that the voice he hears emanates from the face he sees, or the sound from the rattle he shakes.[58] During this development the child also learns to perceive the autocentric sensations of taste and smell as qualities of particular objects. The main motivation in this development toward allocentric perception is not coercion by reality, not an unwelcome demand imposed on the infant by the need for survival. It is, rather, an insatiable curiosity and wish to approach and make contact with the surrounding world in a thousand different ways, and the pleasure in these contacts.

57] Compare D. O. Hebb, *The Organization of Behavior* (John Wiley & Sons, New York, 1949), pp. 31-35, 80-106; and Elisabeth Knoblauch, "Vergleichende Untersuchungen zur optischen Auffassung hochgradig schwachsinniger und normaler Kinder," summarized and quoted by Werner, *Comparative Psychology of Mental Development*, pp. 115-116.

58] For the details of these developments compare Piaget, *The Origins of Intelligence in Children*, and his *The Construction of Reality in the Child* (Basic Books, New York, 1954).

These ever varied and ever repeated approaches take place in *play*—in the playful taking hold and letting go of all accessible objects with hand and mouth and eye, and in the playful producing of and listening to sounds. Such play occurs not when the infant or child is under the pressure of hunger or in discomfort, but when he is freed from the pressure of visceral needs. In this play the child eventually discovers not only the objects but also himself, and the objects eventually are perceived as independent from his actions, with an existence of their own. Both before and after their emergence as independent objects with qualities and a spatial location of their own, they remain endlessly fascinating to the infant and child and he does not tire of exploring them. Thus the initial pleasure in certain sensory stimulations and the wish to prolong and repeat them is increasingly supplemented and overshadowed by the enjoyable, active play in which many different aspects of the objects are discovered and eventually integrated in the emerging allocentric perception of the object. In this development the functional capacities of the child develop together with and as the instrument of his perception of the world around him. It is his activity which opens the world of objects to him.

At a fairly early point in this development, some time during the second or third month and with increasing frequency thereafter, there occurs an important step, the *precursor* of conscious *recognition*. At this point it is not yet a recognition of a full-fledged object, but of a total situation in which one object is prominent and in which visual and auditory factors play a major role. It may be described as a resensing, usually first of the mothering one (mother or nurse). In the third month, perhaps even earlier, there is also resensation of toys or of parts of the crib or other objects which are parts of the more or less constant, immediate environment of the baby. Such resensation is a *pleasurable* event to which the infant reacts by smiling or by some other expression of delight in seeing these familiar objects. That this smile is not an exclusively social response, as C. Bühler assumes, has been shown by Piaget, who observed repeatedly infants in the third month smiling at familiar objects when they could neither see nor hear any person around.[59] "Recognition" consists at first mainly of the pleasurable *affect of familiarity*. The delight of the infant in the first resensa-

59] The same observation has been made by C. W. Valentine, whom Piaget quotes in *The Origins of Intelligence in Children*, pp. 71-74.

tions of something as being familiar is more readily comparable to the adult's pleasure in returning to a beloved countryside or home, or in meeting a friend again than it is to the much more frequent feeling of familiarity with which we barely look at our daily surroundings, only to relegate them to the unnoticed background.[60] In the former experience there is the memory and the anticipation of meaningful and enjoyable experiences and relationships, in the latter the hardly noticed reassurance of orientation in a status quo, without interest and anticipation.

Because of the global quality of the infant's perception of the familiar, the change of even one element in the situation is likely to be experienced by the child as a complete change of the situation, which then no longer is familiar.[61] This is also true of many animals' perception of the familiar,[62] and a similar experience also occurs in adults. When one enters a familiar room in which a piece of furniture that used to be there is missing or in which some of the furniture has been rearranged or a new piece has been added, one may have a sensation that the room "feels" different but be unable to tell what the change has been. This experience may have overtones of not feeling quite comfortable, but these usually disappear when one has found out the nature of the change.

Claparède assumes that the experience of familiarity always involves a feeling of "me-ness."[63] While this may be so in the adult, the first experiences of familiarity in the infant occur during the adualistic stage, at a time when there is as yet no feeling or concept of "I" or "me." The affect of familiarity fuses with the resensing of a global sensorimotor-affective state characteristic of early sensory perception. It probably is more closely related to the feeling of familiarity (or unfamiliarity) which birds and higher mammals have in relation to their habitat and to changes in it, and in their "recognition" of individual members of their species.[64] Rec-

60] Compare below, pp. 169-170.
61] Werner, *Comparative Psychology of Mental Development*, pp. 128-130.
62] See Lorenz, "Comparative Study of Behavior," in Schiller, ed., *Instinctive Behavior*, p. 259.
63] E. Claparède, "Recognition and 'Me-ness,'" in Rapaport, *Organization and Pathology of Thought*, pp. 58-75.
64] Rapaport (*op. cit.*, p. 59, footnote 7) uses the example of the feeding behavior of the mother stork and her young as contradicting the assumption of a similarity between the experience of familiarity in animals and men, or in children and adults. But this example is of an Internal Releasing Mechanism releasing a rigid, innate activity pattern. Recognition by familiarity is always acquired, learned and not innate.

ognition proper, that is recognition at the stage of objectification in the allocentric mode of perception, is a later development and probably a descendant of the earlier affect of familiarity. Piaget, too, believes that "the impression of satisfaction and familiarity peculiar to recognition" stems from the continuity of a subjective schema and "is only the realization of mutual conformity between a given object and a schema all ready to assimilate it. Recognition accordingly begins by being subjective before it becomes object recognition, which of course does not prevent the subject from projecting recognized perception into the undifferentiated universe of his adualistic consciousness (since in the beginning nothing is experienced as subjective)."[65]

At about the same time at which the infant first experiences the pleasurable affect of familiarity in resensation, there occurs another phenomenon, namely a certain *astonishment, hesitation, a slight alarm or anxiety* with the appearance of *new* objects which the infant would like to grasp.[66] The feeling of familiarity is the prerequisite for the experience of the unfamiliar, the new, the strange, and for the emotions linked with this experience. Perhaps this accounts for the observation that young dogs, reared in an extremely restricted sensory environment, are neither bored with nor fearful of the objects they come in contact with when they are brought into a normal environment, whereas normally raised dogs show fear of strange objects and also soon get bored with them. Hebb comments on these observations that the restricted dogs are not smart enough to be either bored or afraid.[67] Perhaps they have first to learn to "recognize" objects, to acquire the affect of familiarity, before they can acquire the affects connected with perceiving the new.

In the growing infant the link between the pleasure of resensing the familiar and the fear of the new or strange is striking. This is especially clear at the time at which recognition proper develops, that is to say at the dawning of the idea of definite objects and of their independent existence. Escalona points out that the so-called "eight months anxiety" (K. Wolf and R. Spitz) is an exacerbation of an apprehensiveness at the contact with strangers

65] Piaget, *The Construction of Reality in the Child*, p. 6.
66] Piaget, *The Origins of Intelligence in Children*, pp. 70-74.
67] D. O. Hebb, "The Mammal and His Environment," *American Journal of Psychiatry*, 1955, 111:826-831, 827.

which, in a lesser degree, occurs much earlier, and that the increase of anxiety at six to eight months "is a consequence of that step forward in the comprehension of the world . . . which enables the baby to perceive that the mother is an independent entity who can decide to be absent or present at will."[68]

The unfamiliar object gives rise to *conflicting* feelings. On the one hand the infant wants to explore it, to grasp it, to see how it feels; on the other hand, he is somewhat reluctant and afraid to do so, whereas in relation to familiar objects the very act of resensing them is enjoyable to him. Before the advent of resensation there exists neither the known nor the unknown, only pleasurable, comfortable, or unpleasurable sensations which come and go. With resensation there arises the division into the *familiar* and the *new*, the unknown. The infant's experience of pleasurable resensation of the familiar thus introduces a conflict which is destined to have a far-reaching significance for the life of man, the conflict between the inclination to remain embedded in the familiar and the desire to expand and deepen his relation to the world by encountering the new.

Freud, who considered every increase in stimulation as unpleasure, saw a conflict between, on the one hand, the basic striving to remain in a quiescent, excitationless state, akin to the fetal state or, in his later writings, to death, and, on the other hand, the activities and detours on the way to that state imposed by reality. I believe that the conflict arises between the wish to remain embedded in the womb or in the mother's care, eventually in the accustomed, the fear of separation from such embeddedness, and the wish to encounter the world and to develop and realize, in this encounter, the human capacities. This conflict first enters the dawning consciousness with the advent of resensation and the ensuing differentiation of the familiar from the unknown. It seems to be inherent in the development of perception and intelligence to the stage where perception begins to become recognition. It can be observed in the play of young cats and dogs as well as in that of the infant. The new object, the *change* from the familiar, gives rise to alarm as well as to the desire to explore. It mobilizes the early tendency

68] Sibylle Escalona, "Emotional Development in the First Year of Life," and the discussion by K. Wolf, B. Spock, and others, in Milton J. E. Senn, ed., *Problems of Infancy and Childhood, 6th Conference, 1952* (Josiah Macy, Jr., Foundation, New York, 1953), pp. 52, 60, 63. Compare also Gardner and Lois B. Murphy, *Experimental Social Psychology* (Harper & Brothers, New York, 1931), pp. 260-263.

to react to all stimuli as a disturbance of embeddedness. But, especially in the youth of the higher vertebrates and most of all in man, it activates, at the same time, curiosity and the desire to explore and relate to the new, thereby expanding and deepening the contact with the environment.

While the lowest animals and the human embryo react to any new stimulus, to any significant and "unexpected" change in the environment with a negative or an avoidance reaction, the higher animals and man react to many changes, in various ways and degrees, with a startle or *alarm* reaction. This alarm reaction differs from the simple avoidance reaction in that it poses a question which can be answered only by further exploration. In contrast to the lower animals, which, upon the appearance of something new, of change, react immediately with escape or a functionally similar response, in the alarm reaction of the higher mammals and birds and of man, the body is mobilized for action,[69] but this action itself is delayed and the field is reconnoitered with regard to the various possibilities of significance of the change, and only then the appropriate motor activity is carried out. As Bally has pointed out, the alarm reaction leads to a momentary widening and loosening of the field which, at this point, is no longer completely dominated by the instinctive activity in which the animal (or infant) had been engaged, or by the interest which the infant, child, or adult had pursued.[70] In this widened field the question "What is it?" arises and leads to attentive exploration. Such exploration may merely go as far as to find out whether the change in the situation heralds something to flee from or something that will fill

69] For the physiological details of the startle and alarm reaction compare C. Landis and W. A. Hunt, *The Startle Pattern* (Farrar & Rinehart, New York, 1939). Perhaps the alarm reaction is one of the origins of the capacity for *delay*.

70] Gustav Bally, *Vom Ursprung und von den Grenzen der Freiheit* (Benno Schwabe & Co., Basel, 1945), pp. 36-40. For this reason it is wrong to assume, as some learning theorists do, that "conditioning" stimuli are effective only because they have the character either of reward or of punishment. The very mild electric shocks used in many of their experiments are not painful. But since they never occur in the animal's natural habitat and way of life, they are quite unknown and therefore alarming. It is this effect which leads to an alerting of attention, a scanning of the environment, and a widening of the field which are conducive to learning. As Muenziger found, rats learn a black-white discrimination not only when shock is given at the choice of the "wrong" stimulus, but also when it is given at the choice of the "right" one. K. F. Muenziger, "Motivation in Learning, I, Electric Shock for Correct Response in the Visual Discrimination Habit," *Journal of Comparative Psychology*, 1934, 17:267-277. Of course when alarm changes to severe anxiety, panic, or a catastrophic situation (Goldstein) it has the opposite effect and prevents learning.

a need, or whether it gives no cause for alarm. But to man it may pose the further question of whether he wants to know this something new more fully for the sake of knowing it.

On the sensory level, with which we are concerned here, the alarm reaction upon the perception of change may be considered as the descendant of the embeddedness principle[71] insofar as it is accompanied by feelings—sometimes hardly noticeable or very slight, sometimes quite marked—of alarm, uneasiness, being on guard, or of discomfort. These feelings always entail a change in tonicity. But the alarm reaction may also be considered as an alerting of attention which offers a challenge or an opportunity for the arousal of *interest,* insofar as it invites contact with and exploration of the new factor which brought about the change. It always leads to a decision, be it of interested pursuit, of flight, of ensuing indifference, of adaptation to the change, or of withdrawal of attention in favor of returning to what one was doing before the new factor entered the situation.

The functioning of all the senses in the service of the embeddedness principle by their quasi-automatic watch for significant change takes place on the autocentric level, guarding as it were the uniform continuation of the environment. From the totality of the constantly impinging sensory stimuli which are registered out of awareness, or on the fringes of awareness, the significant change arouses attention and by focusing attention, at least momentarily, throws the light of conscious perception on the new factor. This is apparent in some of the autocentric senses, for instance the thermal sense, the olfactory sense, but also in the visual and auditory senses in their relation to the totality of the environing field, that is, to the background and the periphery of sensory awareness. We usually do not notice any reasonably comfortable temperature in our immediate environment, but we do notice any marked *change* in temperature. We do not notice the total olfactory background, but we do notice any marked change, the appearance of a new scent as for example of something burning. In the visual background sudden movement will arouse one's attention; in the auditory a sound different in intensity or quality from the general background noise or the sudden ceasing of a continuous background noise will arouse attention. The *alarming* element in such changes is more pronounced in the tactile than in the distance receptors. Unex-

71] For the embeddedness principle, see this volume, pp. 59-61.

pected touch by something or somebody not seen before usually causes a distinct reaction of alarm and often the initial traces of an escape or other defense reaction. Probably the biological function of this difference is that while the distance receptors forewarn us of the possible approach of a new factor so that there is time for exploration and decision, the new factor is already upon us in the unexpected encounter in the contact sense of touch and requires immediate action.

The initial slight alarm reaction of the infant at the visual appearance of something new is usually followed by active exploration of the new thing. Interest wins out over fear of separation from embeddedness in the familiar and widens the infant's scope of sensorimotor-affective experiences. The same conflict can be seen in a somewhat different form later in the child when the element of the fear of the unknown, its possible danger, adds the *thrill of excitement* to the exploration of the unknown, the dark cellars, the mysterious attics, the wide outdoors. Such explorative play takes place more freely and joyfully when it is encouraged by the parents, but the zest for it may be lastingly damaged and curtailed by overanxious parents. At a somewhat later point, however, parental prohibitions often enhance the attraction of the unknown for the healthy child by adding the spice of the forbidden to the dangers that the unknown itself already holds.

In the alarm reaction the active reconnoitering or interested exploring phase is set off by the sensory impinging of a new stimulus, of change. During the first months of infancy, perceptual exploration, apart from the alarm reaction, usually is set off by something that happens to impinge on the infant's sensorium. However, gradually and increasingly the infant no longer merely waits for such impinging stimuli, but initiates exploration by looking about him and, with increased mobility, especially after learning to walk, by moving about and thus widening his range of exploration. Freud attributed such *active* exploration of the environment to the development of attention which, in his view, had the function "periodically to search the outer world, in order that its data might be already familiar if an urgent need should arise." On the perceptual level this meant that attention's "activity meets the sense impressions halfway instead of awaiting their appearance."[72] Meet-

72] Freud, "Formulations Regarding the Two Principles in Mental Functioning," *Collected Papers*, Vol. IV, p. 15.

ing the sense impressions halfway describes active perception, spontaneously initiated by the perceiver, as contrasted with reactive perception, which is set off by an impinging stimulus. In emphasizing the significance of the change from mere passive–reactive to active–exploratory perception Freud recognized the great importance of this advance, but he tried to explain its ontogenetic occurrence by a motivation which, while true for many instances of adult active perception, has no observable basis in the development of the infant's and young child's increasingly active perceptual exploration of the environment.

From the absence of such a motivation in the infant it does not follow, of course, that the phylogenetic cause of the development of active, attentive perception, in the selective process of evolution, may not have been, as very likely it was, that it permitted a better, more economical adaptation to the environment and more effective provision for vital needs, such as food, escape from danger, etc. Following the thought of ethologists who compare instinctive behavior, from the viewpoint of morphology and evolution, to anatomical organs[73] one might say that the development of *feelers* in many insects and some other animals has the function of meeting the sense impressions halfway, of groping around so that the animal will be forewarned of the appearance of obstacles, dangers, food, before the bulk of the animal's body collides with the object. No such organ is found in the lowest animals, which react only to what actually impinges on their bodies. On the other hand, even man uses his hands after the fashion of feelers when deprived of sight, as in groping about in the dark. In higher animals, instead of feelers, active exploration of the environment is seen in appetitive behavior, such as visual scanning of the environment for food. But in many higher mammals, for instance dogs, cats, monkeys, or apes, active perceptual exploration may also serve mere curiosity, an explorative drive, and the desire to orient themselves in their environment. Thus, active perception, meeting the sense impressions halfway, already occurs in the higher mammals in the service of curiosity and not only to provide for future needs and emergencies. In the childhood of cats and dogs, whose vital needs are taken care of by the nursing mother animal, a great deal of their waking time is spent in playful exploration, the motivation for

73] Compare, for instance, Lorenz, "Comparative Study of Behavior," in Schiller, ed., *Instinctive Behavior*, pp. 239-263.

which probably is mainly or entirely the very *need to play* and thus to explore the environment and exercise motor skills.

What is partly true of the childhood period of some higher mammals, especially the altricial ones,[74] is essentially true of human infancy and childhood. The development of allocentric perception and of the motor skills of the growing infant and child take place not because he wants to be able to take care of future needs but because he has a need for and finds pleasure in looking, grasping, listening, tasting, smelling, and exploring all there is to explore around him, just as he has a need for and finds pleasure in learning to sit up, stand up, walk, and run and in manipulating in all possible ways the things he finds.[75] What distinguishes the child's exploratory play from that of the youthful period of some higher altricial mammals and also from the precocial primates is the fact that the kinds of perceptual and motor contact of the young animals are much more limited in the variety of object aspects perceived and of motor activities performed, whereas the infant and child in the movements he performs, in the sounds he produces, and in the object aspects he perceives, shows a variety and richness far beyond anything seen in the animal world.[76] To be sure, the perceptual and motor capacities and skills developed in this kind of play will come in handy at a later time in doing the things parents want the child to do or, still later, in earning a living. But this does not mean that the necessity to cope later in life with the realities of

74] "Altricial" translates the German *Nesthocker*, as contrasted with "precocial," which translates *Nestflüchter*. Altricial birds and mammals go through a childhood period of helplessness during which one or both parents take care of them and—in mammals—play is prominent. Precocial animals are born as the smaller replica of the adult, with all their senses and motor functions ready to function almost from the moment of hatching or birth (e.g., young chicks, ducklings, calves, kids, etc.). Regarding the position of man, who has usually been considered altricial, see the significant findings of Portmann, who describes man as a *precocial born one year too early* (in comparison with his closest phylogenetic relative, the ape, and with the other precocial mammals). This "early extrauterine year" is essential for man's tremendously increased capacity for learning, for flexible adaptation, and for his world-openness. Adolf Portmann, *Biologische Fragmente zu einer Lehre vom Menschen* (Benno Schwabe & Co., Basel, 1951).

75] A similar viewpoint is expressed by G. Murphy, who distinguishes activity drives and sensory drives from visceral drives. Gardner Murphy, *Personality, A Biosocial Approach to Origins and Structure* (Harper & Brothers, New York, 1947), pp. 107-116. R. White, who also emphasizes the importance of the child's exploratory activities and the enjoyable exercise of his growing capacities, questions whether they can be conceptualized as drives and proposes, instead, the concept of competence-motivation. Robert W. White, "Motivation Reconsidered: The Concept of Competence," *Psychological Review,* 1959 (to be published).

76] Compare to this point Portmann, *op. cit.*, pp. 29-30.

parental and societal demands plays a major role in the infant's motivation to acquire and develop these capacities. Insofar as they are not merely phenomena of maturation, they are acquired mainly because the infant and child enjoy their playful exercise. The direction which such exercise takes, of course, is decisively determined by the child's imitation of the parents and by parental influence, prohibiting, encouraging, and teaching. But the main motive power is the enjoyment in the exercise of these manifold capacities.

Perceptually, this development culminates in the shift from looking, touching, etc. for the sake of prolonging or recovering pleasurable sensations to becoming interested in the objects themselves, in wanting to find out what the object is like in allocentric perceptual exploration based on active and expanding interest in a thereby expanding environment. Such exploration is not in the service of urgent present or future needs for food and the like which are taken care of by the mother, nor is it governed by the rigid patterns of instinctive action. It transcends utilitarian purpose and the narrow limits of even the highest animal's *Umwelt* and becomes a quest to learn about anything the exploring child comes upon, in perception and thought. The child wants to find out about the objects and about his own place in relation to them, he wants to get acquainted with the fascinating world around him. He shows a capacity for interest which in most adults is lost in later life and which often goes in many ways beyond the more limited perspective from which many adults later will view the world. The healthy young child is still open toward the world and the world is open for him. Thus, each object may be perceived and encountered by him from many different aspects.

The active turning toward the objects and the wish to expand the boundaries of his world in the encounter with an increasing number and variety of objects is stronger in the healthy infant and child than the wish to remain in the narrow confines of the familiar. Engaged in such activities, the dominant attitude changes from the neonate's prevailing experience of impinging discomfort to that of a world to be explored; the embeddedness principle yields to the transcendence principle of openness toward the world and of self-realization which takes place in the encounter with the world. Where this development does not take place, often because of adverse, anxiety-arousing early experiences in the child-parent relationship, the embeddedness principle may remain pathologically strong, with the result that the encounter with the world is experienced in an autocentric way as an unwelcome impinging of disturbing stimuli. In the perceptual sphere such a basic attitude finds expression not infrequently in an oversensitivity to visual, auditory, and sometimes olfactory stimuli which then are actually felt as distracting, disturbing, or even painful, more frequently and more readily so than by the average person. Often, this occurs in people who, because of their failure to emerge from embeddedness, have considerable difficulties in deciding on and actively striving for goals in their life, difficulties in active self-realization. Just as they often tend unduly to feel victimized in their interpersonal relations, so they may feel bombarded as it were by the overpowering stimuli of the environing reality. The healthy delight in the abundance of the sensory world and the enjoyment in its allocentric exploration are replaced by feelings of being overcome, of their being too much, of too many things impinging all at once, too powerfully, too shrilly, too glaringly, and so forth.[77] This unpleasant experience of being overwhelmed is due to the inhibition or the insufficient development of the capacity to approach, actively and selectively, the objects of the impinging total environment.

The shift from the autocentric to an increasingly important role of the allocentric mode of perception cannot be separated from the development of affect, thought, memory, and communication. It is part of the total mental growth and development of the child. Regarding *memory*, one has to distinguish between the passively experienced reactivation of unconscious memory traces[78] and the capacity for active, voluntary recall. The infant's "recognition" is at first merely the dawning awareness that a total, global sensa-

77] Compare v. Gebsattel's analysis of the perceptual experience of abundance (*Fülle*) and also his remarks about the fear of the new in the obsessional. V. E. von Gebsattel, *Prolegomena einer medizinischen Anthropologie* (Springer Verlag, Berlin, 1954), pp. 55-59, 105-106. Erwin Straus points out that the complaint of many patients of oversensitivity toward noise is a consequence not of a changed function of their auditory nerves but of a disturbance in their communication with the world, because he who withdraws from the world becomes oversensitive to the manifestations of the world that impinge on him. Straus, *Vom Sinn der Sinne*, p. 221. See also this volume, pp. 113-114, regarding the phenomenon of the impingement of the total visual field.

78] Compare Freud's postulate that the process of becoming conscious takes place in a different system than does the leaving behind a memory trace which is necessarily unconscious. Freud, "The Interpretation of Dreams," *Basic Writings*, pp. 488-491; *Beyond the Pleasure Principle* (International Psychoanalytical Press, London, 1922), p. 28.

tion, a complex sensorimotor-affective state feels familiar; the emphasis of this experience is on the subjective side, how the baby *feels;* and of course he is not trying to recall anything, but when the global sensation *"happens"* to him he notices that the feeling is a familiar one. I shall call this type of memory *passive resensing.* On the opposite pole is *voluntary recall,* that is, the recall of constructs which form part of a rationally coherent organization and which are based on abstractions from what has been consciously perceived or on logically coherent thought. Actual adult remembering usually, or probably always, lies somewhere between these two poles and is a mixture of both of them.[79]

However, there is a remarkable affinity between the passive, resensing kind of memory and the autocentric senses or perception in the autocentric mode, and between voluntary recall and the predominantly allocentric senses. Autocentric perceptions are usually not accessible to voluntary recall, or else they are accessible only in the form of very pale, thin, abstract analogues which have little to do with the concrete sensory experience. I can recall that a fruit tasted sweet, or bitter, or sour, but such recall does not enable one to conjure up even a shadow of the actual sweetness, bitterness, sourness, much less of the quantitative degree and qualitative nuance of the real taste experience. The same is true of scents, of the "feel" of a fabric, of pain, of kinesthetic sensations, unless I aid my memory by some initial attempt to resume the motor activity or posture I want to recall, that is to relive rather than merely recall the sensory perception. In contrast to this, it is more nearly possible, though never fully, to recreate by volun-

79] Compare Rapaport's distinction between the drive organization and the conceptual organization of memory, *Organization and Pathology of Thought,* pp. 710-712. While Rapaport, consistent with orthodox Freudian thought, ties the primitive organization of memory to need tension, believing that memories arise originally only with mounting need tension (p. 326, footnote 31), I am inclined to assume that they also can arise, and perhaps more often do, from the feeling of familiarity in re-experiencing a complex, global sensory-motor-affective state, without particular need tension in the sense of a striving for relief from tension. The development of a more distinctly perceptually and, eventually, conceptually organized memory may come about as the attention of the child develops and is more focused now on one now on another sensory aspect of such complex experiences with either positive or negative valences. These recurring aspects eventually are recognized as belonging to an "object," while the feeling aspects of these experiences are recognized as feelings of the perceiver. Such a development could be conceptualized as proceeding from a memory of global, fused, total states to a memory of distinct units with a distinct place in the mental organization of experience. Compare this also to Werner, *Comparative Psychology of Mental Development,* pp. 165-166b, and this volume, pp. 148-149.

tary recall a visual image of a former perception, as one does for example in making a drawing or painting from memory.

On the other hand, autocentric sensory experience often is vividly remembered in the passive, resensing kind of memory. Such memories occur either when actually sensing a similar sensation (taste, smell, etc.), or with the quality of a vivid and prolonged afterimage which continues long after the actual taste or smell stimulation has ceased, or they arise spontaneously in connection with the reactivation of a need, a longing, a nostalgia, or some other "complex" in the context of which the remembered perception originally occurred. The most frequent of these three major ways in which vivid and concrete memories of autocentric sensations occur is that of the prolonged afterimage which may last, with varying intensity, for several hours and which sometimes fluctuates in intensity or disappears and reappears. Lacking the subjective quality of a memory, it is an eidetic "image" of the taste or smell experience which is so much like the actual sensation that the individual experiencing it usually is quite convinced that the external source of the original sensation is still present.[80] For this reason, the phenomenon is usually not regarded as different from actual sensory experience. In the autocentric senses, especially smell and taste, the adult thus resembles the young child in whom, according to the findings of Jaensch and his students, eidetic experiences are the rule and, in sight, often precede the later development of memory images (*Vorstellungsbilder*), and who therefore cannot clearly distinguish present reality, memory, and phantasy.[81]

Because the autocentric senses (and the autocentric mode of perception in all the senses) remain throughout life so much closer to the state of fused perceptions in which there is no clear distinction between subject and object and between sensory quality, pleasure, or unpleasure, they are peculiarly apt to reactivate complex, global sensorimotor-affective states, and, conversely, eidetic experiences in the autocentric senses are apt to arise when such a complex is activated by a need, a wish, a longing, a mood.

Thus, a particular odor or taste or a proprioceptive sensation in

80] This has been pointed out by Henning, who adduces much evidence for his assumption that olfactory sensations are remembered *only* eidetically. Hans Henning, *Der Geruch* (J. A. Barth, Leipzig, 1924), pp. 290-293.

81] E. R. Jaensch, *Eidetic Imagery and Typological Methods of Investigation* (Harcourt, Brace & Co., New York, 1930), p. 85.

an accidentally assumed posture may magically revive with the greatest vividness a distant childhood memory, sometimes merely in the vivid feeling that this is exactly the "smell" of a childhood Sunday afternoon, or of a garment worn by one's mother, or of father's study, sometimes by bringing to mind in vivid detail a whole childhood scene. In Proust's work the recovery of the past is practically always linked to the accidental recurrence of a sensation in the autocentric perceptual mode, the smell and taste of the madeleine, the proprioceptive sensations caused by standing on uneven pavement, the touch of a napkin.[82]

Instances of such vivid revival by an autocentric sensation of past childhood experiences differ from *déjà vu* experiences in that the latter are characterized only by a strong feeling of familiarity, of having experienced exactly the same kind of thing before without, however, being able to recall when and how nor any details. Indeed, the *déjà vu* experience, as Claparède has pointed out, may go together with a *"non déjà vu"* feeling, the feeling of familiarity may appear "bizarre and paradoxical" because, unlike Proust's and similar experiences, it does not evoke anything from the past.[83]

From self-observations and communications from others I incline to believe that *déjà vu* experiences are actually more frequent in the autocentric than in the allocentric senses, particularly in the olfactory, gustatory, and proprioceptive (kinesthetic) senses. They are *déjà senti* rather than *déjà vu* experiences, and even when they are triggered by a visual perception they are not so much a sense of having seen this before as of having felt or experienced all this before, of passive resensing and refeeling rather than of visual recall. The reason for the affinity of *déjà vu* to the autocentric mode of perception lies, of course, again in the fusion between sensory and affective elements inherent in the autocentric mode. The feeling of familiarity is so strong and vivid in these cases because what is revived is a feeling attitude that may once have been fused with the particular sensory experience whereas the latter by itself cannot be recalled. Freud explains the *déjà vu* experience as caused by the arousal of a repressed wish by a present

[82] Compare the discussion in "On Memory and Childhood Amnesia," this volume, pp. 311-312.

[83] Claparède, "Recognition and 'Me-Ness,'" in Rapaport, *Organization and Pathology of Thought*, p. 60 and footnote 8.

perception which, in some ways, is similar to one in the situation where the wish first arose.[84] While this is true of some *déjà senti* experiences, there are others, probably even more frequent, where not a repressed, but merely a forgotten feeling, mood, state of mind is revived, often from an early period of life in which the quality of experiencing differed from that of the adult because it was not yet so thoroughly affected and transformed by the categories of conventional, causal logical adult thought.[85] Perhaps *déjà senti* experiences which are accompanied by a marked feeling of the *uncanny* are particularly likely to derive from a repressed striving which would cause anxiety or panic if it came into awareness.

Just as present autocentric sensations often elicit vivid memories of past experiences, the reverse can happen, too. States of longing, need, day-dreaming, and similar complex, undifferentiated moods connected with past experiences may cause spontaneous eidetic memory images to arise in the autocentric senses, particularly in the sense of smell. The same is true of states of awareness in which secondary thought processes recede because of fatigue, exhaustion, fever, the weakness of convalescence, etc. Conversely, in states of clear, conceptual thinking and alert awakeness, eidetic memories of smell are less likely to occur. As Henning points out, eidetic olfactory images are often, perhaps always, linked with an altered state of experiencing, or state of consciousness, a state which probably resembles the global experience of total states of being characteristic of early childhood.[86]

Allocentric perceptions in sight and hearing lend themselves much more readily to voluntary recall than perceptions in the autocentric sense modalities. A word or a melody heard is readily recalled by many people, and such memories usually do not have eidetic quality. Similarly, many people can recall and describe a house, the features of a person, the form and color of a flower, a

---

84] Freud, "Psychopathology of Everyday Life," *Basic Writings,* pp. 168-171.
85] Compare "On Memory and Childhood Amnesia," this volume, pp. 279-322. Compare also Schilder's explanation of *déjà vu* as the experience of two matching events one of which belongs to the sphere (an undifferentiated mode of experience) while the other (the present one) is fully developed. Paul Schilder, "Studies Concerning the Psychology and Symptomatology of General Paresis," in Rapaport, *Organization and Pathology of Thought,* p. 573 and footnote 274; also p. 502, footnote 17.
86] Henning, *Der Geruch,* p. 295.

leaf, an animal, a tree, and—if they have some talent in drawing—
they can draw from memory a reasonably good likeness of what
they have seen. The reason why voluntary recall of perceptions in
the allocentric mode is more readily feasible than of those in the
autocentric mode lies in the fact that the objectification inherent
in allocentric perception is closely related to concept formation.
Objects are recalled by their outstanding features. These are already abstractions of the full-fledged object. In the visual sphere,
it is the abstracting quality of form and structure which aids voluntary recall, and similarly, in the auditory sphere the conventionally used phonemes of speech and notes of music and the meanings
of words apprehended in listening are the abstractions recalled
from the much more complex actual sounds that the listener heard.
Of course, very often these conventional abstractions, which may
be called schemata or perception concepts, are all that the perceiver
takes in in the first place. Most of the time, most people do not
see the object fully nor do they hear speech or music fully, but
they perceive only the conventional schemata of things which
they expect to see and hear. Hence, it is easy for them to recall
these schemata, which are somewhere halfway between perception
and concept. There are much fewer such schemata available for
the autocentric senses than for the allocentric ones, because our
conscious, conceptual object world is built mostly on perceptions
in the allocentric, objectifying sense modalities.[87]

Obviously, then, the voluntary recall of visual and auditory
perceptions, while richer than that of smell and taste, has considerable limitations. The schemata recalled are shadows of the
real objects, although more substantial than the meager and scant
concepts available for voluntary recall in the sphere of autocentric
senses. Often the perceiver becomes aware of this and feels that
what he can conjure up in his mind by trying to recall what he
saw does not do justice at all to the concrete richness of the
object. But there are others who never become aware of this. They
do not see, and sometimes do not want to see, that there is more
even to a single leaf of a tree than its indented or smooth, pointed
or curving, oblong and thin or roundish outline, its dark or light
green color, and the arrangement of its veins. While most people

87] These aspects of perception and recall are discussed more fully in "On Memory and Childhood Amnesia," this volume, pp. 279-322.

do not particularly notice this kind of detail, even the botanist whose business it is to notice and describe it may not be aware that, no matter how detailed and accurate his description, it cannot encompass the leaf as fully as an act of focal attention does. The allocentric perception in such an act comprises, beyond the noticing of details, a global image[88] of the leaf which eludes all botanical classification and description, no matter how accurate and detailed. This global image is available to recall in a manner that differs from the active, voluntary recall of abstracted features. It need not be eidetic, yet it produces an awareness of something not being quite right whenever the attempt to articulate the memory image, in description or drawing, misses something of the essential quality of the object. Such an awareness often is largely negative: a knowledge that the object is not like what one just tried to represent in drawing or verbal description, that one did not "get" it, that it remains elusive. Yet, such negative awareness presupposes a more accurate and more encompassing, if not readily accessible, memory. From this memory arise the eidetic dream images in which often convincing likenesses of people one knows are seen in concrete richness.

The relation between the two basic perceptual modes and memory recurs in a similar fashion with regard to *communication*. What has been perceived in the autocentric mode, especially olfactory, gustatory, kinesthetic perceptions, eludes precise communication much more than do allocentric perceptions. A smell, a taste, a pain, the feeling of a posture defy description, while language has a much richer vocabulary for what can be seen or heard, especially when what is heard is language itself and the expression of conceptual thought by speech. It is in the nature of the complex, fused perceptions in the autocentric mode that they elude conceptualization and therewith linguistic description. Neither pain nor pleasure can be really communicated by description, but only by the expressive reactions of the cry or groan of pain and of the visible and audible enjoyment or rapture of pleasure. And just as the recall even of allocentric perceptions is limited by the conceptual organization of voluntary memory, so is their communication restricted by the abstractions of concepts in the face

88] Allocentric global perception differs from the primitive global perception of the infant and young child.

of the sensory realness and fullness of reality. Only *art*, by the evocative use of language or by the vision of the painter which transcends the conceptual confines of language, can express more of what man experiences in his sensory contact with the world than the limitations of ordinary speech permit.

8

Secondary Autocentricity

WITH THE HELP OF THE SEEMINGLY BOUNDLESS ENERGY OF THE child's exploratory drive, the great work of the gradual and expanding constitution of the object world proceeds, an achievement made possible by the shift from (primary) autocentric to predominantly allocentric perception. Reality, existing independently of the child, emerges for him. But in the very process of the emergence of the world of objects, on the new and higher level of predominantly allocentric perception, a *secondary autocentricity* develops, destined to play a tremendous role in man's perception of the world. While man could not live without the perspective of this secondary autocentricity, it can block his view of reality and lead to stagnation in a closed, autocentric world. Whether and to what extent he can transcend secondary autocentricity and retain or expand his world-openness is therefore crucial for his experience of other people and of the world around him.

Primary autocentricity in perception is apparent in two major ways: (1) in the close linkage of pleasure-unpleasure feelings with perception and the relative lack of objectification as observable in the lower senses throughout life and in the early stages of perceptual development in all senses; (2) in the negative reaction toward any new stimulus, any change, because it disrupts a state of protectedness and satisfaction of all needs in more or less complete embeddedness, as can be observed in embryonic life and, to a considerable extent, in the life of the neonate. These two major forms of autocentric perception recur on a higher level and therefore in somewhat changed and more complex guises in secondary autocentricity.

(1) Objects are most frequently perceived from the perspective of how they will serve a certain *need* of the perceiver, or how they can be *used* by him for some purpose, or how they have to be *avoided* in order to prevent pain, displeasure, injury, or discomfort. All these purposes and needs may be quite articulately conscious, or they may manifest themselves in vague "background" feelings, or they may not be in awareness at all. When the object is perceived in this way then the predominating feature of the perception is not the object in its own right, but those of its aspects which relate to the perceiver's more or less conscious feelings of the need or purpose which the object is to serve, or of the fear which makes him want to avoid it. In other words, parallel to primary autocentric perception, in which the sensory feeling of the perceiver predominates over the object qualities, is the secondary autocentricity of the perceiver's feeling of need, fear, purpose which exercises a decisive influence on how the object will be perceived and, conversely, on what aspects of the object will *not* be perceived, what will be emphasized and what will be neglected. This is especially apparent in the recurrence of the autocentric perception of "things-of-action" on the higher level of object perception, where it takes the form of the perception of "objects-of-use" and "objects-to-be-avoided" (the latter corresponding to those "things-of-action" which, at the earlier stage, were signals for actions of aversion and flight).

(2) The primary autocentric view of most stimuli as disturbances of embeddedness recurs in the form of the fear and avoidance of a full encounter and of everything new or strange that might disturb the secondary embeddedness in a closed pattern or routine, which may be the pattern of a particular culture, a particular social group, a personal routine pattern of life, or, usually, a combination of all these. These two aspects of secondary autocentricity are closely interrelated and merge into each other. They are discussed separately here for the sake of a clearer presentation.

By "objects-of-use" I mean objects which are perceived chiefly from the perspective of their usefulness, uselessness, or of the need to avoid them, within the framework of the purposes and needs of the perceiver. They belong to a later, more differentiated phase of development than the things-of-action; but to some extent the objects-of-use and the things-of-action shade gradually into each other. The object-of-use emerges with consciously purposive action as distinguished from drive-action. The child who wants to get something which is higher than his arm can reach will climb on a stool or a table to get at it. The stool or the table now become "steps," i.e. objects-of-use for a certain purpose, which, in this case, is a purpose different from the one for which they were made. But to the eagerly reaching child only their "step" aspect may be the decisive perceptual feature at this moment.

In all our daily lives we deal with objects-of-use a great deal of the time. We could not function if we perceived fully every object we deal with. The child learns the object-of-use perspective from the grown-ups. Leaving aside the aesthetic qualities of objects, the object-of-use aspect leads to an adequate perception of most man-made objects, since they are designed to serve a definite purpose. But the objects of nature, too, often become for us nothing but objects-of-use, and we may then become blind to what they are in their own right. Paul Valéry, in his essay on the painter Berthe Morisot, has said that the useful banishes the real and the meaning of objects their form, that we see the future or the past but not the brush strokes of the pure present moment.[1]

Marx emphasizes the crippling effect of the exclusive object-of-use perspective. He writes: "The sense dominated by the raw, practical need is a limited sense only. For a starving man the peculiarly human form of food does not exist, but merely the general quality of food. It could be just as well food in the rawest, most primitive form. His eating activity would be in no way different from the animal's feeding. A man worried, in need, has no senses for the most beautiful spectacle. The dealer in minerals sees only their mercantile value, but not their beauty and their peculiar nature and quality."[2]

Cézanne, too, describes this peculiar blindness; he said (in a conversation with J. Gasquet): "Sometimes I have accompanied a farmer behind his cart driving to the market to sell his potatoes. He had never seen, what we would call seeing; he had never seen

---

1] The essay is at this writing available to me only in Rilke's German translation: Paul Valéry, "Tante Berthe," in R. M. Rilke, *Gesammelte Werke* (Insel Verlag, Leipzig, 1927), Vol. VI, p. 356.

2] Author's translation from Karl Marx, "Nationalökonomie und Philosophie," in Siegfried Landshut, ed., *Die Frühschriften* (Alfred Kröner Verlag, Stuttgart, 1953), pp. 242-43.

Sainte Victoire. They know what has been planted there, along the road, how the weather is going to be tomorrow, whether Sainte Victoire has his cloud cap on or not; they feel it like the animals do, like a dog who knows what this piece of bread is, only from their needs; but that the trees are green, and that this green is a tree, that this earth is red, and that this red rubble and boulders are hills, I really do not believe that most of them feel that, that they know it, outside of their unconscious feeling for the useful."[3]

Cézanne describes here not merely a man who, in the performance of a concrete task and in the pursuit of a specific purpose, sees the objects which he needs for the completion of the task within that context as objects-of-use, not somebody who has this perspective only temporarily and within a limited situation, but a person for whom it has become the only perspective from which he views the entire world at all times. For him the world, instead of being something of which he is an infinitesimal part, has become a world-of-use and he sees it exclusively from the perspective of how it will serve his needs. This demonstrates the important difference between the temporary and situationally conditioned perception of an object-of-use in the service of a particular, passing need or purpose and an enduring, habitual, encompassing perceptual and experiential system in which everything is seen and reacted to from the perspective of how it will fit in with a personal (or collective) frame of reference to which the person clings and without which he would feel lost or adrift. In such a system all objects become objects-of-use because they belong to a "world-of-use" or a "world-of-need." This implies that our "use" of objects extends far beyond the sphere of such use for a limited, practical purpose. For example, when perception stops at mere *recognition* of an object, as it does in most cases, this, too, is perception of "objects-of-use." When one walks along the street on the daily way to work or to home, when one glances around a room at home, and on innumerable other occasions, perception proceeds only to the point of fleeting recognition of the familiar objects, to the point where the recognized object can be filed away by its familiar label, as it were. We look around and say to ourselves, silently and implicitly: "This is the store at the corner

3] Author's translation from Ernesto Grassi, *Kunst und Mythos* (Rowohlt, Hamburg, 1957), pp. 116-17, footnote 2. Compare also Jakob von Uexküll, *Streifzüge durch die Umwelten von Tieren und Menschen* (Rowohlt, Hamburg, 1956).

of X street, this is the red house, this the tree in front of it, these are people going to work, this is the bus stop; this is the chair and the floor lamp, the desk, the window, the bed, etc." While we see all these objects, in this kind of perspective we do not see them fully, in their own right. What is the use we put them to when we just recognize them in this way and then let our glance pass on to some other object which, in turn, we quickly file away as "recognized"? We use the objects for orientation and reassurance that we are moving and being in our familiar, accustomed everyday world. This way of seeing plays a tremendous role in man's life and, in a different way, in the life of animals. It is linked with the often hardly noticeable, but very important affect of familiarity. We take this way of perceiving for granted, and most of the time most people do not question whether there is any other kind of perception; they are implicitly satisfied that what they see in this way is all there is to see about these things with which their daily life is surrounded. Yet, the objects of the world never appear fully in this kind of perception, but only an impoverished, meager, and scanty aspect of them. A comparison of our usual "recognizing" perception of a chair with, for example, Van Gogh's painting of his chair[4] will make apparent the vast difference between a full perception of the object and a perception in which mere recognition of the familiar takes place.

While perception in the service of orientation and reassurance by means of the recognition of the familiar is the most frequently occurring and most important example of the more subtle and pervasive type of perception of objects-of-use, it is by no means the only one. Even beyond the sphere of the reassuring recognition of the familiar objects of everyday life, we tend to avoid the full encounter with the object and instead to perceive only those aspects of it which will permit us to fit it into certain preconceptions and expectations with which we approach it, often without even being aware of these preconceptions. We give it a name, file it away under some label, satisfied that now we know it, when actually by this very process we have barred our way to its full perception and have used it for some other purpose, for example for the purpose of feeling that now we know more, have seen the

4] Reproduced in Meyer Schapiro, *Vincent van Gogh* (Harry N. Abrams, New York, 1950), p. 90.

thing that our friends told us we simply must see so that we, too, can talk about it at the next party, etc.

Perception in the service of *scientific* purposes also usually is perception of an object-of-use. The scientist, in these cases, looks at the object with one or more hypotheses and with the purpose of his research in mind and thus "uses" the object to corroborate or disprove a hypothesis, but does not encounter the object as such, in its own fullness. Also, modern natural science has as its main goal prediction, i.e. the power to manipulate objects in such a way that certain predicted events will happen. This means that only those aspects of the object are deemed relevant which make it suitable for such manipulation or control. Hence, the scientist usually will tend to perceive the object merely from the perspective of his power to control certain events or processes which will affect the object in a predicted way. That is to say that his view of the object will be determined by the ends which he pursues in his experimentation. Thus it becomes an object-of-use. He may achieve a great deal in this way and add important data to our knowledge, but to the extent to which he remains within the framework of this perspective he will not perceive the object in its own right. He may learn to know something very useful *about* the object, but he will not encounter or know the object itself. His knowledge remains "operational," he is only concerned with the question whether a particular approach will "work" toward a particular end, whether it can be used to produce a particular result, and he perceives the object as an "object-of-use" for the operation which he intends to perform with it. Needless to say, not all scientists perceive the objects in which they are interested in this way all the time. Their attitude undergoes changes. But in their attempt as well as in many other people's attempts to fit some object or phenomenon into some system, preconception, or hypothesis, one can often observe a blinding of themselves toward the pure and full being of the object itself. Perception, then, may become almost an act of aggressive violence in which the perceiver, like Procrustes with his hapless victims, cuts off those aspects of the object which he cannot use for his purposes. Instead of approaching the object with complete openness and receptiveness, he approaches it with the determination to see how it will fit into this or that scheme which he has in mind, or whether he can produce this or that effect on it or with it. Of course, such an approach is entirely legitimate and can be very useful for the purposes the perceiver has in mind. I want to draw attention merely to the fact that it cannot lead to the fullest and richest (allocentric) kind of object perception, but only to a limited, one-sided, and sometimes quite distorting perception.

The most important "object" of perception in the life of most men is other people. For this reason the perception of other people is the most significant area for the study of autocentric perception (both primary and secondary). Also, the perception of people either as objects-of-use (and need, or fear) or as persons in their own right, while a very complex process, nevertheless becomes more readily apparent and the connection between the personality of the perceiver and the autocentric distortion occurring in his view of others becomes more transparent than it does, as a rule, in the perception of nature and of man-made objects. This does not imply that the autocentric view of objects other than people is rarer, but rather that it is often more difficult to observe and to demonstrate. By comparing the accounts by different people of how they see the same person, especially if one knows this person well, it can become strikingly apparent how fully or partially, deeply or superficially, clearly or distortedly one person perceives as compared with another. This is as true if the account concerns a person whom they have only *seen* and seen only *once*, so that the impression is a purely visual one, as it is if they have seen and heard the person many times and are quite familiar with him or her. These differences in perception are well known, yet I have the feeling that they have not been taken sufficiently seriously nor considered as palpable and real by the psychology of perception. They appear, again, very strikingly if we compare portraits by different painters. Although the great painters generally have a much fuller, richer, and deeper perception of nature, objects, and people than the average person, still there is even among the most skilled painters an amazing difference in the depth and fullness of perception. A comparison of the best portraits by van Dyck with those of his contemporary and compatriot Rembrandt will show how Rembrandt's eye penetrated to the core of the human being he painted, while van Dyck, however alive and real his portraits are, remains relatively superficial and narrow compared with the depth and fullness of Rembrandt. This difference is not one of technical skill and mastery, in which van Dyck was as accomplished as anybody. It is a difference in depth and completeness of perception, of vision.

The differences in the perception of other people are largely due to the difference in the degree and type of autocentric factors in the perceiver's attitude or the degree to which he is capable of fully allocentric perception. Most people, most of the time, see other people as objects-of-use (i.e. objects of need, fear, or use for some purpose).[5] Socially the most outstanding and widespread examples in our civilization of this kind of perception of other people are the perception of others primarily in terms of their social position, status, "importance," and perception of others in terms of their usefulness as employees or customers or business contacts. Perception of others according to their social position may range from such gross examples as the hunt for celebrities, for getting to know the "important" people, to all the subtle and insidious forms of the wish to mix only with the "right" kind of other people. In all these cases the perceiver's senses are not directed toward and receptive to the other person as a human being, but primarily to the innumerable gross or subtle signs which will indicate to them whether this person is or is not "worth while" in terms of the perceiver's scale of desirable social position and status.

The use for which the employer needs the employee, while different from the use of social position, also results usually in a perception of the employee as an object-of-use. This was, of course, very clearly apparent in a slave economy where the buyer would appraise a slave, that is, view him much the same way he might

5] The concept of people as objects-of-use is related to Binswanger's concept of "taking by" (taking a person by a partial aspect only), just as the allocentric perception of people is related to his concept of the knowledge of their existence (*Daseinserkenntnis*) in the mode of love. Binswanger arrives at his concepts by the method of philosophical (ontological) anthropology. He emphasizes that this method is not, and does not pretend to be, an attempt to explain man's condition in a causal fashion. My main interest is in the attempt to understand genetically and developmentally certain phenomena in human perception. These phenomena come into view only by the effort to observe and describe what the phenomena given in perceptual experience are. The difference in approach accounts for the main differences between Binswanger's view and mine, apart, of course, from the fact that his subject is man's existence (*Dasein*) while mine is limited to perception. That in spite of these major differences we arrive at similar results would seem to corroborate the hypothesis presented here. See Ludwig Binswanger, *Grundformen und Erkenntnis menschlichen Daseins* (Max Nichans Verlag, Zürich, 1953), pp. 300-381, and, regarding man's relation to objects, pp. 275-300. Compare also his more recent book, *Schizophrenie* (Günther Noske, Pfullingen, 1957). See also Erich Fromm, "Man Is Not a Thing," *Saturday Review of Literature*, March 16, 1957, pp. 9-11.

view a work-horse. It is equally apparent when in hiring a worker the only perspective from which he is viewed is whether his actual work output will contribute to the greatest possible profit. In recent times, especially in hiring employees for higher positions or for other than physical labor, there has been an increasing trend to look also at the personality of the job applicant. However, while more aspects of the person are taken into account, this means merely that now the personality is viewed as an object-of-use where formerly only such factors as physical fitness, skill, endurance, industriousness may have been looked for.[6]

The salesman and the advertiser who "size up" the customer are looking for the weak spot which they can exploit in order to persuade him to buy their product. Examples of perceiving people as objects-of-use from which the perceiver hopes to profit in one way or another, financially or in his social position, could easily be multiplied. They all illustrate the culturally patterned autocentric view of people, ubiquitous in our civilization. If this is a person's prevailing or only perspective, it leads to an alienation from the human qualities in others and in himself, because he is likely to see not only others but also himself as an object on the market whose value depends on how much he is "in demand," an object to be used by others for their ends as he uses them for his.[7]

Socioeconomic purposes, however, are not the only ones which lead to an object-of-use perspective on other people (and oneself). The failure to emerge from childlike dependence, with its needs and fears, also leads to an autocentric perception of people as objects-of-use. These two sources of the object-of-use perspective are not unrelated to each other. For example, very often the dependent person, driven to use others as powerful, parent-like protectors, etc., will also be inclined to view people from the perspective of whether their social position makes them more desirable

6] I have shown elsewhere how the very structure and methodology of certain personality tests is affected by the "object-of-use" perspective on the human being. See Ernst Schachtel, "Zum Begriff und zur Diagnose der Persönlichkeit in den 'Personality Tests,'" *Zeitschrift fuer Sozialforschung*, 1937, 6:597-624.

Of course, *any* personality test can be applied with the "object-of-use" perspective, even if this perspective has not been built into the test. The results, e.g. of so-called unstructured tests, are also always dependent on what the tester is looking for. The "object-of-use" perspective affects not only direct sensory perception of people but also the most complex diagnostic procedures and, of course, the whole way of *thinking* about people.

7] Compare Erich Fromm, *The Sane Society* (Rinehart & Co., New York, 1955), pp. 139-149.

and useful for the role of protector and provider and will seek to be adopted by these people. In the psychoanalytic situation, one can see not infrequently patients who not only seek in the analyst a parent who will be better than they felt their own parents were, but also look for social advancement, as though by being "adopted" by the analyst they will be "elevated" to a higher sociocultural sphere.

The autocentric perspective of the dependent personality usually is a result of a narcissistic attitude which blocks the full view of the other person and limits perception to those (real or distorted) aspects which have a bearing on the neurotic demands and fears of the perceiver. He is looking *for* something in the other person rather than looking at the other person. What he is looking for is determined by what he wants to get from the other person and/or what he is afraid of. The effect of this outlook is, at best, that it leads to a very partial view only and, at worst, to a distortion of even those aspects of the other person which have a bearing on the perceiver's needs and fears. The psychoanalytic literature, particularly in the description of transference phenomena, abounds with examples of such partial views and distortions. While these usually are couched in terms of the concept or image which the analysand has of the analyst or of other significant people in his life, it is obvious that they profoundly affect the patient's actual sensory perceptions of other people, their behavior, their bearing, their physiognomic characteristics, their expressive movements, their voices, ways of speaking, etc.

Primary autocentricity, while more radically narcissistic, is usually more accurate in the perception of the narcissistically attracting or repelling and frightening aspects of the other person than is secondary autocentricity. Infants and small children usually can "smell" and sense hostility, tenseness, or anxiousness (or, conversely, warmth, relaxedness, security) in others more accurately than the average older child or adult. They feel it as discomfort or anxiety in themselves or, rather, as a vital sensation (Werner) in which there is no clear demarcation between felt discomfort and the impact of the other person. The older child and the neurotically narcissistic adult are much more likely to get confused by, or fall for, professed attitudes, reaction-formations, or overcompensations, because they orient themselves in their search for the other person as an "object-of-use" more by what they have learned as the conventional and currently acceptable signs of the traits for which they keep a lookout. To them the vital sensation indicating the presence of a pleasurable or unpleasurable, comforting or discomforting attitude in the other person has been replaced by what passes currently as the criteria for a "nice" person or a "not nice" person. Autocentric perception, thus, can be accurate or inaccurate, depending, among other factors, on how close or distant it is from the sphere of "vital sensations"; but even where it is sensitive and accurate, it remains a partial, fragmentary perception, since its viewpoint, rather than giving an allocentric view of the other person, is attuned to the perceiver's narcissistic needs and fears.

The autocentric view of objects and people is part of the human condition, just as is the possibility of and development toward allocentric perception. I emphasize this because I want to avoid giving the impression that the occurrence of secondary autocentric perception, as such, is something "bad" or is always a symptom of neurosis or other forms of mental illness. However, if autocentric perception is, or tends to become, the only mode of experiencing the world and other people, then it is a sign either of mental sickness or of stagnation of human life. Conversely, the greater the role of allocentric perception is in a person's life, the richer and fuller is this person's life and the more truly alive is he. These statements will become more meaningful if we now turn to a more detailed analysis of the second way in which autocentric perception manifests itself, namely as the consequence of embeddedness in a closed world, which leads to the experience of any new stimulus or any change as something disturbing and to be avoided. On the *primary* level, this aspect of autocentricity is characteristic of the intrauterine world and predominates in the world of the neonate and young infant. On the *secondary* level it results from secondary embeddedness in a closed pattern of life, by which man seeks to re-establish something akin to the security of the womb *after* the object world has emerged for him in the exploratory play and learning of childhood.

The problem of autocentric perception due to secondary embeddedness in the closed world of the familiar can be seen concretely when one compares the average perceptual experience of most people in our civilization (and probably in our world) with that of the great artists, poets, scientists, and the great masters in the art of living, and with the perceptual experience of quite a number of people in moments of being fully alive and fully turned toward the object of their perception (i.e. without wanting to *use* it and without being in need of it, that is, dependent on it).[8] The usual perceptual experience is one of recognition of something either already familiar or quickly labeled and filed away in some familiar category. It does not enrich the perceiver, but it may reassure him—usually without his awareness—that everything is "all right," meaning that everything is as expected and accustomed. If the act of perception were to continue it would bore him. Extremes of boredom are avoided, more or less, only by the quick succession of a variety of familiar or easily labeled perceptions or, as in many entertainments such as detective stories, television shows, etc., by the rearrangement of familiar elements in such a way that some suspense or surprise is effected, without deepening or adding to the substance of the perceiver's experience.[9] Compared with this the fullest perception of the object, i.e. the allocentric perception, is characterized by an inexhaustible and ineffable quality, by the profoundest interest in the object, and by the enriching, refreshing, vitalizing effect which the act of perception has on the perceiver. The main reason for this difference lies in the fact that the fully allocentric perception (especially of nature, people, and the great works of art) always breaks through and transcends the confines of the labeled, the familiar, and establishes a relation in which a direct encounter with the object itself, instead of with one or more of its labeled and familiar aspects, takes place.[10] What is seen (heard, sensed, felt, experienced) in

8] Compare A. H. Maslow's as yet unpublished paper "Cognition of Being in the Peak Experiences," read at the September 1956 convention of the American Psychological Association. His "peak experience" is characterized by what I call allocentric perception.

9] Most people in our civilization, especially in their leisure time, live in constant flight from boredom which they barely manage to escape. If they did not escape it but really experienced it, it would assume the unbearable quality of a *negative passion* of which Leopardi said: "The emptiness of the human heart, the indifference, the absence of any passion is boredom, and yet boredom is passion. . . . Thus it is that the living cannot really ever be without passion. This passion, if the heart at the moment is captured by nothing else, we call boredom. Boredom is proof of the uninterrupted duration of passion. Were it not passion, it would not exist when nothing occupies the soul." Author's translation from G. Leopardi, *Zibaldone*, quoted by Grassi in Thure von Uexküll and Ernesto Grassi, *Wirklichkeit als Geheimnis und Auftrag* (Verlag A. Francke, Bern, 1945), p. 127. As Grassi points out, in the suffocation of boredom man experiences, on the one hand, nothingness or nonbeing, and—in the *unbearable* quality of boredom—being.

10] Matisse describes this thus: "Seeing itself is a creative act which demands an effort. All we see in our everyday life is more or less distorted by our acquired

this encounter can never be fully rendered even by the greatest artist. It is to this basic fact that Mallarmé's paradoxical statement refers: "The essential in a work [of art] consists precisely in that which is not expressed."[11] However the artist, poet, and—in a different way—some scientists are what they are by virtue of the fact that they have the avocation and the skill to communicate *some* aspect of what they perceived, beyond the realm of the already familiar, to those who are willing and able to listen to, or look at, their communication. In the moments of allocentric perception at its fullest we always are at the frontiers of our familiar world, breaking through the enclosing wall of explicit or implicit labels and encountering the inexhaustible other, which transcends all labels with which man tries to capture and tame it, so that he may use it and so that its unfamiliarity will no longer disquiet him.

Allocentric perception, thus, always transcends, in some respect, that part of the labeled, traditional, cultural world with which the perceiver is familiar. The more original the mind and personality of the perceiver is, the greater is the likelihood that what he perceives sometimes will transcend *"reality"* as known in the everyday currency of his culture. This touches on the ambiguous and indefinite meaning of the concept of "reality," especially as it is often used in psychiatric parlance and even more often in the advice offered by well-meaning relatives that some idealistic plan or view of the adolescent does not take into account "reality." This kind of "reality" is usually not at all concerned with the inexhaustible reality of the world but is circumscribed by the narrow confines of the familiar, of "public opinion," of the way of life of a certain social group, a class, a family. A person who perceives only what belongs to this kind of "reality" will be blind and deaf as far as allocentric perception is concerned. While such blindness is perhaps particularly widespread in our civilization, it has existed always. Parmenides, about 480 B.C., warned against it: "May habit, well and often worn, not force you on this way: to let rove glanceless eye and noisy ear and tongue. . . ."[12] Parmenides

habits." Author's translation from Walter Hess, *Dokumente zum Verständnis der modernen Malerei* (Rowohlt, Hamburg, 1956), p. 37.

11] Quoted in a letter by Gauguin, in Hess, *op. cit.*, p. 32. The great work of art or poetry conveys the quality of the ineffable and inexhaustible which becomes apparent to perception in the truly allocentric encounter.

12] Compare Hermann Diels, *Die Fragmente der Vorsokratiker* (Weidmannsche Buchhandlung, Berlin, 1906), Vol. 1, p. 115. Compare also Fragment 6, p. 117.

warns the thinker against using eye and ear in the way in which they are usually used, unseeing and unhearing because of the force of habit, that is, seeing and hearing only what habit makes everyone see and hear. He issues this warning in order to let the thinker beware not to consider the ubiquitous opining which has already prejudged everything and anything as *the* way of thinking.[13]

The concept of allocentricity does not imply that allocentric perception excludes primary autocentric elements. Man experiences the world with *all* his senses, his perception is intersensory, comprising both the more allocentric (higher) and the autocentric (lower) senses, and also, within the functioning of a single sense, for example sight, comprising processes in the predominantly allocentric and in a more autocentric mode. To perceive a flower fully, the openness toward the charm of its color is as important as the grasp of its form and the kinesthetic experience[14] of how the stem rises up and is slightly bowed by the weight of the blossom.

Thus, allocentric perception in its most complete form is characterized not by the absence of primary autocentric sensations, but rather by fully turning to and complete openness toward the object. The perceiver, in allocentric perception, is open to the object with all his senses and sensibilities[15] and shows a complete absorption or interest in it which, as long as it lasts, has a timeless quality, i.e. it fills the perceiver so completely that he does not keep track of time, just as he is oblivious of everything else while he is thus fully engaged in the encounter with the object of his perception. The object is perceived in its suchness, without any labeling, naming, classifying, thinking of possible similarities, relations to other objects, etc.

These latter activities may follow the actual act of allocentric perception and they do follow it when we try to articulate the creative experience of such perception and to relate it to other experiences, to our thinking, our knowledge, etc. If great care is

13] The above is taken from Heidegger's interpretation of the Parmenides fragment; the author's translation of the fragment follows Heidegger's German version. Martin Heidegger, *Was heisst Denken?* (Max Niemeyer Verlag, Tübingen, 1954), p. 121.

14] Such kinesthetic experience involves autocentric proprioceptive elements. I have shown elsewhere that in empathic perception, especially of other people, kinesthetic factors play a significant role. Ernest G. Schachtel, "Projection and Its Relation to Character Attitudes and Creativity in the Kinesthetic Responses," *Psychiatry*, 1950, 13:69-100, especially 71-76.

15] Compare to this point p. 227.

not taken, these afterthoughts may obliterate much or all of the experience, because of the ease with which we succumb to the temptation of what seems a felicitous phrase or to a penchant for "making sense" or for a "systematic" or "reasonable" view of things, to the many viewpoints on the object of perception which so readily then usurp the place of the experience itself. In discursive thought we cannot help but think *about* the percept, that is about one or another aspect of it, but we cannot recapture it fully, although, in a sense, it has become part of us.

The effort to preserve the allocentric vision of the true object in recording it in words or paint or sculpture is the never ending struggle of the poet, the writer, the artist. In this effort they have to examine the words and concepts, or the materials used for the work of art and their particular application in canvas or sculpture, as to whether they express truly and precisely the original, intuitive perception. The words and materials now are looked upon as objects of use, in being tested and tried as to their fitness to perpetuate and communicate the artist's vision of the real in its suchness.[16] The reason why sketches often are so much truer to their object than the finished painting is that they are a more spontaneous, direct expression of the original vision. The Japanese ink painting (*sumi e*) forces the artist to render his vision directly, without corrections and without hesitation. This eliminates the trial and error of testing from the artistic object-of-use perspective. Instead, it imposes a lifelong discipline through which the artist eventually arrives at such a profound vision of his object and such a concentrated, yet relaxed mastery of his medium that vision and execution approach each other and, ideally, become one.

Fully allocentric perception has often been described, and the descriptions coincide in saying that in such perception the perceiver establishes a relationship in which he is completely filled with the percept, as though he were one with it, or became the object seen. I want to quote a few such descriptions. Dante wrote: "Who paints a figure, if he cannot be it, cannot draw it." ("Chi pinge figura, si non può esser lei, non la può porre."[17]) Cézanne

16] Compare to the foregoing Joyce Cary, *Art and Reality* (Harper & Brothers, New York, 1958), 31-34, 84-103. The elusiveness of the artist's allocentric vision (see Cary, pp. 94-95) is in some ways similar to that of the dream, because neither fits the conventional conceptual and verbal schemata. More about this below, pp. 279-308.

17] Quoted by Ananda K. Coomaraswamy, *The Transformation of Nature in Art* (Dover Publications, New York, 1956), p. 7.

said: "The artist's will must become silent, he must silence in himself all the voices of prejudice, must forget, become quiet, a perfect echo. Nature out there and in here [he hits his forehead] must penetrate each other. . . ." Braque said: "One must not just depict the objects, one must penetrate into them, and one must oneself become the object."[18]

In Japanese painting this complete turning to and becoming one with the object is a traditional principle, called "living movement" (*kokoro mochi*; in Chinese: *sei do*). This principle is taught to all art students. It requires that the artist at the moment of painting must feel the very nature of his subject. If it is a tree, "he is urged when painting it to feel the strength which shoots through the branches and sustains the limbs. Or if a flower, to try to feel the grace with which it expands or bows its blossoms." If he paints "the sea coast with its cliffs and moving waters, at the moment of putting the wave-bound rocks into the picture he must feel that they are being placed there to resist the fiercest movement of the ocean, while to the waves in turn he must give an irresistible power to carry all before them."[19]

The "oneness" established with the object in the intense relatedness of such allocentric perception is different from the "oneness" with the objects with which autocentric perception starts out in life. The former requires a complete focusing of all the perceiver's perceptual and experiential faculties on the object, so that it is experienced in the fullest possible way; the latter results from the narcissistic situation in which no object exists for the perceiver and all impinging objects tend to be experienced merely as states of the perceiver's comfort or discomfort, as "vital sensations." The former presupposes a temporary eclipse, of all the perceiver's egocentric thoughts and strivings, of all preoccupations with self and self-esteem, and a full turning towards the object; the latter antedates the birth of the self as a conscious object of worry, ambition, fear, need, and antedates the experience of "I" as separate from the world. The oneness of allocentric perception leads not to a *loss* of self, but to a heightened feeling of aliveness.

Freud, and the psychology of perception in general, does not

18] The quotations from Cézanne and Braque are taken from Hess, *Dokumente zum Verständnis der modernen Malerei*, pp. 19, 54.

19] Henry P. Bowie, *On the Laws of Japanese Painting* (Dover Publications, New York), pp. 77-79; compare also pp. 35-37 about the strength of the brush stroke which transmits these feelings (*fude no chikara*).

pay any attention to the very palpable difference between the everyday perception in which objects are merely recognized and thereby disposed of, and allocentric perception, although many people have experiences approaching fully allocentric perception. These experiences differ by their vividness, aliveness, concreteness very distinctly from the more or less gray uniformity of quickly orienting cliché perception. However, Freud deals with the experience of oneness with the outer world at one point, where he states that the "oceanic feeling," i.e. the feeling of being one with the universe, as described by many mystics, is but a recurrence of an early infantile experience which knows of no separation from an outer world of reality.[20] This view seems to me open to question. One has to distinguish between the motivational energy with which man, in his separateness, longs to establish a bond, to be united in some way with the world outside him, and the way in which he tries to realize this striving. It is quite likely that the fact of separation from the mother and the many subsequent experiences of separateness are the original, genetic *reason* why man tries to establish unity again. But such unity can be established not only in a regressive way, by the wish to return to the womb, but also in a new way, on a higher level of development, by loving relatedness to others and to the world.[21] Whether the oceanic feeling is essentially a return to the womb or to a state in which there is as yet no awareness of an outer world, or whether it is a union with the world on a higher level is a question which probably can be decided only on the basis of analysis of the individual experience.

In one respect the problem of the oceanic feeling borders on the experience of oneness in allocentric perception. In the latter, while a concrete object is perceived, it is always perceived not as isolated from the rest of life but as containing in it the *mysterium tremendum* of life, of being. This is as true in the perception of another person as it is in the perception of any object of nature or of a true work of art. This probably is the reason why the object of such perception is always inexhaustible and not to be encom-

20] Sigmund Freud, "Das Unbehagen in der Kultur," *Gesammelte Werke* (Imago Publishing Co., London, 1948), Vol. XIV, pp. 421-431.
21] Compare to this point especially Erich Fromm, *The Art of Loving* (Harper & Brothers, New York, 1956), pp. 7-32. For a historical view of basically the same human problem see Erich Kahler, *Man the Measure* (George Braziller, New York, 1956).

passed, but only hinted at, by any description or label. Here I do not mean that first something is perceived and then connected by thought to related objects or the rest of the world, but that there is a direct perception of life, of being, which permeates this object and vibrates with it. In this sense, the relatedness to a particular, very concrete object in fully allocentric perception is also always a relatedness to something more than just an isolated, separate, single object.

Compared with the intense interest in the world around them which most children show, and with the complete absorption in the object of which man is capable in allocentric perception, it is very striking to even a casual observer of the contemporary world how relatively rare it is that people retain and develop the capacity for allocentric perception and the alive interest in the world that underlies this capacity. One might well say that boredom is the malaise of our civilization with its relative large amount of leisure time and that this sickness is manifested both in the wide spread of acute boredom and in the frantic activities to escape from boredom.[22] The question is all the more puzzling, then, why the fascination with the world that we see in the eyes of all but the very sickest children is lost by most people in later life, when it is quite clear how much richer and more rewarding is a life which retains and develops this capacity than is one which takes place in an orbit in which more or less everything is felt to be known and familiar, while at the same time nothing is ever really seen and known. At this point I want to offer a few speculations and observations which might help toward an eventual clarification of this puzzling question.

Language provides a clue to the problem. In English, that which we recognize readily because we have had prolonged and often repeated acquaintance with it is called *familiar*. The word thus links the family with the feeling we have in recognizing the accustomed, the well-known. I believe that this link is of basic importance in the understanding of the problems of (autocentric) perception of the familiar and (allocentric) perception of the new. The closest translation of "familiar" into German would be *vertraut*. An object that is *vertraut* is one with which one has a long and close acquaintance or, literally, a relationship of trust (*ver-*

22] Compare the central position of the concept of *ennui* in French existentialist thought.

trauen = to trust). Thus, both words refer to feeling "at home," to the feeling of trusting only that which belongs to the world of the family, the things that one has always known, and, by implication, to the opposite feeling: namely the fear and mistrust of that which is not of the family, which is strange and new.[23] Paradoxically, one might add that people usually know least that which is familiar to them, because they take it for granted, they view it always from the same perspective, they no longer see it at all, or only in the most routine manner. Hence the boredom with the familiar, which, if viewed in an allocentric way, is just as new and inexhaustible as any other object in the world. In fact, one might say that creativity consists in the art of seeing the familiar fully in its inexhaustible being, without using it autocentrically for purposes of remaining embedded in it and reassured by it.

The tendency to trust only the familiar and to avoid, or be frightened and alarmed by, the unknown has a long history in evolution. In the lowest animals any change, the appearance of any new stimulus, causes a negative reaction of avoidance. The higher up we go in the evolutionary scale, the more clearly the immediate avoidance reaction changes into an alarm and excitement reaction. In the higher mammals we can observe, side by side with the alarm reaction, a drive to *seek* the unknown, to *explore* the new, and to seek excitement. They show an ambivalent reaction to the new and strange: they seem both to seek out and to avoid the excitement it causes. Hebb and his co-workers have shown that the higher the intelligence of the mammal, the more it is prone to emotional excitement. It will have many more "irrational" fears and excitement in relation to strange and new objects, which the lower animal simply avoids, but it will also seek more excitement.[24] The drive to seek out and explore the new is strongest in the childhood of animals and men, in the period of exploratory play.[25] This is the period during which they get acquainted

23] Compare also the relation between the words *habitat, habitation* and *habit, habitual;* similarly between the German *Wohnung, wohnen* and *gewohnt, Gewohnheit,* and the French *habiter, habitation* and *habitude, habitué.*

24] D. O. Hebb and W. R. Thompson, "The Social Significance of Animal Studies," in Gardner Lindzey, ed., *Handbook of Social Psychology* (Addison-Wesley Publishing Co., Cambridge, Mass., 1954), pp. 532-561. Also, Hebb, "The Mammal and His Environment," *American Journal of Psychiatry,* 1955, 3:826-831.

25] Compare Gustav Bally, *Vom Ursprung und von den Grenzen der Freiheit* (Benno Schwabe & Co., Basel, 1945), and "The Development of Focal Attention and the Emergence of Reality," this volume, pp. 251-278.

with the world in which they are going to live. The youthful curiosity and the exploration in play of the world and of one's own growing capacities to deal with it are essential for the very complex processes of adaptation to the environment. In this period, the higher animal and man are more *open* toward the environment. As they mature we see in the higher mammals and in most men a slackening or ceasing of curiosity, fascination, playful exploration, excitement, enthusiasm: the "open" world has now turned into a variety of objects with signal qualities, or into objects-of-use to which certain adaptive responses are given. As Hebb puts it, the well-adjusted adult lives in the protective *cocoon* of his culture and, within this cocoon, he is "well adjusted," i.e. "relatively unemotional." In line with this, Hebb sees as the goal of moral education the production of an individual that will (1) be stable in the existing social environment, and (2) *contribute to its protective uniformity*.[26]

From my viewpoint, the cocoon aspect of civilization is a telling description of secondary *embeddedness*. The man who lives completely in this cocoon has proceeded from the primary embeddedness in the womb and in the world of mother to the secondary embeddedness in the culture, usually in the subculture of the particular social group to which he belongs. He has proceeded from the primary autocentricity of the infant's perceptual world to the secondary autocentricity of the adult's world of "objects-of-use," in which all objects are reduced to and exhausted by the familiar labels and reactions the culture provides for them. On his way from primary to secondary embeddedness he has passed through a period during which the world seemed open, inexhaustible, exciting, full of wondrous and adventurous possibilities, not to be described by any label. But while the "cocoon" at which he arrived is larger than the womb was, and while within it there are many more objects than the infant ever dreamt of, they have lost their aliveness, just as the man who has "matured" to the state where he does nothing but contribute to the protective uniformity of the cultural cocoon has lost his enthusiasm, his capacity for growth, the essential and specifically human capacity to remain open toward the world, that is, to transcend a closed pattern of reactions and thus to encounter and perceive the new, that which transcends the

26] Hebb, "The Mammal and His Environment."

labels of his "patterned" experience, be it in a new object or in an object encountered many times.

The fact that all men, with the possible exception of the most severely disturbed, completely apathetic children, go through the childhood period of openness toward and fascination with a yet unlabeled environment, might suggest that we deal here, just as in many higher animals' playful learning, with an innate behavior pattern to which is entrusted the essential task of acquainting the organism with the larger environment (compared with the protected maternal world) in which the adult organism will have to live. But such an assumption does not cover fully what we see in man. At best, it might explain why the adult's approach to the world is usually less "open" than the child's and why the range of his discoveries and fresh encounters is usually smaller. But it does not account for the great individual differences, for the fact that some people are always interested, capable of fresh allocentric perception, while others live in an indeed closed world in which nothing vital or new ever happens. It also does not account for the fact that people who have lived in such a closed world can change and experience a reawakening of allocentric interest and perception. The evidence suggests that both in the higher mammals and in man there are side by side the tendencies to seek the new and to be afraid of it and avoid it. The balance between these two tendencies seems to shift from a strong predominance of avoidance of the new in earliest infancy[27] to a strengthening of the tendency to seek the new in childhood; after that it shifts again, in animals, to a predominance of the avoidance of the new, whereas in humans this is true of most, but not of all. The ubiquitous shift toward a strengthening of the tendency to seek the new in childhood may be due to inherent biological structures which in turn are related to the fact that during childhood there is parental care and protection, so that the organism explores while it is still protected. But in man, where the openness toward the world is incomparably greater than even in the highest mammals, we have to try to understand what,

27] This "avoidance" takes place largely by means of the stimulus barrier, but also by actual shrinking from, and discomfort by, such drastic changes as penetrate the stimulus barrier. The concept of stimulus barrier (*Reizschutz*) was developed by Freud. Compare Paul Bergman and Sibylle K. Escalona, "Unusual Sensitivities in Very Young Children," *Psychoanalytic Study of the Child*, Vol. III/IV, 1949, pp. 333-352, where the relevant passages from Freud are quoted and the concept is applied to actual child observation.

in addition to possible inherent biological structures, causes the conspicuous differences between people with regard to their openness or unreceptiveness toward the world and with regard to the loss, the stagnation, or the continuing development of their capacity for allocentric perception and the encounter of the new.

In everybody's life one can observe the effect of the pressure of society, as represented by parents, teachers, peers, toward the formation of a more or less definite, closed view of life and the world, a certain code of behavior as well as often very definite views about things and people and what they are there for. These views may be explicit or implicit. The parents answer the child's endless questions and their answers usually transmit the labels of the culture, the names of things, whether they are useful or useless, good or bad, etc. Inasmuch as the child looks upon the parent as all-knowing, or with fear, he accepts these views and with them very often the implicit assumption that these answers contain all there is to the subject. Obviously, there are great variations in parents with regard to the wish, or the absence of it, to impose their views as the only ones on the child or to further the child's own explorative curiosity; with regard to their own awareness of, and readiness to admit, the limited nature of their knowledge or, on the contrary, their wish to appear as omniscient or as the ones who always know best. The same holds true for teachers. Parents and teachers, in transmitting the current sociocultural views of the world to the child, can help both to open and to close the world for the child. Even if they mostly want to open it, they cannot help but also close it, in some ways, because there is no man who is not to a considerable extent embedded in the culture in which he grew up, the language of his culture, etc.

In addition to the closure of the world which results from the transmission of a familial and/or cultural viewpoint, parental curbing of the child's exploratory drive can also be a factor that interferes with the world-openness of the child and often leads to a more or less powerful strengthening of the tendency to avoid the unknown and remain embedded in the familiar. The more worried the parents are about the dangers of the world, the more likely are they to impart this view to the child. The baby's tendency to put everything in his mouth usually arouses particularly strong reactions in the mother. Probably the powerful emotion of *disgust* has its origin in the negative parental reactions to touching everything with tongue, mouth, and hand. I believe that disgust is primarily the early conditioned fear of intimate contact with certain objects. For this reason it is much more closely connected with the proximity than with the distance senses. The parental tabu on touching, on skin contact, especially since it is usually imparted at a very early age, can have a lasting effect which often interferes quite literally with the person's getting in touch with the world, exploring and trusting it with his hands and entire body.

While the influence of parents and teachers in transmitting the closed perspective of a certain culture is universal, the relative significance of this influence as compared with the influence of the peers of the growing child varies considerably in different cultures. I have the impression that in present-day U.S.A., the relative influence of the young peer group is greater than it was fifty years ago. Moreover, the views of preadolescents and adolescents tend to be, if anything, even more rigorously limiting and "closed" than those of many parents. To have interests, perceptions, thoughts which deviate from those of the peer group carries with it the danger of scorn, ridicule, and ostracism, of social isolation. Thus, the growing child encounters another, decisive pressure toward adopting what one might call the shared autocentric viewpoint of the peer group to which he wants to belong, and thus is discouraged from encountering things as they are, with an open mind and eye. To perceive things differently from the people one knows, parents *and* peers, can be one of the most frightening experiences, if the need for consensual validation is limited, as it is for most people, to the particular social group they live in, and cannot be satisfied by the knowledge that in another place or time there are or have been people whose view of the world and whose thoughts move in a direction similar to, or at least compatible with, our own.

The explicit and implicit influence of parents, teachers, and peers toward the inculcation of a certain perspective on the world is the most obvious pressure on the growing child and adolescent. It determines to a large extent the individual solution of the existential struggle between the two tendencies in man: to remain open toward the world, capable of allocentric perception, or to seek the security of secondary embeddedness in a closed world and in the shared autocentricity[28] of a familiar perspective. Hence, this pres-

28] For an elucidation of this seemingly paradoxical expression see below, pp. 191-192.

sure is also the one that has been studied exclusively by psycho-analysis and that has to be clarified in the psychotherapeutic enter-prise. But it is not the only pressure. *Language* itself, like the par-ents, imparts certain viewpoints which can help or hinder the development of allocentric perception, can open or obscure the world. The word, of course, never can take the place of the object or the quality or the activity which it designates or indicates. But most of the time, when we listen to the spoken or read the written word, we neither perceive nor imagine the referent of the word but are in contact only with the words (or concepts). We behave as if the word were really all there is to the object which it desig-nates. The label (sign) becomes a substitute for its referent, and thus, in listening or reading we are divorced from any experience of that which the words point to. More often than not, the speaker or writer who uses these words is also in contact only with them and not with the objects which they designate. Used in this way language bars the access to the world, obscures the objects, leads to autocentric perception of familiar clichés rather than to allocentric perception of reality. On the opposite pole, language can be *evoca-tive* of experience. The evocative function of language depends usually on the speaker's (or writer's) being in contact with the experience about which he speaks and trying to communicate (i.e. evoke in the listener) this experience, and on the listener's willing-ness and ability to experience (rather than just hearing words) what is being said to him. The way in which language is used can have a decisive influence on whether experiential communication takes place in which both people (speaker and listener, writer and reader) are in touch with the referent of the communication, or whether only words are exchanged and no experience is evoked. The evocative function of the language can be enhanced by avoid-ing clichés and by lifting words out of their most banal, current use and using them in a way that reveals their original meaning, or by using them in such combinations, images, positions as will conjure up most concretely the experience about which one is talk-ing or writing. Good writers and poets excel in evocative use of language; in our day they often have to shock the reader out of the state of mind in which he is capable only of taking in clichés and is blind to experience. I believe that this necessity accounts for much of the seeming obscurity of modern poetry and literature. With the invention of printing and with the constant assault of the modern mass-communication media, language has lost a great deal of its evocative function and the listener or reader merely takes in clichés, which altogether too often is all that the speaker or writer, on his part, was in touch with. This observation is referred to in Goethe's verse:

> Wie das Wort so wichtig dort war
> Weil es ein gesprochen Wort war.[29]

In the spoken word, language can become evocative of experience even if the most hackneyed words are used, provided that the speaker is in touch with their experiential referent. In this case, his tone of voice and the attitude expressed in his whole behavior communicate to the person who is at all able to listen that the words are used not just to make conversation (which in turn can serve a variety of purposes other than communication) but to bring the listener in touch with a significant experience.

Many people believe that if language could only attain the precision of the model of communication found in mathematical symbols then all the complex problems of communication would be solved, people would be really in touch with each other, and the source of all misunderstanding would be eliminated.[30] While precision can no doubt do much to reduce the ambiguity of scientific and other language, the belief that human communication in its entirety could be based on the mathematical model rests on a fundamental misconception of the human situation and the nature of experience. There is no concept, no word, and no sign which completely circumscribes and exhausts an experience in the way in which the mathematical symbol completely represents the mathematical concept. Since human experience always concerns man's relation to "being" in its inexhaustible and unfathomable depth and variety, no symbol or word can take its place and, as it were, limit and fixate that which by its very nature is limitless and always in flux. Conceptual language refers to concepts only. Where the concepts are all that we talk about, as in mathematics, language

---

29] The lines are from the opening poem, "Hegire," of Goethe's *West-östlicher Divan*. Their position emphasizes their importance. In Dowden's translation they read:
> As where the word held sway, and stirred
> Because it was a spoken word.

The West-Eastern Divan, Edward Dowden, trans. (J. M. Dent & Sons, London, 1914), p. 2, by permission of the publisher.

30] The viewpoint of semantics points in this direction.

can be fully and precisely communicative. But where the concepts merely indicate experiences, where we use experiential language, there always remains the unresolvable tension between the evocative word and the inexhaustible quality of the experience. At the point where man were to use nothing but mathematical language he would become a robot and his brain an electronic computer.

In its origins language is always evocative. If we take the pains really to fathom a word, even the most worn one will become pregnant with meaning, the word misused in the most banal cliché will again become evocative of experiences. Really listening to the word and all its implications can accomplish such resurrection of its experiential meaning buried under layers of daily use, and very often a tracing of the history of the word, back to its earliest roots, will recover its evocative impact.

On the other hand, the more a word is used as daily currency, especially if it becomes part of the particular language of a subgroup, such as professional jargon, journalistic headlines, the idiom of advertising, teen-age parlance, the more it loses its evocative power and becomes a cliché which is handed around among the members of the particular group, where it may enhance a spurious feeling of being knowledgeable. However, such knowledge stems no longer from the encounter with the object to which the word refers, but it represents "being in the know," knowing one's way around in the particular group. It stamps one as a member of the group, as belonging. Thus, the use of such "special group" words and of all the most worn words often has a reassuring effect as regards one's sense of belongingness, but has little value as far as a deepening and enlarging of one's experience of the object designated by the word is concerned. On the contrary, these words lead away from allocentric perception, they bar a fresh view of the real object, and they strengthen what I propose to call the *sociocentric* view of the world shared by the particular group for which this word is daily currency.

Sociocentric perception is really a shared autocentricity.[31] This sounds at first paradoxical, since by definition that which is shared with others is no longer autocentric. The paradox is related to that

---

31] Compare to this point Binswanger's remark on the private world of the many, the multitude. Ludwig Binswanger, *Grundformen und Erkenntnis menschlichen Daseins*, p. 557. See also G. Murphy's concept of socially shared autism, *Human Potentialities* (Basic Books, New York, 1958), pp. 119-122.

inherent in the usual concept of "reality."[32] To the average man in the sixteenth and seventeenth centuries, the views of Copernicus and Galileo of the relations between sun and earth appeared crazy, while his own view, according to which the sun circled around the earth, represented reality. Yet, this view was a quite autocentric one, deriving from man's inclination to view himself as the center of the universe. But it had all the earmarks of "reality" because it was a shared autocentric view. If there had been psychiatrists at Copernicus' time and he had told them of his idea, which must have been a central interest of his life, they would at best have dismissed it as an *idée fixe* and at worst would have considered him completely insane because of his "obvious" distortion of reality. The paradox is resolved when we distinguish between two concepts of reality. The prevalent concept of reality rests not on the attempt to encounter reality, but on the reassuring sharing of viewpoints, labels, perspectives which makes superfluous the lonely and precarious struggle with the unknown. To this extent it is shared autocentricity, that is, sociocentricity. It reassures either because so *many* people share it, or—if it represents the viewpoint of a relatively small group—because of the zealousness with which it is adhered to. The other concept of reality takes seriously the fact that reality by its very nature always remains largely unknown and that only partial aspects of it ever become visible when man dares to encounter it, that is, when he does not rest content merely with the shared opinions of the many, with the labels and clichés, but experiences for himself the unfathomable and mysterious reality of other beings, of the objects of which reality consists. The reassuring, defensive character of the sociocentric view has been expressed pointedly by Heidegger when he speaks of the "healthy commonsense and its unhappy irritation" whenever it feels threatened by a questioning of its "obvious" perspective.[33]

Language itself is the expression of the social nature of thought, experience, and perception. But the quality of that which is social,

---

32] See above, p. 178.

33] "[Der gemeine Verstand] beruft sich auf die Fraglosigkeit des offenbaren Seienden und deutet jedes denkende Fragen als einen Angriff auf den gesunden Menschenverstand und seine unglückliche Gereiztheit." Martin Heidegger, *Vom Wesen der Wahrheit* (Klostermann, Frankfurt a.M., 1945), p. 24.

i.e. shared by men when they communicate by language and when they use language in thought, ranges all the way from the conventional label which belongs to the more or less automatic phrases of the common daily speech and blocks the way to allocentric experience, to the evocative word which points to allocentric experience which each person can have for himself. The former refers to the autocentric perspective on the object and to its use for reassurance in a familiar daily world whose familiarity is shared by all; the latter invites to, or recalls, the encounter with the source of all true experience: the immediate and alive contact with the ineffable objects of reality (nature and men).

This immediate contact is dreadful and wonderful at the same time. It can be frightening, as though it were death itself, and yet it is rejuvenating, the deepest source of vitality. Sometimes it is the awful, anxiety-arousing aspects of the experience of the real encounter with its fully allocentric perception that prevail, sometimes the invigorating, exhilarating, vitalizing, and sometimes both are present equally. Since at this point we are mainly concerned with the question why most people more or less lose the capacity for allocentric perception after childhood, why they avoid the direct encounter and do not remain open toward the world but live increasingly in the secondary embeddedness of the closed world of their group, the question arises as to the sources of the anxiety in the encounter with the unknown, unfamiliar, unlabeled aspects of reality, aside from parental and social pressure toward conformity with the familial and group perspective.

The anxiety and awe in the encounter with the unknown have been described by many writers. In the language of religion it is the awe of the unknown God, the nameless God. In Goethe's *Faust* the awe of the unknown is praised as man's highest good if he does not flee from it:

MEPHISTO.
> Bist du beschränkt, dass neues Wort dich stört?
> Willst du nur hören, was du schon gehört?
> Dich störe nichts, wie es auch weiter klinge,
> Schon längst gewohnt der wunderbarsten Dinge.

FAUST.
> Doch im Erstarren such ich nicht mein Heil,
> Das Schaudern ist der Menschheit bestes Teil;

Wie auch die Welt ihm das Gefühl verteure,
Ergriffen, fühlt er tief das Ungeheure.[34]

Rimbaud writes of the poet: "He arrives at the *unknown*, and if, finally, besides himself, he should lose the understanding of his visions, still he has seen them. Let him die in his headlong encounters with unheard-of, unnamable things; other awesome workers will come: they will start at the horizons where he has collapsed."[35] Stephen Spender speaks of the artist's terrifying familiarity with the unprecedented.[36]

Joseph Conrad describes the encounter between a man (the narrator) and a woman who lives in the fear of being deserted one day by her lover. This encounter "had the power to drive me out of my conception of existence, out of that shelter each of us makes for himself to creep under in moments of danger, as a tortoise withdraws within its shell. For a moment I had a view of the world that seemed to wear a vast and dismal aspect of disorder, while, in truth, thanks to our unwearied efforts, it is as sunny an arrangement of small conveniences as the mind of man can conceive. But still—it was only a moment: I went back into my shell directly. One *must*—don't you know?—though I seemed to have lost all my words in the chaos of dark thoughts I had contemplated for a second or two beyond the pale. These came back, too, very soon, for words also belong to the sheltering conception of light and order which is our refuge."[37]

34] Goethe, *Faust II*, Act 1, "Finstere Galerie," in Bayard Taylor's translation (Random House, New York, 1950), p. 54:

> MEPH.
>   Art thou so weak, disturbed by each new word?
>   Wilt only hear what thou'st already heard?
>   To wondrous things art thou so used already,
>   Let naught, howe'er it sound, make thee unsteady!
> FAUST.
>   Nathless in torpor lies no good for me;
>   The chill of dread is Man's best quality.
>   Though from the feeling oft the world may fend us,
>   Deeply we feel, once smitten, the tremendous.

The passage is of special significance for our topic since it occurs when Faust first shrinks back from the descent to the Mothers, that is, to the sources of life itself. He has to face them if he wants to win Helena, to realize his love to the most perfect of all women.

35] Author's translation from Rimbaud, *Lettres à Izambard*, 15 May 1871.

36] Stephen Spender, "Are Critics Too Much with Us?" *The New York Times Book Review*, January 15, 1956. See also Spender's autobiography, *World within World* (Hamish Hamilton, London, 1951), p. 93.

37] Joseph Conrad, *Lord Jim* (Bantam Books, New York, 1957), pp. 202-203.

According to the teachings of Zen Buddhism, which—unlike most other religious systems—pay a good deal of attention to perception, fully allocentric perception of the world in its suchness is achieved only after the obtaining of Satori, of enlightenment, and is preceded by an awful crisis which profoundly shakes the whole person and in which he lets go of any holding on to his "ego," to his thoughts, concepts, prejudices, cravings, involvements.[38]

The anxiety of the encounter with the unknown springs not only from social pressures toward conformity, i.e. from the fear of transcending the socially accepted views of life and the world. It arises also, perhaps primarily, from the person's fear of letting go of the *attitudes* to which he clings for safety, of the *perspectives* which these attitudes give him on the world, and of the familiar *labels* for what he sees in the world. The combination of attitudes, perceptual and thought perspectives, and familiar labels is the descendant, on a higher developmental level, of the infant's experience of familiarity in resensing the global complex of certain sensorimotor-affective attitudes. As the infant and child often show hesitation and anxiety in the face of the new,[39] so man is afraid that without the support of his accustomed attitudes, perspectives, and labels he will fall into an abyss or flounder in the pathless.

Perception cannot be divorced from the *attitude* of the perceiver just as it cannot be divorced from his movements, his posture, his tonus.[40] The attitude determines what will and what will not be perceived and how it will be perceived. An attitude to which one clings will permit one to see only certain limited or distorted aspects of an object and will block a fuller view. Only when this attitude is let go and the person thus set free from having to approach the world in this particular way, is the path free to a different approach and a view thus opened up on hitherto unknown aspects of the object. Letting go of every kind of clinging opens the fullest view on the object. But it is this very letting go which often arouses the greatest amount of anxiety.

This can be observed in changes which impress primarily as

38] Compare the writings of D. T. Suzuki, which give to the Western reader the most comprehensive exposition of Zen teachings.

39] See above, pp. 150-151.

40] See below, pp. 213-214.

changes of physical and motor attitude as well as in those that seem to be primarily changes of mental attitude.[41] In learning to skate (roller-skate or ice-skate) the transition from one mode of relatedness of the moving person to the supporting ground to a new kind of relatedness (attitude) can be experienced and observed very palpably. The clinging to the accustomed attitude of a step-by-step movement, in which one foot is lifted, swung forward and put down again while the other remains on the same spot on the ground, interferes with the learning of the new attitude in which the foot and the whole body glide forward. The more the beginner tries to retain safety by clinging to the accustomed step-by-step movement, in which the static foothold is not fully abandoned before a new one is gained, the less will he be able to change to a new motor attitude. Only when he dares to entrust himself to the new gliding movement, even at the risk of losing his balance and falling, will he learn to skate. There is in this very concrete, physical experience an intrinsic parallel to the New Testament saying: "Whosoever shall seek to save his life shall lose it; and whosoever shall lose his life shall preserve it" (Luke 17:33). From the viewpoint of perception, clinging to the step-by-step movement has two major consequences: (1) it transforms the viewpoint from which the whole environment is seen into a search for possible points of support, thus barring allocentric perception, and (2) it prevents the development of a changed relationship between the person and the ground with its new, primarily tactile and proprioceptive sensations, which open up a whole new way of experiencing the supporting ground and "myself moving on the ground." A very similar process occurs in learning to swim and to dive. As I have pointed out elsewhere,[42] the anxiety connected with learning to dive (or to swim) is not a fear of the water but an anxiety concerning the unknown state of being that will result from giving up the support of the earth and the accustomed motor attitude in standing, walking, resting on firm ground and instead entrusting oneself to a new mode (attitude) of being, the exact nature of which cannot be anticipated but can be experienced only

41] Actually every change of attitude involves the entire person; the distinction of the physical and the mental aspects of the change is due more to the viewpoint of the observer to whom the physical or the mental aspect may be more readily accessible or of greater interest, than it is due to any inherent dichotomy between or predominance of physical or mental factors in the change of attitude.

42] This volume, p. 47.

by risking the leap from the known to the unknown. Although the object "water" is as well "known" to the person learning to dive or swim as anything, in the moment in which he can give up the clinging to the accustomed stance and movement on land, entirely new experiential aspects of water become perceptible to him in being carried by the water or in gliding through the water. Of course it is a simplification to speak of just one leap in learning to skate, to swim, to dive. The required change of attitude takes many leaps, each of which may loosen some of the clinging and open up some part of the possibility of a new way of being in relation to the environment and thus bring about a shift in the perspective on the environment.

In the examples of skating, swimming, and diving the motor attitude is the most conspicuous factor because it is clearly visible, although anyone who has gone through the experience of learning or of teaching to skate, swim, dive, bicycle, etc., will be aware how decisive is the emotional attitude that accompanies the motor attitude. In most cases in which clinging to an attitude prevents perception of the new and in which the fear of the new or unknown is primarily the anxiety aroused by the prospect of letting go of this attitude, the mental (emotional) attitude is the conspicuous factor while the motor elements of the attitude often are very subtle and either visible only to an astute and intuitive observer or hardly visible at all, much less adequately measurable by methods at our disposal at present. The most frequent, significant, and striking examples of this occur in the interference with *full* or with *accurate perception of other people* by an attitude to which the perceiver clings. While usually the perceiver is not aware of this and it becomes apparent only to the observer who listens to the perceiver's description of people known to both of them, in some cases the perceiver becomes acutely aware of his not really perceiving the other person in spite of looking or listening and consciously wanting to see or hear. Thus, one patient complained that she had never really looked at her boy friend and thus never felt that she knew what he really looked like and what kind of a person he was. She had this feeling many times immediately after being with him, looking at him, talking with him, and also after the relationship ended. Often, before seeing him she would resolve that this time she would "really look at him" and, while she did look at him, she would feel afterwards that she had not really seen him. Her whole attitude was one of submissive clinging to him, trying to please him, hoping that by doing so she would gain the power to control him, and fearing many times that by doing something "wrong" she had lost him, which then would turn out not to be true. In being with him she would often experience a fear of looking at him lest she see disapproval in his expression, and when she did look at him she did so, not because she was interested in him but because she was always anxiously searching for signs of approval or disapproval, of love or anger. She could not perceive him fully, in an allocentric way, because she felt in constant, dependent need of him. His face remained unknown to her although she had seen it many times. Her anxiety of the unknown had two components: one, more or less conscious, that she would discover anger, rejection, or ridicule if she really dared to look; the other, more basic, pervasive, and unconscious, that clinging to somebody else and trying to control and manipulate this person by doing what she felt the person wanted her to do was the only way of life known to her; the prospect of giving up this clinging attitude was tantamount to jumping into an abyss in which she did not know how to move. Yet, only letting go of this fundamental attitude could enable her to "really look" at another person.

In cases of *distorted* perception, too, the fear of the unknown which prevents a more accurate perception very often is primarily the anxiety aroused by the prospect of letting go of the attitude which causes the distortion. Thus, one patient, because of his intense wishes to be loved and cuddled like a child and because of a pervasive angry, sad, and depressive attitude caused by the frustration of this wish, tended to perceive the analyst as frowning, angry, bored, or in other ways rejecting and thus giving him cause to continue his own attitude of reproachful sadness and anger. Gradually he began to notice with increasing frequency that the analyst did not look the way he had seen him. On occasions when this became very striking to him, he discovered that he did not *want* the analyst to look friendly and interested in him because that made him feel at a loss what to do. He felt that in being friendly the analyst was "stepping out of line" and he did not want him to step out of line because he was frightened by the prospect of having to let go of his lifelong attitude of angry reproachfulness and hopelessness and then "not knowing what to do." Similar distortions and similar reluctance to perceive others realistically can be observed frequently in people who feel that their main power lies in their anger, which they believe to have some power of control over others; their greatest unconscious fear is of the unknown way of life once they let go of this anger, while consciously they feel that they are afraid of what they perceive, very often distortedly, as rejecting attitudes of others.

According to findings by G. I. W. Smith and others[43] a relaxed, receptive attitude probably increases sensitivity to visually presented subliminal (i.e. not consciously perceived) stimuli. It may well be that the influence of subliminal registration of the fleeting, minute changes which animate the human face and the voice and gestures of people plays a role also in influencing the conscious perceptions which we have of people. Since a tense, over-alert atttitude is usually based on clinging to certain habitual security operations, this would imply that the effect of subliminal registration on perception, too, would be impaired by such an attitude, and that the anxiety connected with letting go of such an attitude would be a powerful force in preventing not only conscious but also subliminal allocentric perception.

Holding on to an attitude, thus, prevents perceptive openness toward the constantly changing flux of life and tends to distort perception in the direction of a closed, one-sided, rigid view of the world corresponding to the rigidity of the attitude held. The person who seeks security in such a rigid attitude thereby inevitably also inclines toward the feeling that if he lets go of this attitude he will flounder helplessly in a chaotic world. The rigid attitude entails the fear of chaos, of the unknown, unmanageable; rigidity and the fear of chaos belong together, just as flexibility, development, transformation, and openness toward the world (allocentric perception) belong together.[44]

Man always lives somewhere between these two poles of clinging to a rigid attitude with its closed world and of leaping into the stream of life with his senses open toward the inexhaustible, chang-

---

43] Gudmund I. W. Smith, Donald P. Spence, and George S. Klein, "Subliminal Effects of Verbal Stimuli." Mimeographed report on an experiment conducted at the Research Center for Mental Health, New York University (1957).

44] See on this point Erich Neumann, "Der schöpferische Mensch und die Wandlung," in *Mensch und Wandlung, Eranos Jahrbuch, 1954* (Rhein-Verlag, Zürich, 1955), Vol. 23, pp. 18-21. Compare also in this context Else Frenkel-Brunswik, "Intolerance of Ambiguity as an Emotional and Perceptual Personality Variable," in Jerome S. Bruner and David Krech, eds., *Perception and Personality* (Duke University Press, Durham, 1949/50).

ing, infinite world. From the beginnings of his life, he turns to others, to tradition, to give him names for the nameless, and while he has in him the striving to transcend that which is already known to him, he is also afraid of getting lost in the as yet wayless world of that which has no signposts and labels. Indeed, if he remains open toward the world, if he expands beyond the familiar, we see him constantly trying to name that which he encounters, to link it up with the already known, to transform the waylessness into territory that is mapped and named. In art and science as well as in other personal discoveries of the individual we see the never ending attempt to take hold of and name, articulate, describe, or symbolically represent the new land which has been wrested from the infinity of the unknown.

In perception itself there is an element of not wanting to remain in the flux of the fully allocentric encounter, but to take hold of the object and fix it, to wrest it from the infinite process of world and life, and to fix it at a definite point where we can take hold of it again, recall it, refind it. The word "perception," from the Latin *per-cipere*, "to take," "to capture through and through," points to this element, as does the German *Wahrnehmung*, "to take as true," "take hold of the truth." The decisive element is in this *taking*, which may be said to be man's ever renewed attempt to subject and make his own that which will always transcend and elude his efforts, that of which he is part, which he can encounter but which he can never capture fully. In this respect perception differs from sensation, which has a much more fleeting character and lacks the attempt to take hold of something. The more rational sense of seeing, especially seeing form, lends itself much more readily to such capturing than do the more primitive senses of taste and smell with their fleeting sensations.

Man's exposure to the pathless, his openness toward the infinity of the world and of its numberless aspects, is his most distinctive difference from the animals, which by their innate organization are more tightly embedded in a much narrower, more closed *Umwelt*. Biologically, the singular position of man, his existential situation, is largely brought about by the degree of his cerebralization and by the fact that, in comparison with those mammals which are most closely related to him in the evolutionary scale, he is born a year too early. This means that processes of maturation which in the highest mammals take place in the uniform environment of the maternal womb, in man take place outside of the womb in an infinitely richer, more varied, and individually differing environment.[45] Thus, at a time when the higher mammals are formed according to developmental laws common to each species in the darkness and the relatively uniform conditions of the womb, with the possibility only of very limited experience, the human infant develops in a unique environment, exposed to a multitude of changing stimuli. In this interaction with the environment the infant develops the distinctly human capacity of upright posture, and of language and insightful action, whereas the higher mammals are already born as more or less complete, small reproductions of the adult animal. In the freedom of the play of his limbs, of his activities, and in the exposure to an open environment, the infant thus finds itself in a very different, wide-open situation. The infant's large cortex, especially the large association areas of its brain, make for a less direct control of behavior by environmental stimuli.[46] This implies that there is much greater choice in the way in which the much more numerous incoming stimuli can be elaborated and connected. The growing infant and child has a strong urge to get in touch with and explore the unknown world around him and to do so in many different ways, in the ever varied and ever repeated actions and perceptions of his play. Thus, it is constantly enriching its object world from ever new perspectives, constantly exploring new territory, new aspects, new ways of relating to the objects of the environment. But at the same time the child is increasingly given to imitation and to demanding answers to his questions from parents or other adults, to imitating not only what they do but especially their speech, and to ask for the names of things. In other words, the child not only explores a pathless and wide-open environment on his own, but also follows the paths which he sees his parents travel, and he wants them to give him names, labels, signs by which he will know not only the many-faceted object itself but also those facets of it to which the traditional word for it points. While in the child's exploratory play the object reveals many different aspects out of which it is eventually constituted as a thing with many qualities and an existence

45] The great significance of this difference has been shown by Adolf Portmann, *Biologische Fragmente zu einer Lehre vom Menschen* (Benno Schwabe, Basel, 1951).
46] To this point compare D. O. Hebb, *The Organization of Behavior* (John Wiley & Sons, New York, 1949), pp. 123-126.

of its own, in learning the object's name the child comes to look at it from the fixed perspective of the traditional culture. Moreover, the child often acts as if by knowing the name for an object, he now knows the object itself, when actually, of course, the naming of the object can never replace the encounter with it. But we must not forget how powerful this magic of names is for the adult, too. When seeing a mountain, a star, a tree, a flower, a person, we often ask for the name and, given it, are satisfied as though now we really knew what still is just as unfathomable as it was before. The name, apart from making communication possible, gives us a fixed point, it seems to delimit and fixate something while the direct encounter with the nameless object takes place in the pathless. Once we know the word for something, we have something to hold on to and very often the knowledge of the word, the name, in giving us the illusion of knowing the object designated by it, makes us quite inert and unwilling to look anew at the now supposedly familiar object from a different perspective. This function of naming is described in mythological language in Genesis. There we find two different accounts of man's relation to nature. In the first version (Genesis 1:28 and 29), God gives man *power* over all animals and plants. In the second (Genesis 2:19), God creates the animals and brings them to Adam "to see what he would call them: and whatsoever Adam called every living creature, that was the name thereof." In this account man is left free by God to determine his own relation to the other creatures. And this is indeed the human situation: nature is to man whatever name he wants to give her. He will perceive nature according to the names he gives to her, according to the relation and perspective he chooses. He feels lost in nameless nature. He both perceives one aspect of her and blocks further perception by the names he gives to her, her creatures, and objects.[47]

In learning the mother tongue, the child on the one hand gets acquainted with the richness of its environment, but on the other hand it has to sacrifice for the newly gained social perspective of language a great deal of its own direct, creative perspective on the

47] Zen Buddhism's interest in the problem of perception is apparent especially in its awareness of the obscuring function of language, and of any systematic, conceptual approach, in that they tend to block the way to direct encounter with the object. Hence the emphasis in its method of instruction on the paradox, on contradiction, and on the Koan exercise. Compare D. T. Suzuki, *Zen Buddhism* (Doubleday Anchor Books, New York, 1956), chapters 5 and 6, pp. 111-154.

objects of the environment and with it the well-known originality which delights or shocks us in so many remarks of children. Every writer and every thinker knows how difficult it is to overcome the power of the familiar perspective of traditional language and concepts and thus to pave the way for a fresh look at the object itself.

While the shared perspective of the language and the fear of transcending it are the most ubiquitous and powerful factors in preventing allocentric perception from penetrating beyond the secondary embeddedness in the culture of the group, the anxiety upon the encounter with the unknown can be demonstrated also in other ways. I want to illustrate this with two examples from everyday life. Both concern the perception of something that cannot be linked up instantly with the familiar environment. The first is the perception of an unfamiliar noise at night. Many people are made quite anxious and disquieted by hearing such a noise, and even where there is no marked anxiety we usually find a more or less intensive, or more or less frantic attempt to guess what this noise could be, that is, to link it up with our known, expected, familiar environment. We can avoid the unknown, unfamiliar by *not* looking, *not* thinking. But when it impinges on us forcefully, as in hearing the strange noise, we very much want to transform it into something known by linking it up with our familiar frame of reference. As soon as we have succeeded in this, as soon as we are convinced that the noise is made by a creaking chair, it no longer alarms or disquiets us; in fact we lose all interest in the specific quality of the noise, we now perceive it under the perspective of the label "creaking furniture" and, reassured, we turn away from it. Usually people are inclined to be more easily disquieted at night, in the dark, than during daytime, by the perception of the unfamiliar. This fact and the very generally unsettling experience of being in darkness in a strange environment is due, I believe, to the loss of the familiar signposts of orientation. If, in a strange and completely dark environment, we suddenly touch something or are touched by something or hear something that we cannot "place" immediately, we can observe in most people a quite distinct alarm reaction. This fear of the dark develops only gradually in the child as it leaves the trusting stage of primary embeddedness and needs the signposts of the familiar world of secondary embeddedness.

The other example of anxiety in the perception of the unfamiliar is taken from a recent self-observation. I had bought a new book-case which was put up in my study, where it covered a fairly large expanse of a hitherto bare, light grey wall in such a way that it was immediately visible from a door by which I usually enter the room. In this wall are also two doors leading to two closets. The first two days after the bookcase had been put up, whenever I went into the study I was struck by the unexpected sight of a "shadow" or of "something dark" where I expected to see the familiar light wall. The first one or two times this happened I noticed a slight, but distinct startle, after which came the thought that somebody must have left the usually closed closet doors open. Each time it took quite a while, a second or two, till I realized that I was looking at the side of the new book-case. The slight, but distinct startle upon the sight of the unex-pected dark "object" (which was not really perceived as a dis-tinct object) is the anxiety when the unknown intrudes where one expects the familiar. Even after this no longer occurred I still did not see the bookcase right away when entering the room but merely an unexpected darkness which then I *explained* to myself as the bookcase before I actually saw it. This probably would have been different had I entered the room not preoccupied with some other thought but with my attention focused on the objects in the room. After a few more days, this sequence changed and when I entered the room I registered the "familiar bookcase," I "recognized" the familiar signpost without really seeing the book-case in the sense of allocentric perception.

Both of these everyday examples, that of the strange noise at night and that of the new bookcase, illustrate the need for embed-dedness in the familiar, the anxiety at the change, at the intrusion of the unknown—an anxiety which, while much less dramatic, is nevertheless related to the anxiety of the man who stands at the frontier of our familiar world and is confronted with the unknown. Both times it is the anxiety aroused by the pathlessness, the ab-sence of the signposts of familiarity. This is one source of our anxiety of the unknown. The other, present often in people who are about to encounter a "frontier" experience, to transcend their familiar orbit in allocentric perception of the new, is the fear of isolation from the shared, sociocentric perspective, if not of ridi-cule or ostracism by their fellow men. These seem to me the two major sources of anxiety, which so often prevent and deflect man from allocentric perception and relatedness to the world.

One major way in which man avoids the threat of these anxieties is by not venturing and by remaining embedded in the familiar. Outwardly this may take the most striking and most readily observable form of literally not moving out of his home, his village or town, his region, his country, his family, his fixed circle of friends, his work, his familiar entertainments. It may also take the less obvious form of not venturing *within* the familiar, that is, to see it always from the same perspective, not to look at it anew, not to perceive the unknown in it, not to encounter it fully but to perceive it autocentrically, using it for reassuring embeddedness and for whatever other needs, without perceiving the familiar people and objects in their own right, their own existence, their own mysterious being. There are many illustrations for this. One is the often observed fact that many people know the city in which they live less well than an out-of-town visitor does. The latter comes to *look* at the city, to savor its atmosphere and to learn to know it, whereas the person who lives there may merely use a small part of the city as a kind of home territory, with certain landmarks of familiarity, but never look at the city for its own sake. The same holds true of many marriages: the marriage partners change from people into landmarks of familiarity; they do not look at each other as persons, each with an inexhaustible life of his own, but as somebody to whom they have become accustomed and who therefore is reassuring and boring at the same time. Of course, such a marriage relationship usually has other elements in it also, such as the use of the marriage partner for other autocentric needs. But in the avoidance of full allocentric perception of the other person and in using him or her for reassurance by the familiar, it resembles the described relation to the home town.

But even when man ventures beyond his familiar environment where one might expect him to encounter the unknown, the new, simply because it would seem to impinge on his senses, he has many ways of undoing, avoiding, preventing the impact of the new, of not encountering and not perceiving it in an allocentric way and often not seeing it at all. As a consequence, his world does not expand and nothing changes in him, in spite of his physically leaving the familiar orbit.

The avoidance of the impact of the new or unknown, once it

impinges on the sensorium, takes place usually by the adoption of special, often quite subtle attitudes of which the perceiver need not be aware. One such attitude is that of quickly labeling the new as though it were just the same as something already familiar or as though it could be encompassed by filing it away under certain familiar categories. The unique mountain becomes just another mountain, the cathedral becomes the "biggest church in X-country" or "an example of Gothic architecture." Or the traveler does not encounter the sights on his journey but collects them like picture post cards or snapshots, and he experiences not that which is before his eyes but the possession and exhibition of something that he will show to his friends at home. In a more subtle way, the adoption of the attitude of "sight-seeing," of "observing strange customs," of "going to the museum" usually prevents effectively the living encounter with the objects one looks at. Many people who visit galleries to see paintings will first quickly look at the name of the painter, thus categorizing the painting as part of art history which they want to know for some reason or other, but again not perceiving that which is painted and hangs on the wall before their eyes. Getting *set* for a new experience, for seeing a new town, a new object, a new country often has a subtle effect of interfering with the full perception, with the spontaneous immersion in the encounter with the new. This is the more likely to happen the more everything is planned in advance and any deviation from the plan avoided. By not entrusting oneself to the encounter with the new, but by holding on to the fixed framework of a certain plan and of a certain preformed perspective on what one is going to see, the new object may never come into view in its suchness, but only in a subtly but pervasively changed perspective, which results from the fear of leaving the familiar framework of one's plan or one's preconceptions. A "jaded" attitude is an insurance against any allocentric perception, because the person who has this attitude is resolved to hold on to his superior "knowingness" which blinds him against seeing or learning to know anything.

The most important instances of preventing or undoing the impact of the new are to be found in the *perception* of other *people*. This refers not only to meeting people one has not known before, but also to being exposed to the constantly changing life of the people one knows. It would require a whole book to describe and analyze the many ways, some habitual, some situational, in which people avoid or undo the full encounter with others with whom they meet and with whom they live.[48] It is the exception when one person perceives the other allocentrically, in the full humanness of his or her being, for as a rule people do not encounter the other person fully but only autocentrically or sociocentrically selected and/or distorted aspects of them, even if the other person should not in his or her turn, wittingly or unwittingly, withhold and conceal himself or certain aspects of himself, or present a façade to the world, all of which most people do most of the time.

The most striking examples of sociocentrically distorted perception of other people and avoidance of full encounter with them are furnished on a large scale by the perception of the enemy in wartime and of the stranger at any time. In wartime a good deal of energy is directed toward depicting the enemy as not human, or not as fully human as one's own people, and usually this effort is quite successful. Indeed, as long as mankind does not wish to abolish war, it has to practice this distortion, because nobody could kill another person if he perceived this person fully in all his humanness. A very similar a priori devaluation is practiced, sometimes quite drastically and openly, sometimes more subtly and covertly, by most people against the stranger. This is most marked in relation to foreign people who speak a different language and have a different culture, but it is also present toward minority groups and very often in the relation of city toward country people and of country people toward city people, and between people from different regions of the same country. It is to be found between different social classes. And in clannish families or circles such dehumanization is directed against every "outsider," that is, against all the rest of the world.

But the dehumanizing perspective on other people appears not only in the overt form of seeing them as more or less subhuman, but also in the more subtle, covert form of a seeming familiarity and equality. When grown men and women consider each other as "the boys" and "the girls," this does not mean that they are closer to each other and experience each other more fully but, on the contrary, that they hide behind the screen of an easy familiarity, deny the seriousness of their common human situation, and do not want to perceive, in themselves or in the other person, their essential humanity, their separateness, and their flight from a real

48] Compare above, pp. 197-199 for two illustrations.

encounter. Similarly, the ubiquitous use of nicknames instead of the person's real name very often conceals beneath the semblance of greater familiarity the desire not to face the full impact of the other person. Of course, the encounter with other people can be avoided equally effectively by the overt practices, more frequent in Europe than in the United States, of hiding behind one's title, social role, or function, and perceiving the other person, too, only in this way.

The described ways of avoiding or undoing the impact of the new and the unknown by avoiding the full perception of and encounter with other people could all be characterized as operations to maintain distance (some of them under the spurious guise of establishing closeness or familiarity) so that one will not be exposed to the full humanity, the real being of others. This attitude could also be described as the autocentric use of others (by pushing them away) for the maintenance of embeddedness in the familiar, often literally in the familial, the most clannish circle. Thus, the auto-centricity of perception of people as objects-of-use and the auto-centricity of wanting to remain embedded in the familiar and not to be disturbed, disquieted by the larger, unknown world are closely related to each other and merge into each other.

The more secondary autocentricity dominates man's perceptual world, the more it interferes not only with the possibility of allo-centric perception but also with the full development and func-tioning of primary autocentric perception on the adult level. The importance of primary autocentric perception throughout life is not limited to the vital functioning of the autocentric senses and of such derivates of the early instantaneous, fused perception of total situations as are found in background and peripheral percep-tion. It is part of the capacity, indispensable for the highest mental development, to open oneself receptively with *all* one's sensibili-ties to the encounter with the world and its objects. Such openness is not regression to a primitive level, but development of a dis-tinctly human capacity which is essential for man's attempt to find his place in the world and his relation to it.[49]

49] Werner emphasizes the vital importance of "primitive" behavior "in support-ing the highest forms of mentality" and considers as "the distinguishing mark of the advanced type . . . that an activity at a higher level is at his disposal which includes, rather than excludes, primitive activity." He seems to feel that man behaves more primitively in "emotional surrender to people and things" than in "sober scientific or practical work." Heinz Werner, *Comparative Psychology of*

The suppression or stunting of the full growth and development of primary autocentric perception is due to the same causes which prevent the growth and expansion of allocentric perception. Socio-cultural and parental pressures and the resulting wish to be like everybody else lead to stereotyping and to restriction of the range of sensibility in the development of the autocentric senses. This is apparent, for example, in national, regional, or group preferences for certain foods, especially strong and rigid in later childhood and adolescence, or in the development of taste preferences where under the pressure of the peer group actual initial aversion is changed to liking, as in learning to smoke or to drink hard liquor. Another example is the general tabu of Western civilization on the sense of smell which is so deeply rooted that in some languages to smell is synonymous with to smell badly, as in English and French.[50]

The social pressure to be busy at all times, the "performance principle,"[51] dominates not only work but also leisure-time activities and prevents the person's staying with anything, hinders the full presence in any encounter which is as essential for allocentric perception as it is for the enjoyment of autocentric sensations.[52] The emptiness and boredom which characterize so many people's lives today and which they try to keep from awareness by frantic attempts to be busy or to seek excitement cripple both allocentric and autocentric perception. The person who, before even tasting of a dish, indiscriminately pours salt and pepper on it as though in order to taste *something* he had to procure an extreme reaction, thereby deadens or prevents the development of any finer sensibilities. The anxiety of the unknown plays as great a role in the autocentric as in the allocentric senses, as we can see, for instance, in Swift's remark on the courage of the first man who ate an oyster.

Perhaps, the stunting and dulling of autocentric sensitivity is even more pervasive and has more far-reaching effects in *proprioception* than in the other autocentric senses. By consciously or unconsciously treating oneself and one's body as an object-of-use

Mental Development, rev. ed. (Follett Publishing Co., Chicago, 1948), pp. 4, 39. While I agree with his view on the continuation of primitive types of behavior in adult man, I have reservations about the implications of the particular hierarchy that he seems to establish.

50] For a fuller discussion of the tabu on smell see this volume, p. 300.

51] See Herbert Marcuse, *Eros and Civilization* (Beacon Press, Boston, 1955).

52] Compare this volume, pp. 65-68.

which has to perform in a certain way, by straining in certain directions and armoring oneself or being on the alert against imagined dangers, the proprioceptive sensitivity which makes the movements of animals and many young children graceful, comfortable, and perfectly suited to their actions is lost. Even though the body may protest by no longer noticed muscular tensions and eventually by pain, the natural capacity for relaxed action as well as for comfortable rest is difficult to regain in the face of the deeply rooted, unconscious purposes which alienate man from himself and use his body in their service. This loss of the body's innocence and its perversion in the service of ulterior unconscious or conscious purposes has been described in a beautiful essay by Kleist.[53]

The pleasure fused with some perceptions in the autocentric mode constitutes an important factor in the link between the person and the objects of reality and in the eagerness with which the activities which are accompanied by this pleasure are pursued. However, if the emphasis shifts from the activity and the object toward which the activity is directed to the sensation of pleasure itself as a goal, then a curiously self-defeating circle is started which eventually destroys the pleasure and interferes with the self-realization of the individual in living. This shift in emphasis changes the perception of the object. From being perceived, in primary autocentricity, as a need-object, or allocentrically, as an object in its own right, it now becomes a mere instrumentality for the creation of a pleasurable sensation, a state of feeling. The use of an object as a mere instrumentality for producing a sensation is different from its use as the object of an appetite; the emphasis changes, for example, from eating because appetite makes the fruit desirable, and in the eating its taste is enjoyed, to a means to produce a taste sensation which becomes the goal. In the proverbial "jaded appetite" which no longer can enjoy anything, the destruction of pleasure by the seeking after pleasurable sensation becomes apparent. The pleasurable or exciting sensation which becomes an end in itself rather than being the accompaniment of a vital activity is a basic phenomenon of *addiction* in its pathological as well as in

53] Heinrich von Kleist, "Ueber das Marionettentheater," English translation by Eugene Jolas ("Essay on the Puppet Theater"), *Partisan Review*, January-February, 1947. Compare also Wilhelm Reich's work on the muscular character armor and its interference, especially with the capacity for sexual activity and pleasure; and Charlotte Selver, *Sensory Awareness and Total Functioning*, General Semantics Bulletin, 1957, Nos. 20 and 21, pp. 5-16.

its more or less "normal" forms, as v. Gebsattel has pointed out.[54]

Addiction usually serves as an escape from a subjectively unbearable condition of life. In such an escape the emphasis may be on the overcoming of inhibitions and feelings of inadequacy by the artificial arousal of feelings of spontaneity and adequacy or grandiosity, as in many cases of alcohol addiction. Or the emphasis may be on a state of languorous, soporific inertia which takes the place of contentment and rest after satisfying activity. This is described in Gide's interpretation of the myth of Theseus and the labyrinth on Crete. In Gide's story the Minotaur who inhabits the labyrinth is not a monster who devours men but a beautiful and witless beast. The real danger of the labyrinth is that it leads through perfumed gardens in which, stupefied by the pleasures of the scents and sights, the visitors are seized by inertia, no longer have the power to move their limbs, and do not *want* to leave this artificial paradise.[55] In the case of alcohol addiction the alcohol itself is no longer the object of an enjoyable taste experience in the satisfaction of an appetite but serves merely as a means to reach the state of intoxication. In the artificial paradises (Baudelaire) of opium, hashish, or mescal the drug is usually taken at first with revulsion and later, although craved for, is not enjoyed for itself but again merely as a means to produce pleasurable sensations.

But addiction may also serve as an escape from a life that is experienced as *empty* because of a failure to turn toward the world in the process of self-realization. Then, to feel anything at all, in order thereby to feel alive vicariously, becomes an end in itself. As in all addictions, however, the obtaining of this end is increasingly self-defeating because larger and larger "doses" are required for the rapidly blunted sensation, whether the sensation be produced by the kind of tasting for tasting's sake that Apuleius describes in the time of Roman decadence, by drugs, by compulsive sexual activity, or by the seeking of thrills and excitement per se.

In the sphere of sex these phenomena are particularly striking. Sexual pleasure is strongest and most satisfying where it results

54] V. E. von Gebsattel, "Zur Psychopathologie der Sucht," in *Prolegomena einer medizinischen Anthropologie* (Springer-Verlag, Berlin, 1954), pp. 220-233. He does not speak of pleasurable sensation, but of an overemphasis on the *zuständliche* (state of being) aspect of existence as compared with active self-realization.
55] André Gide, *Two Legends: Oedipus and Theseus* (Alfred A. Knopf, New York, 1950), pp. 85-95.

from love and desire for the sex partner. But as soon as the goal becomes not the sexual union with the partner but the genital sensations as such, and the partner becomes a mere tool toward the achievement of a sensory pleasure state, there is less satisfaction and enjoyment. And the more often the person merely seeks to feel himself or herself in the excitation of these sensations, the more empty they become, the more similar to masturbation, and eventually they may result in a kind of hangover as do the excitations produced by the use of drugs or alcohol for similar purposes.[56]

Neither excitation as such, as Hebb's neurological theory assumes,[57] nor the absence of it, as Freud assumed, are the goals of healthy human striving. Where they become major goals we deal with pathological or deficient conditions in which man's relation to the world and to himself is disrupted or disturbed and the world is transformed into a mere tool or a mere nuisance for man, rather than being man's habitat in which he has to find the place proper to him by relating to the world with all his capacities.

56] Compare v. Gebsattel about the relations between addiction, masturbation, and sexual perversions. V. E. v. Gebsattel, "Süchtiges Verhalten im Gebiet sexueller Verirrungen," in *Prolegomena einer medizinischen Anthropologie*, pp. 161-212. A similar viewpoint has been expressed by Fairbairn, who says that "explicit pleasure-seeking represents a deterioration of behavior" from the point of view of his object-relationship psychology and that "simple tension-relieving implies some failure of object-relationships." He uses the word "object-relations" for relations to another person. W. Ronald D. Fairbairn, *An Object-Relations Theory of the Personality* (Basic Books, New York, 1954), pp. 139-140.

57] Hebb and Thompson, "The Social Significance of Animal Studies," in Lindzey, ed., *Handbook of Social Psychology*, pp. 532-561, 551-552.

9

General Attitude, Perceptual Mode, and Their Shifts

WHAT CAUSES THE GREATER FREQUENCY OF AUTOCENTRIC OR allocentric perception in one person as compared with another, the prevalence of one or the other in the same person at one moment as compared with another? What causes perception to shift from the autocentric to the allocentric, or from the allocentric to the autocentric mode? These perceptual modes and their fluctuations do not occur alone, restricted to the perceptual function, but as part of a total attitude, a total mode of relatedness of the perceiver to something in the environment, and they shift together with a shift in total attitude. This implies that they also occur together with a particular tonus and motor attitude which may lead to actual movements or to slight changes in posture and expression, or consist merely of changes in muscular and visceral tonus.[1] When I am looking or listening for something rather than looking *at* or listening *to*, the perceptual attitude tends toward the (secondary) autocentric mode. At that moment I am not interested

[1] This observation is consistent with the theories of perception which emphasize the unity of perception and movement. Compare Viktor von Weizsäcker, *Der Gestaltkreis. Theorie der Einheit von Wahrnehmen und Bewegen*, 4th ed. (Georg Thieme Verlag, Stuttgart, 1950); Heinz Werner and Seymour Wapner, "Sensory-Tonic Field Theory of Perception," in Jerome S. Bruner and David Krech, eds., *Perception and Personality* (Duke University Press, Durham, 1949/50), pp. 88-107.

in and receptive toward the person (if a person was the object of my attention), but bent on finding something that corresponds to a preformed expectation. At the same time I am in a state of motoric (tonic) tension, the tension of expectancy. My ear is cocked for the particular sounds I expect, searchingly, hopefully, or fearfully as the case may be. My eye is scanning for a certain expression, movement, gesture. Eye and ear are straining in a certain direction rather than being turned toward the object in receptive openness, and these attitudes are not confined to the muscles controlling the movements and the adjustment of the eye but can be seen in the total facial expression and over-all posture and probably could be observed also in subtle visceral changes.

The presence of such total attitudes, of which a predominantly autocentric or allocentric perceptual mode of relatedness is a part, and the shifts from one type of attitude to another can have many causes. These may be rooted in biological functions such as the diurnal cycle of awakeness and sleep, they may be rooted in character attitudes and change only with a change in character, they may be subject to voluntary control and shift with a change in conscious purpose. Also, the perceptual attitude may reflect, and be the result of, *conflicting* attitudes. For example, character attitudes may conflict with biological needs, conscious voluntary purposes with character attitudes, and such conflicts may interfere with, or influence the quality of, autocentric or allocentric perception or both. I shall give a few illustrations of these connections between general attitude and autocentric and allocentric perception and of shifts and conflicts in attitude and their influence on perception and discuss the attitude underlying allocentric perception.

With the exception of the great ontogenetic shift in infancy and childhood from completely (primary) autocentric to more allocentric perception, the most striking shift in perceptual mode of relatedness is brought about by the diurnal alternation between *awakeness and sleep* and can be observed especially clearly in the state of resting preparatory to falling asleep. In this state there occurs an impressive and comprehensive shift from the usual attitude of awakeness and alertness. Motor activity is reduced to a minimum, muscular tension and tonus change to relaxation, attention is withdrawn from the outside world and directed sometimes toward the conscious enjoyment of the autocentric sensations preceding sleep, and usually toward signalling any disturbance of relaxation and comfort so that these may be restored. At the same time the protective stimulus barrier toward the outside world gradually rises until it reaches a maximum strength in deep sleep. As these changes take place, perceptual functioning returns to the auto-centric mode and this can be seen in the two major ways which characterize ontogenetic and phylogenetic primary autocentricity: (1) in the return to the predominance of autocentric over allo-centric senses, and (2) in the return of sensory functioning as a guardian over undisturbed embeddedness rather than as a means of encountering the objects and qualities of the environment. The daytime predominance of the distance receptors, eye and ear, subsides and gives way to the predominance of two proximity senses, the thermal and touch receptors, and of the proprioceptive receptors, registering comfort or discomfort of bodily position and muscular tonus. Insofar as sight and hearing continue to function, at a reduced level of alertness, they do so in the autocentric mode as they did to a large extent in early infancy: one does not look or listen, one reacts only to too bright light as a disturbing, un-comfortable, almost painful sensation, but one does not try to see the variety of objects. Similarly, sound is reacted to either as too loud and disturbing, or else as lulling, comforting, background noise, but one does not try to discriminate sounds as in listening to speech. The sense of touch does not function in the allocentric mode, for tactile exploration of objects, but in the autocentric mode, as a feeling of comfort or discomfort in being touched by the blanket, by roughness or smoothness, by comfortable or un-comfortable pressure in the contact of the body with the bed. The person preparing for sleep wants to feel warm and snug and free from tensions. The whole sensory emphasis is on how one feels, how the immediate environment affects one, not on what the environment is like.[2] Sleep is a return to the mode of relatedness of primary embeddedness in the immediate environment. We do not turn away from the world in sleep, but we give up our separate, relatively independent position in which, within the world, we

2] Compare Otto Isakower, "A Contribution to the Patho-Psychology of Phe-nomena Associated with Falling Asleep," *International Journal of Psychoanalysis,* 1938, 19:331-345, p. 339.

encounter the world, and become again more completely a part of it, embedded in it as once we were in the mother's womb.[3]

When the capacity to entrust oneself again to the primary state of embeddedness in the daily sleep cycle is disturbed, insomnia may result. In some cases of insomnia one can observe how the attitudes conflicting with the healthy, normal return to primary embeddedness in sleep also interfere with the return to the primary autocentric perceptual mode preceding sleep. A typical example is that of a patient who had a considerable emotional investment in wanting to blame the world for all his troubles while at the same time not wanting to be in a position where he himself could do something to better his situation. In bed at night he was unable to relax and withdraw his attention from the outside world; instead he would tensely listen for any disturbing sound and when he heard even a minor noise, he would get very angry about this disturbance. He remained on the lookout for such disturbances which then would allow him to feel justified in his anger. Another example is of a patient who, on the basis of early experiences with a very tense and destructive mother, would become quite anxious when about to fall asleep and would awaken himself so as to remain alert and on guard. This, too, found expression in a self-induced attitude of general sensory alertness to the outside world, which he would restore as soon as he noticed that he became drowsy. In a milder form, the interference of distrust with return to embeddedness is the reason for the difficulty that some people have in falling asleep in an unfamiliar place. On the other hand, excessive sleep often is the expression of a craving to escape from the encounter with the world into the safety of the womb.

In *resting*, in *convalescence*, and often in *old age* there occurs a similar, but less pronounced shift to the autocentric perceptual mode as in preparing to fall asleep. In resting, for example in relaxing after strenuous and concentrated activity, by sitting in a deck chair in a garden, one usually does not look attentively at one particular object, but either lets one's glance wander idly or gazes with a kind of diffuse over-all background perception. Also, there is increased cathexis of the "comfort" senses: the emphasis is on sitting relaxedly in the most comfortable position, on enjoying the warm sunshine or the soft breeze touching the skin. This

3] This has been emphasized by Erwin Straus, "Die aufrechte Haltung," *Monatsschrift für Psychiatrie und Neurologie*, 1949, 117:367-379, 369.

restful state is particularly pronounced in convalescence and often in old age, both stages in which there is a more or less marked increase of the autocentric perceptual mode either as a habitual one or as one occurring in greater frequency than it does in full health or at a younger age. This partial shift to primary auto-centric perception in convalescence and old age probably is the means by which the organism in its weakened condition insures that its needs are being met.

The shifts toward the (primary) autocentric mode discussed so far occur more or less automatically in the service of physio-logical needs, although they can be aided by conscious purpose, e.g. by the voluntary decision to stop some activity, to relax, and to go to sleep. But there are also shifts from one perceptual mode to the other which are voluntary, consciously controlled, initiated by conscious decision and purpose, although there are considerable individual differences between people regarding the extent to which they can bring about such a consciously initiated shift in attitude.

An example of a *consciously controlled shift of perceptual attitude* can be observed in the sense of touch, especially *manual touch*. If a small object, for instance a pebble, is enclosed in the palm and fingers of the hand then one can feel, at one moment, primarily the pleasant coolness, roundness, and smoothness in the contact, in the way in which palm and fingers are being touched and affected by the pebble resting in them, the way skin and muscles feel in holding it. From this (primary) autocentric atti-tude one can shift to an allocentric attitude in which the intention becomes a desire to explore and recognize the object in one's hand. At this point one successively pays attention to the different areas of contact, moving the pebble around in the hand or, by slightly varying innervation of palm and fingers, exerting changing pressure now at one, now at another point of contact, thus circumnavigating as it were the pebble in the hand and exploring its various surfaces. The attitude has become one of alertness to the structure and quality of the *object*, to its shape, to the distribution of smooth and rough, of perfectly round and of jagged areas. Such allocentric tactile exploration is much more highly developed in the blind than in the average seeing person, since the blind have to rely much more on their tactile sense for their sensory knowledge of the world of objects. The capacity for primary autocentric sensory tactile experience and its enjoyment will be the more highly developed the more the person is able to shift his total attitude to one of giving himself over to the sensation, without the interference of restlessness, impatience, cravings, and tension, i.e. of strivings usually resulting from secondary autocentric attitudes.

The particular sensitivity and pleasure in autocentric tactile experience, quite strong in early childhood, often get lost in later life in Western civilization because of the emphasis on purposive, goal-directed behavior intended to bring about changes in the outer world and to bring success, money, and prestige. In China and Japan, until recently, tactile sensitivity was prized and consciously developed. In both countries people would obtain objects to carry with them in their pockets for the pleasure of handling them. These objects might be perfectly round, smooth stones or they might be pieces of ivory, jade, or bone carved in fine bas-relief. In handling them there probably is an oscillation between autocentric and allocentric perception, with the emphasis now on the autocentric pleasurable experience, now on the subtle exploration of a particular surface area. The cultivation of such tactile sensibility can be seen also in the emphasis on texture in Chinese and Japanese cooking.

Similar, consciously induced shifts of perceptual mode can be observed in *visual* perception. Sitting in a garden one may look at a particular tree, trying to see it fully, to experience as it were the essence of this tree, in the allocentric mode of perception. Then one may give oneself over to the more autocentric experience of the impact of color and light all around one, the refreshing and restful green, the lively colors of clumps of flowers, the blue of the sky. In doing so, one will notice that the shift in attitude is not confined to the visual experience but likely to include a relaxation in muscular tonus, a total shift in the state of consciousness, and an enhancement of the autocentric mode also in the other sensory modalities, which may be similar to the one described in the discussion of resting or may be a more conscious enjoyment of the beneficent effects on our senses of the surrounding nature.

The foregoing examples were of consciously effected shifts from allocentric to primary autocentric perception. The reverse conscious shift, from primary autocentric to allocentric perception, can be observed just as frequently. The same holds true of shifts from and to *secondary* autocentric experience. I can, at one moment, look at an object in the allocentric mode, with the purpose of wanting to see it as fully as possible, and can then, by an act of conscious purpose, shift to look at the same object to see whether it will fit some particular need or purpose of mine, i.e. in the mode of secondary autocentricity. Such shifts may also occur, consciously, but more or less automatically, under the pressure of a particular reality situation. Imagine the situation of a parachutist dropped behind the enemy lines and trying to make his way through a forest to a certain point he wants to reach. In this situation he will perceive everything in the (secondary) autocentric mode. His attention is vigilant rather than focal. He scans everything, not from the viewpoint of wanting to see it fully, but to detect the presence or absence of danger. Every sight and every noise is perceived with the utmost alertness as to its possible danger or safety implications. The sights seen and the sounds heard become potential signals of danger and no longer invite a full turning toward the object. This sensory experience of the forest is drastically different from what it would be if he went for a walk through the woods to enjoy a fine morning, to look at the life of the forest, the trees, the ferns, the moss, the patterns of sunlight on the ground, to smell the morning freshness, to listen to the song of the birds. The conscious experience of danger causes a total shift of perceptual attitude. In walking through the woods to enjoy the morning there is a mixture of allocentric and primary autocentric sensory experiences. In the case of the parachutist there is a shift to a completely one-sided sensory experience, an experience in the secondary autocentric mode. From perception in such a realistic danger situation there is a continuous transition of degrees of awareness to the situation of some neurotic personalities who are not aware of their fears and yet scan their environment in a way which is fundamentally very similar to that of the parachutist behind enemy lines. However, in contrast to him, they may not be aware of the possibility of perception in the allocentric mode because all they have ever experienced is the autocentric view in which the environment is scanned for unknown or anticipated dangers. In less extreme cases, i.e. in most cases, there will be areas and situations in which the person is more capable of allocentric perception and of the enjoyment of primary autocentric sensations so that there is greater likelihood of having or gaining an awareness of how different the world can look and of realizing that the secondary autocentric mode blocks a fuller vision of reality.

It would be a tempting task to explore and describe in detail a larger number of the innumerable intra- and inter-individual differences in sensory perception which result from the manifold combinations, shifts, intensities, conflicts of attitudes with their intrinsic links with the degree, quality, and mixture of the primary and secondary autocentric and the allocentric modes of perceiving. While these differences are subtle and therefore have largely escaped the attention, the methods, and tools of experimental psychology, they are pervasive and instrumental in determining what quite literally constitutes a person's *Weltanschauung* (world view) —and not only his world viewing but also his world hearing, touching, smelling, and tasting. (This sensory world-view may not be at all the same as the person's conscious ideology, and it may even be the opposite.) The present-day situation of the psychology of perception with regard to these perceptual differences may be compared with the situation of the psychology of motivation before psychoanalysis had demonstrated the subtle but powerful role of unconscious motivations and attitudes. The study of the differences of perception in this sense is comparable to the study of expressive movements which, to the trained and capable observer (e.g. a first-rate graphologist), show the person's conscious and unconscious motivations in their intricate patterns of action, conflict, suppression, inhibition, goal-directedness, etc., as expressed in the motoric behavior. It is more difficult because, unlike handwriting, perception leaves no visible record. The only record it leaves is the experience of the perceiver which, outside of our own experience, is only indirectly accessible to us.

The few examples described of shifts in perceptual modes and the resulting differences in perceptual experience demonstrate the inseparable connection between total attitude and perceptual mode. Because of the unique importance of allocentric perception as the highest form of perception reached in phylogenetic and in human ontogenetic development, the question of the *attitude linked with allocentric perception* deserves our special attention now.

I shall designate this attitude as the *allocentric attitude*. From the descriptions of allocentric perception it has already become apparent that this attitude is one of profound interest in the object, and complete openness and receptivity toward it, a full turning toward the object which makes possible the direct encounter with it and not merely a quick registration of its familiar features according to ready labels.[4] The essential qualities of the interest in, the turning toward, the object are its *totality* and *affirmativeness*. The totality of interest refers both to the object in which the perceiver is interested and to the act of interest. The interest concerns the *whole object,* not merely a partial aspect of it; and the perceiver turns toward the object with *his entire being,* his whole personality, i.e. fully, not just with part of himself. The act of interest is total and it concerns the totality of its object. Indeed, one is the function of the other. If one turns to the object with only part of his total being, e.g. with a certain appetite (hunger, sex), or to use it for some specific purpose, then one is interested only in certain aspects of the object and not concerned with the total being of the object. On this hinges the often observed fact that the object, the world, reveals itself to man only according to the degree and quality of the interest he takes in it.

The capacity to become interested in the *totality of any object* and not merely in the immediately need-satisfying aspects of need-related objects is the source of the richness of the human perceptual world. This richness is based on man's capacity temporarily to emancipate himself from being dominated and driven exclusively by the needs he shares with other animals (food, sex, care of the young, shelter, rest, etc.) and to perceive the world around him in its own right and not under the perspective of how it may be used to provide for these needs. It extends in two dimensions: (1) the great variety of objects significant for man, (2) the depth and richness with which he can perceive each single object. Both dimensions distinguish man's perceptual world from the animal's. The biologist Portmann has described this difference with regard to the *multitude* of objects perceived by man. He says that every and any object may concern man, who is constantly on the search for unknown, potentially significant objects, whereas even the most active, indefatigably searching animal never searches for anything but the relatively few significant objects the need for which the animal's organization predetermines. This distinguishes human *interest* from the animal's *appetite* (*Appetenz*).[5] The objects which

4] Compare above pp. 177-183.
5] Adolf Portmann, *Biologische Fragmente zu einer Lehre vom Menschen* (Benno Schwabe & Co., Basel, 1951), p. 64.

may concern man need not have anything to do with either present or future satisfaction of any of the basic needs he shares with the animals.

Man's perception is further distinguished from the animal's by the *fullness and richness* with which he is capable of perceiving a single, particular object. This accounts for the fact that he perceives *objects*, i.e. independently existing things each of which is characterized by a considerable variety of perceptible aspects. The animal perceives the relatively few objects which stand out for it only under certain limited aspects, but neither independently of his need organization nor in the multifaceted way of human objectifying perception in which any and every aspect or quality of the object may become of interest. Furthermore, even on the level of allocentric, objectifying perception there are considerable interpersonal and intra-personal differences which account for the richness with which one may perceive an object at a time when one is fully alive and interested, as compared with another time when one's interest and vitality are subdued or flagging. The great interpersonal differences in the depth and richness of human perception become most apparent in art and poetry, which constitute a living record of human perceptiveness transcending anything that could be explained by a perception limited to the function of providing for the basic animal needs. Human perception is not only in the service of the question, addressed to the object, "How can I use you or protect myself against you?" but—in allocentric perception —it also answers the question, "Who or what are you who are part of this same world of which I am a part?" It is this latter question which concerns the *totality* of the object, while the former always concerns only the need-related aspects of the object.

This view of human perception differs from that of Freud, who believed that the function of man's attentive perceptual exploration of the object world served the purpose only of acquainting man with the data of the world so that these "might be already familiar if an urgent need should arise."[6] Freud's view is supported

6] S. Freud, "Formulations Regarding the Two Principles in Mental Functioning," in David Rapaport, *Organization and Pathology of Thought* (Columbia University Press, New York, 1951), pp. 320-321. See also Rapaport's comment, footnote 22, p. 322, in which he expresses the belief that the richness of the human perceptual world is due to "the attentive-purposive activity by which the organism, even when not in need, notices and organizes its world to provide for the time when the need will arise." For a discussion of the motivation of perception, from the ontogenetic viewpoint, see above pp. 116-158.

by the obvious fact that a great many objects and aspects of objects have been perceived by man because he was looking for some way in which they could be put to use for some need of his. But it does not account for the fact that the richest perception occurs in art, poetry, and in the intuitive glance of some of the greatest scientists. The difference which Freud makes between human and animal perception is that man's attentive search of his environment has as its purpose not only to take care of the present need in tension but also to provide for future emergencies, for the future arousal of an "urgent need." But the mere provision for future needs can be taken care of also by rigid instinctive behavior patterns without any enrichment of the perceptual object world; witness the proverbial hamster, the ant of La Fontaine's fable, the squirrel, the many nest-building birds which provide for the future care of the young, and many other examples from animal life. Freud's view would account for the hoarding of need-satisfying objects, or for a kind of mapping of the environment as to where these objects are likely to be found in the future, but it would not account for the characteristically human capacity of discovering new ways of satisfying needs (new foods, methods of raising and preparing food, invention of tools, new methods of shelter, and so forth), and it would not at all account for man's allocentric quest, for his wish to perceive and know beyond any reference to need satisfaction. Indeed, even the discovery of new ways in which objects might be used for need satisfaction *presupposes* the development of at least a minimal capacity for *allocentric* interest and perception, an extension of perception beyond those aspects of the object which are relevant only for direct need satisfaction, a loosening of the tie between instinctual need and perception, a fuller perception of the object. In order to see even those new aspects of an object which make it suitable for a different way of providing for future needs, perception has to be emancipated from need, man has to stop in his rush to grab the need-object, he has to halt, to step back and to look at the object as it is in itself, from all angles. The presence of a particular purpose to which he intends to put the object narrows rather than widens, binds rather than liberates his glance, and does not permit the object to show itself more fully. Interest in the totality of the object and the allocentric perception implementing this interest develop in *play* rather than in the attempt to provide for future needs.[7] This is a lesson the implications of which present-day man and society are reluctant to learn, as is evidenced by their overriding concern with technology, with know-how, rather than with the basic questions of man's relation to the world, to his fellow men and fellow creatures. It is evidenced even within the field of science, where the basic problems receive much less attention than the invention of new gadgets, weapons, etc., and where in the public mind whatever attention is given to these basic questions can be justified only if it "pays off" in terms of the "conquest" of nature or the conquest of the enemy or financial profits.

Allocentric interest in an object leads to an act of *global* perception in which the object as a whole is perceived. This globality is different from the global perception of early infancy. The latter concerns a state of being or a total situation in which object and subject are not differentiated and in which the emphasis is on the total feeling of the infant. It is also different from the global perception of units in later infancy and early childhood, which leads to a primitive object-globality, without distinct perception of features. Allocentric global perception presupposes objectification and is often based on many preceding acts of perception in which different aspects and details of the object have been explored. It can progress through various stages, global perception repeatedly alternating with attention directed to details. Depending on the personality of the perceiver, the circumstances of the situation, and the nature of the object perceived, the first glance in which the total object is encountered may reveal its essence more truly and fully than later, repeated encounters which may obscure or distort it; on the other hand, a sustained dedication, in many encounters, may eventually disclose the object fully to the perceiver or enrich its quality. Even the perception of particular aspects or features of the object against the background of allocentric global perception differs from the perception of it against the background of special interests or needs, as regards both the act-quality and the object-quality of the perceptual process. The former contributes to the total view of the object, the latter tends to reinforce the particular perspective or bias from which the object is seen.

7] This has been shown by Gustav Bally, *Vom Ursprung und von den Grenzen der Freiheit. Eine Deutung des Spiels bei Tier und Mensch* (Benno Schwabe & Co., Basel, 1945). See also the section on "Focal Attention," this volume, pp. 251-278.

If concern with the totality of the object is one aspect of allocentric interest, *totality of the act of interest,* participation of the total person in the act of interest, a *total turning to* it is the other aspect. The allocentric act of interest thus differs from other acts of interest in which the person turns to the object in order to use it for the satisfaction of a particular need or in the service of a particular purpose.[8] However, it is not only the need-dominated act of interest that excludes the possibility of fully allocentric perception, but also the repression or the more or less conscious warding off, suppression, turning against the demands of some need. It is not possible to turn fully, with complete interest and full attention, toward an object if one is engaged at the same time in a battle against some other impulse, craving, or preoccupation. Under these conditions one may be capable of a cramped but not a relaxed concentration. Only the latter permits the full gathering of all the forces of the personality and their free turning toward the object in the act of total interest. There are many gradations of such relaxed yet concentrated turning toward the object. They range from what Freud describes as "evenly hovering attention"[9] to what in Zen Buddhism is called "right presence of mind" in which the mind, because it is not attached to anything, can freely and fully turn at any moment to anything.[10]

Rilke, who has given much thought to the conditions under which an object will reveal itself to the poet or the artist, writes: "In order to have an object speak to you, you must take it for a certain time for the only one that exists, the only phenomenon which, through your devoted and exclusive love, finds itself placed in the center of the universe . . . ," and on another occasion he writes about the "quietness and sincerity of contemplation" which enables the artist to see the objects in his own way and which is "more generous than he himself" ahead of and beyond all purposefulness by which he works to help it along.[11]

8] For a discussion of such need- or purpose-dominated interest and its effects on perception see above, pp. 166-212.

9] Freud, "Recommendations for Physicians on the Psychoanalytic Method of Treatment," *Collected Papers* (Basic Books, New York, 1959), Vol. II, p. 324.

10] Compare the description of this state of the fullest presence of mind which results in the capacity for the fullest allocentric "egoless" attention, in Eugen Herrigel, *Zen in the Art of Archery* (Pantheon Books, New York, 1953), pp. 58-59.

11] Author's translation from Rainer Maria Rilke, *Briefe aus Muzot 1921-1926* (Insel-Verlag, Leipzig, 1935), pp. 17-18 and 121-122.

Rilke touches here on the relations between allocentric interest and love. In the allocentric attitude, which is the foundation of allocentric perception, there is an element of affirmation. Every act of allocentric perception has this affirmative quality which acknowledges the object of the act as existing in its own right. In Hegel's thought it is the movement from knowledge to acknowledgment which constitutes love.[12] Only when interest is defined as partial, serving a particular purpose or need, as a special interest, does it stand in the way of allocentric perception. But total interest is identical with the allocentric attitude in which the very being of the other, of the object, is affirmed, and it is only on the basis of such affirmative interest that allocentric perception becomes fully possible. This is the reason why love sees more than hatred. Hatred can be astute in perceiving every possibility for attack, but even though such astuteness may lead to penetrating insights as well as distortions, they remain partial in the literal sense of this word: they always concern only part of the other and they are "partial" to those parts which will serve as the points of attack. But hatred is unable to see its object in its totality. When, on the other hand, it is said that love is blind, this is true only for infatuation and desire, but not for love which wants to affirm others in their total and unique being. Such affirmation does not presuppose nor does it foster blindness for the other person's limitations, weaknesses, and shortcomings, which are the lot of man.

In the allocentric attitude the object is affirmed as part of the same world of which man is a part. While this attitude becomes most readily apparent in the kinship of all men, it can extend to every part of nature. This is expressed in the Indian *Tat tvam asi* (That is you), or in Goethe's lines:

> Du führst die Reihe der Lebendigen
> Vor mir vorbei und lehrst mich meine Brüder
> Im stillen Busch, in Luft und Wasser kennen.[13]

12] In this movement, according to Hegel, love and reason become one, as is suggested also in the Biblical Hebrew word *jadoah*, which means both to have sexual intercourse and to know. Compare Ludwig Binswanger, *Grundformen und Erkenntnis menschlichen Daseins* (Max Nichaus, Zürich, 1953), pp. 493-498.

13] "The ranks of living creatures thou dost lead
   Before me, teaching me to know my brothers
   In air and water and the silent wood."
Faust I, "Forest and Cavern," Bayard Taylor, trans. (Random House, New York, 1950), p. 124.

This affirmation of the other person in the act of allocentric perception is possible only where there is an experiential realization of the kinship between oneself and the other. Such realization is made difficult or impossible by fear and by arrogance—by fear because then the need to protect oneself by flight, appeasement, or attack gets in the way; by arrogance because then the other is no longer experienced as akin, but as inferior to oneself. An example may illustrate the concrete effects of such interference in perception. A person who, for reasons of his life history, feels unacceptable to others and to himself responds to the anxiety which this arouses in him by a basically defensive attack. He feels attacked and so he counterattacks. Both his hostility and his anxiety find, like every human emotion, visible and audible expression in his features and his behavior. But another person, who for reasons of his own is particularly afraid of rejection by others, that is, who is particularly dependent on being accepted and approved of, is likely to look at a person like the one just described not in an allocentric way, but in order to satisfy his own need for acceptance. This need may have the effect that he can see only the manifestations of hostility, but not those of anxiety. He becomes unable to experience kinship with the other because his preoccupation with the hostility does not let him see the whole human being, with whom he has in common the human predicament.

The allocentric attitude is a relative rather than an absolute concept, a matter of emphasis rather than of the exclusion of all and any autocentricity. Obviously man cannot transcend his sensory equipment. The fact that he is affected by colors and scents in the very act of perceiving the world around him does not preclude, but is included in, his fully turning toward this world. Nor can he make himself immune to fear and many other feelings which might interfere with allocentric perception if they become too strong or if he wants primarily to protect himself against them. It is the attempt to escape from such feelings, rather than the existence of them, which prevents man from turning fully, with his whole being, toward the object.

The allocentric turning toward the object presupposes the readiness to *expose oneself* with all one's sensibilities to its presence without shielding oneself by any of the numerous protective devices which man has at his disposal. They range all the way from selective inattention or from "disposing" of the object by some kind of classification to effective neutralization of the object's impact by attitudes of indifference, distance, intellectualization, pseudo-objectivity, etc. Whether they serve protective or other purposes, they preclude an essentially allocentric perception of the object. Such attitudes may be part of the personality structure and thus habitual, or they may be part of a transitory mood. A few examples will illustrate the connection between personality, mood, and basic perceptual mode. They concern attitudes which prevent fully turning toward the object in allocentric perception and therefore lead in different, subtle, but pervasive ways to a relative loss of realness which, in extreme cases, can approach the loss of reality found in depersonalization. They all hinge on the intrinsic connection between degree and quality of interest and degree and quality of the richness, realness, and fullness of the object.

The first example is that of the *pseudo-realist*, ubiquitous in modern civilization. He knows all the answers, knows how to handle everything, often even knows what is "behind" everything. Nothing astonishes him, nothing gives cause for wonder, nothing is mysterious to him. He knows his way around and, indeed, his way always leads him around, but never *to* the object, although he is often very good at pursuing his objective. The objects never speak to him, never reveal themselves to him, because he does not stop to listen to them or to look at them since he already knows all there is to know. Thus, he turns away from them, sometimes indifferent or bored, sometimes satisfied that, because he knew the right "angle," he got just what he wanted, sometimes proud of his "realism" and his knowledge which, without his knowing about this, are the veiled nihilism of the commonplace. His perceptual gesture is not that of seeing or looking but, in Nietzsche's telling image, that of blinking.

"Behold! I show you the last man. 'What is love? What is creation? What is longing? What is a star?'—so asketh the last man and blinketh. . . . 'We have discovered happiness,'—say the last men, and blink."[14] The pseudo-realist disposes of all objects as already known. They have nothing to offer to him except how they may be used by him. His world consists of objects-of-use. Thus, he succeeds in avoiding the disquietude and anxiety of the

14] *Thus Spake Zarathustra*, Prologue, 5. Thomas Common's translation (Tudor Publishing Co., New York, 1934), p. 9.

unknown which the full encounter would cause him, although he is not aware of this. He treats the objects as completely familiar, but this familiarity, too, is a pseudo-familiarity, since all he knows of them are "angles." This is very different from the global familiarity which the infant and young child come to experience in their immediate environment and is also different from that which slowly grows from the intimate contact of a life or of many years spent in the same home, the same village, the same neighborhood. His is a secondary embeddedness among objects which never were anything but objects-of-use, so that he would feel helplessly out of his depth if ever he encountered them in a different way. He is protected against such an encounter because he has failed to develop those sensibilities and capacities which go beyond a mere practical, intellectual know-how.

Related to, but also different from, the pseudo-realist is the *pseudo-detached* personality, not infrequently an intellectual, often with a real or a pseudo-scientific bent. He tends to believe that he is very objective and very rational with regard to the world at large, to other people and to his own life. Actually, he often is lacking in sensitivity and has a knack of riding roughshod over other people, sometimes with complete unawareness of what he is doing, showing a naive surprise if others do not agree that his behavior is completely rational. While he believes that he perceives reality very clearly and in a quite unbiased way, he actually is out of touch with life around him as well as with his own life. His detachment is due to massive processes of intellectualization and isolation which render him incapable of turning to the world fully with his whole personality and thus of allocentric perception. The scope of what he perceives often exceeds that of the pseudo-realist, but while more objects may come into his view he, too, remains separated from them by an invisible barrier which lets him see only their shadows, a skeletal, bloodless reality, or one of biased constructs instead of the living world around him. His detachment differs from the kind that has no personal stake, no axe to grind, no special interest, as contrasted with total interest. The latter kind of detachment can be the basis of a fully allocentric attitude and can go together with an undemanding and uncontrolling love, provided that it is not built upon repressed needs.

A barrier different from those which prevent the pseudo-realist and the pseudo-detached personality from turning fully toward the object gets between the perceiver and the world in the *aestheticist* attitude. The aestheticist perceives images and pictures of reality, instead of encountering it. By thus transforming it he can avoid the full encounter with a three-dimensional and alive world and, furthermore, selectively screen out, underemphasize, or turn against those aspects of reality which do not fit into his peculiar world of images. The subtle derealization which takes place in the transformation of the object into an image not only serves the purpose of creating a distance and barrier between perceiver and object; very often the unconscious "composition" of these images also has the function of magic wish-fulfillment. Then the type of image perceived may have a soothing or a stirring quality, or a self-complementary or a self-reflecting quality. In the latter case, the reflection is apt to be of a self-ideal rather than of the real self. The self in these cases becomes an image, too. This self-image does not follow Goethe's precept for self-knowledge—to act and meet the day's demands so that one may see what there is to one—but arises from narcissistic wishes and phantasies and usually has as its secret and sometimes unconscious counterpart an equally distorted negative self-image. The person who cannot love another as she or he really is, tends particularly to create such images which may have hardly anything to do with the beloved on whom they are projected. This is the quality of "love" described by Proust in the narrator's relation to Albertine and in Swann's to Odette. Both seek an image built out of their own needs, and are rudely awakened from their dreams when the real person bears no resemblance to the image, or—in her real or spiritual absence—are tortured by the fear that this very moment the elusive image that they want to hold on to and possess might escape them forever. In a similar way, many people perceive images of nature or of the social world which, although they seem the very opposite of the pseudo-realist's view of the world, are just as far removed from the richness of reality and just as effectively prevent the full encounter with it.

The aestheticist transformation of reality has no intrinsic relation to art. On the contrary, the true artist could not create the work of art if he did not fully see the real world or some aspect of it. The work of art arises from the ever repeated encounter in which reality yields its secrets to the patient and receptive eye of the artist, although they may not yet be visible to his contemporaries. The aestheticist has more in common with the sybaritic attitude of the seeker after pleasant sensations[15] than with the artist. His addiction is to images and daydreams rather than to drugs. But he shares with the addict the need to escape from his own and the world's reality. Just as the luminous images of the mescalin intoxication are bought at the price of a temporary paralysis of the capacity to act and to take any interest in other people,[16] so the aestheticist transformation of the world into images is a substitute for the alive encounter and arises from the necessity to repress the impulses which would interfere with one's fully turning toward the world.

If the real world appears uniformly pale, unsubstantial, lacking in aliveness and brilliance, this results from the stunting of the capacity for allocentric interest which can be brought about, needless to say, as much by the pressures of poverty or of an impersonal daily grind as it can by neurotic conflicts. The greater vision of the artist, with which Huxley compares the effects of mescalin, need not be bought, as in the mescalin intoxication, at the price of a paralysis of his life as an acting and feeling man. Man's wishes, strivings, and feelings interfere with allocentric perception only where they prevent his turning fully, with total and intensive interest, to the totality of the object.

The pseudo-realist, the pseudo-detached, and the aestheticist thinning of perception usually is not conscious, since the perceiver does not know any other way of perceiving. On the contrary, the pseudo-realist often feels that only he sees the world as it really is, and the aestheticist may pride himself on his sensitivity or sense of beauty; both may look down with contempt or irritation on anyone who does not acknowledge the superiority of their perspective. It may happen, occasionally, though, that they remember how much more vivid and interesting the world appeared to them when they were children and it may also happen that at some time in the course of their lives they experience boredom and the peculiar pallor which it casts over everything.

Since *boredom* and its relative, *mild depression,* in the form of temporary moods are known from personal experience to most

15] See above, pp. 210-212.
16] See the account of the effects of mescalin on perception in Aldous Huxley, *The Doors of Perception* (Harper & Brothers, New York, 1954).

people, the changes in perception brought about by them are more readily accessible to recall and awareness than those due to more enduring factors in the structure of the personality. In boredom and depression the world loses its valences to the degree that the person loses his interest and does not turn toward the world. Usually he is at the same time angry at the world because he feels that it fails him in some respect, but his anger need not necessarily be conscious. A striking contrast is observable between the dreary, deadened, dull, grey, uniform world which the depressed and the bored perceive and the presence, clarity, impact of a vivid world, full of contrasts, colors, light and dark, which the interested person perceives. In Rorschach's test this contrast often finds expression in a decrease or absence of color responses in the depressed or bored. While usually they are aware of the color, it has no, or less, impact on them and appears less vivid than it does in a different mood. Because of their withdrawal of interest from the world, they not only are unaffected by the objects around them no matter how varied, beautiful, ugly, stimulating, attractive, or repellent these may be, but they also suffer an impairment of the ability to really grasp the structure and quality of the objects. While they perceive the "same" objects as others (although often not as many), these objects have undergone a marked change of quality. Their conceptual referents remain the same, but their appearance and living significance have changed. They have lost character and outspoken qualities. Both the allocentric and autocentric senses suffer the same fate in boredom and depression. Many depressed patients complain that food tastes no more, just as the visible world appears dull or shadowy to them. The depressed and the bored are incapable of allocentric as well as autocentric interest, they can neither turn to the world fully nor pursue the search for need-objects with eagerness. Sensory communication with the world has palled for them.

Such disruption can be produced artificially by the removal both of sensory stimulation and of the possibility of establishing active contact with the world. This is the case in the torture of solitary confinement, especially when at the same time vision of the world without is barred, as in the medieval dungeons and their modern counterparts of the twentieth century, or in the recent experiments on boredom at McGill University.[17] A milder, but widespread form of artificially enforced disruption of contact with the world exists in some types of monotonous work in which, at the same time, communication with others is made impossible.

But in the cases of boredom and depression which occur either as a passing *mood* or as a more lasting *disposition,* the disruption of sensory and other communication with the world is not enforced from outside but originates in the personality of the perceiver. The world appears dull and empty to him because he cannot establish contact with it and at the same time he undergoes a relative loss of self, he does not feel quite alive. He can no longer be reached by, be receptive to, the richness of the sensory world because he feels unable to turn toward it. The capacity which distinguishes the maturing and growth of human perception from that of the fetal state of total embeddedness, the capacity to turn toward the world or, in Freud's words, to meet the sense impressions halfway, has suffered a setback which results in a pervasive change of the over-all quality of perception. The barren desert into which the perceptual world is transformed in boredom and depression illustrates perhaps more drastically than anything else the change from the state of fetal embeddedness in which every stimulus was felt as disturbance to that of emergence from embeddedness into the individuation of separate, wakeful life. The suffering of the bored and the depressed, their negative passion,[18] arises from the very fact that they dwell as shadows of their alive selves in a world emptied of life and holding no prospect of stimulation, comparable to the Hades of Greek mythology in which the sun never shines. Far from feeling stimulation as a disturbance, they reproach the world for not giving them the stimulation they crave, while at the same time they reject what the world has to offer.

This becomes apparent when boredom turns into restlessness and depression into manic or hypomanic excitement. In restlessness and excitement a frantic effort is made to escape from the emptiness of self and world experienced in boredom and depression.

17] W. H. Bexton, W. Heron, and T. H. Scott, "Effects of Decreased Variation in the Sensory Environment," *Canadian Journal of Psychology,* 1954, 8:70-76; Woodburn Heron, "The Pathology of Boredom," *Scientific American,* January, 1957, pp. 52-56.
18] Compare Leopardi's remark on boredom, quoted above, p. 177, footnote 9.

But the frantic nature of the effort defeats its purpose. The contacts made are pseudo-contacts. They are not the result of turning to the world with interest, but with an impatient and angry demand. They are essentially destructive. This is manifest in manic rage, but it is true also of the angry dissatisfaction with everything encountered in the restless search of the bored, although the anger may be disguised or repressed. In the French words *ennui, ennuyant,* which signify both tedium and annoyance, the intrinsic connection between boredom and anger finds expression.[19] Imprisoned in the empty shell of a self and a world which have lost their alive substance,[20] the bored and depressed, in the restless and excited phases of their affliction, desperately and angrily beat at the invisible walls of their prison demanding to be given what in reality they can reach only if, first, these walls are broken down, that is, if *they* can turn to the world with interest. Even where the restless search of the chronically bored for stimulation seems to be successful, their temporary feeling of relief has the character of distraction from emptiness, rather than of overcoming it by the resumption of alive contact with the world. Perception, even in these moments of distraction, does not become fully allocentric because the capacity to turn to the world with interest is not regained. The person seeks for such stimuli as will distract or divert him, passively, from his plight, because he feels unable to gather his own resources. Hence, the peculiar fitness of suspense, thrills, excitement for the purpose of escaping from boredom. They grip the person but do not lead to the finding of world and self in the act of allocentric encounter.

Before concluding this account of various forms in which the capacity for allocentric perception is disturbed and the full encounter with the object world disrupted or attenuated, I want to quote a short passage from the moving account of a manic-depres-

19] Compare also Fenichel's patient who felt mainly angry when he was restless and bored. Otto Fenichel, "On the Psychology of Boredom," in Rapaport, *Organization and Pathology of Thought,* pp. 349-361.

20] v. Gebsattel has pointed out the affinity between depression and depersonalization and derealization. V. E. von Gebsattel, "Zur Frage der Depersonalisation," *Prolegomena einer medizinischen Anthropologie* (Springer-Verlag, Berlin, 1954), pp. 18-46. A similar affinity prevails between boredom and depersonalization and derealization. While these do not usually reach the degree of acute feelings of estrangement from self and world, the loss of substance and aliveness of self and world in prolonged boredom seems to me a milder form of depersonalization and derealization.

sive patient of v. Gebsattel, who came to treatment after two years of severe depression with depersonalization feelings. After two years of treatment she describes an experience she had while walking in the garden: "I discover a leaf of a beech tree, I feel it between my fingers, I feel the smooth and the rough surface like something entirely new. It was a moment only, the slender little leaf, it gave me a thousand times more than at Easter the faces of my children. [The experience took place in August.] At that time I took their heads in my hands so as to feel them, but I felt nothing —my hands, between them: nothing. The little leaf, suddenly I discovered it, and then it was gone again. I saw an earthworm, a little while ago, a dumb earthworm on the garden path. I stopped and looked at it as if at something unheard of—an earthworm who wriggled. People, alas, are nothing to me as yet, only nature I have discovered, not as a whole, but in its smallest parts only. That is a great wondering, a great quietness after all the restless rushing."[21] The discovery made by this patient who had been, and still was, severely disturbed, is one that many "normal" people in our time never make, at least not after childhood. The pseudo-realist and the pseudo-detached often are among them, although they are perfectly sane in the clinical sense of the word.

The analysis of the changes and differences in perception due to changes and differences in moods and basic attitudes is a task which psychology has yet to perform. The instances just discussed and those mentioned earlier (the pathological oversensitivity to sensory stimuli, transformation of perception in the "sensation seeker"[22]) represent only a few sketchy examples from an as yet uncharted field, in the exploration of which the concepts of primary and secondary autocentric and of allocentric perception may prove helpful. How much of such research is accessible to present-day experimental methods remains to be seen. The difficulty lies mainly in the fact that we deal with subtle, although pervasive and profound changes and differences of which the perceiver often is not aware, and that the methods of the laboratory are likely to change the very attitude which is to be studied by them. This is the reason why clinical and phenomenological methods so far have contributed more than experimental ones to this field.[23] It should

21] Author's translation from v. Gebsattel, *op. cit.,* p. 25.
22] See above, pp. 158, 210-212.
23] Compare especially the work of E. Straus, v. Gebsattel, E. Minkowski, G.

be possible, however, to devise experimental methods, for example, for the study of various sensory thresholds in which not only the absolute limits of sensory capacity are measured, as has been done in earlier research, but in which changes of thresholds in different life situations and different attitudes are studied, including the variations in the autocentric and allocentric modes of perception. From animal psychology instances are known in which changes in mood or in different types of instinctive activities lead to drastic changes in sensory functioning. Thus, bees discriminate color when in search of food, but not otherwise. Male grayling butterflies following a female prior to mating respond equally to dummies of different colors, but when seeking food they seek out yellow and blue flowers only.[24] The changes in perceptual functioning discussed in this paper do not lend themselves to such simple description, but some of them are at least as drastic while others are more subtle, yet very significant for the understanding of the person and his perceptual world.

Bachelard, K. Goldstein, L. Binswanger. For an experimental approach see Klein's work on the "leveling" and "sharpening" attitudes and their relation to reactive behavior and passive drifting, and autonomous, aggressive behavior, respectively. George S. Klein, "The Personal World through Perception," in Robert R. Blake and Glenn V. Ramsey, eds., *Perception: An Approach to Personality* (Ronald Press, New York, 1951), pp. 328-355.

24] N. Tinbergen, quoted by Henry W. Nissen, "Phylogenetic Comparison," in S. S. Stevens, ed., *Handbook of Experimental Psychology* (John Wiley & Sons, New York, 1951), p. 350. N. Tinbergen, "Psychology and Ethology as Supplementary Parts of a Science of Behavior," in B. Schaffner, ed., *Group Processes, First Conference, 1954* (Josiah Macy, Jr., Foundation, New York, 1955), pp. 112-113.

10

Perception as Creative Experience

Critique of the Concept of Regression in the Service of the Ego

THE PHYLOGENESIS OF PERCEPTION IS CHARACTERIZED BY THE INcreasing amount, variety, and enrichment of sensory experience. It culminates in man's allocentric mode of perception, in which independently existing objects are perceived (objectification). Because of man's openness toward the world the number of possible objects of human perception and the variety of their aspects are infinite and inexhaustible. To what extent man realizes his potentiality of allocentric perception depends on the stage he reaches in his ontogenetic development. During this development he explores, in the playful encounters of childhood, an expanding environment and an increasing variety of object aspects in exercising his growing sensory-motor capacities. While part of this exploration takes place in the spontaneous and immediate encounter with the objects, an important part consists in the increasing acquaintance with their meaning in the culture. Such learning on the one hand enriches the object world of the growing child to a degree which could never be reached by an isolated individual. On the other hand, it also increasingly supplants the child's original approach to the objects and, especially in our time, entails the danger of *closing* his openness toward the world and of reducing all experience to the perception of such preformed clichés and "angles" as make up the world of "reality" seen by the family, peer group, and society in which he grows up. The perspective from which objects are perceived may narrow to "what they are there for" and "how one deals with them." Nature may no longer be seen as the mother of all living creatures including man, but may become an enemy to be conquered or a mere object to be exploited and used. Other people, too, may be seen from a similar viewpoint, the viewpoint of secondary autocentricity.

Where the perspective of secondary autocentricity becomes the only one and dominates all perception, allocentric as well as primary autocentric perception tend to stagnate and atrophy. In our time this stagnation tends to take the form of an alienation of man from the objects and from his own sensory capacities. The danger of this alienation is that man's dulled senses may no longer encounter the objects themselves but only what he expects and already knows about them, the labels formed by his society. The closed world of this perspective ceases to hold any wonder. Everything has its label, and if one does not know it the experts will tell him.

Another facet of such closure of the world appears in the often observed fact that older people frequently tend to feel that only the "good old times" offered any worth-while experience, that, for example, only the authors, actors, or singers they admired in their youth or young adulthood were great, only the sights seen in their youth were wonderful and exciting in a way to which the contemporary world offers no parallel. This complaint probably is as old as the human world. Its cause is not that the world has become duller, but that the capacity for allocentric interest has shriveled with the decreasing openness toward the world and the extended confinement in the familiar world of secondary autocentricity.

The world of secondary, socially shared autocentricity bears a certain resemblance, on the higher level of objectification, to the closed worlds of the animals predetermined by their relatively few needs and their innate organization, which serves the satisfaction of these needs as does their learned behavior. This resemblance is highlighted, perhaps inadvertently, by a remark in the account of an interesting recent experiment with dogs. The results of this experiment indicate that in normally raised adult dogs the curiosity with which they explore something new wears off very quickly—they become bored and lie down or turn their back on it. This is not true of puppies in the stage of playful exploration, nor is it true, as these experiments showed, of dogs raised in an environment with very restricted sensory stimulation, for these animals persist much longer in lively exploration than do the normally raised dogs. The experimenters, although emphasizing that their research does not have any bearing on humans, nevertheless comment that the normally raised dog acts more intelligently because he can satisfy his curiosity more quickly and that while "there may be something delightful about a child who can spend an hour completely absorbed in a clothespin . . . this is not intelligent, adult behavior."[1] However, the parallel drawn in this remark between dog and man obscures a crucial difference. *Only* the adult who is able to be completely absorbed, again and again, often for many hours and days, in an object that arouses his interest will be the one who enlarges his, and sometimes man's, scope of perception and of experience. A painter may spend many days, weeks or months, or even years, in looking at the same mountain, as Cézanne did, or at blades of grass or bamboo leaves or branches of a tree, as many of the Chinese and Japanese masters did, without tiring of it and without ceasing to discover something new in it. The same is true of the poet's or writer's devoted love for his object, of which Rilke speaks,[2] of the true naturalist's perception of the plant or animal with which he has to live for long periods of time in order to acquire that intimate knowledge from which eventually new meaning and understanding will be born. This applies to all men who want to learn to know something or somebody truly and deeply. Of course, the length of time spent in such repeated encounters will bear fruit only if it does not become a blind routine in which the perceiver closes himself off from, rather than opens himself toward, that which is before him so that he merely sees the same aspect over and over again and becomes increasingly blind to the nature of the object. In the latter case he will be bored, like those who quickly turn their back on anything new. Like the experienced and mature dog, he will remain within a limited world and quickly close it again in the unlikely event that he should catch a glimpse of the

1] William R. Thompson and Ronald Melzak, "Early Environment," *Scientific American*, 1956, 194:38-42. Hebb comments that "the restricted dogs . . . haven't the brains to be bored." D. O. Hebb, "The Mammal and His Environment," *American Journal of Psychiatry*, 1955, 111:826-831.

2] See above, p. 225.

vastnesses and depths unknown to him. Only if the concept of intelligence is restricted to mean adaptation to the status quo is it more intelligent to be done quickly with anything new. But if man's highest capacity is that of allocentric interest to which the world never becomes a closed book, then the greater intelligence may be that which does not quickly dispose of or deal with an object but wonders at it and does not tire easily of contemplating and exploring it even if to others it may be the most familiar thing imaginable.

In such perception the glance dwells on the frontiers of human experience and becomes creative, revealing hitherto unknown vistas. It has been compared with the child's glance when it is said that the artist[3] and the wise man resemble a child. The resemblance consists in the freshness, spontaneity, interest, and openness with which the object is approached and reacted to. Just as these qualities and attitudes in the child are the prerequisite of expansion and progress in the encounter with the world, so they are in the adult. They make the encounter creative, be it in the sense of growth and enlargement of personal experience, or in the sense of enabling the artist or the scientist to add to the scope of human experience. Such openness toward and interest in the object is part of the phenomenon of creative experience which takes place in the whole human being with all his capacities and reactions even though one or the other may play a more dominant role in any particular act of creative experience. Thus, what we have seen in studying the ontogenetic development and the nature of allocentric perception can be of help in clarifying the nature of creative experience.[4]

The problem of *creative experience* is essentially the same for all the human capacities such as perception, thought, feeling, and motor activity, comprising, in the widest sense, not only the hand that moves the brush in painting or manipulates the object to be explored or to be fashioned, but also the eye, the head, the body that approach the object from different angles, etc. It is the problem of the open encounter of the total person with the world, that is,

3] The word "artist," here and on the following pages, always refers not only to the artist but to the poet or writer or composer as well. Furthermore, I am considering mainly modern art and literature, from the Renaissance to the present day.

4] The unity of the problem of creative experience will become more apparent as it is taken up in the chapters on focal attention and on memory. See this volume, pp. 251-278 and 279-322.

with some part of the world. Of the different aspects of allocentric perception the *openness in turning toward* the object is the most basic and important one; the fullest interest in an object is possible only if the person opens himself fully toward as many object aspects as possible, that is, optimally toward the totality of the object.

The openness toward the object in creative experience is apparent both in the motivation for the encounter and in the way in which the encounter takes place. The main *motivation* at the root of creative experience is man's need to relate to the world around him, a need which, as we have seen, becomes particularly strong and striking when urgent physical needs such as for food and rest have been stilled. This need is apparent in the young child's interest in all the objects around him, in his ever renewed exploration of and play with them. It is equally apparent in the artist's lifelong effort to grasp and render something which he has envisaged in his encounter with the world, in the scientist's wonder about the nature of the object with which he is concerned, and in the interest in the objects around him of every person who has not succumbed to stagnation in a closed autocentric or sociocentric world. They all have in common the fact that they do not remain in a closed, familiar, labeled world but that they want to go beyond embeddedness in the familiar and in the routine, and to relate to another object, or to the same one more fully, or from another angle, anew, afresh. In such acts of relatedness man finds both the world and himself. This does not imply that other needs may not also play a role in and color or codetermine the creative experience. It only means that without the basic need to relate to the world, without openness toward the world, the experience will not enlarge, deepen, and make more alive the person's relation to the world, that is, will not be creative.

The *quality* of the encounter that leads to creative experience consists primarily in the openness during the encounter and in the repeated and varied approaches to the object, in the free and open play of attention, thought, feeling, perception, etc. In this free play the person experiences the object in its manifold relations to himself and also tentatively tries out, as it were, a great variety of relations between the object thus approached and other objects, ideas, experiences, feelings, objects of imagination, etc. In characterizing this activity as play I do not mean that it is playful rather than serious, but that it is not bound by rigorous rules or by conventional schemata of memory, thought, or perception. It may at times be playful, too; but that is not its main characteristic. It resembles the child's free play in his encounter with the world where playfulness, too, is not the main feature but the openness, the intensity of the interest, the repeated and varied approaches, which range all the way from the grave and serious, the absorbing and tantalizing, to the playful and the fleeting.

In the earliest stages of infancy the play of the child with the objects of the environment is at first limited to and determined by what happens to impinge on his senses. Later on it increasingly expands as the child can turn actively from one object to another. From then on it may at times range freely, at other times be focused more on a particular object, idea, feeling. In such focusing, relations may be established between the specific object and others that have been encountered in ranging more widely. In the creative process the person usually focuses more and more sharply on a particular area or object. As he approaches it from various angles in the tentative play of thought, senses, and motor behavior, he also connects it with other experiences. His relatedness to the object is intensified and he becomes more open to its different aspects and possible links.

What has been learned in such unfettered and open intercourse with the world may enlarge unnoticeably and gradually the person's experience and contribute to his growth, or it may crystallize suddenly in an insight, or in a new vision of something that seemed long familiar, or in an "inspiration." But it is truly assimilated and becomes consciously and freely available to the person only if it is either fashioned into an objective work, as in artistic or literary creation, or is otherwise elaborated by connecting it with, and making it part of, the conscious total life and experience of the person. This usually is a more laborious process than either the long incubation period of the many encounters between person and object or the subsequent flash of insight, vision, or inspiration. Both the period of immersion in the ever renewed encounters and the period of articulating and connecting the experiences won in the free play of the varied approaches are essential for the growth and expansion of the person's relation to the world through creative experience.

In Freud's work and in post-Freudian ego psychology, especially in the work of Kris, the view is expressed that such experience, especially as it leads to artistic creation, is always the product of a *repressed libidinal or aggressive impulse* and of a *regression* to infantile modes of thought or experience, to the primary process, albeit in the service of the ego. Freud considered it probable that the artist has a constitutionally given "looseness of repression"[5] and he ascribed certain "achievements of special perfection" to the temporary removal of the repression of an unconscious impulse which, for the particular occasion, becomes ego-syntonic and manifests "a resistance in the face of opposition similar to that of obsessional symptoms."[6]

This resistance in the face of all opposition, it seems to me, is the resistance not of an Id drive but of the conviction of the truth of artistic or scientific creation in the face of the opposition by the shared autocentricity of conventional perception and thought. Such truth is more likely to be encountered by the person who has continued and expanded the child's openness toward the world on the adult level and whose sensory and intellectual capacities have not entirely succumbed to the pressure of the accepted way in which everyone perceives the "realistic" world of the conventions of the day, the era, and the society. Just as the amnesia for early childhood is not due primarily to the repression of forbidden sexual impulses but to the transformation of the total manner of perceiving and thinking,[7] so the unseeingness which in all of us, in varying degrees, stands in the way of a more creative vision is due more often to the encroachment of an already labeled world upon our spontaneous sensory and intellectual capacities than to the repression of a libidinal impulse.

Freud assumed that the artist suffers from too strong drives in craving honor, power, wealth, fame and to be loved by women and that, since he does not have the means of obtaining these satisfactions, he turns his back on reality and tries to obtain them in his phantasies, which, if he is worldly successful with his creations, in the end will get him what he originally wanted.[8] While these

5] *Lockerheit der Verdrängungen*, S. Freud, "Vorlesungen zur Einführung in die Psychoanalyse," *Gesammelte Werke* (Imago Publishing Co., London, 1940), Vol. XI, pp. 390-391.
6] S. Freud, "The Unconscious," *Collected Papers* (Basic Books, New York, 1959), Vol. IV, p. 127.
7] See this volume, pp. 279-322.
8] *Gesammelte Werke*, Vol. XI, p. 390.

drives may play a role in an artist just as well as in a businessman or in anybody else, they are in no way specific for the artist nor are they unusually strong in all artists. However, what *is* essential for the artist is that he experiences and expresses more precisely, and without being blindfolded by the sociocentric view, what happens in his encounter with the world or some aspect of it. His need to relate to the world must not be channeled as completely by the conventional patterns and schemata of his culture as is the case for most people in our time, so that his senses, his sensibilities, and his mind can be more open, more innocent, like the child who, in Andersen's tale, saw and said that the emperor was naked and did not have the beautiful clothes that everybody else had persuaded himself to see or, at least, to profess having seen. Thus, the "looseness of repression" of which Freud speaks has to do more with the artist's vision not being fettered and molded completely by the conventional views, with his being more open toward the world and himself, than with the looseness of the repression of any particular libidinal impulse.

Kris makes the additional point that in the genesis of the work of art a *regression to primary-process thought* takes place. Unlike the regression in dreams or in pathological cases, it is controlled by, and in the service of, the ego. According to him, it is this regression which permits the discharge of the repressed impulses mentioned by Freud. The regression to primary-process thought takes place, according to Kris, both in fantastic, free-wandering thought processes and in creative processes, in the former under a condition of ego weakness, in the latter in the service of the ego.[9] But the seeming similarity emphasized by Kris is deceptive, and regression to primary-process thought is not typical of the creative process.

Primary-process thought uses freely displaceable cathexes in the unrestrained tendency toward full discharge of the tension of id drives by the path of (phantasied or hallucinated) wish fulfillment, that is, in the service of the striving to return to a tensionless state.[10] There are daydreams, reveries, and idly wandering thoughts which are correctly or approximately described by the concept of pri-

9] Ernst Kris, "On Preconscious Mental Processes," in David Rapaport, *Organization and Pathology of Thought* (Columbia University Press, New York, 1951), pp. 474-493, especially 485-491.
10] Compare Rapaport, p. 694.

mary-process thought. What the early stages of the creative process have in common with such reveries is mainly the fact that they, too, wander freely without being bound by the rules and properties of the accepted, conventional, familiar everyday world. In this free wandering they center, however, on the object, idea, problem which is the focus of the creative endeavor. What distinguishes the creative process from regression to primary-process thought is that the freedom of the approach is due not to a drive discharge function but to the openness in the encounter with the object of the creative labor.

This openness means that the sensibilities of the person, his mind and his senses, are more freely receptive, less tied to fixed anticipations and sets, and that the object is approached in different ways, from different angles, and not with any fixed purpose to use it for the satisfaction of a particular need, or the testing of one particular expectation or possibility. It seems likely that greater mobility of cathexis is found not only in mental processes serving primarily the discharge of an id drive but also in the described free play of all one's faculties in the open encounter with the world. In the latter case the function of the mobile cathexis is not primarily the discharge of an id drive in order to abolish tension but, on the contrary, the contact with a manifold, inexhaustible reality and the steeping of the person in many different aspects of the world, which takes place by means of thoughts and phantasies as well as by the play of the senses and the motor functions. Of course, the discharge of drive tension and the striving to make contact with some aspect of reality may also occur in the same train of phantasy or freely wandering thought. There may be constant transitions from one to the other, so that at one moment one may predominate, at the next the other.

The relatively undirected, freely wandering play of perception, thought, phantasy, thus is not necessarily regressive but can be and often is progressive. Developmentally, the tendency to mere drive discharge and the tendency to relate to the world in many-sided sensory-motor-affective-thinking contacts move in opposite directions: the former tends to decrease, the latter to play an increasingly important role during early childhood. The free play of senses and mind in the open encounter with the world is capable of continued development as more and more aspects of the world are assimilated, while thought serving primarily discharge of tension is indeed in the service of the regressive tendency to abolish the encounter with reality and return to a state of rest and satiation.

Perhaps the idea of a regressive tendency in the creative process not only stems from the mistaken notion that freely wandering thought in the early phases of the creative process mainly serves the purpose of the discharge of libido and aggression (primary-process thought), but has received support also, perhaps unwittingly, from the tendency to judge human activity solely on the basis of the performance principle, of a quasi-industrial standard of the "goods" that the activity delivers.[11] Compared, for example, with the strictly purposeful modern manufacturing process, which regulates uniformly every movement of machine and human hand in order to avoid any waste motion and thus produce the finished product in the shortest possible time and with the smallest expense of energy, the creative process, and especially its earlier phases, may seem like an incredible waste. The analogy is easily extended to the kind of perception and thought that are directed merely to the quick recognition of any object or to its relation to the conventional schemata of familiar reality and to its use for some definite purpose within this framework. But even if the work of art, of poetry, or creative thought is acknowledged as a worth-while end in itself, expanding as it does the range of conscious human experience, the perspective of the performance principle may lead to the view that there is something "regressive" in the period of free, mobile, and open play of the mind, the senses, the hand with the many possibilities and aspects of the objects only some of which may enter ultimately into the creation. Yet, it is clear that the incubation period as well as the period of execution of the work are equally important, and that the former provides the foundations for the latter.

The notion of a regressive factor in the creative process may have still other, unacknowledged ancestors. From the standpoint of a closed system, any fresh groping which in some way runs counter to the "realistic world as we know it" may appear as childish. When, for example, the cognitive functions of the ego are considered primarily as adaptive to a world already known, to familiar concepts and percepts, then the loosening of the familiar

11] The concept of "performance principle" is taken from H. Marcuse, who understands it as a principle by which the members of our contemporary civilization are stratified according to their "competitive economic performances" and which is part of modern society's reality principle. Herbert Marcuse, *Eros and Civilization* (Beacon Press, Boston, 1955), p. 44.

features in an open and fresh approach may be viewed as regressive in the sense of not serving the quick adaptation to known reality for immediately useful purposes.[12] Such a definition of cognition would already imply that anything short of the immediately useful orientation in the world as already known falls short of the cognitive, adaptive function of the ego, and perhaps for that reason is apt to be labeled "regressive." In such a view not the openness of the mind toward the world, but its ready recognition and use of the familiar "handles" of "reality" would be the highest cognitive and adaptive function of the ego.

The decisive shortcoming of such a view of man's coping with reality lies in the overlooking of his openness toward the world. This oversight may be facilitated by a concept of normality, of the nature of man, which derives its normative yardstick from the greatest number, from the average rather than from the full realization of man's potentialities in the course of healthy development and maturation. One of the merits of psychoanalytic theory has been its emphasis on the developmental viewpoint. This has led to a definition of normalcy in terms of stage of development reached (or stage regressed to). According to this definition, normalcy is identical with maturity. This viewpoint is shared by all the different psychoanalytic schools regardless of whether they define development and maturity, as Freud does, in terms of the stage of libido development and ego development or, as Sullivan does, in terms of the development of the capacity for love and respect of self and others or, as I would, in terms of the degree and stage of emergence from total embeddedness. But once the concept of normalcy is thus defined developmentally, the analyst finds himself confronted with the odd discovery that, according to his criteria, most people never reach maturity and thus do not seem to be normal. In Freud's work this discovery is evident in "The Future of an Illusion." In his concept of collective neuroses he makes ex-

---

12] This seems to be the position of Bellak, who reformulates the concept of regression in the service of the ego as "a brief oscillating reduction of *certain adaptive* functions of the ego in the service of (i.e. for the facilitation of) other, specifically the synthetic ego functions." He describes this process as a decrease of cognitive, selective, adaptive functions with a consequent weakening of the "sharply defined boundaries of figure and ground, of logical, temporal, spatial and other relations," permitting a reordering into "new configurations with new boundaries under the scrutiny of the again sharply functioning adaptive forces." Leopold Bellak, "Creativity, Some Random Notes to a Systematic Consideration," *Journal of Projective Techniques,* 1958, 22:363-380, 367. In such a view the concept of regression to primary-process thought no longer retains its original meaning of thought processes serving the discharge of repressed drive impulses.

plicit the conflict between a norm based on the greatest number, the average man, and one based on an idea of human nature and human potentialities.[13] Sullivan doubted very much that most people reach maturity according to his criteria of the capacity to love and respect others and oneself. Fromm discusses this problem in developing his concept of the "pathology of normalcy."[14]

While man's openness toward the world is clearly apparent in the child's wonder at the many objects in his environment and in his encounters, in which he discovers ever new aspects of the world, in most people the stress of life and the patterns of their culture and social group soon stifle the eager, youthful quest and close the once open mind so that it will encounter only the same, familiar objects. To their knowledgeable "realism" the suggestion of a different approach may appear unrealistic, or a regression to childish modes of behavior, or useless for the serious business of adaptation to reality as they know it. Even if they allow for the possibility of a different view of the world such allowance may be a mere word or thought without weight and substance.

Yet, in contrast to the animals, man is capable of continued growth and development throughout his life if he succeeds in remaining open to the world and capable of allocentric interest. Such openness is the basis of progress and of creative achievement in individual life as well as in the history of mankind.

On the one hand, man lives always in the world of the objects-of-use, in the perspective of secondary autocentricity. He could not exist without this perspective. In providing for his needs the objects-of-use perspective largely replaces the instinct-organization of the animals. But if man ceases to develop the allocentric mode of perception, if he loses that openness of senses and mind which transcends the object-of-use perspective and enables him to relate to others and to the world for the sake of the relationship itself, then his development stagnates in the closed world of secondary autocentricity, and the ontogenetic trend of development toward objectification and allocentric interest comes to a standstill. The basic difference between animal and human mental organization, man's openness toward the world, can be increasingly realized only if man retains and develops the allocentric mode of perception, the first appearance of which is the most important step in the development of perception in the growing child.

13] S. Freud, *Civilization and Its Discontents* (Hogarth Press, London, 1953).
14] Erich Fromm, *The Sane Society* (Rinehart & Co., New York, 1955), pp. 12-21.

III

ON ATTENTION
AND MEMORY

11

*The Development
of Focal Attention
and the Emergence
of Reality*

THE THEORY OF ATTENTION IS CRUCIAL FOR AN UNDERSTANDING OF
both consciousness and repression. In developing a dynamic theory
of attention, Freud formulated this insight by saying that "the
act of becoming conscious depends upon a definite psychic function—attention—being brought to bear."[1] Not all acts of attention,
however, shed the full light of consciousness on the matter attended. For instance, something that strikes one's attention may
lead to flight, to a turning away, if it arouses anxiety; and it may
lead to an act of *focal attention* if it arouses one's curiosity. By
"focal attention," as distinguished from other forms of attention,
I designate man's capacity to *center* his attention on an object
fully, so that he can perceive or understand it from *many sides*,
as clearly as possible. In this presentation, I shall attempt to show

1] Sigmund Freud, "The Interpretation of Dreams," *Basic Writings* (Random
House, New York, 1938), p. 529. William James's concise formulation, "My experience is what I agree to attend to," also stresses the dynamic, motivational
character of attention and experience. William James, *The Principles of Psychology* (Henry Holt, New York, 1931), see especially Vol. I, p. 402.

(1) that focal attention is the main instrument which, as it gradually develops, enables man to progress from the primitive mental activity of wishing or wanting (primary-process thought) to a grasp of reality (secondary-process thought); and (2) that man's grasp of reality is not merely based on his wish to satisfy primary, biological needs—is not merely, as Freud assumed, a detour on the path to wish fulfillment—but that it also has as a prerequisite an autonomous interest in the environment. Focal attention is the tool of this interest; it appears first in the child's exploratory play and requires relative freedom from need and anxiety. In discussing these topics, I shall describe the structure of acts of focal attention, briefly sketch the development of focal attention, discuss the bearing of this development on Freud's theory of repetition compulsion, and examine the basis of man's grasp of reality, reviewing critically Freud's theory of the origin and nature of thought.

The Structure of Focal Attention

Acts of focal attention are distinguished from developmentally earlier forms of experience by a number of factors which bring about a change in the nature of consciousness and of experience. The emergence of acts of focal attention does not, however, prevent the survival and continued significance of these developmentally earlier forms throughout man's life. Focal attention superimposes a new kind of experience on them; it also changes the earlier forms of experience. But it does not extinguish or replace them completely, and it is, in its turn, affected by them.

The most important of the distinguishing characteristics of focal attention are these: (1) Acts of focal attention are *directional;* they do not concern the total field[2]—that is, they are not global, as the most primitive forms of experience are, but focus attention in a particular direction. (2) They are directed at a *particular object,* which may be an external object or an internal object, such as a thought or a feeling.[3] (3) They take hold of

2] By "field," I designate, in this context, both the external and internal fields in their interaction—that is, the environment as well as the thoughts, feelings, impulses, tensions, and needs of the person.

3] The object-directedness of attention has often been described. See, for example, K. Koffka, *Principles of Gestalt Psychology* (Harcourt, Brace, New York, 1935), p. 358. Phenomenologists have discussed this problem in terms of intentionality of acts. Intentionality (*Intentionalität*) does not mean purposiveness or purpose-the object and aim at its active mental grasp. (4) Each focal act, as a rule, consists of not just *one* sustained approach to the object to which it is directed but *several renewed* approaches. These approaches explore different aspects and relations of the object. Not only are they made from different angles, as it were, but often they are made repeatedly from the same angle and directed at the same facet of the object in an attempt to assimilate it more thoroughly. They also usually—probably always—alternate or oscillate between a more passive, receptive, reactive phase and a more active, taking-hold, structuring, integrating phase. The relation of these two phases to each other and their relative predominance vary considerably both inter- and intra-individually. (5) Acts of focal attention *exclude* the rest of the field (environmental and internal) from that form of consciousness which is designated as focal awareness.

These factors are essential for an understanding of the change of consciousness and experience brought about by the gradual development and maturation of the capacity for focal attention in infancy and childhood. It is a change from (1) a diffuse total awareness of well- or ill-being, in which at first there is no distinction between the infant and the environment, through (2) a diffuse, more or less global awareness of an impinging environment, to (3) a state in which distinct needs and feelings become increasingly differentiated and discrete objects emerge from the environment. Ultimately, these objects are conceived by the child to have an existence of their own that continues even when the object does not impinge on the child's receptors. In this way focal attention plays a most important role in the gradual emergence and constitution of the object world (reality) and of the sense of self. It plays an equally decisive role in the development of the capacity for delay and drive control, by virtue of its *exclusion mechanism*. This mechanism excludes, for the duration of the focal act, the rest of the field from focal awareness. Thereby it delays the discharge of all those impulses which are motivated by the rest of the field and require focal attention for their execution. It also delays and/or mitigates the impact of the rest of the

fulness. It refers to an essential aspect of consciousness—namely, that every act of consciousness has an object, that an object is "given" in every act of consciousness. Compare Edmund Husserl, *Logische Untersuchungen* (Max Niemeyer, Halle, 1913), see especially Vol. 2, part 1, pp. 343-507.

impinging field—which is excluded from focal awareness—by reducing vigilance, diffuse awareness, and fringe awareness. The
degree of such mitigation depends on, among other factors,
the intensity of the act of focal attention and the strength of the
need *not* to become aware of the rest of the field—that is, the
distribution of hypercathectic and countercathectic energies during any particular act of focal attention. This implies that the
temporary exclusion mechanism of focal attention often, perhaps
always, is structurally and dynamically similar to repression. It is
distinguished from repression by its brief duration and by the
fact that the person is able to terminate it, whereupon attention
can be directed to that which before had been excluded from
focal awareness.

The temporary shutting-out of the rest of the field during acts
of focal attention directed at a particular object is not the only
relation between focal attention and repression. With the full
development of focal attention, focal awareness becomes the
highest and the predominating form of consciousness in the waking life of man. What is not focally perceived is not in full awareness. What is not accessible to focal awareness for reason of man's
limited horizon remains unknown to him. If the inaccessibility
is due not to the general limitations of man, but to anxieties rooted
in the individual life experience, it constitutes repression proper.

The Development of Focal Attention

The first change in man's life—and the most profound, comprehensive, and abrupt one—occurs at birth, and consists of the
transition from a foetal, prenatal existence to a separate, postnatal one. Before birth all of the embryo's needs for food, liquid,
and oxygen are supplied by the mother's blood stream through
the placenta. The foetus lives in the moist, nurturing, evenly warm
interior of the mother's body. This form of existence, as Ferenczi
especially has pointed out, resembles in many ways that of the
sea animals,[4] particularly the lower ones such as the protozoa,
whose needs for oxygen and nourishing minerals are supplied by
the sea water, and whose existence may be characterized as predominantly drifting, receptive, without active motility, without

4] S. Ferenczi, *Versuch einer Genitaltheorie* (Internationaler Psychoanalytischer
Verlag, Leipzig, 1924).

direction, passive. In foetal existence, because of the constant supply from the mother's body of all food and oxygen needs and of warmth, relatively few need tensions arise, and probably there is no differentiation of needs, or at least no felt differentiation.

Only after birth does the marked and constant alternation begin between rising need tension and satisfaction of the need which continues throughout life. It is probably the experience of this alternation and of variations in it which gradually produces an awareness in the infant of his own body as different from the mother who satisfies the needs.[5] The emergence of mother or mother's breast as something different and separate from the infant cannot be pictured as the full-blown and distinct idea of mother as a separate person. This idea comes much later, after the capacity for focal attention has matured. At first, the infant probably has only the vaguest feeling, like: "There is something out there which has to happen, which has to come, to make me feel good." This is different from foetal existence in which there was no *there*—no outside, separate from the foetus. The *something*, at this first, postnatal stage, must not be understood as an "object," or a "person," but is entirely vague and nondescript. The something is characterized only by the fact that it has to happen in order to make the infant comfortable and that the infant wants it to happen; there is a first glimmering of the notion that this something that has to come from somewhere *outside* the baby's body will then produce, for example, the satisfying state of "nipple-in-lips."[6] At the same time, the change from continuous gratification of all needs *in utero* to a state in which need-tensions mount until they are satisfied, at intervals, also leads to a *differentiation of needs and of the felt experience of these needs*. Being hungry feels different from being cold and from being sleepy, and so on. Furthermore, discomfort felt in different regions of the body leads to further differentiation. Thus, in addition to global feelings of comfort and discomfort, there arise

5] Therese Benedek, "Adaptation to Reality in Early Infancy," *Psychoanalytic Quarterly*, 1938, 7:200-215.

6] Compare Harry Stack Sullivan, *The Interpersonal Theory of Psychiatry* (Norton, New York, 1953), pp. 66-73, 80-91, 110-122. His analysis of the nursing situation and of the emergence of "good mother" and "bad mother" personifications conveys an idea of the complexity and significance of the processes going on *before* the idea of the mother as *one, separate* person is eventually developed by the child.

increasingly differentiated feelings of *particular* need tensions, vague awareness of different body regions, and strivings *directed* toward satisfaction of the *particular* needs and alleviation of the particular discomforts, mainly by means of crying, which calls forth the mother's need-satisfying activity.

In this stage of the infant's development, *vaguely directional* (that is, not sharply focused, but not completely global) experiences assume increasing importance. They can also be observed in the reaction to impinging light and noises. While not yet being able to *look at* anything or to *listen* to anything, the infant does experience the coming of light or noises from a vaguely perceived, general direction. At four weeks, a vacant, diffuse stare is still the most typical behavior. In the fifth and sixth weeks, although the infant still stares vaguely, he stares in a certain direction—for example, at the window or at the wall—and for the first time he also occasionally focuses his eyes and looks at people and objects in his environment. Following the fifth week, this focused looking at people and objects is an increasingly frequent behavior; at first the infant focuses only for brief moments, but from approximately ten weeks on he focuses on the same object for a prolonged period. Together with the development of focal regard, the infant starts to follow a moving object with his eyes —that is, to hold on to it and *keep* it in focus.[7] The infant now no longer depends entirely on what happens to fall into his line of vision. An object no longer necessarily disappears—ceases to exist for the infant—when it moves, but the infant begins to be able to keep hold of the object by following it with his eyes and turning his head. Toward the end of the first year (from approximately the seventh or eighth month on), the infant also

7] The age levels given above are taken from Arnold Gesell and Helen Thompson, *The Psychology of Early Growth* (Macmillan, New York, 1938), pp. 170-172. There a detailed description of the development of focal regard during the first year is given for different types of objects. According to a personal communication from Lois B. Murphy of the Menninger Foundation, the baby starts to look at things with interest even before the ability to focus has fully matured. This looking takes place only when the baby is neither hungry nor sleepy, as described later in this chapter. She has observed it already on the ninth day and describes it as involving "a comprehensive bodily effort; the whole body is still and the energy is concentrated in holding the head up for a moment or two and the baby keeps its gaze or stare steadily on one object, something bright generally, for some seconds." Similarly, Stirnimann reports interested, attentive looking of some infants from the first or second week on. F. Stirnimann, *Psychologie des neugeborenen Kindes* (Rascher Verlag, Zürich, 1940), p. 59.

becomes increasingly capable of, and interested in, focusing on very small objects. In the period of vague directional staring, only large areas impressed the infant's vision; and in the early stages of focal vision, he focused only on objects which were relatively large or which loomed large directly in front of his eyes —especially if they also impinged upon his attention in some other way, as a rattle might impinge by producing a noise, or as an object might impinge which was moved back and forth in front of his eyes. Attention to very small objects is another important step—a change from attending only reactively to what impinges, to attending actively to an object which arouses curiosity and interest. It is at about the same period, between the ages of nine and twelve months, that another decisive step in the development of focal attention takes place: the birth of the idea that an object may continue to exist even if it ceases to impinge on the baby's receptors, and that this object may be made to appear again by means of appropriate motor behavior. This is in contrast to the way in which he has made the experience of being nursed, the nipple-in-mouth situation, recur by means of crying. Between the ages of five and eight months the child grasps an object which he sees, but he immediately loses interest in it and does not seek for it if, in front of his eyes, one covers it with a cloth or places a screen in front of it. But from eight months on the child will seek the object underneath the cloth which covers it.[8]

Beginning with this first glimmering of the idea of object constancy, focal attention gradually during the next years becomes increasingly capable of being used in *thought*, instead of being tied completely to focal perception. The first step in this devel-

---

8] Jean Piaget, "Principal Factors Determining Intellectual Evolution from Childhood to Adult Life," in David Rapaport, ed., *Organization and Pathology of Thought* (Columbia University Press, New York, 1951), pp. 163-164. While the behavior described above may be conceived of as the birth of the idea of an object's continuing to exist even if not impinging on the receptors, at this stage the object still remains very closely tied to the child's motor activity, as Piaget shows. Just as crying produced mother's nipple, so now diving underneath the pillow produces the object hidden under it. Piaget describes how, between nine and ten months, the baby who has succeeded in finding an object hidden under a pillow to his right, if the next time it is placed, in front of his eyes, under a pillow to his left, will continue to seek it under the pillow to his right. The baby's experience at this time seems to be *diving under pillow to right will produce the object that I can't see*, rather than the experience of realizing that the object has an autonomous place in space, which is independent of the repetition of a particular action such as crying or diving under the pillow to the right.

opment is that the child not only becomes able to focus attention via the senses on an object seen, touched, and so on, but also becomes able to focus attention on the *idea of an object.* This focal attention to thoughts develops in the second year, together with the learning of speech—without which the capacity to have ideas of objects could not go beyond an extremely primitive stage. Gradually not only objects but also their *relationships,* real or fancied, to the child and to each other become the objects of focal attention in thought. The child's reflective focusing on his own feelings and experiences constitutes the last step in the development of focal attention, and accompanies the development of the idea of "I" and the autobiographical memory—that is, the concept of the continuity of the self. During the time when the instrument of focal attention is developing, and also after it has reached maturation, the object world and the person's inner world are explored and assimilated so that they become part of the consciously known world of man, part of the sphere of his focal awareness. This work, which takes place through ever repeated acts of focal attention, is of truly staggering proportions during childhood. No later period in life compares, in the scope and variety of exploration by means of focal attention, to the age of discovery—the age of early childhood; for children, unless they are very disturbed and succumb to apathy, always show great curiosity and desire for exploration.[9] People vary considerably, however, in the degree to which they retain this desire in later life, ranging from those for whom there is nothing new and who are incapable especially of seeing the new in the familiar, to those who are always interested and to whom even the familiar is full of unexplored aspects, of hidden depths, of surprising facets.

Focal Exploration and Repetition Compulsion

The structure and development of focal attention, as described here, shed new light on certain phenomena in the child's behavior which Freud looked upon as early manifestations of the repetition

9] The degree and quality of exploratory curiosity and play vary considerably in children because of hereditary and congenital factors as well as the child's early interpersonal experiences. However, in spite of these variations there is no doubt that the drive to explore is much stronger, as a rule, in children than it is in adults. The same seems to hold true for young monkeys as compared with adult monkeys. See Robert A. Butler, "Curiosity in Monkeys," *Scientific American,* February 1954, pp. 70-75.

compulsion. Although Freud states that the repetition compulsion can serve as an instrument for the active mastery of experiences, he characterizes it mainly by its conservative nature and considers it to be the expression of an inertia principle, of a drive to return to an earlier state, and, in the final analysis, of the death instinct.[10]

I want to discuss briefly here only one often observed fact: a child's pleasure in, and insistence on, being read or told the same story over and over again. This discussion will (1) serve as an example for a more detailed description of the exploratory function of focal attention, and (2) show that the child's insistence on repetition is not due primarily to an inertia principle but, on the contrary, is essential for the productive work of exploring and assimilating the objects of the environment—in this case, an object of the cultural environment.

Adult observers have often been struck by the disturbance a child may show at the slightest change—even one word—in a story which has been repeated for the child. This disturbance does not seem to make much sense to the adult mind. What is the difference if a minor episode or a mere word is changed, as long as the main drift of events is retained in the story? This viewpoint overlooks the enormous difference in meaning which the repetition of a story has for the child who listens to it with absorption and for the adult who is bored by it. One tries in vain to encompass the child's experience with categories of the adult mind which are not suitable for grasping the meaning of the situation for the child.[11]

What are the decisive differences between the child's and the adult's experience in listening to the same story over and over again? The age at which such repetition is desired and enjoyed by the child is roughly from two to five years, with considerable individual variation. At the beginning of this period, the child has already learned to perceive distinct and concrete objects, but this learning must necessarily continue, for the object world of the child is constantly and rapidly expanding, and increasingly includes such complicated objects as words and pictures which

10] Sigmund Freud, *Beyond the Pleasure Principle* (International Psychoanalytic Press, London, 1922).

11] For a more detailed analysis of the problem of using adult categories for the understanding and remembering of early childhood experiences, see "On Memory and Childhood Amnesia," this volume, pp. 279-322.

denote or represent other objects. However, the manner in which discrete objects are perceived by the young child differs a great deal from the manner in which they are perceived by the older child and the adult. The young child perceives objects much more globally and concretely than the older child or adult. This implies that "any phenomenon known in terms of qualities-of-the-whole, rather than in terms of strictly articulated qualities, is apt to be seen by the young child as undergoing a complete change, even if no more than minor details in the situation are altered." From the young child's viewpoint, none of the many elements making up the global situation "need be more essential than any other, since all of them contribute to the characteristic coloration, or tone, of the situational totality."[12]

Since a story contains not only many different objects but also many different relationships among these objects, which unfold in a definite sequence of events, it is much more complex than even the most complex objects in the child's environment. For the young child to grasp and digest a story requires an amount of attention and of effort at understanding which the adult is incapable of imagining, since his grasp of a story rests not only on years of training but also on a quite different, much more abstractive kind of perception and understanding. Only by repeated acts of focal attention, which at one time turn more to one part, at other times to other parts, can the child very gradually come to understand and assimilate a story. A particular part of the story may become something to wonder about even if on some other day it seemed already familiar or not worthy of special attention. To encompass all of it is no small achievement. What if the story should change as the child tries to get hold of it? Any change makes it elusive and frustrates the child's effort to master it. The attempt to assimilate a particular story requires a complex labor of attention and thought; in fact, it usually involves the child's learning the story by heart. This learning-by-heart is a by-product of the child's innumerable acts of focal attention toward the story as a whole and toward its different parts, and of the child's feelings about the story. The fact that this learning-by-heart comes as a by-product—much in contrast to later learning-by-heart in school—indicates the difference in de-

12] Heinz Werner, *Comparative Psychology of Mental Development*, rev. ed. (Follett Publishing Co., Chicago, 1948), pp. 128-130.

gree and quality of attention between the young child's and the older child's or adult's listening to a story.

The young child who listens to the story not only is engaged in assimilating its complex fabric but, in addition to that, is confronted with the equally or even more difficult problem of finding his way in the puzzling distinctions between reality, representations of reality, possibility, and sheer phantasy. Just as the task of learning that a picture can represent a real object but that it is different from the real object is not an easy one and takes considerable time and effort to master, so it is a difficult task to learn about the various possible relations between a story and reality. Furthermore, it is of great importance to the child that he can *rely* on the story—that it does not suddenly disappear, that it is still there. This is just as important as to be able to rely on the fact that a toy in which the child is interested will not vanish overnight. Before the child can read, the only way to be sure that he can rely on a story is by having it reread or retold to him and making quite sure that it is really the same story.

A change in the story is about as upsetting to the child as it might be to an adult to discover that overnight the table in the living room had changed its shape. The idea that one can *make* a story, hence also *change* it, dawns much later on the child than the earlier implicit conviction that a story is a piece of reality on which one can rely, so that any change of it interferes drastically with the important task of getting thoroughly acquainted with this particular piece of reality.

When Freud says that the child's need to hear the same story over and over again is a trait which disappears in the adult, he refers, probably without being aware of it, to a phenomenon which is characteristic only of large segments of the adult population in modern Western civilization, but which is not true of all men or of all times. For the greater part of man's history, people read or listened to the same stories many times. This is as true of the Bible as it is of *The Arabian Nights;* and it is equally true of the sermons of Buddha, which employ in a most impressive way literal repetition of the same stories and phrases—a device which is frequent in Oriental poetry. The modern need to read the latest best-seller, to look at a new movie or television show, to consume enormous amounts of always new mysteries, magazines, and comic strips, is peculiar to our time and culture.

Moreover, a proper comparison, I believe, of a child's attitude toward a story can be made only with an adult's attitude toward an object of *similar significance*. The story, to the child, is at first strange country which he gradually explores and in which new discoveries are always possible. A comparable relationship exists in our culture between the appreciative adult and a work of art, a piece of music, or a poem. One does not tire easily of looking again and again at a cherished painting, of listening many times over to a beloved piece of music or a poem. Every renewed encounter may reveal new aspects and lead to deeper understanding. Any change in the poem, the painting, the music would destroy it. Because of the quasi-organic, lifelike character of the real work of art, such a change would indeed make it into something very different.

In other words, if the adult matures to a stage where he is capable of meaningful encounter with a significant human creation, then his relationship to this creation is likely to require many contacts with it, just as the child's relationship to the story does. The meaning of such significant encounters is very different from the kind of reading or listening which has the purpose of killing time, of being entertained passively or thrilled and titillated. For inherent in every real encounter with a work of art, a myth, a fairy tale is an active effort of the total personality, which is also inherent—in a somewhat different way—in the child's attempt to gradually assimilate the story. The motive of inertia seems to me considerably stronger in the adult who wants to see a new movie or read a new mystery every night than in the child who wants to hear the same story retold. The former avoids meaningful and enriching experience; the latter seeks it.

Thus the child's insistence on repetition of the same story serves primarily the purpose of assimilating it, of getting fully acquainted with all its aspects by many acts of focal attention,[13] and of making quite sure that it is still there and can be explored and enjoyed with some measure of dependability.

The story as an object is different from other objects, such as the baby's own body and toys, in that it is not available without

13] For a related viewpoint with regard to other repetition phenomena, compare Piaget, "Principal Factors Determining Intellectual Evolution from Childhood to Adult Life," in Rapaport, *Organization and Pathology of Thought*, p. 162. Also Paul Schilder, "Studies Concerning the Psychology and Symptomatology of General Paresis," *ibid.*, pp. 574-575, footnote 285.

a cooperating adult who reads or tells it. Exploring the story, thus, depends on such cooperation. The same holds true of all those *play* experiences in which the child plays *with* an adult. These experiences, too, require many repetitions in order to be fully explored and assimilated. For these repetitions, the child is dependent on the cooperating adult. Such interpersonal play has special significance since it is perhaps the most important situation experienced by the young child in which his own contribution is as important as the adult's; in other words, it is a situation in which he and the adult integrate as partners, rather than as one person who is in need and helpless and another who is powerful and can satisfy the need. While the emphasis in rehearing a story is on the exploration of the story, which only *incidentally* requires the cooperation of the adult, the emphasis in interpersonal play is on the give and take of the play situation, which *essentially* consists of the participation of two people, the child and the adult.[14]

Once the infant no longer lives in the primitive world of foetal and neonatal existence, it becomes of vital importance to him that the world outside, especially the mothering one, can be *depended on* and does not suddenly disappear without returning. Because of the infant's helplessness, the only way in which he can assimilate and accept the at first painful realization that the mothering one is not always present when needed is by realizing that he can depend upon her reappearance.[15] Similarly, it would be well nigh impossible for him to become oriented in the environment, which assumes increasing importance during the periods of late infancy and early childhood, if he could not rely on the fact that the more significant objects of the environment continue to exist and remain identical—that is, *do not change*—even when they are not visible or touchable. Learning about object constancy, thus, is probably closely linked emotionally with the degree to which the infant experiences the constancy—that is, dependability—of the most important object, the mother. The more helpless a person feels, the more likely he is to require an extreme degree of object constancy, and the less able he is to tolerate any change

14] The significance of the bedtime story very often lies more in the reassuring integration of an interpersonal situation than in the story as something which the child wants to explore.

15] If the infant cannot depend on the reappearance of the mothering one, his development very often will suffer and pathology may develop.

in the environment. This can be observed not only in the emotionally disturbed child who cannot tolerate his mother's absence or the absence of a toy, but also in many neurotic patients and especially some patients with brain lesions,[16] who are frightened by change and, to reassure themselves, insist on a rigid constancy of environmental conditions.

In the play described by Freud[17] of a boy of one and a half who made a spool fastened to a thread disappear behind the curtains of his bed in order to pull it out again and joyfully greet its reappearance, the mastery of the experience of the disappearing and reappearing mother was a decisive factor. Since it is highly probable that the infant's first inkling of the fact that the objects of reality are separate from his body comes about through the painful realization that his mother is not always present when needed, the gradual development of the important insight that objects continue to exist, even though they disappear, may well remain closely linked in many children, for a considerable time, with the experience of the absence of the mothering one.

Thus manifold interrelations exist between the following: (*a*) the discovery of object constancy; (*b*) the power to make an object reappear—be it mother, by crying, or the spool, by pulling at the thread; (*c*) the capacity to recover an object by going after it and finding it in reality; (*d*) the confidence that an object will continue to exist and eventually will be available again even if, for the time being, one can neither make it reappear nor go and look for it; and (*e*) the capacity to keep hold of an object in *thought*—that is, to develop focal attention to the idea of an object even when the object is not available for present need satisfaction, manipulation, perception, and exploration. Not all of these interrelations can be explored here, but I want to emphasize that even quite apart from the need for, and confidence in, the reappearance of the mother, the importance for reality orientation of learning about object constancy leads the child to quite extensive and often repeated experimentation with disappearing and reappearing objects. Such experimentation is likely to proceed the more productively, the less the child is worried about the dependability of the mothering one.

16] Compare Kurt Goldstein, *Human Nature in the Light of Psychopathology* (Harvard University Press, Cambridge, 1947), pp. 103-104.
17] Freud, *Beyond the Pleasure Principle*.

Thus, much of what impressed Freud as repetition compulsion in the child's need to repeat a story or a play activity over and over again turns out to be neither the result of a desire to return to an earlier state nor the effect of the principle of inertia, but an essential requirement for the gradual exploration of the environment, the world of reality, and the child's relations to it. Exploration by many acts of focal attention is possible only if the object of exploration is repeatedly available and is unchanged; and orientation in the environment would become quite impossible if one could not depend on its relative constancy. This does not mean that no other motives are present in the child's need for repetition of experiences. The enjoyment in doing that which one already masters, as compared with the hazards of any new venture, are ever present competitors in man's life. Their relative strength may result in an empty, fear-conditioned inertia which dreads the new and prefers the familiar, or in the victory of the desire to explore something new and to have significant experiences. Already in the child the tendency to prefer the safe mastery of the familiar to the challenge of the unknown often plays a role, especially if his natural curiosity and desire to venture have been inhibited or stifled by an overanxious or forbidding parent. In the child's insistence that not a single word be changed in a story, there may also be the desire, born of anxiety, to control the situation and the reading adult. But the possible presence of such other motivations must not blind one to the fact that exploration and discovery of unknown aspects are constantly going on in what may ostensibly impress one as mere repetition.

The Emergence of the Object World (Reality)

The child's exploration of the object world depends not only on the continued availability of the objects but also on the child's relative freedom from too strong need or anxiety tensions. The emergence of the object world is inseparably linked to the temporary *abeyance* of needs. In the infant, this abeyance is brought about by the satisfaction of needs through the mothering one. But, in the course of development, it is also increasingly brought about by the child's capacity to *delay* need satisfaction. The more secure the infant or child feels in being able to *depend* on the mother for eventual need satisfaction—and, later, on his own capacity to satisfy his needs—the more adequately this capacity to delay need satisfaction is likely to develop. Focal attention is the instrument which plays a decisive role both in the development of the capacity for delay and in the grasp of reality, of the object world. Only by means of focal attention do distinct objects emerge from the impinging environment so that they can be perceived and understood as independent of human needs. This is possible only because the rest of the field is excluded for the duration of the act of focal attention—that is, the claim of all other needs and impulses for attention is delayed or abated.

The understanding of this development has suffered from a semantic difficulty arising from the different meanings of the word "object" in psychoanalytic and general usage. Originally, object was that which is *ob-jectum*—that is, the thing thrown before the mind, the thing which one encounters. Derived from this original meaning is the general meaning of object as anything presented to the eye, the senses, or the mind—anything which is objective and not merely subjective. But object means also that which is one's purpose, goal, or aim. Psychoanalytic terminology has made use only of this latter meaning and has further restricted it to include only the need-satisfying object—primarily the object of libido, of sexual desire. Here, the word *object* is used only for the objective object, for the object that exists independent of man's needs.[18] This object is more than just something which satisfies a particular need; it has aspects other than the one which makes it suitable to satisfy the need. It has an existence of its own. It does not come into existence because the need which it may satisfy is in tension, nor does it cease to exist because the need has been satisfied (unless it is swallowed because it satisfies hunger or is killed because it arouses fear). The reverse is true of perception of the "object" in a field characterized by high need tension. That is, the hungry animal sees only the prey, and as soon as the hunger is satisfied, the field completely changes its character, and the animal no longer pays any attention to what before was the outstanding "object." In contrast to the temporary and single-aspect-dominated character of the need-satisfying object, the emergence of the real object is predicated on two characteristics of the process of focal attention: (*a*) focal attention permits one to hold on to the object in one's mind while

18] Whenever the psychoanalytic meaning is referred to, "object" will be put in quotation marks or specifically designated as a need-satisfying object.

excluding need tensions from focal awareness, so that one is not propelled by a need in high tension, and (*b*) it permits one, in holding on to the object, to approach it from a variety of angles and repeatedly, so that many other aspects of it become apparent besides those which make it suitable to satisfy a need. In the world of biological needs, the "object" arises with the need and disappears or perishes with its satisfaction. In the world of focal attention, the object can be seen from all sides and obtains constancy—that is, it is perceived as continuing to exist even though the interest in it may slacken. The perceiver or thinker knows that the object may be contemplated again, perceptually or in thought, if he wishes to do so; it continues to exist. Indeed, it may be said that the object arises only when strong need tension subsides, for one cannot see the independent, objective object as long as one is driven by a strong need. The primary, biological needs, especially when they are strong—that is, in a state of high tension—prevent the experience of the object because they produce an overwhelming pressure toward need satisfaction. Thus the object emerges when the need tension is relaxed.

These considerations cast some doubt on the adequacy of Freud's theory of the origin and nature of thought, especially of the relation of secondary-process (reality) thought to primary-process thought. According to Freud, thought has only one ancestor, the attempt at hallucinatory need satisfaction. Thought, thus, is the child of want, of an id drive in tension which clamors for satisfaction and obeys only the pleasure principle. It originates in the hallucinatory perception of the need-satisfying object, such as food, when satisfaction is delayed and the need tension rises. Since this attempt at hallucinatory need satisfaction succeeds only to a very limited degree and does not really satisfy the need, a more reality-oriented thinking develops—secondary-process thought. But Freud makes it quite clear that secondary-process thought "merely represents a roundabout way to wish fulfillment made necessary by experience" and that "thinking is nothing but a substitute for the hallucinatory wish."[19]

19] Freud, "The Interpretation of Dreams," in *Basic Writings*, pp. 509-510, 535. Also compare Freud's "Formulations Regarding the Two Principles in Mental Functioning," in *Collected Papers* (Basic Books, New York, 1959), Vol. IV, pp. 13-16. Freud's view that thought is nothing but a substitute for hallucinatory wish fulfillment parallels his view that the ego is merely an offshoot of the id— a part of the id which, under the influence of the environment via the perception

In contrast to Freud's view, I believe that thought has two ancestors rather than one—namely, motivating needs *and* a distinctively human capacity, the relatively autonomous capacity for object interest. Focal attention is the tool, the distinctively human equipment, by means of which the capacity for object interest can be realized.[20] There is no proof that the wish for need satisfaction alone would ever lead to object perception and to object-oriented thought—that is, to a relatively objective view of reality. On the other hand, it can be shown that the more urgently need-driven perception and thought are, the less able they are to grasp and understand the object.

One of the main proofs offered for the assumption that hallucinatory need satisfaction is the cradle of object representation in thought is the observation of the dream process, of the illusions of people suffering hunger or thirst, and of the hallucinations of cases of Meynert's amentia.[21] However, this argument overlooks the fact that all of these examples are taken from people in whom the capacity for focal attention has been fully developed. And once the world has been perceived by means of focal attention— that is, structured in terms of objects—objects will continue to be seen as such, regardless of whether their perception follows the drive or the reality organization of thought, whether the objects are evoked by the needs or fears of a hallucinating psychotic patient or by a motivating dream impulse, or whether they are seen

system, has been gradually differentiated from the id. Compare Freud's *The Ego and the Id* (Hogarth Press, London, 1927).

This view has been opposed by Hartmann, Kris, and Loewenstein, who assume that the ego and the id both arise from a common, undifferentiated phase, thus emphasizing a relatively greater autonomy of the ego. The views presented in this chapter lend support to their assumption rather than to Freud's. See Heinz Hartmann, Ernst Kris, and Rudolph M. Loewenstein, "Comments on the Formation of Psychic Structure," in *The Psychoanalytic Study of the Child*, Vol. 2 (International Universities Press, New York, 1946).

20] I shall not attempt at this point to give a detailed analysis of the meaning of object interest in man, which perhaps parallels the meaning of love, although a brief analysis is made later in the chapter. It is likely that this human capacity, too, has one of its evolutionary ancestors in the animal world—namely, in the *curiosity* of monkeys. The work of Harlow, Butler, and Walker has shown that the monkey's curiosity is not motivated by a desire for food or other rewards, but is a primary motivation containing its own reward. For a summary of this work, see Butler, "Curiosity in Monkeys," *Scientific American*, Feb. 1954, pp. 70-75. Compare also Tolman's observations on rats: Edward C. Tolman, "Freedom and the Cognitive Need," *American Psychologist*, 1954, 9:536-538. Tolman, starting from a quite different approach, arrives at conclusions similar to mine, regarding the incompatibility of strong need- or fear-pressure and the pursuit of truth.

21] Compare Rapaport, *Organization and Pathology of Thought*, p. 690.

by a person idly glancing out of a window. The drive organization of thought, the primary process at this stage, uses imagery which, in its turn, has developed only *after* focal attention has matured, after the world of objects has emerged, after secondary-process thought has furnished the raw material out of which this imagery is built.

Freud assumes that the *perception of food is an essential constituent* of the infant's experience of the satisfaction of hunger, and that, therefore, when the infant again is hungry, a psychic impulse which may be called a wish will re-evoke the former food-percept.[22] This is highly improbable. The available evidence shows that at the earliest stages, specifically before focal attention develops, no objects are perceived by the infant. He perceives neither the milk, nor the mother, nor the mother's breast as a separate and distinct object. All the infant "perceives" at this stage are global feelings of well- or ill-being, of satisfaction or need tension, of the disturbing or pleasant impact of an environment which is as yet neither clearly differentiated from the infant nor structured in itself. And even after there slowly dawns on the infant the distinction between his own body sphere and the something "out there"—from which pleasant or unpleasant things seem to impinge on or happen to the body—there is no differentiation of the environment into distinct objects, such as food, or mother's body, or blanket. Sullivan refers to this primitive, egocentric, global stage of experience as "prototaxic," and describes it as consisting of "instantaneous records of total situations."[23] While the psychic activity going on at this stage is largely a matter of conjecture and inference, there is definite evidence that no objects are perceived at this stage.[24] How can one picture, then, the mental activity of the infant when need tension arises, when he longs for satisfaction of the need? One can picture it only as a longing for the return of the total state of the former need-satisfying experiences. If one can speak of hallucinatory activity at all,

22] Freud, "The Interpretation of Dreams," *Basic Writings*, p. 509. See also, more recently, Anna Freud, "Some Remarks on Infant Observation," in *The Psychoanalytic Study of the Child* (International Universities Press, New York, 1953), Vol. 8, pp. 12-13.

23] Patrick Mullahy, "A Theory of Interpersonal Relations and the Evolution of Personality," in Harry Stack Sullivan, *Conceptions of Modern Psychiatry* (Norton, New York, 1953), p. 252.

24] See the section above on "The Development of Focal Attention" and the data presented there which show that no visual perception of objects takes place.

it must be a kind of hallucination which is different from that known to us from dreams or psychotic hallucinations. It cannot consist of the hallucination of visual images of objects or of distinct sounds. It can only be a reactivation of the memory traces of the "total situation"—for example, of the total feeling of well-being while being nursed. It is a longing for, and, perhaps, a hallucinatory reactivation of, an "instantaneous record of a total situation," and this situation is not to be conceived as consisting of differentiated objects, but of how it feels to be comfortable, to be nursed, and so on.

That the infant does not long for or hallucinate food, but, rather, longs for or hallucinates the recurrence of a total situation of well-being is consistent also with the modern concept of instinct and instinctual action. Konrad Lorenz has shown that it is not the "object"—such as the prey or the mating partner—but the instinctual action itself which is the goal of the animal; the "object" merely releases this action and is its environmental substrate.[25] Similarly, the "goal" of the infant is not mother's breast or the milk, but the repetition of the total experience of being nursed or, in terms of the parallel to the biological concept of instinctual action, the satisfying sucking and being held experience.

The ancestral role of hallucinatory experience in relation to thought, then, is merely that it constitutes primitive mental activity of a wishing or longing character. It is the cradle of primary-process thought, but there is no path that leads from it to secondary-process thought, to the emergence of the object world. Indeed, Freud does not indicate any steps which lead from primary-process to secondary-process thought, but merely states that another type of thought has to develop, since the primary-process thought is not equipped to bring about the satisfaction, but merely to evoke the hallucinatory image of the need-satisfying object or, as I would prefer to say, of the diffuse, global need-satisfying experience.

Where, then, must one seek for other ancestors of thought, especially of object- or reality-centered thought, of secondary-process thought? Objects become distinct parts of experience only when they are encountered in a field sufficiently relaxed from need tension to permit the infant to approach and explore the object *playfully*—that is, without having to incorporate it as nour-

25] Konrad Z. Lorenz, "Ueber den Begriff der Instinkthandlung," *Folia Bio-theoretica*, 1937, 2:18-50.

ishment. In exploratory "play" (which is at this stage, and for a long time to come, the most important way of *learning*) the infant or child approaches, grasps the object, and lets it go again, in ever renewed encounters and from different angles. That infants like to put objects in their mouths and sometimes will even swallow them does not mean that they do this because the need tension of hunger drives them. It means that of the great variety of exploratory, playful contacts which can be had with an object, contact through the mouth is the earliest and therefore for some time the most important one, which later is equaled and then superseded in importance by contact with the hands. The object gradually emerges as the thing which can be felt, touched, tasted, seen, let go, recaptured, patted, squeezed, hit, pulled, and so on—which not only is known as satisfying hunger but also can be experienced in a great many different ways, from different angles, and which remains the focus of all these different experiences and makes them possible.

In the need-dominated approach, the whole field receives its character from the need, and the "objects" in the field are perceived only as signals pointing toward food, prey, danger, or escape, as the case may be. The action is completely directional: toward or away from. In the *play* of young dogs or cats the object is approached and then let go, approached again and released again, turned around, chased, abandoned, watched, picked up again, in ever repeated and ever varied approaches. The playing child discovers that different kinds of actions can be performed and different kinds of contacts had with the toy-object and with his own body. These varied actions become possible only when the object is *not* approached or fled from under the overriding impact of need or fear. The great variety of the playful approach, as contrasted with the narrow directedness of the need-driven approach, lets the child perceive many aspects, facets, qualities of the object which would never be revealed to him if he used it only for the gratification of a basic biological need. Urgent desire and fear make one blind rather than able to see; they alert one to the immediate possibilities of need satisfaction and to danger; but they do not lead to knowledge and appreciation of the object. Gustav Bally has shown that only the tension-relaxed field permits play, and that only play permits the recognition of an object world. Only those animals which, because of a prolonged period of parental protection and care, experience relative security from too great need tension show the beginnings of play; and man, in whom the parental satisfaction of the young's vital needs is most prolonged and who therefore is least exposed to overwhelming need tension, has developed play to an extent unknown in the animal world. His relative freedom from urgent need tension is the basis of the richness of his object world, which could not have developed if he had not been free, in play and thought, to explore objects without having to use them for immediate need satisfaction.[26]

In the brief outline I have presented of the main structural aspects of focal attention, I mentioned the fact that focal acts usually consist of several approaches from different angles to the object and/or renewed approaches from the same angle, and that these approaches oscillate between receptive exposure to the object and active taking hold of it. This aspect has essentially the same character as the back and forth of the child's playful exploration of the world around him. It can be observed as easily in focal attention to something visually perceived as in focal attention to a thought or feeling. In attentively looking at an object, such as the pencil lying in front of me on my desk, my glance does not remain fixed on any one point of the pencil for any long period of time. It wanders, goes back and forth, sometimes slowly, sometimes quickly shifting from one point to another, and then returning again to a point looked at before. Thus I receive a variety of impressions, each of which is then integrated more or less completely into my total experience of the pencil. This behavior takes place in *all* acts of focal, visual attention. When the glance remains fixed on only one point for any length of time, it very soon turns into an unseeing stare which no longer has the character of active visual exploration but of passively being held by the point stared at.[27] If maintained long enough, this kind of stare may lead to a trancelike experi-

26] Gustav Bally, *Vom Ursprung und von den Grenzen der Freiheit: Eine Deutung des Spiels bei Tier und Mensch* (Benno Schwabe, Basel, 1945). It is regrettable that this excellent and thoughtful study has not yet been translated.

27] This unseeing stare plays a considerable role in difficulties in concentration and thinking. The blind, unmoving, fixed mental "staring" at a word or a thought is one of the ways in which active and productive thought is interrupted. The passive "stare" replaces active thought when other needs or anxiety interfere with the thought process—that is, when one experiences "working difficulties."

ence, which is the reason why many hypnotists use a very small, bright object to help in inducing a trance. The person looking at a small, bright metal disk very soon stares unseeingly at the bright spot; his glance becomes fixed on the brightness. An object showing many features would be unsuitable for inducing a trance, because it would invite the eye to explore it, to circumnavigate it actively, and to wander over it. The exploring, wandering-back-and-forth nature of focal, visual attention is also characteristic of focal attention to a thought. The object of thought is viewed from many different angles and in repeated approaches; it is considered in its various real or possible relations to other objects, in different contexts, and so on. Without this back-and-forth movement, thought becomes sterile and fruitless. Just as the completely need- or fear-governed action (and the instinctual action) never really encounters the object, so the thought which is under the pressure of either too much fear or anxiety, or under the pressure of too urgent or narrow a goal, does not do justice to its object. Only thought which is sufficiently free from the pressure of urgent needs or fears can contemplate its object fully and recognize it in relative independence from the thinker's needs and fears— that is, as something objective. Thus focal attention is incompatible with severe anxiety. The starving person does not think about what he eats, but grabs at anything.

But even outside the sphere of urgent biological needs, it can be shown that too strong need pressure interferes with productive thought. In thinking about a problem one is usually successful only if one does not press too hard for a solution; that is, one is more likely to be successful if the thought is truly object-centered, free to contemplate the object from all sides, than if the thought is goal-centered, under the pressure of *having* to produce a solution immediately. In teaching diagnostic testing, I have been impressed many times with the fact that the students who feel under the pressure of having to know, at all cost, whether this person is schizophrenic or that person is hysterical are much less likely to learn something about either the person, or schizophrenia, or hysteria than are the students who are able to take in and contemplate the data in front of them, without the pressure of the narrow goal idea of having to find a diagnostic label.

The development of focal attention and the emergence of the

object world presuppose relative freedom from basic need tension, so that the object can be perceived under many different aspects, rather than apprehended merely as something that will satisfy hunger or that arouses fear and has to be fled from. And even after focal attention is fully developed and the environment is perceived as consisting of distinct objects, the need-driven (as opposed to the object-interested) perceiver or thinker will not see the object as fully in its own right as will the person who contemplates it in relative freedom from acute need tension. Curiosity, the desire for knowledge, the wish to orient oneself in the world one lives in—and finally the posing of man's eternal questions, "Who am I?" "What is this world around me?" "What can I hope for?" "What should I do?"—all these do not develop under the pressure of relentless need or of fear for one's life. They develop when man can pause to think, when the child is free to wonder and to explore. They are not, as Freud would have us believe, merely detours on the path to gratification of basic biological needs, any more than thought is only a substitute for hallucinatory wish fulfillment. They represent man's distinctive capacity to develop *interest*—the autonomous interest which alone permits the full encounter with the object. That man is capable of autonomous interest does not, of course, rule out the fact that he also remains subject to his biological and other needs, and that these may interfere with his quest for truth, or may further it, as the case may be. Just as the infant first encounters the object *not* when he is hungry or afraid, but when he is free to play and explore, so does man, on each successively higher level of understanding, discover new aspects of the object world and of himself when he is not driven by consuming need or fear, but when he can devote himself to the object. The relation of autonomous interest to need-dominated interest is similar to the relation of love to sexual desire, and to neurotic need of the "love-object." Like love, autonomous object interest is potentially inexhaustible and lasting, while need-dominated interest subsides with the satisfaction of the need, and revives only when the need tension, such as hunger or sexual desire, rises again. Moreover, while need satisfaction, according to Freud, is related to tension discharge, both love and object interest find their fulfillment not in a discharge of tension but, rather, in the maintenance of it, in sustained and ever renewed acts of relating to the beloved person or to the object of interest.[28]

Focal attention to people is slower and longer in developing than focal attention to other objects of the environment. Even after the child has developed the capacity for object-centered focal attention with regard to his peers or to some adults, his own parents still may not be seen focally—that is, from all sides and in all their aspects. The reason for this is, of course, that the parents, especially the mother, are of such overwhelming significance as the need-satisfying and also as the anxiety-arousing "objects" that they are relatively slow in emerging for the child as people with an existence of their own, independent of the child's needs and fears. To this is added another factor: Many parents prevent the child from seeing them in all their different aspects, focally, as they really are. They do this out of their own needs and anxieties, in order to perpetuate the child's dependence on them, or in order to maintain in their own and their children's minds an idealized image of themselves as the good or model parents. To this end they discourage, consciously as well as unconsciously, the child's focally attentive and explorative approach. The parents must not have any weaknesses or shortcomings; the child must not be critical of them; they must be exempt from the realistic curiosity of the child. Thus the idea that parents are people about whom one may have opinions and whom one may critically judge—that they are people like other people—may come as a shock to the child, or, indeed, may never occur to him. If the parent, by forbidding gestures or other manifestations of the parental tabu on focal attention to the parent as a person, arouses sufficiently severe and pervasive anxiety in the child, such anxiety will interfere effectively with any focal attention toward the parent and, possibly, toward people in general. Thus people will continue to be experienced predominantly as anxiety-arousing and need-satisfying "objects" by the person whose focal attention to the parents has been disrupted and diverted by anxiety. Actually, this is the case, to a greater or lesser extent, in most neurotic and psychotic patients. This same strategy of arousing fear in order to

28] The capacity for autonomous interest, or object-centered focal attention, is the basis of what Fromm has called productive thought, which in his view, too, parallels love. Erich Fromm, *Man for Himself* (Rinehart, New York, 1947), pp. 96-107.

discourage focal attention toward a person, a problem, a situation —to discourage exploring them from all angles, objectively—has always been and continues to be favored as an instrument of *social power;* it is used by all those who have a stake in hindering or preventing man's search for truth and freedom, who thereby maintain their own irrational authority unquestioned.

The psychoanalytic patient-therapist relationship shows clearly the difference between perception in a need-dominated field and in a field sufficiently relaxed from tension to permit the emergence of the object and the development of autonomous interest. First, the relationship is designed to lessen anxiety to the point where focal attention, rather than need- or fear-driven alertness, can develop sufficiently to enable the patient to see himself. Second, in the transference relationship the patient uses and sees the therapist at first largely as a need-satisfying object and/or as a danger against which he has to protect himself. This perception changes gradually, and to the extent that the patient no longer sees the therapist as a need-satisfying or as a threatening object, the patient becomes able to see the therapist objectively as a person. Similarly, the therapist's perception of the patient will be an objective one only to the extent to which the therapist has autonomous interest in the patient and is not blinded by his own needs and anxieties.

Autonomous object interest and object-centered focal attention in man are everywhere and at all times closely interwoven with need-driven perception and thought. Man's capacity for autonomous, object-centered interest—and with it, his search for truth —has forever to disentangle itself from his fears and needs. This constitutes one of man's limitations. It also makes it difficult to keep clearly in mind the essential difference between these modes of relating to the world. Yet, without recognizing the emergence of this capacity which is not to be found in the animal world, it is not possible to understand man, to understand his relation to others and to the objects in the world around him.

The viewpoint presented here does not imply that man's capacity for object interest and his desire for truth are not the results of evolution. No doubt these capacities have developed because they enable man to know more about his environment, to adapt more effectively to it, and to change it, which he could not do were his behavior dominated by instinctive needs and fears to the extent characteristic of animals. But one would succumb to what

Julian Huxley has termed the "nothing but" fallacy if one assumed that because these capacities have developed in the service of more effective adaptation, they have remained nothing but servants of man's biological needs.

The "nothing but" view of man permeates Freud's work. It underlies the theory of the pleasure principle as well as that of the death instinct, just as it underlies the libido theory, the concept of sublimation, and the theory of thought as being nothing but a detour toward instinctual need-gratification. It sounds like a distant echo of God's angry words after man had eaten from the tree of knowledge, "For dust thou art and unto dust shalt thou return," and of the bitter and pessimistic pathos of Ecclesiastes, "The thing that has been, it is that which shall be; and that which is done is that which shall be done; and there is no new thing under the sun." If one views the revolutionary discoveries of Freud in the context of the nineteenth century's image of man, then the strength of his genius—in this respect similar to Nietzsche's—lies in the destruction of a shallow and self-satisfied optimism which believed that man was an entirely rational being and that if he had not achieved the best and most reasonable of all worlds, he had come close to achieving it. Freud showed the dark, powerful, and complex subterranean forces which give the lie to such a soporific view of mankind. But in emphasizing these forces, in the course of discovering man's individual prehistory and its tremendous impact on his life, Freud tended to overlook the fact that the movement of evolution as well as of history does create "new things under the sun," and that man is not only the slave of his past, but, with all his limitations, also the potential master of his future.

Freud has been accused of being too biologically oriented. And his view of man as "homo natura,"[29] with its relative disregard of social and historical factors, supports this criticism. But the biological view of man, if aware of its own limitations, is a legitimate and fruitful one. What seems to me a more basic criticism of Freud is that *within* the biological framework he was more impressed by death than by life, more impressed by the return of all organisms to the inorganic than by the miracle of life devel-

29] Compare Ludwig Binswanger's essay on this aspect of Freud's work, "Freuds Auffassung des Menschen im Lichte der Anthropologie," in *Ausgewählte Vorträge und Aufsätze*, Vol. 1 (A. Francke A. G., Bern, 1947), pp. 159-189.

oping from inorganic matter. His penetrating glance was turned toward the frustrating and tragic spectacle of man's being bound by his phylogenetic, his ontogenetic, and his biographical past. But the discoverer of a method of therapy which did more than any other method so far to free the individual from these shackles, averted his eye from the perhaps even more wondrous sight—which can be seen in biology and evolution as well as in history and in individual development—of the creative powers of life.

12

On Memory and
Childhood Amnesia

GREEK MYTHOLOGY CELEBRATES MNEMOSYNE, THE GODDESS OF
memory, as the mother of all art. She bore the nine muses to
Zeus.[1] Centuries after the origin of this myth, Plato banned poetry,
the child of memory, from his ideal state as being idle and se-
ductive. While lawmakers, generals, and inventors were useful
for the common good, the fact that Homer was nothing but a
wandering minstrel without a home and without a following
proved how useless he was.[2] In the Odyssey the voices of the
Sirens tempt Ulysses:

> For never yet hath any man rowed past
> This isle in his black ship, till he hath heard
> The honeyed music of our lips, and goes
> His way delighted and a wiser man.
> For see, we know the whole tale of the travail
> That Greeks and Trojans suffered in wide Troy-land
> By heaven's behest; yea, and all things we know
> That come to pass upon the fruitful earth.[3]

1] The words "muse and "mnemosyne" derive from the same root $\mu\epsilon\nu$ or $\mu\alpha\nu$.
Ludwig Preller, *Griechische Mythologie* (Berlin, 1872), Vol. 1, p. 399, footnote
1. In German, too, the words *Gedächtus* (memory) and *Dichtung* (poetry) derive
from the same root *denken* (think); compare also *gedenken* (remember).
2] Plato *Republic* 599, 600.
3] Homer, *Odyssey*, William Morris, trans. (Oxford University Press, New York,
1925), Book XII, ll. 189-196, by permission of the publisher.

Their irresistible song, in evoking the past, promises a delight which will allow no future and will be the end of Ulysses' plans to return to an active life and to resume the rule of Ithaca. He prevents his shipmates from listening to the alluring voices by plugging their ears with wax, and he, too curious to renounce the pleasure, has himself chained to the ship's mast so that he will not be able to yield to their song and abandon the future.

This ambivalent attitude toward memory, especially toward its most potent form as embodied in the song, the epic, the tale, in poetry, music, fiction, and in all art, has accompanied the history of man. The modern, popular attitude, so widespread in the United States, the country of the most advanced industrial and techno-logical civilization—that all art and poetry is "sissy"—is the latter-day implementation of the Platonic taboo. But with this difference: the contemporaries of Plato, and before them the shipmates of Ulysses, were susceptible to the promise of happiness that the song of the Sirens and of the muses contains, so that Ulysses and Plato, concerned with planning and not with the past, had to forcefully prevent their listening. Today the masses have internal-ized the ancient fear and prohibition of this alluring song and, in their contempt for it, express and repress both their longing for and their fear of the unknown vistas to which it might open the doors.

The profound fascination of memory of past experience and the double aspect of this fascination—its irresistible lure into the past with its promise of happiness and pleasure, and its threat to the kind of activity, planning, and purposeful thought and behavior encouraged by modern Western civilization—have attracted the thought of two men in recent times who have made the most sig-nificant modern contribution to the ancient questions posed by the Greek myth: Sigmund Freud and Marcel Proust.

Both are aware of the antagonism inherent in memory, the con-flict between reviving the past and actively participating in the present life of society. Both illuminate the nature of this conflict from different angles. Proust, the poet of memory, is ready to re-nounce all that people usually consider as active life, to renounce activity, enjoyment of the present moment, concern with the future, friendship, social intercourse, for the sublime happiness and profound truth recaptured in the most elusive of all treasures that man has hunted for, the "Remembrance of Things Past." He pursues this conflict between activity and memory into its most subtle manifestations. He knows that, as the awakening dreamer may lose the memory of his dream when he moves his limbs, opens his eyes, changes the position of his body, so the slightest motion may endanger and dispel the deep pleasure of the vision of the time in Combray recaptured by the flavor of the *madeleine*, or the image of Venice conjured up by the sensation and the posture which the unevenness of the pavement in the court of the Guermantes town house brought to him as the unevenness of the pavement of San Marco had years ago.[4] He does not dare to stir, for fear that the exhilarating vision may disappear. Bodily movement is the basic and simplest form of all activity endangering memory. Action itself, the attitude of activity, even the activity of enjoying the immediate present are seen by Proust as the antagonists, the incompatible alternative of memory.[5] From here it is only one step to the insight that the memory which reveals the true vision of something past, the memory celebrated by Proust, is very different from the voluntary, everyday memory, the useful instrument needed by man every hour and every minute to recall a word, a figure, a date, to recognize a person or an object, to think of his plans, tasks, intentions, the eminently utilitarian memory characterized by the very fact that it serves the purposes of active and conventionally organized life in society. Proust speaks of the artificiality and untruth of the pictures that this memory furnishes, of its flat and uniform quality which cannot do justice to the unique flavor and the true qualities of anything remembered.[6]

While for Proust the antagonism between society and memory of the significant past can be resolved only by renouncing either one or the other, Goethe seeks to reconcile the two. When, at a party, a toast was proposed to memory he objected vehemently with these words: "I do not recognize memory in the sense in which you mean it. Whatever we encounter that is great, beautiful, significant, need not be remembered from outside, need not be hunted up and laid hold of, as it were. Rather, from the begin-

---

4] Marcel Proust, *A la recherche du temps perdu, VIII, Le temps retrouvé* (Librairie Gallimard, Editions de la Nouvelle Revue Française, Paris, 1927), Vol. 2, p. 8.

5] *Ibid.*, p. 14.

6] *Ibid.*, pp. 11-12.

ning, it must be woven into the fabric of our inmost self, must become one with it, create a new and better self in us and thus live and become a productive force in ourselves. There is no past that one is allowed to long for. There is only the eternally new, growing from the enlarged elements of the past; and genuine longing always must be productive, must create something new and better."[7]

Freud, not unlike Proust, approaches the problem of memory not from wondering what, or how well, or how much man remembers, but how hard it is to remember, how much is forgotten and not to be recovered at all or only with the greatest difficulty, and how the period richest in experience, the period of early childhood, is the one which usually is forgotten entirely save for a few apparently meaningless memory fragments. He finds this surprising since "we are informed that during those years which have left nothing but a few incomprehensible memory fragments, we have vividly reacted to impressions, that we have manifested human pain and pleasure and that we have expressed love, jealousy and other passions as they then affected us."[8] The few incomprehensible memory fragments left over from childhood he considers as "concealing memories" (*Deckerinnerungen*),[9] and his painstaking work to decipher their language bears more than a superficial resemblance to Proust's attempt to decipher the hieroglyphic characters of the images of a cloud, a triangle, a belfry, a flower, a pebble—a most difficult undertaking, but the only way to the true memories enclosed in these signs which seemed to be only indifferent material objects or sensations.[10] It was Freud who made the discovery that a conflict, leading to repression, is responsible for the difficulty of this work of deciphering and for the difficulty of remembering the past. His well-known explanation of infantile amnesia is that the forgetting of childhood experiences is due to progressive repression of infantile sexuality, which reaches the peak of its manifestations in the third

7] Author's translation from *Goethe's Gespräche* (Herausgegeben von Flodoard Freiherr von Biedermann, Leipzig, 1910), Vol. 3, p. 37 (November 4th, 1823). Compare with this Proust's "Les vrais paradis sont les paradis qu'on a perdu." Proust, *op. cit.*, p. 13.

8] Sigmund Freud, "Three Contributions to the Theory of Sex," *Basic Writings* (Random House, New York, 1938), p. 581.

9] Freud, "Psychopathology of Everyday Life," *Basic Writings*, pp. 62-65.

10] Proust, *op. cit.*, p. 24.

and fourth years of life. This repression is brought about by the "psychic forces of loathing, shame, and moral and esthetic ideal demands."[11] These forces have the sanction of society, they are the product of society, they are part of and serve the purposes of the same conventionally organized life of society which molds the functions of all social activity and of that "uniform" memory in which Proust saw the irreconcilable antagonists of the true remembrance of things past.

It is the purpose of this chapter to explore further the dynamics of this conflict in memory which leads to the striking phenomenon of childhood amnesia as well as to the difficulty, encountered by Proust though more hidden to the average eye, of recovering *any* true picture of past experience. To speak of a conflict in memory is a convenient abbreviation. Formulated more explicitly and accurately, the intention of this presentation is to shed light on some of the factors and conflicts in man and his society which make it difficult, if not impossible, for him really to remember his past and especially his early childhood.

Obviously, the concept of memory which such an approach presupposes cannot be the impersonal, artificial, isolated, and abstract concept implied by experimentation on the recall of digits, nonsense syllables, and similar material, a concept which seems more appropriate for the testing of the capacity of some mechanical apparatus than for the understanding of the functioning of memory in the living person. Nor is such a concept fundamentally changed when logically meaningful phrases or perceptually organized "Gestalten" are substituted for nonsense syllables and memory is investigated for its capacity to reproduce those, rather than meaningless material. Nobody doubts that it is easier to remember meaningful than meaningless material and that the function of

---

11] Freud, "Three Contributions to the Theory of Sex," *Basic Writings*, p. 583. Freud asserts that the development of these forces during the latency period is organically determined and that it "can occasionally be produced without the help of education." It is surprising that the man who discovered, explored, described, and emphasized over and over again the conflict between culture, society, and sexual instinct should have ascribed the ontogenetic origin of sexual inhibitions to organic factors as though he wanted to explain as natural those inhibitions which a culture, hostile to pleasure and to sex, has created, deepened, and strengthened in every imaginable way. The only explanation for such a strange and questionable hypothesis lies, to my mind, in Freud's and every great discoverer's tragic conflict between a powerful and lucid mind searching for truth and the person who never can entirely extricate himself from the thousand threads with which he is captured and tied to the prejudices, ideologies, falsehoods, and conventions of his time and society.

memory has not developed in order to make possible the recall of nonsense. Memory as a function of the living personality can be understood only as a capacity for the organization and reconstruction of past experiences and impressions in the service of present needs, fears, and interests. It goes without saying that, just as there is no such thing as impersonal perception and impersonal experience, there is also no impersonal memory. Man perceives and remembers not as a camera reproduces on the film the objects before its lens; the scope and quality of his perceptions and experiences as well as of their reproduction by memory are determined by his individual needs, fears, and interests. This is the more apparent the more significant an experience has been for the person.

With this concept of memory in mind, the puzzling problem of childhood amnesia seems to become more transparent and accessible to understanding. No greater change in the needs of man occurs than that which takes place between early childhood and adulthood. Into this change have gone all the decisive formative influences of the culture transmitted by the parents, laying the fundament of the transformation into the grown-up, "useful" member of society from the little heathen, who is helpless but as yet sees nothing wrong with following the pleasure principle completely and immediately and who has an insatiable curiosity and capacity for experience. An explanation of childhood amnesia that takes into account these changes leads to the following tentative hypothesis:

The categories (or schemata) of adult memory are not suitable receptacles for early childhood experiences and therefore not fit to preserve these experiences and enable their recall. The functional capacity of the conscious, adult memory is usually limited to those types of experience which the adult consciously is aware of and is capable of having.

It is not merely the repression of a specific content, such as early sexual experience, that accounts for the general childhood amnesia; the biologically, culturally, and socially influenced process of memory organization results in the formation of categories (schemata) of memory which are not suitable vehicles to receive and reproduce experiences of the quality and intensity typical of early childhood. The world of modern Western civilization has no use for this type of experience. In fact, it cannot permit itself to have any use for it; it cannot permit the memory of it, because such memory, if universal, would explode the restrictive social order of this civilization. No doubt the hostility of Western civilization to pleasure, and to sexual pleasure as the strongest of all, is a most important factor operative in the transformation and education of the child into an adult who will be able to fulfill the role and the functions he has to take over in society and will be satisfied by them. Freud has not only called attention to the phenomenon of childhood amnesia but has also singled out a decisive factor in its genesis. I believe, however, that two points are important for a more adequate understanding of the phenomenon.

First, it is not sufficiently clear why a repression of sexual experience should lead to a repression of all experience in early childhood. For this reason the assumption seems more likely that there must be something in the general quality of childhood experience which leads to the forgetting of that experience. Second, the phenomenon of childhood amnesia leads to a problem regarding the nature of repression, especially repression of childhood material. The term and concept of repression suggest that material which *per se* could be recalled is excluded from recall because of its traumatic nature. If the traumatic factor can be clarified and dissolved, the material is again accessible to recall. But even the most profound and prolonged psychoanalysis does not lead to a recovery of childhood memory; at best it unearths some incidents and feelings that had been forgotten. Childhood amnesia, then, may be due to a formation of the memory functions which makes them unsuitable to accommodate childhood experience, rather than exclusively to a censor repressing objectionable material which, without such repression, could and would be remembered. The adult is usually not capable of experiencing what the child experiences; more often than not he is not even capable of imagining what the child experiences. It should not be surprising, then, that he should be incapable of recalling his own childhood experiences since his whole mode of experiencing has changed. The person who remembers is the present person, a person who has changed considerably, whose interests, needs, fears, capacity for experience and emotion have changed. The two mechanisms of forgetting suggested here shade gradually and imperceptibly into one another. They are neither alternatives nor opposites, but rather the two ends of a continuous scale. It might be theoretically interesting to follow up this viewpoint to see how much it could clarify the much used but not too clear concept of repression and the processes underlying repression. However, this would lead too far away from the immediate problem of a more concrete understanding and testing of the suggested general theory of early childhood amnesia.

A closer examination and comparison of the content and quality of adult and childhood memories may be helpful for the purpose of such an understanding. Both Freud and Proust speak of the autobiographical memory, and it is only with regard to this memory that the striking phenomenon of childhood amnesia and the less obvious difficulty of recovering any past experience may be observed. There is no specific childhood amnesia as far as the remembrance of words learned and of objects and persons recognized is concerned. This type of material is remembered because, in contrast to the autobiographical past, it is constantly reexperienced and used and because it is essential for the orientation and adaptation of the growing child to his environment. In the recall of this type of material we have to deal with memory serving the immediate, practical use of knowledge and perception (recognition) mainly. The memory of the personal past—of one's past experiences, which also contain the material that has gone into the formation of one's character—is a much less efficient and reliable servant than the memory of learned material, on the whole, seems to be. Yet the separation of the "useful" from the "autobiographical" memory is, of course, an artificial abstraction. Actually this distinction of the content of remembered material is not clear-cut, and the two types of material indicated by it are continuously and everywhere interrelated.

The autobiographical memory shows in most persons, if not in all, the amnesia for their early childhood from birth to approximately the fifth or sixth year. Of course, there are considerable gaps in the memory of many people for later periods of their lives also, probably more so for the period before than after puberty; but these gaps vary individually to a much greater extent than does the ubiquitous early childhood amnesia. Freud's observation of this amnesia has not stimulated others, as far as I can see, to significant investigations of the adult autobiographical memory. Yet it would seem that an awareness of the main differences between the type of material remembered from early childhood and that remembered from later life might help in an understanding of the phenomenon of childhood amnesia. If one believes Proust, life after childhood is not remembered either, save for the elusive flashes of a vision given only to the most sensitive and differentiated mind as the rare grace of a fortunate moment, which then the poet, with passionate devotion and patient labor, may try to transcribe and communicate.

Freud contrasts the presumable riches of childhood experience, the child's great capacity for impressions and experience, with the poverty or total lack of memory of such rich experience. If one looks closely at the average adult's memory of the periods of his life after childhood, such memory, it is true, usually shows no great temporal gaps. It is fairly continuous. But its formal continuity in time is offset by barrenness in content, by an incapacity to reproduce anything that resembles a really rich, full, rounded, and alive experience. Even the most "exciting" events are remembered as milestones rather than as moments filled with the concrete abundance of life. Adult memory reflects life as a road with occasional signposts and milestones rather than as the landscape through which this road has led. The milestones are the measurements of time, the months and years, the empty count of time gone by, so many years spent here, so many years spent there, moving from one place to another, so many birthdays, and so forth. The signposts represent the outstanding events to which they point— entering college, the first job, marriage, birth of children, buying a house, a family celebration, a trip. But it is not the events that are remembered as they really happened and were experienced at the time. What is remembered is usually, more or less, only the fact that such an event took place. The signpost is remembered, not the place, the thing, the situation to which it points. And even these signposts themselves do not usually indicate the really significant moments in a person's life; rather they point to the events that are conventionally supposed to be significant, to the clichés which society has come to consider as the main stations of life. Thus the memories of the majority of people come to resemble increasingly the stereotyped answers to a questionnaire, in which life consists of time and place of birth, religious denomination, residence, educational degrees, job, marriage, number and birthdates of children, income, sickness, and death. The average traveler, asked about his trip, will tell you how many miles he has made (how many years he has lived); how fast he went (how successful he was); what places he has visited—usually only the well-known ones, often he visits only those that one "simply must have seen"—(the jobs he has held, the prestige he has gained). He can tell you whether the driving was smooth or rough, or whether somebody bumped his fender, but he will be quite unable to give you any real idea of the country through which he went. So the average traveler through life remembers chiefly what the road map or the guide book says, what he is supposed to remember because it is exactly what everybody else remembers too.

In the course of later childhood, adolescence, and adult life, perception and experience themselves develop increasingly into the rubber stamps of conventional clichés. The capacity to see and feel what is there gives way to the tendency to see and feel what one expects to see and feel, which, in turn, is what one is expected to see and feel because everybody else does.[12] Experience increasingly assumes the form of the cliché under which it will be recalled because this cliché is what conventionally is remembered by others. This is not the remembered situation itself, but the words which are customarily used to indicate this situation and the reactions which it is supposed to evoke. While this ubiquitous and powerful tendency toward pseudo-experience in terms of conventional clichés usually takes place unnoticed, it is quite articulate in some people and is used widely in advertising. There are people who experience a party, a visit to the movies, a play, a concert, a trip in the very words in which they are going to tell their friends about it; in fact, quite often, they anticipate such experience in these words. The experience is predigested, as it were, even before they have tasted of it. Like the unfortunate Midas, whose touch turned everything into gold so that he could not eat or drink, these people turn the potential nourishment of the anticipated experience into the sterile currency of the conventional phrase which exhausts their experience because they

12] Tolstoi gives a masterful description of how, in an adolescent girl during a visit to the opera, the experience of what happens on the stage changes from a genuine, naive, and fresh view to the conventional "appreciation" of the opera habitué. His account of her initial perceptions, by the way, is a surrealist description of opera more than half a century before surrealism. Tolstoi, *War and Peace*, part 8, chapters 9 and 10.

have seen, heard, felt nothing but this phrase with which later they will report to their friends the "exciting time" they have had. The advertising business seems to be quite aware of this. It does not have to promise a good book, a well-written and well-performed play, an entertaining or amusing movie. It suffices to say that the book, the play, the movie will be the talk of the town, of the next party, of one's friends. To have been there, to be able to say that one has been present at the performance, to have read the book even when one is unable to have the slightest personal reaction to it, is quite sufficient. But while Midas suffered tortures of starvation, the people under whose eyes every experience turns into a barren cliché do not know that they starve. Their starvation manifests itself merely in boredom or in restless activity and incapacity for any real enjoyment.

The burial and distortion of experience in the process of memory under the cliché of the conventionally accepted finds an interesting confirmation in Bartlett's experiments on memory.[13] In one of them he showed to his subjects, who were educated adults, five picture postcards, on each of which was the representation of the face of a naval or army officer or man. He asked them to look at each card for ten seconds "noting carefully as many of the characteristics of the faces as you can, so that later you may be able to describe the faces, and to answer questions about them." Half an hour after the exposure of the cards, each subject described them and answered questions about some of the details. This was repeated after a week and then after longer intervals. Reporting the outcome of this experiment, Bartlett says, among other things: "Obviously, complicating the perceptual pattern were all kinds of conventional notions about soldiers and sailors of a given rank. . . . A particular face often at once aroused a more or less conventional attitude appropriate to the given type. Thereupon, the attitude actively affected the detail of representation. Even in immediate memory the features of the face often tended to be made more conventional, while in subsequent recall they tended to approach yet more closely the conventional pattern." He summarizes the results of this experiment by saying that it "seems certain that attitudes may strongly influence recall

13] F. C. Bartlett, *Remembering: A Study in Experimental and Social Psychology* (Cambridge University Press, Cambridge, 1932), see especially pp. 53-54, 89, 125, 171-173.

and may tend in particular to produce stereotyped and conventional reproductions which adequately serve all normal needs, though they are very unfaithful to their originals."

In another experiment he used a North American Indian folk tale, "The War of the Ghosts." Each subject read the story twice. Then he reproduced it after fifteen minutes and again, several times, after considerably longer intervals. In these reproductions a most important role is played by a factor which Bartlett calls "rationalisation"; the function which he attributes to it is "to render material acceptable, understandable, comfortable, straightforward; to rob it of all puzzling elements." With one of his subjects all mention of ghosts disappeared in the very first reproduction of the story "in spite of the fact that special attention was called to the title. The same thing occurred at some stage in *every* series obtained with this story as a starting point. This omission illustrates how any element of imported culture which finds very little background in the culture to which it comes must fail to be assimilated."

However, conventionalization affects not only elements of "imported culture," but everything recalled. Bartlett gave newspaper reports of a cricket game and a passage from a review of Tilden's book *The Art of Lawn Tennis* to Cambridge undergraduates for repeated reproduction. In still another experiment he used a passage, "The intellect is vagabond," from Emerson's essay, *Self-Reliance,* with entirely similar results. In one chain of reproductions of the latter "every bit of general reasoning had disappeared. The whole point of the original is lost. All that is left is a bald record of a personal incident, and one general opinion. This opinion is the exact opposite to the original from which it is derived, but is no doubt more in accord with common views." In his summary of the experiments using stories and similar material, Bartlett comes to the conclusion that "all the stories tend to be shorn of their individualising features, the descriptive passages lose most of the peculiarities of style and matter that they may possess, and the arguments tend to be reduced to a bald expression of conventional opinion. . . . Where the opinions expressed are individual they appear to tend to pass over into opposed conventional views; where the epithets are original they tend to become current, commonplace terms. The style gets flattened out and loses any pretensions it may have had to forcefulness and beauty."

The processes of memory thus substitute the conventional cliché for the actual experience. It is true that the original experience or perception usually is already, to a large extent, determined by conventional cliché, by what the person expected to see or hear, which means by what he has been taught to expect. However, everybody who has paid attention to these processes in himself and others can observe that there is, especially at first, some awareness of the discrepancy between the experience itself and the thought or words which articulate, preserve, and express it. The experience is always fuller and richer than the articulate formula by which we try to be aware of it or to recover it. As time passes, this formula comes to replace more and more the original experience and, in addition, to become itself increasingly flat and conventionalized. Memory, in other words, is even more governed by conventional patterns than are perception and experience. One might say that, while all human experience, perception, and thought are eminently social—that is, determined by the socially prevailing ways of experiencing, perceiving, and thinking—memory is even more socialized, to an even higher degree dependent on the commonly accepted categories of what and how one remembers. Bartlett's experiments confirm this. As time passes, the remembered story loses more and more of its original flavor until nothing remains of its essence and a banal cliché is substituted for it. "Rationalization," as psychoanalytic theory knows it, is but one type of such transformation of actual experience into individually and socially acceptable clichés. One important reason why memory is even more susceptible than experience and perception to such conventionalization is that experience and perception always are in *some*, however flimsy, immediate relation to the situation experienced, the object perceived, while memory is distant from it in time and space. The object of memory has less chance than the objects of experience and perception have to penetrate and do away with part of that glass, colored and ground by the social mores and viewpoints, through which man sees everything or fails to see it. Memory is a distance sense, as it were, and—to an even greater degree than the two other distance senses, vision and hearing—less immediately related to its objects than the proximity senses of smell, taste, and touch, and more influenced and molded by the categories of the mind. Also like sight and hearing, only more so, memory is a phylogenetically and ontogenetically more differentiated, later, and more "spiritual" development than smell, taste, and touch. All this predestines memory to lose contact with actual experience and to substitute preformed, conventional patterns of thought for it. And, as will be seen later, it has significant bearing especially on the problem of early childhood amnesia.

How well is the average highly conventionalized adult memory equipped to contain and recall the time and the experiences of early childhood? Very poorly or not at all. This will become more apparent through consideration of the quality of early childhood experience. The adult amnesia for this period prevents direct knowledge. Observation of little children and imagination are the only means of learning something about this subject. It is safe to assume that early childhood is the period of human life which is richest in experience. Everything is new to the newborn child. His gradual grasp of his environment and of the world around him are discoveries which, in experiential scope and quality, go far beyond any discovery that the most adventurous and daring explorer will ever make in his adult life. No Columbus, no Marco Polo has ever seen stranger and more fascinating and thoroughly absorbing sights than the child that learns to perceive, to taste, to smell, to touch, to hear and see, and to use his body, his senses, and his mind. No wonder that the child shows an insatiable curiosity. He has the whole world to discover. Education and learning, while on the one hand furthering this process of discovery, on the other hand gradually brake and finally stop it completely. There are relatively few adults who are fortunate enough to have retained something of the child's curiosity, his capacity for questioning and for wondering. The average adult "knows all the answers," which is exactly why he will never know even a single answer. He has ceased to wonder, to discover. He knows his way around, and it is indeed a way around and around the same conventional pattern, in which everything is familiar and nothing cause for wonder. It is this adult who answers the child's questions and, in answering, fails to answer them but instead acquaints the child with the conventional patterns of his civilization, which effectively close up the asking mouth and shut the wondering eye. Franz Kafka once formulated this aspect of education by saying that "probably all education is but two things, first, parrying of the ignorant children's impetuous assault on the truth and, second, gentle, imperceptible, step-by-step initiation of the humiliated children into the lie."[14]

Most children go through a period of endless questioning. While at first they desire an answer, gradually their search turns into an almost automatic repetition of the same seemingly senseless question or into the related ritual of countering every answer with a new question. It is as though the child no longer really expected or wanted to obtain information by this type of questioning, but expressed only the last stubborn assault against the unbroken wall of adult "answers." The child has already almost forgotten what he wanted to know, but he still knows *that* he wanted to know and did not receive an answer. The automatic questioning may have the unconscious purpose of driving this point home to the adult. It is chiefly during the period of early childhood that the quality of the world around him changes for the growing child from a place where everything is new and to be explored—to be tasted, smelled, touched and handled, wondered about and marveled at—to a place where everything either has received a name and a label or is potentially capable of being "explained" by such a label, a process which will be pursued systematically in school. No experience, no object perceived with the quality of freshness, newness, of something wonder-full, can be preserved and recalled by the conventional concept of that object as designated in its conventional name in language. Even if, in modern Western civilization, the capacity for such fresh experience has largely been deadened, most people, unless they have become complete automatons, have had glimpses of the exhilarating quality that makes fresh experience, unlabeled, so unique, concrete, and filled with life. They can realize, if their attention is called to it, the great difference between such experience and one which merely registers the label of things seen, of the furniture of the

14] In view of the inadequacy of the author's translation, the German text is given here: "Wie ja allerdings wahrscheinlich alle Erziehung nur zweierlei ist, einmal Abwehr des ungestümen Angriffs der unwissenden Kinder auf die Wahrheit und dann sanfte unmerklich-allmähliche Einführung der gedemütigten Kinder in die Lüge." Franz Kafka, *Beschreibung eines Kampfes; Novellen, Skizzen, Aphorismen aus dem Nachlass* (Verlag Heinrich Mercy Sohn, Prag, 1936), p. 317. The passage is taken from an earlier version of what probably was the last story Kafka wrote, "Forschungen eines Hundes" (Researches of a Dog).

room, the familiar faces, the houses on the street. Yet this difference is small when compared with the difference that separates the young child's fresh experience and discoveries from the adult's recognition of the familiar clichés into which the automatic labeling of perception and language has transformed the objects around him. Since adult memory functions predominantly in terms of recalling clichés, the conventional schemata of things and experiences rather than the things and experiences themselves, it becomes apparent how ill-equipped, in fact incapable, such conventionalized memory is to recall the experiences of early childhood in their freshness, in the real significance which they had at that time. The age of discovery, early childhood, is buried deep under the age of routine familiarity, adulthood.

The incompatibility of early childhood experience with the categories and the organization of adult memory is to a large extent due to what I call the conventionalization of the adult memory. Conventionalization is a particular form of what one might call schematization of memory. Voluntary memory recalls largely schemata of experience rather than experience. These schemata are mostly built along the lines of words and concepts of the culture. Also the so-called visual or the auditory memory reproduces schemata of visual or auditory impressions rather than the impressions themselves. Obviously the schemata of experience as well as of memory[15] are determined by the culture which has developed a certain view of the world and of life, a view which furnishes the schemata for all experience and all memory. But the range and differentiation of a culture like that of Greece, India, China, or modern Western civilization is of considerable scope. It offers highly differentiated and subtle as well as very conventional, banal, and commonplace schemata. By conventionalization of the memory (and experience) schemata I understand those memory processes which are subject to the most conven-

15] The term "memory schemata" is taken from Bartlett's study, *Remembering*, but used in a somewhat different sense. Bartlett rightly emphasizes that remembering is "an affair of reconstruction rather than mere reproduction." According to him, this reconstruction serves as a justification of the present attitude toward past experience. Such reconstructions he calls schemata, and these are determined by sense differences, appetites, instincts, and interests. In this essay, however, the concept of memory schemata is used only to designate socially and culturally determined patterns of reconstruction of the past, as contrasted to individually determined patterns. Obviously the greater part of all individual memory schemata in Bartlett's sense are culturally determined.

tional schematization and which, therefore, are not capable of reproducing individual experience, but can only reproduce what John Doe is supposed to have experienced according to the Joneses' and everybody else's ideas of what people experience. Every fresh and spontaneous experience transcends the capacity of the conventionalized memory schema and, to some degree, of any schema. That part of the experience which transcends the memory schema as preformed by the culture is in danger of being lost because there exists as yet no vessel, as it were, in which to preserve it. Even if the schemata of experience have not prevented the person from becoming aware of or sensing that quality of his experience which transcended these schemata, this quality, if it is to be preserved and to become a productive part of the personality, has to overcome the second handicap of the memory schemata, which tend, as time goes on, to supplant this fresh and new element of experience with some preformed notion and thus to bury it. The process of schematization and conventionalization and its effect on the raw material of experience, especially childhood experience, can be well observed in two of its specific developments which take place as the child learns to make use of his senses and to speak.

Language, in its articulating and its obscuring function, may be considered first since the adult, too, encounters the problem of the incompatibility of experience with language and the consequent forgetting of experience or its distortion by the cliché of language. The fact that language is adult language, the language of an adult civilization, and that the infant is molded only very gradually from his natural existence into a member of the civilization into which he is born makes the discrepancy between his precivilized, unschematized experience and the categories of civilized, conventional language much greater. Yet between this discrepancy and that existing between the adult's experience and his language, there is a difference of degree rather than of kind. Everyone who has honestly tried to describe some genuine experience exactly, however small and insignificant it may have seemed, knows how difficult, if not impossible, that is. One might well say that the greatest problem of the writer or the poet is the temptation of language. At every step a word beckons, it seems so convenient, so suitable, one has heard or read it so often in a similar context, it sounds so well, it makes the phrase flow so smoothly. If he follows the temptation of this word, he will perhaps describe something that many people recognize at once, that they already know, that follows a familiar pattern; but he will have missed the nuance that distinguishes his experience from others, that makes it his own. If he wants to communicate that elusive nuance which in some way, however small, will be his contribution, a widening or opening of the scope of articulate human experience at some point, he has to fight constantly against the easy flow of words that offer themselves. Like the search for truth, which never reaches its goal yet never can be abandoned, the endeavor to articulate, express, and communicate an experience can never succeed completely. It consists of an approach, step by step, toward that distant vantage point, that bend of the road from which one hopes to see the real experience in its entirety and from where it will become visible to others—a point which is never reached. The lag, the discrepancy between experience and word is a productive force in man as long as he remains aware of it, as long as he knows and feels that his experience was in some way more than and different from what his concepts and words articulate. The awareness of this unexplored margin of experience, which may be its essential part, can turn into that productive energy which enables man to go one step closer to understanding and communicating his experience, and thus add to the scope of human insight. It is this awareness and the struggle and the ability to narrow the gap between experience and words which make the writer and the poet. The danger of the schemata of language, and especially of the worn currency of conventional language in vogue at the moment when the attempt is made to understand and describe an experience, is that the person making this attempt will overlook the discrepancy between experience and language cliché or that he will not be persistent enough in his attempt to eliminate this discrepancy. Once the conventional schema has replaced the experience in his mind, the significant quality of the experience is condemned to oblivion.

The discrepancy between concepts, language, and experience can be looked upon as a model and as part of the discrepancy between memory schemata and experience. This close relationship, of course, is not accidental, since voluntary recall and communication of recalled experience are essentially dependent on conceptual thought and language. While there is also recall of experience without the vehicle of language, a great deal of what we recall, especially of what we recall voluntarily, is recalled in terms of language and in concepts formed by language. This has considerable bearing on the problem of childhood amnesia. The infant and small child has to undergo and assimilate the comparatively greatest amount of new experience at a time when his language, his concepts, and his memory schemata are poorest or as yet entirely undeveloped. Only very gradually does he acquire the faculty of language, learn the conceptual schemata of his culture, and develop a memory and memory schemata. The experiences of the infant are inarticulate and complex. In a term coined by Sullivan, they are instantaneous records of total situations.[16] They are also as yet unformed and untainted by the experience schemata of the culture which, from the viewpoint of the culture, justifies Freud's remark that the small child is "polymorph perverse." He is a little animal, a little heathen, and his experiences are only gradually and increasingly forced into the Procrustean bed of the culturally prevalent experience schemata which allow for certain experiences, forbid others, and omit a great many for which the culture has either no frame of reference or only an unsuitable one. It is true that only by learning and developing the schemata of language, conceptual thought, experience, and memory prevalent in the culture can the child progress from the phase of complex and inarticulate experience to that of specific and articulate experience. It is true that the complex and inarticulate experience of infancy and early childhood, because of the very lack of schemata for detailed articulation, is often prevented from reaching awareness or else soon removed from awareness and forgotten. But, on the other hand, the schemata provided by the culture and gradually acquired by the growing child cannot accommodate his experience in its entirety, but will distort and bias it according to the patterns of the culture. Two major trends thus operate toward eventual early childhood amnesia. First, the schemata for articulate experience and for recall of such experience are relatively slow and late in developing. They are entirely lacking in the earliest

16] Patrick Mullahy, "A Theory of Interpersonal Relations and the Evolution of Personality," in Harry Stack Sullivan, *Conceptions of Modern Psychiatry* (W. W. Norton, New York, 1953), p. 252.

period of life and one could say generally that as they develop, experience gradually loses its character of newness and acquires the quality of familiarity and recognition. The tremendous amount of experience which the small child undergoes does not, therefore, find a proportionate variety of suitable vessels (schemata) for its preservation. Second, the quality of early childhood experience does not fit into the developing schemata of experience, thought, and memory since these are fashioned by the adult culture and all its biases, emphases, and taboos.

Both these trends become even more apparent if one considers them in connection with the development of the *senses* in the child. Such a consideration also shows how closely biological and cultural factors are interwoven in the causation of early childhood amnesia and how difficult, if not impossible, it is to draw a clear borderline between the two. What might have been a cultural factor in man's prehistory may well seem to the present observer like a biological development. Phylogenetically as well as ontogenetically the distance senses, sight and hearing, attain their full development later than the proximity senses, smell, taste, and touch. Sight and hearing are more highly differentiated and more closely linked up with the human mind than smell, taste, and touch. The latter senses, especially smell and taste, are neglected and to a considerable extent even tabooed by Western civilization. They are the animalistic senses *par excellence*. Engaged for thousands of years in a battle for control and mastery of nature outside and inside himself, man, and especially Western man, does not want to be reminded that he is not only man but also nature, also animal. Because of the cultural taboo on smell and taste—smell even more than taste, but the two are inseparable—it is even possible for the adult to realize clearly the effect which the discrepancy between experience on the one hand and language and memory schemata on the other hand has on the capacity for recall, especially voluntary recall. English, like the other Western languages, is conspicuously poor in words for the description of smells and tastes. Even in dealing with the flavor of wine or of a dish, language is quite incapable of expressing any but the crudest difference in taste, in spite of the great material and historical role of drinking and eating. A wine is said to be dry, sweet, robust, fine, full, and so on, but none of these words enables one to imagine the flavor and bouquet of the wine. Compared with this poverty of words, the vocabulary for the description of the visible world and its forms and colors is much richer. Even poetry has never succeeded in conjuring the flavor of a smell or taste, although it sometimes enables the imagination to evoke a visual image. For these reasons, the experience schemata for smell and taste sensations are relatively undeveloped. This is true even more of the memory schemata. A taste or a smell is usually remembered only involuntarily; that is, the former experience may be recognized by renewed encounter with the same stimulus. But it is difficult or impossible for most people to recall voluntarily the taste of a particular wine or the smell of a particular flower, animal, or person. In fact, most people are hardly aware of the differences in smell of different people.

Both pleasure and disgust are more intimately linked with the proximity senses than with the distance senses. The pleasure which a perfume, a taste, or a texture can give is much more of a bodily, physical one, hence also more akin to sexual pleasure, than is the more sublime pleasure aroused by sound and the least bodily of all pleasures, the sight of something beautiful. No other sense produces the emotion of disgust more easily and violently and provokes reactions of nausea and vomiting more readily than the olfactory sense. The infant is not disgusted by his feces; he quite likes their smell. Very many, if not most, adults do not have the reaction of disgust to the smell of their own excretions; many do not show it with regard to the body odor or the excretions of a beloved person. As everybody knows, animals, especially dogs, are best able to tell one person from another and one dog from another by body and excretion smell. The infant, long before he knows and remembers how his mother looks, knows how she smells and tastes. Very likely, angry or frightened mother tastes and smells rather different from good or comfortable mother to the infant, just as she will look very different to him as he grows older.[17] In his growing experience of the world around him, the proximity senses at

17] Groddeck, speaking about the paramount importance of the sense of smell in infancy and early childhood, asserts that, even more than the dog, the child judges people and objects largely by their smell and, since the child is small or is being held on the lap, this means chiefly the smell of legs, lap, sexual and excretory organs. G. Groddeck, *The World of Man* (C. W. Daniel Co., London, 1934), p. 132.

first have primacy over the distance senses. He tastes and sniffs and touches earlier and better than he perceives with eye and ear. In order to get really acquainted with something or somebody, he has to touch it and to put it in his mouth, as he first did with his mother's nipple. Only very gradually and slowly does the emphasis shift from the proximity to the distance senses. This partly biological and phylogenetically determined shift is helped along powerfully and the development of taste and smell discouraged by the stringent taboos of the significant adults, who do not want baby to take everything in his mouth and who, in cleanliness education, drastically and persistently show their disgust with the most important objects of smell, those of the body and its excretions, so that the child cannot but feel that he has to refrain not only from the pleasure given by body and excretion odors but even from the discriminating perception of them.[18] The proximity senses, which play such a great role in relations between animals and, if not repressed, in the sexual relations of man, are otherwise tabooed in interpersonal relations the more a culture or a group tends to isolate people, to put distance between them, and to prevent spontaneous relationships and the "natural" animal-like expressions of such relations. The emphasis on distance and the taboo on smell in modern society is more outspoken in the ruling than in the laboring class, distance being also a means of domination and of imposing authority. Disgust arises where the repression has not succeeded completely and a powerful deterrent is needed in order to bolster it.[19]

Whatever the social and cultural reasons for the discouragement and neglect of the proximity senses, the shift from their initial predominance to that of the distance senses, which takes place progressively during infancy and early childhood and which is a result partly of these cultural factors and partly of biologi-

---

18] Freud links fetishism with a repressed coprophilic smell desire; feet and hair become fetishes after the now unpleasant sensation of smell has been renounced. "Three Contributions to the Theory of Sex," *Basic Writings*, p. 567, footnote 3. On another occasion he suggests that the sense of smell which attracts the male to the menstruating female animal became the victim of organic repression as man started to walk erect and that this was the origin of the emotion of disgust. *Das Unbehagen in der Kultur* (Internationaler Psychoanalytischer Verlag, Wien, 1930), p. 62, footnote.

19] Something of the importance of the deeply rooted taboo on smell in Western man comes to the surface in the vituperative and hateful use that is made of body odor in interracial conflicts.

cal and phylogenetic factors, necessarily entails for the child a far-reaching change in the whole way of perceiving and experiencing the people and the world around him, a change which the adult mind is quite unable to imagine concretely. Much less is the adult memory capable of recalling experience that occurred before the shift in the organization of the senses was made, since this change altered the entire mode of perception and experience.

Together with and continuing after the shift in the organization of perception from the primacy of the proximity senses to that of the distance senses, a comprehensive development in the direction of specialization and differentiation takes place in the child's apparatus for experience. This, too, brings about considerable changes in the mode of experience. As ontogenetic development of the child from conception to adulthood repeats the phylogenetic development of man from his farthest ancestors in the most primitive living organisms to his present state, the development of consciousness is a relatively late stage in this process, beginning only some time after birth and continuing for a long period. Within the development of consciousness, the consciousness of self comes latest, and neither individually nor in the history of the race has man as yet ever reached anything approaching full consciousness of self. Memory, especially voluntary memory, is an important part of consciousness. It seems probable that in the infant and child the development of memory starts with a recognition of certain complex, undifferentiated states of his own body-feeling, primarily states of comfort, satisfaction, and pleasure, and states of discomfort, tension, and displeasure. Since the infant has as yet no cognition, one cannot properly speak of recognition either; rather one should speak of a resensing, a re-experiencing of certain complex and dimly perceived states of his own well-being or ill-being. The differentiation between body and mind, body and psyche, also develops gradually and becomes more accentuated in the course of time. The infant, at first, is not capable of distinguishing between himself and whatever persons or objects of his environment come sufficiently close to him to affect him.[20] The mother's

20] This was the opinion of Descartes, who said: "In early life the mind was so closely bound to the body that it attended to nothing beyond the thoughts by which it perceived the objects that made impression on the body; nor as yet did it refer these thoughts to anything existing beyond itself, but simply felt pain when the body was hurt, or pleasure when anything beneficial to the body oc-

breast is not, at first, part of "another person"; it belongs to the undifferentiated little world of the infant, is part of his "own cosmic entity," as Sullivan puts it.[21] The whole concept of self and others does not make sense at this earliest period, and nothing corresponding to this concept exists for the small infant. It is not chance, then, that much later in life those rare instances of a whole vision recalled by involuntary memory are often stimulated by some body-sensation, that is, by the resensing of a sensation of long ago. They are memories of the body, as it were, or of the unexplored realm where body and psyche are identical, and it is here that Proust's involuntary memory flashes, occasioned by the taste of the *madeleine*, by the unevenness of the pavement, have their earliest origin.[22] The perception of the environment as something separate, a changing configuration of various *objects*, develops only very gradually in the infant and small child. Objects can be handled and eventually controlled to some extent, but life in the early stages of infancy, as well as in the lower forms of the fauna, begins with a state in which the living organism is merely affected by his environment and experiences this as a change in his own bodily state, not—as the growing child and the adult will perceive it later—as the actions of people and objects outside himself.

In this context it is significant that the olfactory sense, so important in infancy, throughout life is least, practically not at all, capable of objectifying stimuli, whereas the more spiritual and later developed sense of vision cannot but objectify the stimuli by which it is affected. In this respect also, the olfactory sense retains more of an earlier stage of development, a closer, less alienated, and less differentiated relationship to the environment than the distance senses and even the sense of touch. As the specialization

---

curred. . . . And afterward when the machine of the body, which has been so fabricated by nature that it can of its own inherent power move itself in various ways, by turning itself at random on every side, followed after what was useful and avoided what was detrimental, the mind, which was closely connected with it, reflecting on the objects it pursued and avoided, remarked, for the first time, that they existed out of itself. . . ." *The Method, Meditations and Philosophy of Descartes*, John Veitch, trans. (M. Walter Dunne, Publisher, Washington and London), pp. 329-330.

21] Harry Stack Sullivan, "Conceptions of Modern Psychiatry," *Psychiatry*, 1940, 3:1-117, p. 15.

22] See also Ernest G. Schachtel, "The Dynamic Perception and the Symbolism of Form: With Special Reference to the Rorschach Test," *Psychiatry*, 1941, 4:79-96, p. 85, and footnote 16.

and differentiation of the apparatus for experience continue—including the sensory apparatus and the slowly developing consciousness—the initial lack of distinction between organism and environment gives way more and more to the division that is of such fundamental importance in the history of man, that of subject and object, a division that comes about slowly and gradually, but one that the adult mind cannot possibly discard even in phantasy, and certainly not in perception and rational thinking. It becomes so predominant that it completely blots out the earlier kind of experience and whatever remains subterraneously, as it were, of this early way of experiencing the environment in later life. In the slow development of consciousness, the sharp differentiation between sleep and being awake also comes about only gradually. Memory is a relatively late product of this whole process of differentiation and specialization. Autobiographical memory—that is the ability for voluntary recall of one's past life—is one of the latest developments in childhood, which is not surprising since it is part of the awareness of self, a capacity found only in man, and even in adult man usually not very well developed. According to Stern,[23] memory up to the third year refers almost exclusively to the visible world of objects and events. The life of the small child is naturally oriented toward the present and the future, not toward the past. The concept of "I" hardly develops before the third year, which is but another expression of the fact that the division between subject and object is a gradual, relatively late development. Yet the significance of this division and its particular quality in a particular society, culture, and stage of historical development can hardly be overestimated. It partakes of and is determined by all the fundamental attitudes in the relation of man to his fellow men, to nature, and to his material environment as they have developed in a specific society and culture.

The late development of the autobiographical memory and of the concept of "I" or "self" as a subject preserving one's identity in time is but another aspect of early childhood amnesia. The child lives much more in the present moment than the average adult does. His life is so much more filled with the exploration of the environment and of his own growing capacities that the past has

23] William Stern, *Psychologie der frühen Kindheit bis zum sechsten Lebensjahre* (Quelle & Meyer, Leipzig, 1914), p. 166.

not much interest for him. And even with the appearance of the first traces of autobiographical memory and of the concept "I" in the third year of life, the quality of childhood experience is still so different from that of the adult that the memory schemata of the adult cannot accommodate the greater part of this experience.

The fact that autobiographical memory develops so late in childhood should be considered with the question of its usefulness for life and especially for life in Western civilization. Considered from this angle it becomes apparent that autobiographical memory is of much less immediate use for orientation in and adaptation to the environment than the development of the senses, of the mind, and of "useful" memory—that is, memory in the service of the recognition of objects, the learning of words, and similar functions important for survival. Biologically and culturally, autobiographical memory thus finds little encouragement. In a culture oriented toward efficient performance of profitable activities, a society in which everybody has to fit like a cog in a machine and where powerful pressure is exerted to make people equal, in the sense of uniform, autobiographical memory is discouraged in its development and predestined to atrophy. It is of no use for the reliable and efficient performance of the worker at the machine, the clerk at his desk, the surgeon at the operating table; in fact, it would interfere with their activities. It would stand in the way of the process of equalization and uniformity since its very function is to preserve individual experience rather than repeat cultural and conventional schemata of experience. If Ulysses gives in to the song of the Sirens, his active life will have reached its end and his plans will come to naught. The pseudo-memory of the adult, which reproduces not his real experience but the experience schemata furnished by the culture, is a more reliable and conservative servant of the culture than the true memory which would preserve the real experience before it has been filtered through the memory schemata of the culture and thus cleansed from all that transcends the ubiquitous pattern.

In one other area of life, namely in the realm of *dreams*, one finds a general amnesia, although it is not quite so pervasive as that pertaining to early childhood. A closer study of the recall of dreams and especially of the period of awakening from a dream, when quite often one can observe its disappearance from memory or its transformation or fragmentation, may therefore add to, disprove, or corroborate the hypotheses developed so far for the phenomenon of early childhood amnesia and of adult forgetting of trans-schematic experience. It is probable that the majority of dreams are not remembered at all. A great many others are recalled in fragments only. Of those that are still remembered at the time of awakening, very many are forgotten in the course of the day, quite often in the first few minutes or the first hour of beginning the daily activities of rising, getting dressed, and so on. The relatively small proportion of dreams surviving in memory undergo a rapid transformation and fragmentation and usually they, too, are forgotten after a few days. If they are not forgotten, they are transformed in a way which is rather analogous to the transformation of the Indian story in Bartlett's experiment. That is to say, they lose increasingly their peculiar dream quality, and the peculiar language of the dream changes in the direction of conventionalization and rationalization. Even persons sensitized to awareness and recall of their dreams, for example psychoanalytic patients, find it difficult or impossible to counteract this powerful tendency toward forgetting or conventionalizing the dream unless they record their dreams as soon as possible after awakening. The dreams that make such a profound impression on the dreamer that they survive all these obstacles, although not without some damage, are rare indeed. Thus the question arises: What are the causes of this usual, general *dream-amnesia?* Why does one forget by far the greater part of his mental life going on during sleep, a life that in most people, judging from the fragments recalled, seems to be far more original, interesting, spontaneous, and creative than their waking life? It shares these latter qualities with early childhood, which, from all one can observe, seems to be the most fascinating, spontaneous, original, and creative period in the life of most or perhaps of all people. Is it because of these qualities that the conventionalized memory schemata cannot reproduce the great majority of dreams and their real character?

Freud devotes a whole section of "The Interpretation of Dreams" to the problem of the forgetting of dreams. His purpose in this section is to defend the validity of dream interpretation against the objection that one does not really know his dreams because he either forgets or distorts them. Freud's answer to the problem is that the "forgetting of dreams depends far more on the resistance [to the dream thought] than on the mutually alien character of the waking and sleeping states" and that the distortion of the dream in recalling or recounting it is "the secondary and often misunderstanding elaboration of the dream by the agency of normal thinking" and thus "no more than a part of the elaboration to which dream thoughts are constantly subjected as a result of the dream-censorship."[24] I think that the question should be raised whether "resistance" and "mutually alien character of the waking and sleeping states" are really, as Freud seems to assume, mutually exclusive and contradictory explanations of dream amnesia and dream distortion by waking thought. Or whether, as I believe, "resistance" is operative in the awake person, not only against the dream thought but against the whole quality and language of the dream, a resistance, to be sure, of a somewhat different character, yet fundamentally related to that which represses and censors those dream thoughts which are intolerable for consciousness.

In sleep and dream, man's activity in the outer world is suspended, especially his motor activity. Attention and perception are withdrawn from outer reality. The necessity to cope with the environment is interrupted for the duration of sleep. The stringent rules of logic and reason subside—rules which during waking life are geared to useful, rational, adaptative, conventional control of behavior and thought. The psyche receives leave, for the period of sleep, from the demands of active life in society. As Freud expresses it, endopsychic censorship is reduced. And the psyche makes good use of this short leave from the demands of reality. Its productions, seen from the usual, realistic viewpoint, seem utterly useless. It is true that other, older civilizations did not always share this viewpoint, but attributed considerable importance to dreams, sometimes greater importance than to waking thought. But measured with the yardstick of modern Western civilization with its emphasis on useful, efficient production and work, dreams are really quite useless.

During sleep, motor activity, most essential for dealing with the outer reality of objects and people, is reduced to a minimum. Movements are not performed actively. But in the dream a world of movement is perceived. Rorschach has called attention to the fact that dreams are primarily kinesthesias, that is, kinesthetic pro-

24] Freud, "The Interpretation of Dreams," *Basic Writings*, pp. 470-485, especially pp. 476 and 472.

duction.[25] Rorschach's experiment has demonstrated that even in waking life kinesthetic perception, that is, a most creative factor in perception, is invariably inhibited or made altogether impossible by an attitude of cramped attention, by the straining of will-power in the direction of control and good performance, and that it is facilitated by an attitude of giving in to one's ideas, to what will occur to one, without straining for ambitious performance. The dream, of course, is a mental production without any conscious effort and one in which the dreamer passively gives in to the images evoked by his phantasy. In that sense the dream is the opposite of *work* as it is known to Western civilization, the opposite of efficiency. When awakening, it is often possible to catch hold of a dream, as Rorschach has pointed out, if one lies perfectly still and does not open his eyes. But the first movement, especially an active one like jumping out of bed, will very often chase the dream into oblivion. In other words, the return to the outer world through motor activity and reshifting of attention and perception to the environment leads to forgetting of the dream. This process is a quite general one and, as far as I have been able to observe, bears no relation to specific dream content. Therefore it seems to stem from the incompatibility of the extroversive attitude of waking with the introversive attitude of dreaming, rather than from resistance to specific strivings which are expressed in the dream thoughts. The antagonism between motor activity and dream recall brings to mind Proust's words, that he could recapture his former being only "dehors de l'action, de la jouissance immédiate"[26] and that in such a moment he did not dare to budge lest he lose the refound memory of the past.

But even without the described effect of the resumption of motor activity on the voluntary recall of dreams, it seems obvious that the experience and memory schemata developed and formed by man's life in his society are much less suitable to preserve the fantastic world of the dream than to recall conventional waking experience. The awakening mind has to cope again with outer

25] Hermann Rorschach, *Psychodiagnostics: A Diagnostic Test Based on Perception* (English edition by Paul Lemkau and Bernard Kronenberg) (Hans Huber, Berne, 1942), p. 72. Since dreams are the most creative mental production of the average person, this sheds an interesting light on one of Rorschach's significant findings, that of a close kinship between kinesthesia and mental creativity, and seems to corroborate this finding.

26] Proust, *A la recherche du temps perdu*, Vol. 2, p. 14.

reality, and to this end has to remobilize all the patterns and schemata useful for, and developed by, the conventional social forms of life and work. Attention has to be paid to the environment. And the attitude of attention is to the mind what purposeful motor activity is to the body.

In the forgetting and distortion of dreams during waking life it is important to distinguish between that which is due to the resistance to and repression of a specific dream thought or dream content and that which is due to the incapacity of the conventional memory schemata to retain the phantastic general quality and the strange language of dreams. The distortion of a dream thought which resistance wants to keep from awareness has to be distinguished from the process of conventionalization which, more or less, *all* dream elements undergo because the medium of the dream language is incompatible with the medium of the conventional world of waking life. In the degree of this incompatibility there are, of course, considerable variations between different people and, even more so, between different cultures. But modern Western civilization with its streamlined efficiency, uniform mass culture, and emphasis on usefulness in terms of profitable, material production is particularly and strikingly at the opposite pole from the world of dreams.

Dream amnesia and early childhood amnesia are due to related causes. Experience and thought transcending the conventional schemata of the culture are found in relatively few people. Yet they are universal in early childhood and in the dream: in early childhood because the spontaneity of the child has not yet been deadened or channeled into the conventional patterns of the culture; in the dream because the hold of these conventional patterns, the hold of reality, can be relaxed to some extent since the dreamer temporarily is cut off from active commerce with outer reality by the suspension of perception and motor activity. It is the trans-schematic quality of early childhood experience as well as of dreams which makes it difficult or impossible for the memory schemata to preserve and recall voluntarily such experience. Yet it is also this quality in which potentialities of progress, of going beyond the conventional pattern, and of widening the scope of human life are forever present and waiting to be released.

The main subject of my considerations so far has been to discover the causes of the forgetting of early childhood and other trans-schematic experience. What, then, are the qualities of that relatively rare remembrance by which the individual past, the lost experience is recalled, and what are the conditions favoring such recall? The veil of amnesia which hides former experience under the memory schemata of voluntary recall is sometimes lifted and the lost experience recovered. A dream, already forgotten, is suddenly remembered. A scene from childhood, buried under layers of years of a conventional life, reappears as though it had been yesterday. The recent age regression experiments in hypno-analysis show in dramatic fashion how forgotten experiences of many years ago, secreted in the unconscious, are recalled and relived during hypnosis and again lost when amnesia returns after awakening from the trance. But this is a more striking demonstration only of the classical teaching of psychoanalysis about the memory traces of the unconscious which usually are immune to voluntary recall but may be approached by the special techniques of dream interpretation, free association, and recall under hypnosis or under the influence of resistance-reducing drugs.

The hidden quality of these lost memories, their separation from the rest of life, their inaccessibility, and their incompatibility with voluntary memory and with conventional, purposeful, daily activity are described lucidly by Proust. He compares the recesses of the lost memories to a thousand vases distributed on the various altitudes of the past years of one's life, filled with the particular atmosphere of that period of his life, and containing sometimes a gesture, a word, an insignificant act which, however, may be the key to the recapturing of the lost experiences, the lost past of his life. According to him, the very fact that the experience, the past time, has been *forgotten* and thus has remained isolated as at the bottom of a valley or on the peak of a summit, gives it an incomparable air of freshness and aliveness when it is recovered, *because it has not been able to form any link with the present.*[27] In other words, it has not been distorted by the memory schemata, by the needs and fears of the present, by the routine of daily life. Proust's view, here, is almost identical with that of Freud, whose theory of memory postulates that *only* that which is unconscious can leave a permanent memory trace and that "becoming conscious

27] *Ibid.,* pp. 12-13.

and leaving behind a memory trace are processes incompatible with each other in the same system."[28]

The memory trace that has been secluded from contact with conscious present life thereby often acquires in the isolation of the unconscious the character of *strangeness* to one's present life. Hence the surprise when it is recovered. Again, Proust makes an illuminating contribution to the understanding of this phenomenon. He describes how, in the library of the Prince de Guermantes, he finds a book, *François le Champi*, that his mother had read to him when he was a child. The memory is painful at first. In the shock of sudden recall of the forgotten childhood scene he asks himself angrily who causes him such pain, and in the same moment he discovers that he sees *himself* as a child, he is the stranger. In reading the title of the book, *François le Champi*, he suddenly finds himself transposed into the remote past and he reads with the eyes of the child, of the person that he was then, with the same reveries and the same fear of the next day that he had felt then.[29] The reason for the strangeness of such sudden and vivid recollections of hitherto forgotten experience is that such experience is in contrast to and alien to one's present state and conscious preoccupations. The voluntary memory schemata accommodate the familiar and the conventional only, in terms of the present life. The involuntary recovery of the forgotten past very often intrudes on this present life like a strange, alien element. The person that one was then, the child that Proust sees in the scene recalled, has long since been buried under the years of social routine, of changed needs and interests, of the preoccupations of the present. He has become a stranger. But this stranger may also assert a life and wishes which had been starved and suffocated by the time gone by and the pressures it brought.

In Proust's work the recovery of the forgotten past is characterized as the supreme satisfaction, carrying with it a sense of exhilarating happiness and constituting the very core of the work of art. This is not the place to discuss the profound meaning of his evaluation which, three thousand years after the Greek myth, again celebrates memory as the mother of art and poetry. Be it

28] Freud, *Beyond the Pleasure Principle* (The International Psychoanalytical Press, London, 1922), p. 28. See also, "The Interpretation of Dreams," *Basic Writings*, pp. 488-491.

29] Proust, *op cit.*, pp. 30-38.

sufficient to say that in the conflict of modern society between efficient adaptation and activity, on the one hand, and the preservation and recovery of the total personality, which to him seems possible only by the fullest awareness of the individual past, Proust sides against his society and with the "lost paradises" of his own past. And it is true that each genuine recovery of forgotten experience and, with it, something of the person that one was when having the experience carries with it an element of enrichment, adds to the light of consciousness, and thus widens the conscious scope of one's life.

Such widening of the personality by the recovery of lost ground and its liberating and exhilarating effect has to be distinguished from what I propose to call the *possessive* attitude to memory, or to one's past, an attitude that occurs much more frequently than the instances of genuine recovery of the past. The possessive attitude to one's own past, particularly to past feelings, more often imagined than real, seems to me the essence of sentimentality. The person who has this attitude pats himself on the shoulder as it were and feels what a fine fellow he is for having had such feelings or such experience. It is the same attitude that leads also to a kind of proprietary satisfaction about one's character. Character, feelings, the past are looked upon as prized possessions enhancing the prestige of their owner. On closer analysis, it usually turns out that these treasures are spurious.[30] The possessive attitude toward the past prevents rather than furthers the gain in consciousness and the widening of the scope of life by the rediscovery of forgotten experience.

Since the lost experience is inaccessible to voluntary recall and incompatible with the conventional memory schemata, the question arises as to what the conditions are under which such forgotten experience may be recalled. Of course, a definite and complete catalogue of these conditions cannot be given. But it may be useful to consider some situations which typically favor the rediscovery of a past that has been forgotten. Proust attributes to bodily sensations and to perceptions the greatest importance,

---

30] The possessive attitude toward the (pseudo-) remembered past is closely related to and finds its counterpart in the acquisitive anticipation of (pseudo-) experience, already described, in which not some event is experienced, not some object perceived, but instead the motions are gone through and a preconceived cliché replaces actual experience because the performance of such pseudo-experience promises an increase in prestige.

in fact exclusive importance, as carriers of such significant memories. The accidental recurrence of a bodily posture or of a sensory perception which he had experienced in the past, on some occasions brings with it the entire vision of that past, of the person he was then and of the way he saw things then. It is a sensation—feeling of a body posture or sensation of the perceptive apparatus—not a thought, as in willed recall, which revives the past. In Proust's account, visual sensations are far outnumbered as carriers of such memories by those of the lower, more bodily senses, such as the feeling of his own body in a particular posture, the touch of a napkin, the smell and taste of a flavor, the hearing of a sound—noise or melody, *not* the sound of words. All these sensations are far from conceptual thought, language, or conventional memory schemata. They renew a state of the psychosomatic entity that, in some respect, this entity had experienced before, felt before. It is as though they touched directly the unconscious memory trace, the record left behind by a total situation out of the past, whereas voluntary recall tries to approach and construct this past indirectly, coached and deflected by all those ideas, wishes, and needs which tell the present person how the past could, should, or might have been. Just as the infant's recall probably starts out as an automatic recognition or, rather, resensation of a certain state of his body—pleasurable or unpleasurable, satisfied or needy, comfortable or tense—and not as conscious recall of former experience, such resensation, more differentiated than in early infancy, seems to be one basis and one condition of involuntary recall of forgotten experience. By revival of a former sensation the attitude of the former self that first had this sensation is remobilized. And thus is made possible recall of the objects and feelings closely connected with the former sensation—objects and feelings which the present self would otherwise not perceive or experience in the same manner since it thinks, feels, behaves differently and since, therefore, the conscious memory schemata are not prepared for the ready reproduction of material stemming from a historical past in which the person was different, moved by needs, interests, and fears different from those that move him now, especially from those of which he is aware at present. But all experience leaves a record behind, as it were, a memory trace, inaccessible, as a rule, to the consciously, purposefully searching mind, revealed sometimes by the repetition of a sensation that had occurred at the time when the record was first made.

This hypothesis of one type of involuntary recall of forgotten experience seems to fit in with two data from psychoanalytic theory and therapy. One of them concerns Freud's "screen" or "concealing" memories (*Deckerinnerungen*) from early childhood; the other, therapeutic findings of Wilhelm Reich. Freud calls attention to the "fact that the earliest recollections of a person often seemed to preserve the unimportant and accidental, whereas . . . not a trace is found in the adult memory of the weighty and affective impressions of this period."[31] He distinguishes regressive, encroaching, and contemporaneous or contiguous concealing memories. The indifferent, unimportant recollection, according to Freud, conceals the forgotten, significant emotional experience. If the image recalled has preceded the significant experience, he speaks of a regressive concealing memory; if it has succeeded the experience, he terms it an encroaching memory; if they belong to the same time, the concealing memory is a contemporaneous or contiguous one. To simplify matters I shall speak only of the contiguous screen memory. The question relevant for the problems presented in this chapter concerns the nature of the associative connection between screen memory and forgotten significant emotional experience. It is my impression that usually, if not always, this connection is very similar to the one described by Proust between the taste of the *madeleine* and the recall of his childhood, the sensation of uneven pavement and the recall of Venice, and all the other instances in which a seemingly quite indifferent object arouses most significant forgotten memories. In the analysis of such seemingly indifferent memories, such as the recall of a piece of furniture, a corridor, a stove in the parental home, of a piece of apparel worn by the child or by his parents, I have often found not only that it is possible to rediscover the forgotten emotion "behind" this screen memory, but that what seemed merely a screen, an indifferent object, was not so indifferent after all. Quite often the feelings with which this particular object was seen, the perceptual "aura" of the object was a condensation of significant emotions in the interpersonal relations of the child at that time. There was a time, in other words, when the way in which the now indifferent object

31] Freud, "Psychopathology of Everyday Life," *Basic Writings*, p. 62.

was perceived contained in a complex, condensed, inarticulate manner the essence of the life of the child at that time. That a simple perception should contain such condensed material is not as astonishing as it may seem. Rorschach's psychodiagnostic test is based on the fact that the way in which a person sees *is* the person and that it is possible to reach significant conclusions as to structure and conflicts of a personality by analyzing the processes of his visual perception. In many, possibly in all, cases of contiguous screen memories, the indifferent object is not so much the significant element as the perceptual aura of this object in childhood—the perception itself, its individual qualities and characteristics which contain the child, as it were, that once saw this object, the little stranger of whom the adult Proust speaks when the perception of the book *François le Champi* suddenly brings with it the whole atmosphere of the time when this book was read to him by his mother. In the course of growing up, the language label and the corresponding conventional memory schema replace the living perception of the object. Thus the significant individual perception is lost, the object loses its aura, and only its name remains; and its indifferent, conventional cliché or picture may be recalled voluntarily by the conventional memory schemata. But sometimes it is possible, by insisting, to revive the former alive perception, the childhood aura of the object, and in this way to arrive also at the significant emotional experiences of that time which endowed the object with its unique aura. Once the cliché quality of the object or scene recalled consciously in the screen memory is discarded, one can penetrate to the memory trace left behind by the living sensation, the individual perception of this object as experienced by this person in his past. The memory of the conscious, conventionalized mind thus gives way to the memory of the body, of the psychosomatic entity in which the old sensation left a record not only of this object but of the total emotional configuration in which the object was seen and which gave to it the aura that made it peculiarly fit to become a symbol for the period and event to which it refers.

The subjective element in perception, the individual perspective under which the seemingly indifferent object once was seen, thus turns out to be the associative link between screen memory and significant experience. From this viewpoint, the screen memory loses its seemingly indifferent and accidental character. The object of the screen memory and the significant emotional experience belong together. The significant experience constituted the atmosphere in which the object was perceived and which thus became part of that object. Significant experience and "accidental" object are no longer separate; they belong together and often shade imperceptibly into one another. The perceptual attitude was closely akin to, or identical with, the general attitude of the child in his experiences.

If the screen memories show how this attitude may be recovered by reviving the former unschematic perception of the object and by reviving therewith the attitude of the child at that time, Reich's vegetotherapeutic technique has shown how, starting not from an object recalled, but from the bodily residua and encrustations of childhood attitudes in posture, expression, and muscular armor, one can recover forgotten experience.[32] Reich has found that "the dissolution of a muscular rigidity . . . brings back into memory the very infantile situation in which the repression had taken place." According to him, the repressed affect and the defense against this affect produce muscular fixations and changes in the vegetative behavior. By analyzing and dissolving the muscular rigidity, it is possible to revive and bring to awareness the defense against the repressed affect, the affect itself, and the memory of the experience which had originally produced the affect. In other words, the body remembers, as it were, what the mind has forgotten and repressed.

The discussed instances of recall of previously forgotten or repressed material have in common that they all point to a "location" of involuntary memory, not in the conscious, purposefully remembering mind and its memory schemata, but in a sphere which is more adequately if vaguely described as memory of the body or, rather, of the psychosomatic entity. The forgotten experience is revived by the recurrence of a sensation which has left a record, a trace behind; or it is revived by the understanding and reliving of the bodily attitudes, muscular and vegetative, which the forgotten experience produced.

Another condition favorable for the recovery of forgotten experience which the conscious mind is unable to recall voluntarily is furnished by the psychoanalytic method of free associa-

32] Wilhelm Reich, *The Function of the Orgasm* (Orgone Institute Press, New York, 1942), see especially chapter VIII, pp. 266-325.

tion. The relevant factor of this method is indicated by the word "free." Three components may be distinguished in the freedom of association. One is the attempt, never entirely successful, to follow the fundamental rule of psychoanalysis: to eliminate rational, logical, and conventional control and censorship of one's thoughts in communicating them and to give in to whatever thought or feeling occurs. How well or how poorly one succeeds in this attempt is dependent chiefly on the two other factors important in free association, the general inner freedom of the person associating and the interpersonal relationship between him and the analyst. The more rigid, controlled, and automaton-like a person is, the more all his thinking is under the grip of the conventional schemata of thought, experience, and feeling, the less will he be able to associate freely, and the more difficult will it be for him to recover any experience that does not fit into the conventional patterns which govern his life. The same is true if he cannot relax from the purposeful, "useful" pursuit of some activity or thought and let his thoughts wander. In other words, the more a person is dependent on and a prisoner of the socially prevalent pattern of useful efficient activity—from which the usual highly uniform leisure-time pursuits are distinguished more by the fact that they are not profitable than by a fundamental difference of attitude—and the more his experiences and mode of living are conditioned by the conventional experience schemata of the culture, the less will he be able to escape the hold of these schemata, to relax and approach that state of relative freedom in which a forgotten experience may break through the armor of his conventionalized thought processes and memory schemata. As Alexander has pointed out, the recovery of memories is not the cause, but the result of therapeutic progress.[33] The loosening of rigid control and of defenses, the greater inner freedom brought about by the therapeutic process, gives the repressed and forgotten material a chance to reappear because the conventional thought and memory schemata have no longer such exclusive predominance in the mental life of the patient.

Freedom, which the psychoanalytic situation seeks to establish by controlled, purposeful procedure, is an essential condition for

33] Franz Alexander, "Concerning the Genesis of the Castration Complex," *Psychoanalytic Review*, 1935, 22:49-52. See also Franz Alexander and Thomas M. French, *Psychoanalytic Therapy* (The Ronald Press, New York, 1946), pp. 20, 163.

the possibility of true, that is, nonschematic, recall of experience. This freedom may be brought about in different ways. The relaxation of censorship in sleep brings greater freedom. The memory schemata, which so largely govern voluntary recall in a state of wakefulness, lose their hold and relax their function during sleep, so that in dreams experiences which otherwise have been forgotten may be recalled, usually in somewhat changed and distorted or in symbolic form. The artist, the writer, the poet, if they have any real claim to their vocation, must be capable of nonschematic experience. They must be perceptive; that is, they must experience, see, hear, feel things in a way which somewhere transcends the cultural, conventional experience schemata. The relative freedom from these experience schemata is also freedom, to whatever extent, from the conventional memory schemata. And memory, the Greek myth tells us, is the mother of the muses.

Memory and forgetting are components of the nature of man, who is both a biological and a cultural, social, historical being. In memory and forgetting the conflicts between nature and society, as well as the dynamics and antagonisms of society, play a determining role. To investigate abstract memory phenomena is to investigate an artifact, something that does not exist. This has become apparent at each step of these considerations, which now have led to a point where it is possible to formulate their main results.

Early childhood amnesia may be considered a *normal* amnesia. It shares this quality with most, though not all, of dream amnesia and with the constant forgetting of those parts and aspects of experience which do not fit into the ready patterns of language and culture—trans-schematic experience. Normal amnesia is both akin to and different from pathological amnesia. Their likeness consists in their causation by a conflict between nature and culture or by intracultural conflict. Their difference consists chiefly in the fact that the conflicts causing normal amnesia are ubiquitous in a culture and their solution is part of the development of the personality in that culture; whereas in pathological amnesia, by and large, the conflict is due to individual traumatic experience which, although caused also by the stresses and conflicts operative in the culture, has become traumatic because of the particular history of the individual person. One might say that the normal amnesia, that which people usually are unable to recall, is an illuminating index to the quality of any given culture and society. It is that which does not serve the purposes of that society and would interfere with the pattern of the culture, that which would be traumatic to the culture because it would break up or transcend the conventions and mores of that culture. Early childhood amnesia is merely the most striking and dramatic expression of a dynamism operative throughout the life of people: the distortion or forgetting of trans-schematic experience, that is, of experience for which the culture provides no pattern and no schema.

Cultures vary in the degree to which they impose clichés on experience and memory. The more a society develops in the direction of mass conformism—whether such development be achieved by a totalitarian pattern, or within a democratic framework by means of the employment market, education, the patterns of social life, advertising, press, radio, movies, best-sellers, and so on—the more stringent becomes the rule of the conventional experience and memory schemata in the lives of the members of that society. In the history of the last hundred years of Western civilization the conventional schematization of experience and memory has become increasingly prevalent at an accelerating pace.

Even within a culture different *groups* may show marked differences in the degree to which conventional schemata of experience and memory prevent the recall of actual experience. Such a difference seems to exist, for example, between European men and women. There is some reason to assume that European men usually show a more extensive and pervasive amnesia for their early childhood than women.[34] A plausible hypothesis for the explanation of this difference would have to take into account the marked difference in the social status of the two sexes in Europe and, specifically, the difference in what one might call the social self-ideal of man versus that of woman. This idea of what the grown-up person, the respectable citizen, ought to be emphasizes the cleft between childhood and adulthood much more in men than in women. All things pertaining to the rearing

34] Personal communication from Ruth Benedict. In interviewing a number of European men and women Benedict found consistently that the women recalled quite a few details of their lives before they reached the age of 6 while the men recalled hardly anything. The people interviewed by her did not constitute a representative sample of the population, yet the consistency of the phenomenon in all the people interviewed seemed indicative of its more general significance.

of children and to the home are the domain of the women, and the average man would consider it beneath his "dignity" to know much about them or to be much concerned with them. Hence, to recall details of early childhood would be consistent with the social self-ideal of women whose interests are supposed to center around children, kitchen, and home. But to a man these things are not supposed to be sufficiently "important" to deserve much attention. To approximate the social self-ideal is important for his self-esteem; and the further removed from, and opposed to, the image of childhood the grown-up man's social self-ideal is, the more difficult will it be for him to recall experiences showing that once he was an infant and little boy. In general, more extensive childhood amnesias are to be expected in those groups, cultures, and historical epochs which emphasize the belief that childhood is radically different from adulthood, than one is likely to find where the continuity between childhood and adult life is emphasized.[35]

Mankind's belief in a lost paradise is repeated in the belief, held by most people, in the individual myth of their happy childhood. Like most myths this one contains elements both of truth and illusion, is woven out of wishes, hopes, remembrance, and sorrow, and hence has more than one meaning. One finds this belief even in people who have undergone cruel experiences as children and who had, without being or remaining aware of it, a childhood with hardly any love and affection from their parents. No doubt, one reason for the myth of happy childhood is that it bolsters parental authority and maintains a conventional prop of the authority of the family by asserting that one's parents were good and benevolent people who did everything for the good of their children, however much they may have done against it. And disappointed and suffering people, people without hope, want to believe that at least once there was a time in their life when they were happy. But the myth of happy childhood reflects also the truth that, as in the myth of paradise lost, there was a time before animalistic innocence was lost, before pleasure-seeking nature and pleasure-forbidding culture clashed in the battle called education, a battle in which the child always is the

35] For the general significance of continuity and discontinuity between childhood and adulthood, see Ruth Benedict, "Continuities and Discontinuities in Cultural Conditioning," *Psychiatry*, 1938, 1:161-167.

loser. At no time is life so exclusively and directly governed by the pleasure principle as it is in early infancy; at no other time is man, especially civilized man, capable of abandoning himself so completely to pleasure and satisfaction. The myth of happy childhood takes the place of the lost memory of the actual riches, spontaneity, freshness of childhood experience, an experience which has been forgotten because there is no place for it in the adult memory schemata.

Childhood amnesia covers those aspects and experiences of the early personality which are incompatible with the culture. If they were remembered, man would demand that society affirm and accept the total personality with all its potentialities. In a society based on partial suppression of the personality such a demand, even the mere existence of a really free personality, would constitute a threat to the society. Hence it becomes necessary for the society that the remembrance of a time in which the potentialities of a fuller, freer, and more spontaneous life were strongly present and alive be extinguished. In memory's service of this purpose one may distinguish two processes which overlap and shade into one another. One process leaves the culturally unacceptable or unusable experiences and the memory thereof to starvation by the expedient of providing no linguistic, conceptual, and memory schemata for them and by channeling later experience into the experience schemata of the culture. As the person, in the process of education, gradually comes to live more and more exclusively within the framework of the culturally and conventionally provided experience schemata, there is less and less to remind him of the possibility of trans-schematic experience. As his memory schemata develop in accordance with the schematized experience, they become unfit to preserve and recall trans-schematic experience. Only if a person has escaped to some extent this process of schematization of experience and memory, only if he is more differentiated and more free than the average person, will he be in a position to break, at some point, the hold that the memory and experience schemata have on his life and his perceptiveness. But usually it needs special, fortunate circumstances to make possible the escape from the memory schemata and the recall of trans-schematic experience. In a highly developed culture this process resulting in amnesia for culturally undesirable or unacknowledged experience by means of providing memory schemata only for culturally acceptable experience is exceedingly complex, flexible, subtle, and all-pervading.

Compared with this process, the dynamism of the tabu and of repression of individually or culturally tabooed experience and strivings is like the nightstick of the policeman compared with the gradual, slow, insinuating process of education in which some things are just not mentioned and others are said to be for the best of the child. But the dynamism active in normal amnesia is even more subtle than what is usually called education. It is an education of which the educators are not aware and of which the child is too helpless and too inarticulate to have more than the vaguest feeling that something is happening to him. On the other hand, those strivings, qualities, and potentialities of the child which are too strong to be left behind to die by the side of the road of education and which endanger the current social and cultural pattern have to be battled by the more drastic means of taboo and repression. In this sphere sexuality and the conflict with parental authority play central roles. One might say that taboo and repression are the psychological cannons of society against the child and against man, whereas in normal amnesia society uses the method of blockade and slow starvation against those experiences and memories which do not fit into the cultural pattern and which do not equip man for his role in the social process. The two methods of warfare supplement each other and, in the siege conducted by society against the human potentialities and inclinations which transcend the cultural pattern, the cannon helps to maintain the blockade, and the blockade and ensuing starvation make it less necessary to use the cannon.

Hesiod tells us that Lethe (Forgetting) is the daughter of Eris (Strife).[36] Amnesia, normal and pathological, is indeed the daughter of conflict, the conflict between nature and society and the conflict in society, the conflict between society and man and the conflict within man. Lethe is the stream of the underworld, of forgetting, the stream which constantly flows and never retains. In the realm of Lethe dwell the Danaïdes, who are condemned eternally to pour water into a leaking vessel. Plato interprets this as the punishment of those unwise souls who leak, who

36] Hesiod *Theogony* 227.

cannot remember and are therefore always empty.[37] But Mnemosyne is an older and more powerful goddess than Lethe. According to Hesiod she was one of the six Titanesses from whom all gods stem. And it was one of the world-founding deeds of Zeus that he begot the muses on her. Memory cannot be entirely extinguished in man, his capacity for experience cannot be entirely suppressed by schematization. It is in those experiences which transcend the cultural schemata, in those memories of experience which transcend the conventional memory schemata, that every new insight and every true work of art has its origin, and that the hope of progress, of a widening of the scope of human endeavor and human life, is founded.

37] Plato *Gorgias* 493 c 2. For the mythology of Mnemosyne and Lethe, see Karl Kerényi, "Mnemosyne-Lesmosyne," in *Die Geburt der Helena* (Rhein Verlag, Zuerich, 1945).

Index